AF270343

LITTLE
KINGDOMS

To Dettori,
the queen of my little kingdom.

LITTLE KINGDOMS

AN A-Z OF EARLY MEDIEVAL BRITAIN

ALEX HARVEY

PEN & SWORD HISTORY

AN IMPRINT OF PEN & SWORD BOOKS LTD.
YORKSHIRE ~ PHILADELPHIA

First published in Great Britain in 2025 by
PEN AND SWORD HISTORY
An imprint of
Pen & Sword Books Ltd
Yorkshire – Philadelphia

Copyright © Alex Harvey, 2025

ISBN 978 1 03612 581 3

The right of Alex Harvey to be identified as Author of
this work has been asserted by him in accordance with the Copyright,
Designs and Patents Act 1988.

A CIP catalogue record for this book is available from the British Library.

Typeset in Times New Roman 10/12 by
SJmagic DESIGN SERVICES, India.
Printed and bound in the UK by CPI Group (UK) Ltd.

The Publisher's authorised representative in the EU for product safety is Authorised
Rep Compliance Ltd., Ground Floor, 71 Lower Baggot Street,
Dublin D02 P593, Ireland.
www.arccompliance.com

For a complete list of Pen & Sword titles please contact
PEN & SWORD BOOKS LIMITED
George House, Units 12 & 13, Beevor Street, Off Pontefract Road,
Barnsley, South Yorkshire, S71 1HN, England
E-mail: enquiries@pen-and-sword.co.uk
Website: www.pen-and-sword.co.uk

or

PEN AND SWORD BOOKS
1950 Lawrence Rd, Havertown, PA 19083, USA
E-mail: uspen-and-sword@casematepublishers.com
Website: www.penandswordbooks.com

CONTENTS

REVIEWS

of a people easily categorized by ethnicity or nationality. Instead, Harvey breathes life into a sweeping miscellany of little kingdoms, some familiar and prominent in our early medieval histories, others mysterious and elusive. Whether it's in reports of strange weather (mole rain) or references to undead islands (a misinterpreted place-name), the reader of Little Kingdoms will find more than a little to explore in a richly complex medieval Britain."

Simon Elliott, author of *Sea Eagles of Empire:*

"Post-Roman Britain is a land of myth, legend and wonder for many, and a true dark age for others. A place which could easily sit in the Middle Earth of J.R.R. Tolkien, not surprising given it was the inspiration for many of his best-known plot lines.

Yet here Alex Harvey skilfully brings this little-known period of British history to vibrant life, showing in striking detail how events then set in place the multiple identities of Britain today. Using true academic rigour, matched with a wonderful ability to tell a story, he introduces readers to kingdoms large and small, some only short-lived but many still recognisable today within the political geography of Britain. In that sense, this is also an important book for our age, when self-identification is at the forefront of the national debate."

Steve Brusatte, University of Edinburgh paleontologist and New York Times/ Sunday Times bestselling author of *The Rise and Fall of the Dinosaurs*

"Fun, readable and informative, Alex Harvey's *Little Kingdoms* is a celebration of some of the most obscure and odd kingdoms, fiefdoms, territories, and settlements of British history. Infused with enthusiasm and written in a conversational tone, this is the type of pop history I love to read."

Christopher Hadley, author of *The Road:*

"I really liked the decision to structure the book in sixty-two alphabetical entries. It could so easily have been shaped thematically with endless case studies, but that would have made the book less accessible to the general reader and taken the focus off the kingdoms and their stories. And yet, while reading this only as a gazetteer is a delight -- with its intriguing pen portraits of long forgotten little realms teased out of clues in charters, old poems and traces in the landscape -- it would be a missed opportunity. Read together in sequence the entries allow the reader to watch Alex Harvey use his furious curiosity to puzzle out a much more complete portrait of this fascinating period of history, its people and places. In fact, Little Kingdoms invites different readings: by all means begin with a pick and mix approach, then read it through in alphabetical order while making sure to jump backwards and forwards between the cross references.

Harvey is not afraid to ask questions that are impossible to answer, but his attempts not only make for an enjoyable read, but gradually form answers to much bigger questions about the past: about settlement, identity, change and continuity -- how these kingdoms emerged and disappeared and why that matters.

Process is an important part of the reading experience, the story of how we know what we know about these lost kingdoms is half the pleasure.

Little Kingdoms shows what can be achieved with a combination of archaeological expertise, a way with words, an enquiring mind and an imagination fed on manuscripts and long barrows. It is essential reading for anyone interested in the period, in what can be made of the traces that remain, in how to do history well. Essential and absorbing.

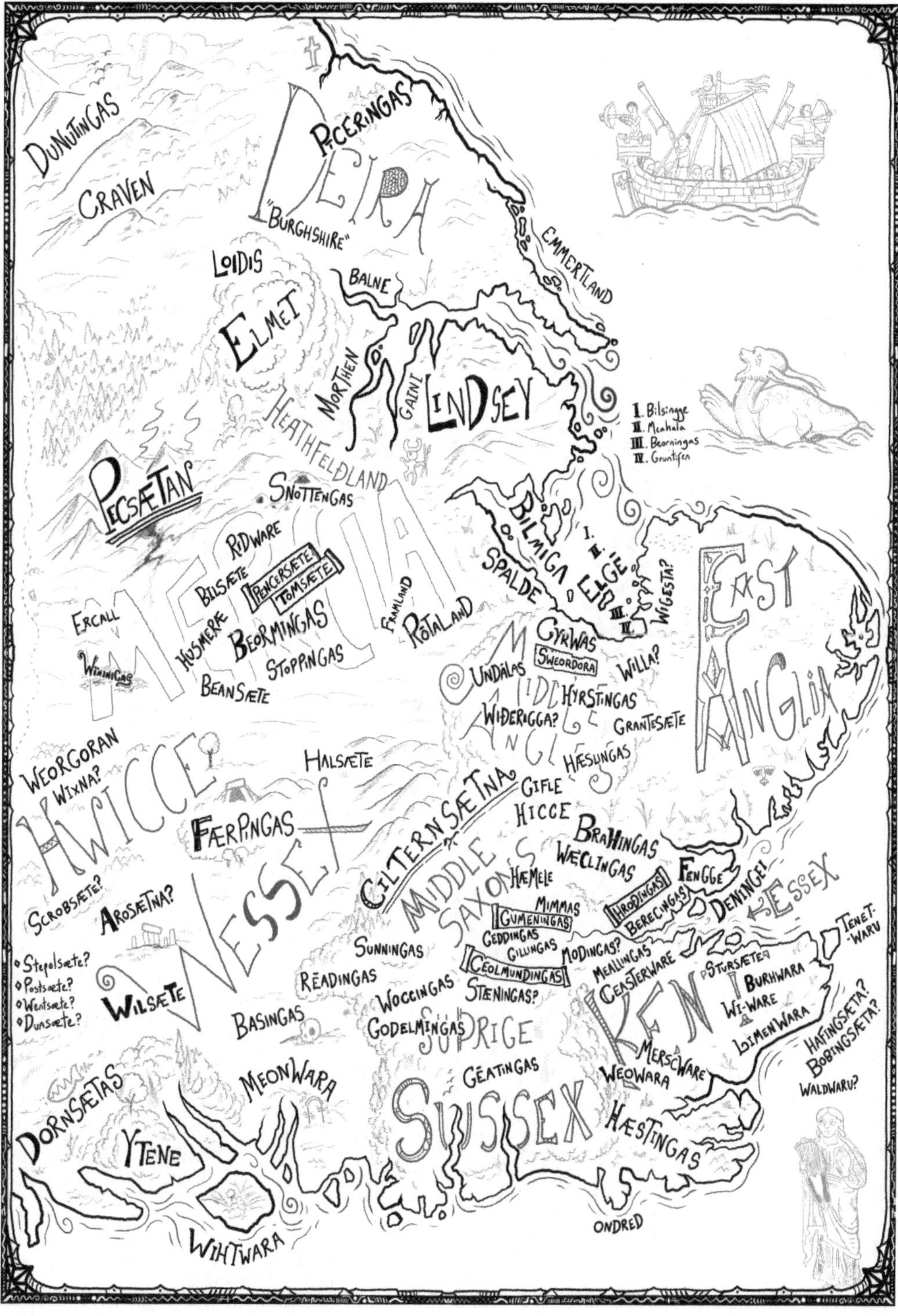

DUNUTINGAS
CRAVEN
PÆRINGAS
DEIRA
"BURGHSHIRE"
EMMERTLAND
LOIDIS
BALNE
ELMET
MORTHEN
GAINI
LINDSEY
HEATHFELDLAND
PECSÆTAN
SNOTTENGAS
RIDWARE
BILMIGA ELGE
SPALDE
BILSÆTE
PENCERSÆTE
TOMSÆTE
HOSMERE
BEORMINGAS
FRAMLAND
ROTALAND
ERCALL
WININGAS
STOPPINGAS
BEANSÆTE
GYRWAS
SWEORDORA
WILLA?
UNDALAS
HYRSTINGAS
WIÐERIGGA?
GRANTESÆTE
HÆSLINGAS
WEORGORAN
WIXNA?
HALSÆTE
GIFLE
HICCE
EAST ANGLIA
HWICCE
FÆRPINGAS
CILTERNSÆTNA
BRAHINGAS
WÆCLINGAS
MIDDLE SAXONS
HÆMELE
FENGGE
HRODINGAS
SCROBSÆTE?
WESSEX
MIMMAS
GUMENINGAS
BERECINGAS
DENINGEI
HESSEX
AROSÆTNA?
GEDDINGAS
GILUNGAS
MODINGAS?
MEALLINGAS
CEASTERWARE
TENET-WARU
STEPOLSÆTE?
SUNNINGAS
CEOLMUNDINGAS
STÆNINGAS?
STURSÆTE
BURHWARA
POSTSÆTE?
READINGAS
WI-WARE
WENTSÆTE?
WOCCINGAS
LIMENWARA
DUNSÆTE?
WILSÆTE
BASINGAS
GODELMINGAS
SUÞRIGE
KENT
HAFINGSÆTA?
BOBINGSÆTA?
MERSCWARE
WALDWARU?
DORNSÆTAS
MEONWARA
GEATINGAS
WEOWARA
YTENE
SUSSEX
HÆSTINGAS
WIHTWARA
ONDRED
I. Bilsingge
II. Mcohala
III. Beorningas
IV. Gruntifen

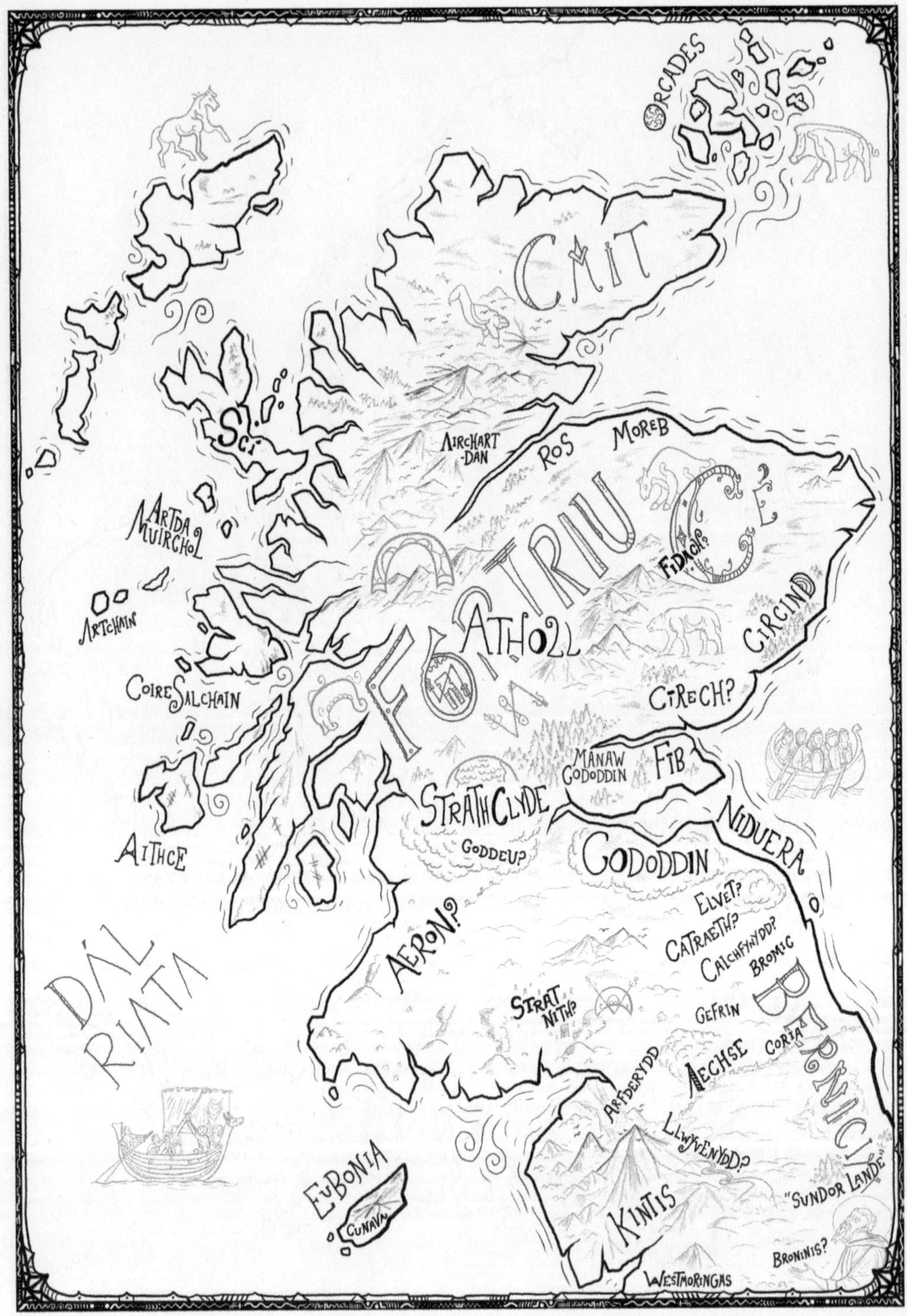

ORCADES
CAIT
SCÍ
AIRCHART-DAN
ROS
MOREB
FIDACH?
TRIU
FORTRIU
CE?
ARTDA MUIRCHOL
ATHOLL
CIRCIND
ARTCHAIN
CIRECH?
COIRE SALCHAIN
MANAW GODODDIN
FIB
STRATHCLYDE
NIDUERA
AITHCE
GODDEU?
GODODDIN
DÁL RIATA
AERON?
ELVET?
CATRAETH?
CALCHFYNYDD?
BROMIC
STRAT NITH?
GEFRIN
BRNICI
AECHSE
CORIA
ARFDERYDD
LLWYFENYDD?
EUBONIA
CUNAVA
"SUNDOR LANDE"
KINTIS
BRONINIS?
WESTMORINGAS

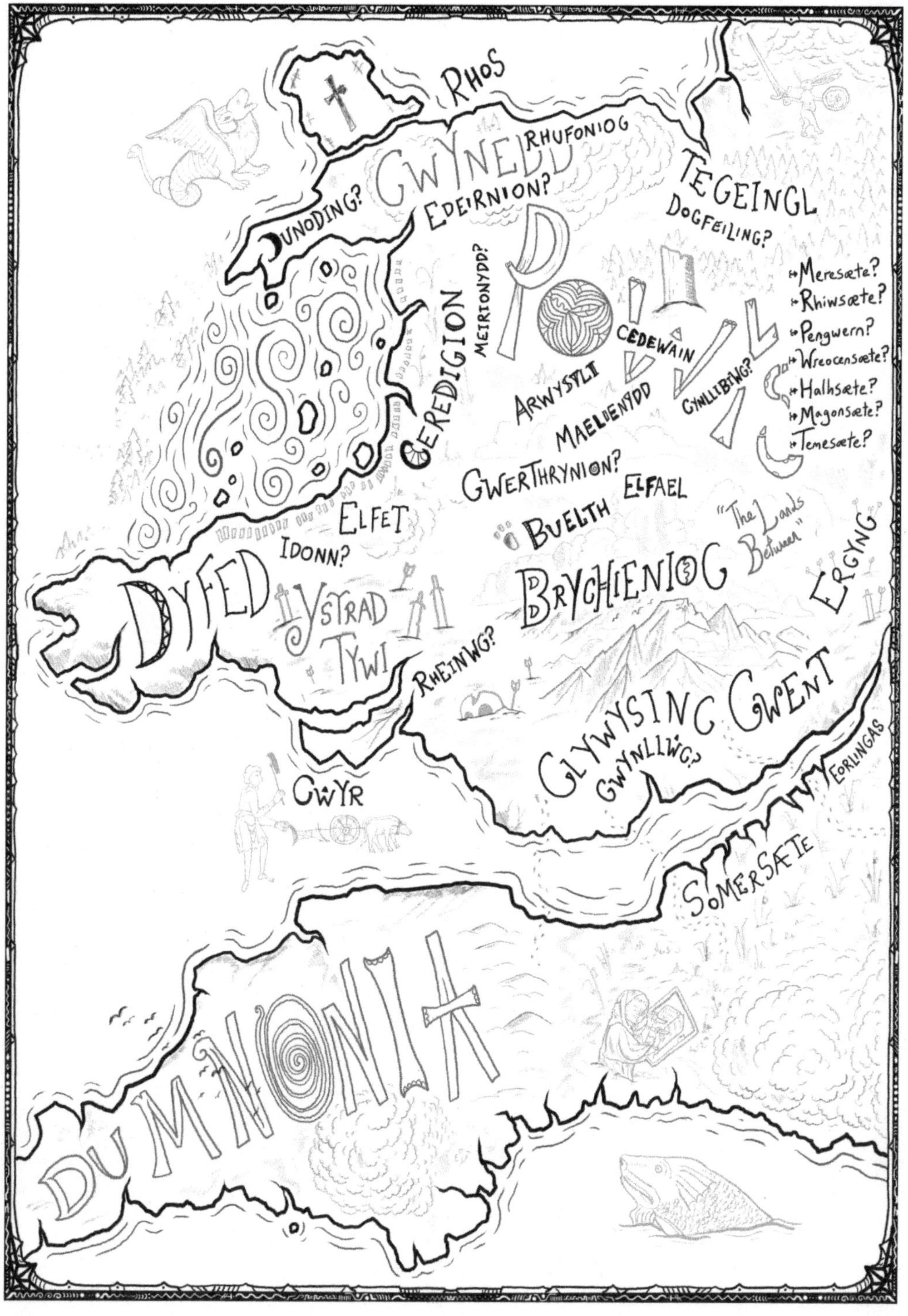

RHOS
GWYNEDD
DUNODING?
EDEIRNION?
RHUFONIOG
TEGEINGL
DOGFEILING?
MEIRIONYDD?
CEREDIGION
CEDEWAIN
ARWYSTLI
MAELIENYDD
CYNLLIBIWG?
GWERTHRYNION?
ELFAEL
BUELTH
ELFET
IDONN?
DYFED
YSTRAD TYWI
RHEINWG?
BRYCHEINIOG
"The Lands Between"
ERGYNG
Meresæte?
Rhiwsæte?
Pengwern?
Wreocensæte?
Halhsæte?
Magonsæte?
Temesæte?
GWYR
GLYWYSING
GWENT
GWYNLLWG?
SOMERSÆTE
EORLINGAS
DUMNONIA

A COMMENT TO START

'Go forth and journey for four months, till you reach the city of Bartīniyah. It is a great city on the shore of the Western Ocean, ruled by seven kings', says the ninth-century *Book of Precious Records*, an Arabic compendium describing the travels of Hārūn ibn Yahyā rendered through the voice of Ibn Rusta.[1] Bartīniyah is Britain and it had seven kings who ruled seven kingdoms. Or at least, it did in the eyes of outsiders, ever-interested in our island from afar and keenly invested in the politics, economies and networks that shaped us, but unaware of the neighbourhood schisms, the communities within communities, the local hotspots and deep-rooted historical allegiances, the whispers and back alleys. There were undoubtedly more than seven kingdoms, but a belief in a heptarchy must have been widespread enough to be recognised in Córdoba, Constantinople, even Baghdad. Hiding in the gaps between these 'seven kingdoms' would have been innumerable regional identities and administrative districts, their forms chiselled from the bones of older realms, remnants of past authorities and recycled regimes. Following the footsteps of Hārūn ibn Yahyā, let us cross the same seas, walk the same roads, observe the same kings and see just how many 'kingdoms' can really be found here in 'the last land'.

This is a book about little kingdoms. It has little chapters and is arranged into alphabetised vignettes. While it is intended to be read in the order in which it is printed, the almanac-style affords readers the ability to pick and choose. Let's say you're about to visit the Brecon Beacons, or Leeds; why not have a gander at the chapters on Brycheiniog and Loidis, just to check what's what?

I have wanted to write this book for years, being obsessed with these tiny territorial entities which emerged or persisted between the gloom of the Romans and the Normans, traditionally called the 'Dark Ages'. Some of these kingdoms will be familiar, like Wessex and Kent, whereas others might only raise seasoned eyebrows, such as Lindsey, Deira and Elmet. I hope there are an equal number of chapters completely alien to people. Have you heard of Craven? Eirch? Gŵyr? As it was not possible to devote thousands of words to each territory, many chapters serve as avenues to further study, so I have tried to cherry-pick the most interesting aspect, site or object from each and use it to weave a short narrative. Some chapters unravel the condensed chronology of a kingdom whereas others offer a whistlestop tour of interesting places. As I am an archaeologist, I have tried to place readers on the ground floor of these locations and each chapter should, where possible, begin with the unique geography of the region and how people adapted to it before diving into other forms of evidence like charters, poems and chronicles. And sure, this book *can* be read in a scattershot manner, picking up a chapter on Ytene and then going back to Ceredigion and forward again to the Middle Saxons, however, I have used the alphabetised order to 'on-board' some of the more obtuse concepts and disciplines in the hope of stacking layers of complexity as the book goes on. My use of italics normally designates archaic place names, like *Eoferwic*, and the presence of an asterisk (as with **Lindēs*) indicates a reconstructed name that can only be estimated. I use the Old English letters 'ð' ('eth') and 'þ' ('thorn') which both produce unvoiced *th-* sounds, along with Portable Antiquities Scheme (PAS) and Sawyer-charter references. These are indicated by brackets with the PAS ID or Sawyer tag (for example, S 112).

There is never *too* much information on any one kingdom but rather mini-narratives spread across several. The aim is that, by the time you put this book down, you've got a rough idea of England, Wales and Scotland during their formative years. However, this is not a book about their unification – that is a different story altogether – but rather the individual histories of entities that once existed within them. I wanted to approach them all on their terms rather than viewing the little kingdoms as roadblocks on the way to something else. Therefore, the themes and topics – unity, connectivity, otherness, togetherness, multiculturalism – chiselled themselves as I was writing. I let the little kingdoms tell their own stories. In that respect I am but their humble compiler, a collector of tales, trinkets and treasures from the tip of Atlantic Scotland to the Isles of Scilly, and, just as no book is written alone, neither is a kingdom built by one.

I have my parents and wife Dettori to thank for consistent encouragement and, above all else, tolerance, listening to me day after day make comments like 'I've nearly finished this chapter' and 'that chapter'. The innumerable people I have informed about this book have no doubt, through rolled eyes, wished for it to be released just so I stop talking about it. I apologise for such enthusiasm. Amy Jeffs, Thomas Williams, Hana Videen and Christopher Hadley are the authors who inspired this particular book, but I must also thank scholars like Guy Halsall, Neil McGuigan, Catherine Cubitt, Max Adams, James Harland, David Petts, Sarah Sunne and Russell Ó Ríagáin who, throughout this book's development, have been there for random conversations, pieces of advice or directions towards sources. Will Swales, Tania Styles, Diana Whaley, John Baker and the good members of the Society for Name Studies in Britain and Ireland (SNSBI)[*] were vital sounding boards for many ideas, lines and commentaries from this book's early prototype at a conference in October 2024.

Some acknowledgements must be direct and others less so. A random conversation I had with Jay Smith years ago about the etymology of 'Axholme' prompted me to ponder my home's history which led to my first book, which led to my second, which led to this one. Mike Farrington let me borrow a few studies

---

[*] Most toponymic information is derived from the English Place-Name Survey or the SNSBI's website: https://www.snsbi.org.uk/.

on the Yorkshire Dales which prompted several sections of this manuscript. Harry Ellerd-Cheers and Donato Sitaro read many of these chapters in their earliest forms and David Johnson reviewed my first draft. I am grateful, also, to Steve Williams for conversations about the book's cover artwork. Then there are people like Hidetaka Miyazaki, Cormac McCarthy and Joseph Delaney who don't know me but whose work has had a massive impact throughout my life, influencing my own flair and creative motifs. A major theme of this book is tracing material styles (something once used to pinpoint ethnicities on maps). All of these artisans' styles proliferate through my work but this does not mean that I *am* Steven Moffat, for instance. Each chapter is punctuated by a piece of artwork which I hope brings out either a key artefact, visual or manuscript, about the kingdom to which it relates. Please forgive any errors with these illustrations and, indeed, the entire book. Whilst I have been blessed with the edits and professional support of Jon Wright, Laura Hirst and Richard Doherty, I hold myself responsible for any mistakes across these pages.

Likewise, I take only some credit for the theories contained within as I am standing atop a monumental pile of papers and books, all cited in a bibliography indicated by superscript references. Where relevant there are also footnotes which tease out further information.

Above all else, this book represents *my* little kingdom, the life I have led up to this point, the influences that have inspired me and the ideas that have been generated after I've already written something. There are undoubtedly kingdoms I have missed but I hope the attached stylised maps, which list everywhere mentioned in the book, will suffice. It is important, I think, to approach the Early Medieval Period on a local level, rather than viewing it as a grand narrative. *Little Kingdoms* contains sixty-two histories stacked alongside one another like a patchwork quilt.

The first few chapters introduce these topics and concepts through their narratives, so I will bore you no longer. This is a winding road to walk and it begins in …

AECHSE

What brings people together? What forms the foundation for commonality, togetherness, community? For some, it is the distinctiveness of their surroundings – geography that separates them from others. But is that it? Are communities formed because of the differences between themselves and others, or because of shared similarities within a group? Where lies the distinction between *us* and *them* and is this what forges societal ties that knot landscape, subsistence and community together?

The United Kingdom is made up of England, Wales, Scotland and Northern Ireland. Each of these countries consist of shires, districts, provinces, subdivided into towns, villages; streets, shops, houses; rooms. Our loyalties to *our space* vary in size although the larger the space the more threads we invent to connect us to those who share it. It is perhaps through shared ideals that we define territory, or through a sense of belonging to what we as individuals have known since our inception.

In the Stone Age, communities amassed through tightly-knit family groups, sometimes led by a single figure whose leadership was inherited or hard won. Near Scarborough, at the site of Star Carr, multiple generations converged on the same spur of land, interacting with one another. On the edges of Lake Flixton these people grew a sense of community, something that defined *their area* and separated them from others. A woodsman preparing an antler frontlet may have seen rising pillars of smoke in the distance – *others*. It is through 'othering' that we distinguish where *our* land ends and another's begins. This process has continued throughout history, names of places spoken into the world. The Mesolithic is a good place to start to observe this phenomenon. Our transition from hunter-gatherers to seasonal farmers brought with it a change in how we approached and manipulated the land: no longer part of nature but a separate force capable of imposing something upon it. Later, territories became immortalised through names: Yorkshire, Lothian, the Isle of Wight, unique areas labelled for passers-by to notice.

But why would people come together and create boundaries and how would they remain static amidst a fluctuating world? Crises have a confounding impact on group identities. They fracture and divide, splintering into sub-groups, or they find unity in chaos. This is how territories are born.

In the late fourth century, the arm of the Roman Empire that extended over the British Isles had become economically and politically fraught, fading out of importance over several decades. Rome's 'fall' should be regarded as a long-drawn-out affair, involving a series of complicated socio-political impacts and a growing sense of economic distance between elite centres in *Britannia* and the wider Empire. The fact that *Britannia* was already on the edge of Imperial interests from its inception led to an alleged societal collapse perpetrated by Irish and Saxon 'barbarians' in 367 and multiple foreign takeovers, notably Magnus Maximus in 387 and Constantine 'III' twenty years later. These events all happened before *Britannia* was officially abandoned; the province had long been crumbling, with several watershed moments later becoming preserved as '*the* fall'. These events, like the 'barbarian conspiracy', then became embedded in folk memory. Two centuries later writers were still bemoaning their impact. A breakdown in taxation networks had a negligible effect on the ninety-per-cent of society who lived a localised agrarian lifestyle, clusters of farmsteads beholden to no one. However, now lacking oversight, fortunes could change, territories could be reshaped. In the wake of Imperial authority, communities carved out territory across *Britannia* in areas that had previously been tightly defined administrative districts. Even these districts, established in the first century, were often based around tribal groupings with Iron Age roots. After Rome, some kingdoms were forged anew and others were reshaped entirely.[2]

Innumerable territories from this post-Roman twilight have been neglected, their lights extinguished through political expansionism, some as small as an island, others as nebulous as a name. How can we find these lost realms? An enduring tool is that of place names, called toponyms, and the linguistic elements that form them.[3] Take 'London', from the hypothetical pre-Roman **Londonjon*,[4] the name of the fortress positioned on the Thames. **Londonjon* became rendered in different languages following its establishment; *Londinium, Lundenwic, Lundenburh, Lundunaborg, Lundene*, London, each adding a new linguistic vestige – Latin, Old English, Old Norse, Middle English. The *-wic* suffix of *Lundenwic* indicates that the site became a trading port; *-burh* reveals it was later fortified. The very fact that the name evolved through a Celtic language into Old Norse over eight centuries affords us a glimpse of the changes that transpired here.

Changes were happening everywhere. The British Isles were as they have always been, a multi-ethnic melting pot of language, culture, ideas and ownership. And with that, borders and barriers but also bridges. Links that tied kingdoms together, divisions that caused others to be nemeses. What even *is* a kingdom, anyway? It implies royalty and statecraft, but the truth is many of the earliest territories in this post-Roman haze were simply clusters of families occupying spaces along riverbanks. It might be best to use the catch-all term 'polities' to describe them, but even that implies some kind of political awareness. Some of the communities in this book were just that: communities. As small as a valley or as large as a mountain, these groups shifted over the centuries to form the countries that exist today. Others disappeared entirely.

Approaching these tiny territories from a modern perspective is to do them an injustice. The formation of the United Kingdom was not predestined. Most of these places were, at one point, the centre of their world. Some remained self-serving until they entered the radar of regionally ambitious warlords, others are preserved only in song or immortalised in stone. Some kingdoms were centred around unique topography, others emerged through competition. Some were liminal, others central, many both.[5] In approaching Britain's domains in this light, the intention is to give an equal share of the stage to everyone but, in doing so, afford each but a few pages.

And some won't even get that far. Our first, Aechse, is mentioned only in a single piece of literature, the eighth-century *Life of St Cuthbert*.[6] In it, we follow the eponymous bishop on his travels across England. Somewhere between Hexham and Carlisle, tracing the crooked spine of Hadrian's Wall, Cuthbert stopped to preach at a place called Aechse (or *Ahse*). Upon hearing of his arrival at an unnamed gathering point, the locals left their hillside farms to hear the word of God. Cuthbert is modelled on the literary ascetic archetype, so the event is cast in doubt, but Aechse itself was real, positioned somewhere near Haltwhistle. The *Life* is a hagiography, many of which will appear throughout this book; they are stories about saints designed to exemplify their greatest attributes and exaggerate their feats, often with extreme political or religious biases but they do contain lots of very useful supplementary details like the names of territories. With Aechse, the nearest Roman fort is *Aesica*, now Great Chesters in Northumberland. By the seventh century *Aesica* and Hadrian's Wall would have remained immutable, cast in stone, retaining their importance, though their purpose had changed. As with London, *Aesica* became Aechse through dialectal shifts. In the shadow of a wall-adjoined fortlet, indomitable even three centuries after Imperial decline, a community came together to a place where they shared commonality.

Here, 'in a *regio* which is called Aechse', the locals listened to Cuthbert.

Regio is a term typically used to describe petty territories or districts, small administrative divisions under the autonomy of another. In this case, the *regio* of Aechse was centred around the old Roman fort jutting from Hadrian's Wall. Economically, it would have been a client of a larger polity. Fully autonomous kingdoms are usually referred to as *provinciae*, people as *populi* and nations as *gentes*, various strengths of legal and political glue. Hadrian's Wall, which had once been but one cog in the mighty Roman machine, became a belt of individual communities, no longer serving international ambitions but local needs. It summarises beautifully the transformations occurring all over the former Empire between the fourth and seventh centuries, a well-connected network fragmenting into self-serving territorial units, like *Britannia* but, on this micro-scale at the wall, fortlets like Birdoswald, Vindolanda and *Aechse*. Kingdoms rise but they also fall and their spheres of influence and interaction shrink.

And so it is in the tiniest example that we see what makes a little kingdom. Aechse has been used here as an introduction, a tease as to how these realms may have functioned, how they can be analysed and how they can be discussed. For the farmers he met along his seventh-century journey, Cuthbert was an intruder: he had crossed the boundaries of their *regio* and struck at their centre, a communal space which crystallised some kind of shared identity, an economic core that brought disparate farmers together over hills and hollows. Aechse was not alone. It is this model, in some form or another, that was mirrored all over early medieval Britain.

AERON

There is no better kingdom to start our exploration than enigmatic Aeron. It evades identification, is mentioned only sparsely and has been vigorously debated since it was first studied. If Aeron can be recognised for one thing, then it is for how well it synthesises the difficult quest to identify little kingdoms; we know nothing about Aeron's bounds, its policies, its origins or its downfall. All this must be inferred through multiple disciplines. The puzzle of Aeron is one to be guessed, though never solved, through linguistic study, analyses of poetic material, place names and scant archaeological traces. In truth, there is more to be said about what we do *not* know.

In 1265, an anonymous poet compiled thirty-eight sheets of parchment in a candlelit monastery in Wales. We will never know the compiler's name nor the exact place of origin for the manuscript. What we can be reasonably sure of, however, is that contained within these folios is a handful of poetic verses stylistically traceable to the ninth century. Coldly designated Cardiff MS 2.81, the *Book of Aneirin* contains poems written in two dialects from Wales's linguistic past, Old and Middle Welsh. Old Welsh was widely spoken within Wales from the ninth century until sometime in the twelfth as it evolved into Middle Welsh. We know more about Middle Welsh, its sentence structure, pronunciation and application than we do its precursor. Still, the presence of both within one manuscript gives us a start and end date for its creation. It is unlikely to have been written *beyond* the point at which Middle Welsh stopped being used and, because it contains Old Welsh, preserves poems already ancient by 1265. We are guilty of looking at history through sepia lenses, at 'the olden days' rendered in jittery monochrome frames, at cold visages of dead monarchs and the faded grandeur of frayed tapestries. Like us, those compiling the *Book* in 1265 had a history; they, too, looked at the distant past with some concocted mix of reverence, fear and distaste, flavoured by their contemporary perceptions. They may have seen their forefathers as ignorant and that their modern age, eight centuries ago, afforded them the comfort and privilege to look back through time at those even older than them.

Among the poems in the *Book* the most famous is *The Gododdin*, a soaring lament to the noble defeat of various semi-legendary figures from the histories of Scotland and Wales, a memory of a great battle fought in the sixth or seventh centuries.[7] *The Gododdin* is one of many works hailing from the literary tradition of *Gwŷr y Gogledd* or the 'Men of the North'. This framework encompasses elegies, bardic poetry and genealogies, all intertwined in describing one perception of Britain's past. The perspective shared across much of this literature is a Welsh one, but Welsh only in the sense of being British.

For the Early Medieval Period, an often-parroted shorthand is that the British were Welsh, the Scots were Irish, the English were German and the Picts were British. Normally, these four are rendered down into a dichotomy; the 'Anglo-Saxon' English versus the 'Britons' or 'Celts'. These are oversimplifications. The poet attributed with the original verses of *The Gododdin* is Aneirin, an orator praised by a near-contemporary historian from the ninth century. Aneirin's verses are written in Middle Welsh, despite being originally spoken in Old Welsh and yet Aneirin himself was probably born in Scotland and his genealogy (if we can trust it) refers to antecedents from northern Britain. Old Welsh is a Celtic language and this was one of many traits shared between Wales and Scotland, linguistically distinct from the Germanic languages spoken in the east. We have, then, a shared identity and it is this identity that the literary tradition of the 'The Old North' harnesses. *The Gododdin* is only one example; its sweeping eulogies unite kingdoms from both Wales and Scotland's past, but also areas like Cumbria, Cornwall and Lincolnshire.

All these areas are hinted at through careful readings of *The Gododdin*. The actual focus of the poem is peculiar, however. It is a series of off-hand mentions to something that was once well-known, so well-known to the point that the poet failed to describe it, assured by the fact that audiences would simply pick up on the allegories and work it out for themselves. Twelve-hundred years later, this task is significantly more difficult and interpretations of the poem range from a conflict fought between Celtic-speaking northerners and Germanic-speaking enemies, or rival British kingdoms altogether, with Germanic-speaking allies on both sides. Nevertheless, even the location of the battle cannot be accurately assessed, although many place it at Catterick.

It is in this context we can discuss Aeron, mentioned as one of the myriad kingdoms whose warriors were present at a military disaster that remained fossilised in poems and spoken in courts until it was, in 1265, finally preserved.

> The men went to Catraeth; they were renowned;
> Wine and mead from golden cups was their beverage;
> That year was to them of exalted solemnity;
>
> Three warriors and three score and three hundred,
> wearing the golden torques.
>
> Of those who hurried forth after the excess of revelling,
> But three escaped by the prowess of the gashing sword,
> The two war-dogs of Aeron, and Cenon the Dauntless,
> And myself from the spilling of my blood, the reward of my sacred
>   song.

How would tall tales find their way from the battlefield to the bard's lips? And from there to the monk's quill? While a brave death in battle was commendable, it is only through survivors that we can learn of their feats and in the above quote the heroes of Aeron are said to have fled the conflict. Not shunned but celebrated just like the war-dead; noble soldiers who persevered against an unstoppable enemy. The identity of the enemy does not matter. Aeron and its allies were on the losing side.

Cynon led Aeron's retinue that day alongside two other 'sovereigns of the Brythons' and Cyndilig, 'one of the Novantian heroes'. Whether these individuals were real or not also does not matter. Their names hint at gnashing dogs, snarling wolves: they were the 'war-dogs of Aeron' although clearly their bark was bigger than their bite. Several elements of *The Gododdin*, like Aeron's battle-hounds, were recycled to suit new audiences as the poem was retold over hundreds of years. In the above translation, the men of Aeron drink wine out of golden cups, yet in other, earlier, poems, mead from horns is the beverage of choice. Swords are mentioned where otherwise they would be spears; Aeron is listed as one of many areas under the overlordship of the legendary Urien, but other times absent, reflecting the changing tastes of poets and their audiences. A twelfth-century elegy for a Welsh noble compared him to this popular past: 'one battle-leader like the battle-hound of Aeron',[8, 9] but the core of *The Gododdin* is one of defeat. Aeron does not, then, have the most glowing of reputations. Such is the problem with relying solely on literature. Aneirin's Aeron is a petty territory whose bravest warriors fled from a battle where they were only ever playing lapdog. Still, Aeron's limited literary stature does not make it uninteresting.

Over the years, debates have percolated concerning the kingdom's exact location. One of the more enduring suggestions is within Ayrshire, Scotland.[10] Here, in the southern uplands, the boundless hills give way to the crashing waves of the North Channel, which batter Lendalfoot Coast in the shadow of Ailsa Craig. This land has chiselled many champions over the years, like Robert the Bruce. Cyndilig, one of the few named figures of Aeron, is referred to as one of the *Novantæ*, a Caledonian tribe mentioned in Roman sources. The modern bounds of Ayrshire fall within land that was once briefly governed by Emperor Antonius Pius (138-161 CE) following the partial creation of the Antonine Wall. This boundary, a stretch of Roman administration, was soon abandoned. Legionaries withdrew to Hadrian's Wall within a few years, the 'barbarians' to their north remaining a deadly limiter. That the Antonine limit had even been established in the first place indicates that the residents *south* of it were more valuable than those to the north. Ayrshire is sandwiched here, in what was evidently a more 'Romanised' area of Scotland.

By the time Aeron's war dogs had fled from their legendary battle, the Antonine Wall was but a scraped row of broken teeth in the landscape. When Aneirin let loose his rendition of *The Gododdin* to expectant crowds in days of yore, those rotted nubs had sunken into the earth. By 1265 the Antonine Wall found itself amongst more recent ghosts and, in our age, we can add Robert the Bruce to Ayrshire's hall of fame. Like almost everywhere in the United Kingdom, Ayrshire is steeped in history.

But Aeron-as-Ayrshire has never been agreed upon. While the shoe fits, there are alternatives. Rachel Bromwich argued for a placement around Airedale, in West

Yorkshire.[11] Here, Aeron's war dogs would not rub shoulders with the Antonine Wall, but the Aberford Dyke, the Aire Gap and the untamed forests along the southern edge of the Yorkshire Dales. The Aire Gap is a natural topographical doorway, funnelling movement from the Vale of York into the uplands. Strategically, rivers and routeways along this passage would be easily guarded. Most conflicts in the Early Medieval Period occurred along Roman roads, like Spittal Hardwick Lane which cuts between Monkhill and the river Aire, once linking fortresses together in an unyielding web. In the centuries following the decline of *Britannia*, the roads retained their importance and so, wherever the conflict within *The Gododdin* took place, we can be confident that it occurred with pre-existing networks in mind. A 'River Aeron' is even mentioned as being filled with the corpses of the heroic dead. Both Airedale and Ayrshire have rivers but only the former is particularly well endowed with preserved Roman roads.

But the Roman Empire was not the first entity to scar the landscape of the British Isles. Before it, in the ages that preceded, people working with flint, copper, bronze and iron left barrow mounds, standing stones and routeways to serve as temporal markers. The early medieval perception of pre-Roman prehistory is a difficult thing to decipher as unexplained monuments were re-used in new ways: a standing stone to a fertility goddess might, centuries later, find itself re-purposed as the precipice for a judicial assembly; a tomb for a bronze-laden warlord might become a territorial limit.

Dog-headed people have appeared frequently throughout historical mythology. Several adorn the Kyiv Psalter from 1397 (pictured above), but there is also an Arthurian tale that places half-wolf warriors in Edinburgh, originating from the far north of Scotland. Hounds have long been associated with strength, cunning and battle-prowess. Aeron's affectation for canines reflects a broad trend.

These remnants were important in staking claim to land and dividing territories from one another. So, too, were ancient names. The speculative *Agronā* has been proposed for the origin of Airedale and Ayrshire but this can only ever be guesswork. It also doesn't help us with placing Aeron. Nor does the fact that an Aeron Valley *and* a river Aeron both exist near Cardigan Bay, Wales.

This Aeron has been argued to come from the Middle Welsh word *aer-* meaning 'slaughter'.

Whatever the case, there is no reason to believe that placing Aeron in either Ayrshire, Airedale or Wales limits its dogs' ability to roam. Early medieval warlords were peripatetic and, before substantial economic systems were established, the act of journeying along these roads, striking out and harvesting tribute and the means of social reproduction was the backbone of kingship. Whether Aeron's dogs were beasts of the Scottish moors or sentries of the Aberford Dyke, they were well known, although mentioned in praise poems for other kingdoms entirely. 'A hundred armies would tremble in Aeron' at the sight of Gwallog, a fearsome butcher we will visit later.

We get the impression of Aeron as a tenacious but secondary territory, always under the shadow of its more substantial neighbours. Wherever it may be placed, Aeron was remembered through lamentation. It was secondary to Urien and Gwallog, rock stars of the Welsh poetic corpus, and its heroes were afforded little fanfare. But maybe Aneirin was misremembering. Another trope of Middle Welsh poetry is the specifically chosen numbering system: 'three warriors and three score and three hundred' marched to battle in *The Gododdin*. There is good reason to believe that these numbers were picked because of alliteration; they hint at enormity without ever committing. Even so, and even when we consider the likelihood that they do not reflect anything real, of the three who returned from the three hundred war-dead, *two* were from Aeron.

AROSÆTNA

How polities ended is interesting enough, but what about their inception? What is the first step in the creation of a kingdom? In England some territories used their Roman past, reshaping themselves to suit emergent social pressures. Others were brand new; migrants arriving on the shores of old *Britannia*. What did they seek? Were they merely groups of ramblers, wandering in the hope of finding something suitable? Or did they strike out with intent?

The current curriculum would have it that, in the absence of *Romanitas*, aliens called the 'Anglo-Saxons' conquered eastern England from the fifth century. This is a blurring of facts, a symptom of centuries of shaky ethnonyms:[12] people labelled 'Anglo-Saxons' did not exist during the period in which our little kingdoms were formed. People who spoke different Germanic languages had served in *Britannia* as foreign mercenaries since at least the second century but they were not the 'Anglo-Saxons'. They were based in forts and along roads and later became official Roman citizens; some were even granted ranks and titles, lands and status. The Empire was, after all, wholly multi-ethnic and, with that, came people from all over the world and beyond its edges. 'Anglo-Saxon' is a label grouping together people from the Angeln Peninsula, Saxony, Jutland, the Low Countries and elsewhere. They were referred to without care as *Saxones* by Roman authors, often conflated with the *Franci* from France, roaming North Sea pirates. Eventually, these pirates became soldiers and then settlers and this process was already occurring whilst *Britannia* was part of the Empire. Indeed, many of the legionaries guarding its shores would have been of northern stock.

In the absence of state-authorised economic and military control, new forms of expressing power and rank were needed. No longer could someone wear a toga and live in a royal bathhouse if there was nobody to repair the pipes or to appreciate civic trappings. In a collapsed economy the rich and materialistic upper classes would have found fewer means to purchase markers of identity and therefore that identity would have faded in importance as the vast majority of the populace whose surplus they lived off adapted to newer, progressive hierarchies with newer forms of expression. (In the past those different forms of expression would have been assigned terms like 'Celtic' or 'Anglo-Saxon', but they are all responses to similar things). Now, status came in the form of good old-fashioned strength, a much more malleable *and violent* form of power. We see this in extravagant burial assemblages, swords, shields, brooches and buckles, the Sutton Hoo helmet. These are not ethnically diagnostic but indicative of new material expressions, the idea of Rome expressed through mercenary activity. After all, material culture exists as a means to extend and express ideas, beliefs, practices, and personal relationships. One's territory also exists as an extension of that identity, shared between others in a mutual habitat. This applies to the 'Britons versus Anglo-Saxon' debate which might best be reframed as different 'Late-Roman' parties with different ways of expressing their heritage and identity. So, when we see the trappings of 'Anglo-Saxon' material across fifth-century archaeological layers, what we are seeing is not a mass wave of migrants but the proliferation of a new identity that became prominent amidst social, economic and political upheaval. Many burials aren't even the burials of warriors, either. Weapons existed as ideological extensions, the aspirational goods of a dead person, not necessarily their tools. These ideas and the concept of 'ethnogenesis' originate not in historical study but in social science, although ethnicity remains a fraught and difficult concept to discuss.[13] Groups all over the globe will continue to ceaselessly shift, change, rise, and fall, alongside one another, as they have for centuries. This creates the notion of 'tightly formed ethnic identities'; however, rigid ethnicities cannot be applied to the past and are defined by social closure, political salience, group acceptance, cultural differentiation (or perceived differentiation) and a sense of historical stability through recognisable traditions and legal systems.[14, 15] Identity can also be affected by someone's location. A traveller abroad might feel more 'English' than they otherwise would in England where they feel closer to a specific region. All these factors contribute to the idea of an ethnicity, and shifting ethnicities reflect and create gradual social change. They represent renegotiated social identities; they are contradictory, kaleidoscopic, dynamic.

In short, applying ethnonyms like 'Celt' or 'Anglo-Saxon' to the past simplifies much more interesting discussions.[16, 17]

However, people and ideas *were* travelling to these shores both during and after Roman administration, as revealed through genetic evidence and continental goods. Whatever we call them, many newcomers spoke languages different from those of the natives and how they perceived the world will remain a tempting puzzle. Nevertheless, some factors can be rightly asserted: Germanic place names are different from Celtic ones, which gives us some indication of the spread of dialects. Saying that, seminal linguist Peter Schrijver has proposed that Old English was *adopted* by Lowland Celtic speakers; the linguistic extinction favoured by previous scholars no longer holds. Germanic dialects were folded into Celtic tongues, probably with accents.[18] They may *already* have been the dominant language for most of the isles before the fifth century.

In some cases there is direct continuity between Late-Roman and 'Anglo-Saxon' settlements for they are often the same with no gaps, as is the case for the sites of Spong Hill and Wasperton. Here, there is evidence for fourth-century Romano-British settlement and then overlapping funerary evidence belonging to a different archaeological signature, distinct from the pre-existing insular material but not opposed to it. These 'migrations' were not ethnic wipe-outs, but changes in fashion. Periodising history is a useful teaching tool but can create unnecessary blockades for discussion: the dichotomy between 'Roman' and 'Dark Ages' is one and between 'Briton' and 'Anglo-Saxon' is another.

Other dichotomies are useful, however. Some areas of land are pleasant, others are not and this depends on the purpose of settlement. To impose tribute successfully from an unreachable fortlet, mountains are best. For reliable farmland, river valleys top the list. Typically, arable pastures form territorial cores with marginal land acting as the border. It is no wonder, then, that most of the earliest communities started along rivers or in marshlands. Economies which could juggle both arable and pastoral farming were at an advantage, doubly so if they could also support marine subsistence. By extension, hubs held greater financial value for overlords. A document known as the *Tribal Hidage*, an economic assessment of about a dozen territories, records the 'hide' count for each one. A hide is the average family's unit of wealth, cattle, a small piece of land, foodstuffs, ready for taxation. The *Hidage* is useful in elucidating further details about little kingdoms and will be referred to repeatedly.[19] It is relevant here for its inclusion of five territories all ending in variants of *-sæte*, Old English and Old Frisian for 'inhabitants', 'settlers', 'settlements', 'dwellers' or 'sitters'.

While the *Tribal Hidage* is useful, it is unknown when or where the document was compiled, nor do the contents reveal when each of the polities were created. Our earliest existing copy dates from the eleventh century but is thought to reflect information from the seventh, albeit written in a garbled hand. The *-sætna* territories have been especially debated. Are they longstanding kin groupings, the original

settlers of areas like the Wrekin and the Chiltern Hills? Or are they administratively applied judicial units[20] or established colonies, created by that ever-recognisable Midlands kingdom, Mercia, as bulwarks against an enemy? Were they settlers or sitters?

Arosætna is one, a community valued at 600 hides based around either the river Arrow between Warwickshire and Worcestershire or its twin between Powys and Herefordshire. Both nourish the surrounding soil and would have provided attractive terrain for newcomers, whether fifth-century migrants or seventh-century Mercian colonists, winding blue ribbons, teeming with frogspawn and cattails, perfect for bankside farming and weir-fishing. Buzzing midges, wet loam, turgid algae, the sound of oars hitting the water, strakes being drawn up on shingle, traders advertising their wares. Wealth.

But rivers change: not just their courses through the topography, but also their role in the development of post-Roman polities.[21, 22] On one hand, rivers are a source of life, harvest and subsistence but also act as the perfect boundary marker: 'here lies our land, there lies yours'. Territories that were established hugging riverbanks are typical of the earliest period of settlement when a need for reliable subsistence on one's doorstep took precedence. As the Early Medieval Period progressed, the idea of itinerants and overlords led to tribute and taxation, economies which could rely upon the hard work of others rather than insular labour. Rivers were no longer the 'core' of a territory, but the border.

ATHOLL

Where Aeron and Arosætna are split between geographic identifications, the kingdom of Atholl can be securely placed in the Scottish Highlands, between Drumalban and Argyll. Mentioned first in *The Annals of Ulster* and *Tigernach*, Irish chronicles compiled between the late sixth and fifteenth centuries, Atholl's name has more in common with Norway than it does England or Wales.[23] Norway's etymology has been convincingly argued to hail from 'the Northern Way', a reference to the jagged coastline linking Agder to Tromsø. A well-travelled thoroughfare, the communities along the gulping fjords eventually became known collectively: Norway. This bears useful parallels to identifying what Atholl means, but before that, there is another origin to consider.

In the *Annals* Atholl is referenced alongside its ruler Talorcan as *Athfoitle*. Elsewhere, in the Old Irish poem *Seven Children of Cruithne*, which recounts the legendary ancestry of the Picts, the character of 'Fotla' is recalled. The affairs and history of Pictland were of interest to Irish poets and chroniclers. Some linguistic work can better interrogate why.

> Seven of Cruithne's offspring
> Divided Alba into seven shares
> Cait, Ce, Círig, children with hundreds,
> Fife, Fidach, Fotla, Fortriu.

In this poem, the fabled ancestor of the Picts divides his realm between his sons. His second, Fotla, founds a kingdom in his name. Again, like Aeron's war dogs, the reality of these literary motifs matters not. When this poem was composed, a Pictish origin myth for multiple kingdoms was recognised in Ireland. The relevance of Fotla stems from the fact that the same word appears in Gaelic languages as *Fódla*, one of the names given to a tutelary deity of Irish mythology. 'Fódla' is sometimes synonymous with 'Ireland', the god imagined as a foundational figure. The linguistic similarities are telling, doubly so when considering the Gaelic *ath-* means the same as the English *re-* (repeat, replay, redo …). Therefore, *Athfoitle* becomes Atholl, meaning 'Another Ireland'.

Links between Ireland and Scotland were common, the Irish Sea acting as a crossroads for language, beliefs, trade and warfare since prehistory. Rome had failed to penetrate too far beyond the Antonine advance, nor had it reached Ireland in any great capacity beyond Meath and Tara. What connected these areas was not Roman roads and Latin but water and Gaelic dialects, variations of those spoken elsewhere across Britain. The *Scoti*, from Ireland, were labelled as perpetrators in the 'Barbarian Conspiracy' of 367 CE along with the *Picti*. In the later *Life of St Patrick*, we understand that Irish raids along the west coast were frequent enough to warrant minimal explanation.[24] Patricius, that famous saint of Ireland, was followed by figures like Colmcille (St Columba), who used the Irish Sea to spread the good word from his monastery on Iona. This water was a nexus. Several dedications to Ionan monks have been found across Atholl, at Pitlochry and Fergna in Moulin parish, along with Irish-style Christian bells and a sixth-century burial of a man with a quernstone. This individual, who had lived on a diet of salt-sprayed sheep and freshwater fish, had emigrated to Atholl from further north.[25] He ended his days in a long-cist burial, a funerary rite typically associated with the spread of Roman Christianity and found all over northern Britain, including nearby on the Isle of May. In this regard, Rome *did* leave an impression beyond the Antonine Wall; the religious trappings of premier society flowed over its limits.

Whether he came to Atholl because he recognised it as a heritage hotspot, because pirates kidnapped him or for a more mundane reason, the 'Blair Atholl Man' is but one example of the criss-crossing nature of the early medieval Irish Sea. And what are most useful for travellers? Directions.

Finally, we return to the similarity with Norway's etymology, following the footsteps of historian James E. Fraser.[26] Other legendary sources rich with detail are the Pictish king lists, which include a slew of characters from both Irish and Scottish mythology. Among these, and relevant details mentioned in the fourteenth-

century *Chronicle of the Kings of Alba*, *-ch* is written instead of *-th*. Like us, early medieval writers were prone to scribal errors: Atholl becomes **Áthfochla*, changing the meaning of the word. Instead of 'Another Ireland', *fochla* is Old Irish for 'north' and *áth* would therefore be 'ford': 'north ford', or 'north pass'.[27] Another northern way for travellers to recognise and embed into the landscape.

We have two origins for Atholl. One rooted in pseudo-history and the name of a fictitious antecedent, another based on useful everyday geography. The latter seems more plausible, with the former an invention to explain a place name or, more interestingly, to stake contemporary claims to parts of Scotland. '*Ath-Fotla*' was certainly in currency by the eleventh and twelfth centuries; an Irish origin placed in the past, marking central Scotland as a place of alleged early Gaelic settlement. This was not uncommon: West Saxon chroniclers invented primogenitor figures to solidify their ownership of the Isle of Wight, as if to say, 'we have always owned this land because it is named after our ancestor'. More probably is that Atholl's name arose through a need for travellers to recognise what parts of the landscape led where, and its similarity with the word '*Fódla*' was noticed only later – this 'northern pass' between Drumochter and Killiecrankie: the gates of Atholl.

And its gatekeepers were the Picts, as best we can understand. The phrase *rex Pictorum* first appears in the 680s, displaying that a Pictish identity was recognised and used by rulers of the highlands. There was no single ethnically consistent area of the British Isles, though: these 'Picts' spoke a similar language to their southern neighbours and contingents were made up of Gaels too. The original usage of *Picti* may just mean 'barbarian', differentiating those who were less Romanised than others, regardless of linguistic or cultural background. Thus, the term 'Pict' is a Roman invention. They were the 'other', with this label becoming adopted and repurposed over subsequent centuries.

Scotland was never a backwater. Luxury items and tableware from the Mediterranean arrived in the highlands via complex long-distance trade routes from the sixth century onwards. The 'northern pass' had a role in these networks, linking Scotland to Constantinople and the Rhine, with natural features like Schiehallion guiding travellers ever northward. This conical peak of Perthshire, sometimes called the centre of Scotland, has been used as a guiding point for centuries. When Colmcille and his Ionan monks traversed Scotland, they did so through Atholl. By the eighth century Northumbrian historians regarded it, Mar and Moray as central to the Pictish *principatus*, a network of monastic and secular power spreading through the northern pass. The *Life of St Columba* even refers to a *regio* to the west of Ayrshire, near the Hebrides.[28] This was 'the rough and rocky region called Artda Muirchol', remembered in Ardnamurchan.[29] Several such *regiones* existed across Scotland,* and while we do not have a firm grasp on what Pictish kingship looked

---

* From the *Life* alone, we have Coire Salchain (Morvern), 'the little land of Aitche' (Islay), Airchart-Dan (Glen Urquhart, Inverness), Artchain (Tiree), 'the district which borders on the Lake Crogreth' (somewhere near Loch Creran), Delcros (somewhere 'thorny' near Iona) and Cainle (an unknown mountain realm).

like, many rulers must have been sponsoring Ionan monks for there to have been such a closely-tied network of interlinked communities. Rulers like Talorcan may have acted as patrons, his bloodline tied with fellow kings, en route to creating some kind of hegemony in the eighth century, led by a *rex Pictorum*. In a near-contemporary poem written about Colmcille, he is referred to as converting 'the arrogant ones who surrounded the great king of the Tay'.[30] Whomever this was, they represent the knots that bound Irish monasticism to Pictish might.

Whether it be an interchange for travellers like the Blair Atholl Man, religious institutions like Colmcille's Ionan monks, luxury imports from Rome and Constantinople, or the marching armies of Pictish overkings from Moray, Atholl has always been central to Scotland.

BERNICIA

Our sources for the previous realms were sketchy, mistranslated poems, excerpts from legendary genealogies and the tattered ends of old manuscripts. The best textual records from the Early Medieval Period are chronicles and annals. But even these are riddled with biases and those who wrote them were not trained as are modern historians but instead in the art of biblical philosophy. Chronicles are never sterile accounts of what happened when and who was where but are instead narrative histories, overly imbued with personal or regional affectations, with attached parable truths or moral lessons hiding twisted details to suit contemporary politics. They all need taking with a pinch (or handful) of salt. This is not a criticism of these writers: they were, and still are, immensely influential. Chief among them is the Venerable Bede.

Bede is a legend even amongst those with a vague idea of English history. Not a legend like Arthur, Gwallog, or Fotla, but a real person whose efforts have left behind a tremendous legacy: he popularised our current dating system, for one. On Thursday 26 May 735, this great man died after struggling 'with frequent attacks of breathlessness' for some time. Allegedly, according to one of his disciples who wrote down his final words, Bede remained spritely up till his last breath, dictating to scribes what to write and singing the praise of God. An often-quoted poem is attributed to his final hour, the so-called *Death Song*, but the authorship is uncertain. We can be more confident about the works that Bede wrote while he was alive, scrawling with a quill in a corner of his monastery at Jarrow. He is responsible for biblical commentaries, geographies, scientific and computing treatments; he compiled books of hymns, hagiographies, dedications and lists of abbots and monks he admired; he wrote about epigrams, philosophy, his love for poetry and his thoughts on both the beginning and end of the world. All of it was rendered through a devout Christian lens. Bede's world was multicultural; his mentor, Benedict Biscop, had undertaken five journeys to Rome and brought back continental artisans and ideas which became embedded in Jarrow. The red-striped concrete that made up the monastery, the glass used in the windows, and even the chanting styles of the chorists were deeply Roman. So, too, was Bede.

But he was also an ardent Northumbrian, a people he claimed were formed from all who were north of the river Humber, that great artery that bisects central eastern England. A natural boundary, prior to industrial drainage the Humber was surrounded on nearly all sides by impenetrable marshes. Because of this, while it separated overland travel, it was vital for maritime trade. The etymology of Northumbria leaves a geographic origin clear, although there is good reason to believe that the actual limit was farther south, based around Dore and Whitwell, or the Isle of Axholme.[31]

In Bede's time, Northumbria was beset by civil strife and political tension, its heyday long passed. As a result, his work languishes in the glory days. But Northumbria was not always united; instead, it was split between two halves. The most famous of Bede's works is the *Ecclesiastical History of the English People*, an account of the sixth and seventh centuries from a Northumbrian perspective.[32] The word 'Northumbrian' frequently appears, although as a broad descriptor of generic peoples above the Humber, not as a defined political entity. Therefore, there is good reason to believe it was a new term in Bede's time, with 'Humbrian' having been common a century prior. Still, Bede used it and held a special passion for his half of the kingdom: Bernicia.

Coterminous with much of Northumberland, the legendary origin of Bernicia centres around a figure called Ida, who sailed his army from Angeln and captured the fortress of *Din Guaire* from the locals, founding a mighty dynasty. His grandson would later gift this fortress to his wife, Bebba. It became Bebba's fort: *Bebbanburg* – Bamburgh.

While the Britons are positioned as the nemesis to the Idings, it is quite clear from linguistic studies that the kingdom has a native origin. Another early medieval historian, writing in ninth-century Wales, described Bernicia as *Brynaich*,[33] 'the land of the high passes', and many of the toponyms across the county are of Old Welsh descent. History is rewritten to suit the times: while Bernicia was undoubtedly forged out of a pre-existing British polity, it was remembered as an Anglian powerhouse. To Bede, Bernicia was the rightful birthplace of Anglian might: the dynasty of the Idings included the man responsible for one of the earliest proto-states: Oswald.

The territories in this book vary in size, strength, scope and scale. Some are simply a cluster of huts outside a Roman ruin, others are sprawling webs of interconnected peoples united by an ideology. Northumbria was arguably the first regime of England – a unified collection of core territories – and a large part of that is down to Oswald. Taking his place on the throne in 633, Oswald was the first English monarch to gift land in perpetuity to the church, then a rapidly developing power. In doing so, this 'book land' outlasted Oswald's death and became a source of governance. Oswald was a charismatic ruler, succeeding in knitting together the power of the individual with the power of the community. He operated within the economic and socio-political bounds expected of contemporary leaders, establishing a true continuum of power. Where beforehand kings were largely peripatetic and generated wealth through tributes, Oswald created something that would endure through interregnums. The church, now insured by land, had the influence to install future rulers and to maintain the establishment *in-between* rulers. The church also destabilised local and pagan power groups, reducing those with the power to install authority to a small number: joining the church was joining *the club*. In this regard, Oswald knitted society and an ideology together. Bernicia, Northumbria, was no longer simply a cluster of kin groups but a lordship.[34]

Like us, Bede thought much of this, and of Oswald. His *Ecclesiastical History* is dripping in Bernician flair, with mentions of other kingdoms often underplayed.

As far as Bernicia goes, it was a little kingdom that engulfed those around it under the reigns of Oswald's father and his successors, notably his brother Oswiu, his queen Eanflæd and their son Ecgfrith. Its power can still be seen in archaeological remains: the site at Yeavering features timber halls and a grandstand built for preaching and inspirational speeches. Huge enclosures for corralling cattle were found here and, nearby at Millfield, arenas to parade victors' spoils. Millfield is one of the only sites in Bernicia with unique burial evidence; elsewhere the cemeteries are indistinguishable from northern British ones. It is increasingly clear that

Bernicia was not an Anglian invention but a poly-ethnic one. The internationally significant monastery established on Holy Island was one too, the fortress of *Bebbanburg* another. Here, over four-hundred individuals excavated at the 'Bowl Hole' display diverse isotopic origins, found amongst the dunes south of the castle. The skeletal remains classified on the Bamburgh Digital Ossuary hail from West Scotland, Cumbria, elsewhere in Northumbria, several from Scandinavia and at least one from far to the south beyond Brittany. As people came to Bernicia from far afield, Christian stone sculpture blossomed outwards, influenced by Irish styles from the seventh century; as a result, standing crosses dotted across places as far as Nithsdale owe their origins to Northumbrian expansion. After Oswald's day, his brother would even decide the fate of Christianity in the north. Bernicia was not just a kingdom but a realm of kings, a furnace that forged Oswald, Oswiu and Ecgfrith: Northumbrian dynasts with imperial ambitions.

At its greatest extent, Northumbria stretched from the Firth of Forth down to Nottinghamshire and Lincolnshire, imposing overlordship across territories in Lancashire, Cumbria and the Midlands. The *Lindisfarne Gospels* are a masterpiece of scripture and illumination and only one example of many a candlelit folio born from the rich artistic and educated culture that, momentarily, united northern England together under banners of learning, church and visions of Empire.

By 26 May 735 this supremacy had started to wane. Northumbria had first buckled under a disastrous defeat against the Picts in the late seventh century and infighting had wilted what remained. Bede's final glimpse of Bernicia was of one fraught half of a greater whole, a whole that would continue to crumble under both insular and foreign pressure into the ninth century. In the Viking age, the two halves of Northumbria would re-emerge in bastardised forms, Bernicia retaining its fierce independence long into the tenth century, although drastically diminished.

The Northumbrians on Bede's pages, by contrast, remain proud and imperial, beholden to a manifest destiny. Nowhere is this more apparent than in the quests to recover pieces of Oswald following his brutal dismemberment in 642. His arm, viewed as incorruptible, became the basis for an enduring Christian cult embedded with pagan undertones, one that would spread across Europe. Grisly pieces of the past; shards of a powerful king and his powerful kingdom. The fear of 'what comes next' is one of the most effective means of coercion available, security in the *here and now* doubly important. Oswald understood this and ensured that the church created a tangible administration out of both to ensure a brighter future for Northumbria.

It is no wonder Bede looked to the past.

ʘBILMIGA & SPALDE

There is no recorded past to look back to when it comes to the rarely-discussed territories of Bilmiga and Spalde, once recorded in the *Tribal Hidage* only to fade into obscurity, appearing only in dimly remembered place names. Spalding Moor and Spaldington, East Yorkshire and Spalding in Lincolnshire; Billinghay, Horbling and Billingborough too, and Billingham on the Tees. These are both small judicial entities, 'the dwellers of the ditch' and 'Billa's folk' respectively, who shared similar territory and may have moved northwards, into Bernicia, at similar times.

Bilmiga appears in the earliest versions of the *Hidage* but is later spelled with extra syllables as *Billmiligas, Birmiligas, Biliniligas* and *Silimligas*. The *Hidage*'s information was repeated in a twisted manner, so misspellings are a plausible explanation for these discrepancies. However, it is possible that 'Bilmiga' and 'Billinga' are two separate territories. We can only guess at the location of the latter.

The place names Billinghay, Horbling and Billingborough, all from South Lincolnshire, point to a dispersed kin-grouping associated with a common ancestor. The locations line up with distributions of important cremation and inhumation cemeteries, along with the archaeologically-identified production centres at Sleaford and Garwick, so it is likely they represent a small *regio*. Over nine hundred continental amber beads and bag-rings fashioned from elephant ivory are known from the Sleaford site, along with a *pressblech* die at Garwick used in the stamping of designs onto foil. These were rich trading centres of Kesteven, evidenced by the sheer quantity of seventh-and-eighth-century coins found which dwarf the amount recovered from the rest of Lincolnshire.

Whilst this land was almost all tidally bound, a few islands would have crested above the waves, encircled by brackish peat. One is known from the silt of Holland, adjoined to dry land via the old Roman road of King Street. There may have been an administrative centre here, perhaps near Wykeham, which developed into a small, organised hub of commerce in the fifth and sixth centuries, profitable enough to justify the 600-hide value attributed to Spalde. This was a territory judged individually, valued the same as the Arosætna, representing a distinct *regio* within a larger Lincolnshire or Cambridgeshire-based *provincia*. Both Wykeham and Garwick may have been the respective *-wics* of Spalde and Bilmiga. Archaeologically, a distinction between Holland and South Lincolnshire is evident, based on cemetery placements and old watercourses of the river Glen. These lands were separated. Several large and important cremation and inhumation cemeteries tied with North Sea populations and burial rites extend around Lincoln[35] but there are none in Holland, where the available evidence points to a much more subdued form of interment. As Caitlin Green has argued, it might be that the Spalde's affiliations were local: the Christian Brythonic burial tradition was unadorned and can be archaeologically invisible, unlike the lavish Lincolnshire and Kesteven cemeteries.[36] The people of Spalde, then, are a mystery. The *Death of St Guthlac*, written in the eighth century and usually referred to as 'Guthlac B', describes an unacculturated army of Britons dwelling in these marshes 'as far north as the sea',[37] but the Kesteven cemeteries of Baston and Aberg display Jutish and Kentish material culture, like great gilded square-headed brooches. Whether they swung this way or that, to local or overseas customs, the rich traders of Spalde and the Bilmigas eventually moved northwards.

But we don't know *when* this happened. The earliest attestation of Lindisfarne, *Lindisfarena*, means 'the travellers of Lindsey', a district of Lincolnshire with historical roots; this was a kingdom annexed by Northumbria in the seventh century. It is plausible that the first migrants to Lindisfarne and the Bamburgh region originated *from* Lindsey, an area which was indeed significant for the later development of Northumbrian lordship. This is made more interesting when we consider the place names of Billingham, Spaldington, Spalding Moor and Jarrow, all of which seem to be named after kin groups from Lincolnshire: the *_Billingas_, the *Spalde* and another we will visit later. Arguments abound about the push-and-pull factors for migration between these areas. It might be that the first monks of Lindisfarne were specifically selected from Lindsey, or perhaps those lords Bede so admired originated not from Angeln directly, but Lincolnshire. Ida, the Bernician progenitor, may very well owe his ancestry to Holland's silt. Even Jarrow, where Bede composed most of his *Ecclesiastical History*, owes its etymology to the 'mud people' of the Cambridgeshire marshes.

Overlooked by many, even Bede, these fens and their dwellers played a central economic role in the sixth and seventh centuries.

Used for making foil mounts, this die, recovered from Garwick, would have been a useful tool for an artisan working and selling wares on the western North Sea rim (LIN-4F6CE7).

BRAHINGAS

The Rib Valley has been inhabited for over two millennia, a verdant strip of lazy rivers and arrogant lakes, boasting their supply of freshwater fish. At its centre is the river Rib, fed by tributary streams like the Quin, itself fuelled by subterranean springs. Hertfordshire bursts with life in springtime and on hazy summer evenings the Rib Valley takes on an otherworldly appearance. One can see why this would be an attractive place to settle.

So, too, did the Brahingas, a group first recorded in a ninth-century charter. Their name means 'the people of Braha', from Old English -ingas. This is one of the most interesting Germanic linguistic elements, observable in hundreds of toponyms across England, such as the Hertfordshire village of Braughing. Wherever -ingas is present, at the end or in the middle of a word, it usually relates to a group named after or in honour of a single individual, whether real or otherwise, a landmark, or a judicial division.* A great example would be Eaton Farm, Surrey, first recorded as *Getinges* in a seventh-century charter ('the people of Gēat', S 1165). Gēat appears in various legendary genealogies[38] and can be understood to be an aspirational composite of Germanic-speaking folk from Sweden and its environs – ergo, not *one* individual, but the *idea* of an individual, an invented rockstar to name a community after.[39] As for Braha, their name is all we know, real or not. We also do not know much about the people he inspired; they may have named their community after him because he was a powerful leader, because he was buried nearby, or like with the *Getinges*, because he was a recognisable icon from contemporary pop culture. Toponyms with the -ingas element have been argued to be from the seventh or eighth centuries, but they reflect much earlier land claims.[40] It was in the ninth when the Brahingas were first mentioned, in a document referring to the gifting of ten hides of land on the promise that once the landowner died these lands would fall under the jurisdiction of the monastic community of St Albans. The *Tribal Hidage* does not list the Brahingas. It does mention polities that existed in the same area, however. The Brahingas, then, probably had already been absorbed by a larger neighbour before the seventh century although they remained in the landscape as a tightly-knit communal or administrative identity.

---

* Or, in broader texts and tales, to signify a specific 'race'. The fire-breathing *Healfhundinga* ('half-hound people') are said to hail from unknowable India in the Old English *Book of Monsters*.

They were not alone, either, for nearby were the Wæclingas, remembered in today's Watling Steet and St Albans. Bede names the city Wæclingacaester and a charter from the last decade of the tenth century even states 'Verulamium, which our ignorant call Vaeclingacaestir' indicating that, as with the Brahingas, the Wæclingas remained a recognisable community. Both groups occupied well-drained soils at opposing ends of the Rib Valley, flanked by a more extensive *regio* in the Chiltern Hills. Much as the Brahingas had been engulfed by these larger polities, so, too, were these *regiones* absorbed. By the time that ninth-century charter was drawn up, the Brahingas were being juggled between Mercia and Wessex. This process of annexing and then owning others' land would have resembled protection rackets; Brahing territory became a gift that could be patronymically given.

Given these changes in ownership, it is worth pondering if the tenth-century Brahingas and Wæclingas were descended from the original kin who settled their respective sites or if entirely different people inhabited the soils, keeping the name. This would have had some precedence because the core territory of the Brahingas seems to have been centred around an extant Iron Age hub.

The Braughing site is extensive, its history as long as the Rib Valley. It features circular buildings with chalk floors, rectangular structures occupied between 50 BCE and 60 CE, encircled by ditches of variable length acting as tax barriers or defences. Pottery from Gaul and Italy made their way to Braughing long before Roman legionaries stamped their authority over the place. This was a locally important centre which became internationally promising once they did. However, by the second century, Braughing's sphere of interaction had shrunk, the commercial requirements of Imperial exchange not met. Still, Braughing remained important within *Britannia*'s southern lowlands. Spindle whorls, used in textile operations, litter the archaeological layers, along with complex moulds for casting and strips from worked lead and bog-iron.[41] Nearby, Baldock and St Albans display tantalising evidence of Late Roman continuity,[42] as does Welwyn. These areas retained their administrative importance into the post-Roman period,

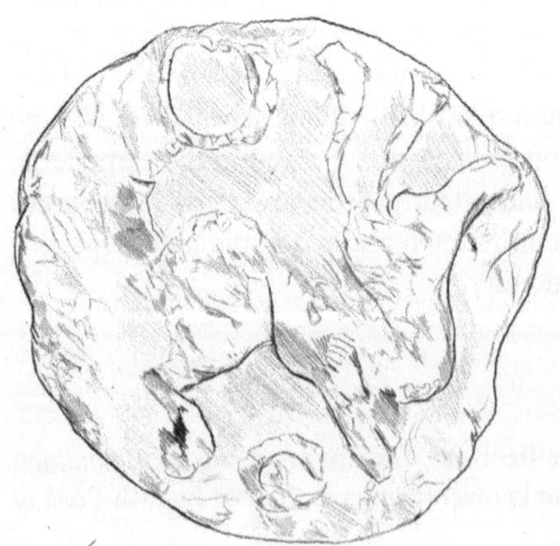

Coins such as the above have been found all over Braughing and Puckeridge, from both Iron Age and Roman layers of occupation. These coins symbolise the Catuvellauni tribe.

re-purposed as minsters or farms. This was productive land, overflowing with yield, making it popular not just to Iron Age settlers but also to those who followed.

But who were these people? Did Braha and the boys sail down the Rib one afternoon to find an abandoned Roman establishment, overgrown with vines and pockmarked by moss and mud? Or were the 'settlers' of fifth-century Braughing already present and did these people maintain continuity with their heritage and location well into the tenth century? The Brahingas may have been here all along or, if they were a migrant group, they clearly were not the first to take advantage of the Rib Valley's bounty.

BRYCHEINIOG

Granite peaks and wooded valleys, heather moors squelching underfoot, roaring gorges and heavy skies, the mist-laden fastnesses of the marcher lords, waiting waterlogged in the black mountains. Brycheiniog.´

The Brecon Beacons ascend out of south-east Wales destined for greatness, touching the sky at Sugar Loaf, Pen y Fan and the Skirrid. This land has long served as a formidable blockade between England and Wales, where the Forest of Dean gives way to open plains and shadowed vales, where Geoffrey of Monmouth compiled bastardised versions of history in the twelfth century. He spun tales about a king called Arthur who was destined to reclaim *Lloegr*, the lost lands of the Welsh: England. From this same literary soup sprang Brychan the 'little badger', the legendary founder of Brycheiniog, who had wrestled the former kingdom of Garthmadrun from his wife and renamed it in his honour.[43] Brychan makes frequent cameos in Irish and Welsh hagiographies and, in the twelfth century, is mentioned alongside Arthur and Guinevere in the war against King Gundleus of Gwynllŵg.[*] Gundleus had kidnapped one of Brychan's twenty-four daughters, who were, along with his twenty-four sons, responsible for the spread of Christianity throughout Wales, expanding outwards from their royal residence at Talgarth. From the Old Welsh *tâl-* and *-garth* for 'end of the ridge', Talgarth proudly displays its origins as the heart of Brycheiniog on its roundabout. Rightly so, the town has much to celebrate. The annual Talgarth Festival held in August is one of many reasons to visit this Welsh hubbub: a modern celebration, but one with striking parallels to the kind of artificial rituals forged in the Early Medieval Period, made to celebrate ancestors real or otherwise, claims and victories from imagined histories.

The history of Brycheiniog, as written above, is suspicious. Aside from a strong possibility that Brychan is a Welsh rendition of the Irish Broccán, thus revealing the kingdom's overseas origins, we must rely on archaeology to learn about Brycheiniog's past. Thankfully, the Brecon Beacons are littered with it. Be it the Roman fort of *Gobannium* or the plentiful *ogham* inscriptions scattered across the Usk and Severn valleys, Brycheiniog tells a story through its landscape a thousand-times richer than anything Geoffrey could invent. This story, like the archaeological

---

[*] Gwynllŵg's historicity is uncertain but, if it was real, it was probably based between the rivers Rhymney and Usk. It was traditionally viewed as a district within Morgannwg, itself a merger of two earlier kingdoms.

record of all these little kingdoms, is dominated by high status sites, a discovery bias that leads to each realm being characterised by one or two locations: the Iron Age hub of the Brahingas, Mither Tap and the Bailies of Bennachie, the dolphin-laden entrepôt of Flixborough. Like every territory in this book, Brycheiniog is more than just one type-site, more than the legends of Brychan and Arthur.

Removing legend from the equation has no impact on Brycheiniog's historical importance either. Listed in the *Antonine Itinerary*, the fort of 'Gobannio' is joined by two more near Usk and Kentchester, linked together by a network of military staging posts founded in the first century to quell local resistance. Elevated ground along the river Gavenny afforded the legionaries of *Gobannium* an opportunity to press the iron hobnails of Rome upon the untamed valleys; sling-shot ammunition and bronze military equipment have been found in excavations of the site, along with everyday items of habitation; Samian-ware pottery sherds, evidence of granaries and postholes, Augustan coins and timber ditches. Like Northumberland's *Aesica*, *Gobannium* remained long after legionaries withdrew. At the dawn of the eighth century, faded moth-eaten maps of *Britannia* were painstakingly analysed by a cleric hundreds of miles away in sun-kissed Ravenna who compiled a list of place names from Ireland to India. *Gobannium* was on that list, as *Bannio*, as were most Roman forts and locations across *Britannia*. *Bannio* is joined alongside *Alabum* and *Cicutio*, other Welsh fortresses linked by milestones. This cosmographer was not simply selecting names at random, working from the earlier *Antonine Itinerary*, but deliberately following charters and maps in a zig-zag formation, moving from the south of *Britannia* to the north over months of careful research.[44] The cosmographer described landscape features, roads and forts. The fact that there are so many in Wales reveals that there was a need to consolidate and enforce rule upon the rowdiest and westernmost of *Britannia*. *Gobannium*, then, is one amongst many, not just the many Roman forts of Wales, but also the bountiful archaeology of Brycheiniog. By the time the cosmography was compiled, the political landscape around *Gobannium* had changed, morphing from a militarised frontier to a fledgling kingdom.

In that time new features had erupted across Brycheiniog, markers of peoples new and old staking their claim to these high hills. In the Late Roman Period, there is archaeological evidence for activity centred around the fort of *Cicutio*, near Aberyscir; it was re-fortified sometime in the late fourth century as an early residence within what would become the heartlands of the kingdom. Other possible fortified sites include a hillfort near Llyswen, based on speculative earthworks and a sub-circular enclosure upon the slopes of Pen-Rhiw-Wen. The Old Welsh element *llys-* usually denotes a 'royal residence', so this attestation holds. Equally important for Brycheiniog was Llangorse lake, located along the upland bends of the river Llynfi, itself fed by the Wye which drains into the Severn estuary. Because of these rivers, Brycheiniog was not quite the landlocked liminal space it first resembles.[45] A recent and continuing upheaval in archaeological research has been our collective perception of and approach to water – rivers, oceans, swamps, fens. These are not always boundaries but may also be bridges. For Brycheiniog, what was once perceived as a barren upland kingdom, cut off from opponents on all sides, can now be appreciated more honestly as an interconnected polity tangibly linked with the rest of Wales and the Irish Sea through rivers and lakes.

With this in mind, the Irish Sea is the most likely source for Brycheiniog's origins. Whilst no mass migration occurred from Ireland to Wales, from the third century there was a general extension of an Irish Sea milieu, with coastal-dwelling locals on either side borrowing cultural elements from their neighbours. Importantly, cultural discourses like this were not just occurring in south-west Wales but also in Cornwall and Scotland. Indeed, cross-pollination between people on both sides of a body of water characterises the North Sea, too, where art, ideas and languages ping-ponged over the gulping waves. Epigraphic script can be found on stones and markers dotted across the Brecon lowlands, some in Latin, others in an Irish script called *ogham* and many featuring both. Ogham is a vertical language based around horizontal lines etched into wood and stone which emerged from the third century through interactions with Latin script, the same time that runic and Pictish iconographic script developed. The permeation of ogham across the countryside of Brycheiniog opens a window into Irish influences along with individual dedications and ecclesiastical activity. The spread of this writing form, and others, points towards local rulers actively imitating learned Latin communities, but in an independent, regionally expressive way. Some ogham inscriptions mention the rulers of other kingdoms while others indicate the sites of unexcavated monasteries. Contemporary with Geoffrey of Monmouth, the *Book of Llandâf* preserves documents and law codes from earlier Welsh history, among which are eighth-century references to *reges Brecheiniauc*, the quality of arable farmland, the quantity of monastic sites and the distribution of fisheries. Whilst a controversial source, the *Book* – when treated alongside available archaeology – is a useful frame for mapping the realm of Brycheiniog, especially its most bountiful sites.

It is easy, then, to get carried away when discussing the crannog at Llangorse Lake. This was an island site, easily visible from the shore. Over twelve-hundred crannogs are known from across the British Isles with a significant concentration in the south-west of Ireland, again pointing to a probability that the building style originated over there. When was the crannog built? Dendrochronological dating, the study of tree rings, indicates that Llangorse Lake was crowned with its timber precipice sometime between 889 and 893, during significant tension with Mercia, Wessex and Scandinavian raiders. We must not view Llangorse as automatically militarised, however. Palynological analyses, the study of microscopic, fossilised pollen, have revealed that residents were cultivating sorrel, corn spurrey, ribwort, dandelion and other species of plant for local subsistence. Some of the seeds may have even come from imported foodstuffs. Llangorse Lake functioned as a central place, perhaps *the* core of Brycheiniog.[46] Bream and pike filled the nets of fishermen as cranes flew overhead. The crannog sits closest to the lake's northernmost shore and may have been reached by dugout log boats, like one discovered in 1925.

This boat was dated to the ninth century and was probably one of many types used for the variable riverine routes of early medieval Wales, stretching from the old Roman quay at *Isca* (Caerleon) to the upland streams. Even rivers we nowadays view as impassable may still have been navigable with tiny leather-bound bowl-like

vessels called coracles, which were frequently used across the Irish Sea. People and goods followed Brycheiniog's waterways and so did religious ideals. There is a strong possibility that a monastic site lurks under the soil near Llangasty-tal-y-llyn, on the southern shores of Llangorse Lake. The nearby Neolithic cairn of Ty Illtud also displays evidence of being used as a Christian hermitage in the ninth century. This was a religious *and* secular landscape. A farmer carrying bushels of wheat on the crannog would be able to wave to her secret admirer, a chastised monk living in a tomb, over on the shore at Llangasty. Sound would also carry across the water. We overlook the experiential aspect of different senses in archaeology, but a vital study in this regard would be Rebecca Rennell's holistic analysis of the visibility and audibility of sites on the Hebrides.[47] A distant island might *look* isolated but wind can carry messages across with ease, the spread of news, jokes, warnings.

For 916, the [A] version of *The Anglo-Saxon Chronicle* records how a Mercian army stormed a place called *Brecenanmere* with fire and fury. The king at the time, Tewdr, soon acknowledged Mercian overlordship. One wonders how news of the enemy's approach would have travelled over the Brecon Beacons. Were messages guided by firelit cairns like a scene from *The Lord of The Rings*?

Published in 1989, Raymond Williams' historical fiction *People of The Black Mountains* is more relevant to Brycheiniog. The many narratives contained within cover thousands of years of history and are sprawling and disparate, much like this book. All coalesce around a body of water called Leucara, Llangorse Lake. Waterways characterise the region today; canals link Blaenavon to Gilwern to Crickhowell, vital for the region's upkeep. Brycheiniog is more than just water, however, more than just Brychan and Leucara, legends crafted by talented authors. Still, it is difficult to avoid these temptations, these type sites, these treasures. There is a reason they so often characterise the place. Perhaps Brychan does distantly immortalise an Irish takeover of a pre-existing kingdom.

This chapter opened with Roman sources of buildings and networks across Wales. Another itinerary, written in 1191, will serve to end it. Writing about the waterways surrounding that ever-central legendary lake, Gerald of Wales remarked that it 'supplies plenty of pike, perch, excellent trout, tench and mud-loving eels for the local inhabitants'. Maybe Llangorse has always been Brycheiniog's heart.

CAIT

> Near the island Britannia are many islands, some large, some small,
> and some medium-sized. Some are in the sea to her south and some
> in the sea to her west, but they abound mostly to the northwest and
> north [...]

This extract is taken from *On the Measurement of the World,* written by a scholar named Dícuil.[48] Dícuil had taught in the schools of Louis the Pious in France and Germany, often perusing vast libraries containing the works of Virgil, Homer and Julius Caesar, all familiar to him. Aside from schooling students and contributing astronomical works, in 825 Dícuil wrote the above treatment. Like Ravenna's cosmographer, he was fascinated with the far-flung regions of the world and was well-read and well-travelled: '[...] among these I have lived in some, and have visited others; some I have only glimpsed, while others I have read about.' He may have spent time in the Hebrides alongside Ionan monks. An important Columban monastery at Portmahomack, flanked by the nearby elite centre at Burghead, may have been visited on his northward voyage, since it was the foremost ecclesiastical site in ninth-century Scotland. It was Pictland's equivalent of Lindisfarne, sharing a symbiotic relationship with Burghead much as Holy Island did with *Bebbanburg.* Further north, and indeed the focus of Dícuil's comments, were scattered monastic cells dotted amongst the tumbling blue of the North Atlantic: Christian anchorites clinging to island chains like Orkney and the Hebrides, Fair Isle and Shetland, even the distant Faroes, humbled in service of God.

The windswept northern coasts of Ireland and Scotland and all the islands in between, were a seascape of activity long before an infant Julius Caesar even dreamed about conquest. As with Brycheiniog's rivers, the waters of the North Atlantic were a lubricant for mobility and exchange, from the brochs of Shetland to the roundhouses of the machair plains. At the dawn of the sixth century, a cleric called Gildas compiled a woeful polemic against several kings and the state of the British Isles. This is the famous *On the Ruin of Britain* which, alongside Bede, is one of the most widely cited textual sources for our period.[49] In his candid biblical rants, Gildas describes the 'terrible hordes of Scots and Picts eagerly coming forth in their tiny crafts across the Irish Sea'. While he is describing a pseudo-fictitious version of events, he recognised the Picts for their aquatic affinity. This also has archaeological precedence.

Portmahomack, for instance, was suitably placed to launch naval expeditions from the Firth of Forth and stone carvings indicate widespread use of the coracle across Scotland. At Dunbeath the discovery of two Christian inscribed stones was followed by the excavation of an ecclesiastical site. Here, stone channels and rectilinear cobbled outlines point to a small pottery-producing stead.[50] This is one of the few pre-Scandinavian archaeological sites across Caithness, the rest of the territory (and toponyms) swallowed by Old Norse influence in the ninth century. Nearby is the speculative Iron Age nucleus at Latheron, which included rectilinear longhouses, a fortified multi-storey stone building and a rare example of a compound roundhouse. These roundhouses form a 'figure of eight' when looking from the top down and are barely understood; another was excavated at Cnip on Lewis, tentatively dated to the third and fourth centuries. Were you to gain an eagle's eye view of early medieval Latheron, you might have seen activity but, unfortunately, the site is undated. Similarly fragmentary is a site at Lambsdale Leans on the north coast, where long-cist burials underlie a later seaside structure. Over the Irish Sea, on Ireland's east coast are suggestions of a seventh-century water mill at Strangford Lough. Parallels may also have existed in Scotland, and at least one is known from the slightly later Faroese site of Toftanes. In most cases, these sites are marginal and forgotten.

In contrast, nowhere is a better location for a high-status site within Atlantic Scotland than the Brough of Birsay. People cast metal here, illuminating the overcast skies of Orkney with sparks from salted forges. Hammer and tong worked overtime to bring bubbling crucibles out of the blacksmith's pit, to pour liquid flame into steatite moulds, casting the beautiful jewellery of early medieval Scotland.[51, 52] The art of metalworking was an extraordinary thing. Our tendency as archaeologists is to focus on elite jewellery, the Hunterston Brooch, for instance, but most metalworkers crafted mundane everyday things: horseshoes, iron nails for ships, repair work to steady buildings. On the Brough, a few pieces of eighth-century material have been excavated underneath a later Norse layer. They include a selection of cross-slabs and grave markers, adorned with symbols, pointing to a significant Christian settlement that existed right here atop the crown of the British Isles. Three cloaked warriors armed with spears and shields march in a silent procession on one slab, their heads shadowed by a sea-eagle and Pictish symbols. Who these individuals represented, whether they were part of a kingdom or not, they were heralded, etched in stone. These figures represent the idealised version of a warrior. Specimens of the north.

Further north still, on St Ninian's Isle, Shetland, was found an assorted hoard of metalwork, forged by artisans similar to whoever was spouting flame on Orkney. Twenty-eight silver and silver-gilt objects were found in 1958, among them two-headed beast and penannular brooches, sword pommels, hanging bowls and a porpoise jawbone.[53, 54] The objects range from the secular to the spiritual, perhaps a distinction here is unnecessary, and from the Midlands to the North Atlantic. Out here, Shetland was connected to an elite exchange network, a ley line that allowed island-dwelling elites to interact with the goings-on of the mainland. Consider the brooch makers who forged these items; did they create their masterpieces knowing the recipient in advance? It is easy to observe adornments from an external perspective; they are designed to be seen by others. Many details on the St Ninian Isle's brooches are tiny, however, and could only be fully appreciated by the individual wearing them, looking down at his or her cloak. While a display of ostentatious wealth, many of these items would be important only to the wearer: a hushed prayer here, a gentle touch of the brooch there, intimate moments lost forever. Consider the process of brooch making, the artistic inspirations preserved in the maker's mind, the slate drawings and template designs before the final product, as known from Argyll and Shetland. Consider the heat of the forge and the howling wind outside the door; the anticipation ahead of gifting the brooch, the maker expectant and nervous, itching for a glowing review.

Out here in the North Atlantic people were as intimately woven into these networks of gift-giving as anyone on the mainland. Let us not forget them, be they the silent monk clutching a porpoise jaw or the island queen smiling down at the brooch on her chest.

Moving away from archaeology, in a study of Scottish place names,[55] William Watson postulated that the ancient territory of Cait means what it sounds like: 'Cat'. This name, while not explicitly tied to the aforementioned islands, is generally mapped onto Atlantic Scotland. It is preserved in toponyms like Caithness and *Innse Catt* (Shetland), Gaelic for 'isles of the cat people'. *Innse Orc*, which gives us Orkney, may have meant the 'isles of the boars'. On the topic of animals, unique Pictish symbols are found across northern Britain, among them highly-stylised depictions of bulls, boars and even dolphin-horse hybrids. These symbols and others are carved into stonework, like the 'Burghead Bulls', or metalwork like an immense silver chain from Whitecleugh, Lanarkshire. These names and artwork may have been connected to some kind of Iron Age totemic system that continued into the Early Medieval Period; they could even be the equivalent of 'brand logos' for certain dynasties. The etymology of Caithness and Shetland suggests that a shared identity existed across both areas but did the settlers recognise each other as members of 'the kingdom of Cait' or as brooch-sporting individuals?

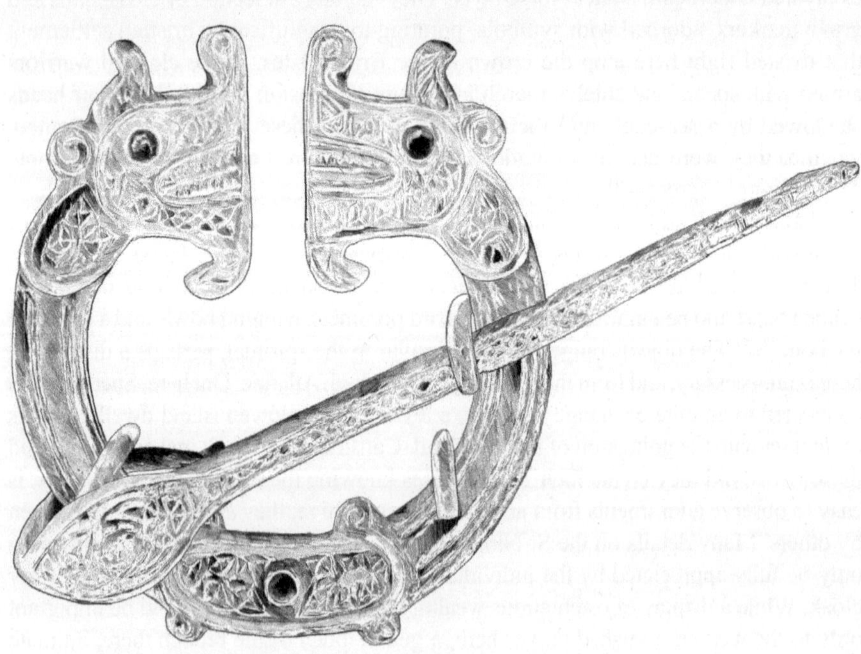

CATRAETH?

Having covered a diverse collection of realms, it seems fitting to return to Aeron and the other 'kingdoms' mentioned in *The Gododdin*, none as irritating as Catraeth.

For a long time, Catraeth was placed at Catterick due to a clear etymological similarity. Catraeth linguistically evolved into Catterick over several centuries, right? Wrong. Well, possibly, but the result is the same. The Latin form of Catterick, *Cataractonium*, means 'confluence of two rivers' or 'place of waterfalls', the latter

making little sense given the nearby geography, though the Swale does burst into rapids when deluged. *Cataractonium* has been assumed to be a Latinised form of an existing name that sounded to Roman ears like *cataracta* (meaning 'waterfall') despite the fact there aren't any. So, what did legionaries mishear? It has been hypothesised that the word was something like *caturatis* which means 'battle ramparts', which later became Latinised into *Cadarachta*, only to then be re-Celticised in the fifth century into short, mutated forms like *Cadract* and then anglicised in the seventh century into *Cetrecht*, before finally settling into the Old Welsh *Catraeth* by the ninth.[56] Gibberish? To most, it will be. The short version is that Catraeth *could* be Catterick.

In placing the conflict of *The Gododdin* here, Catterick can be evaluated as a geographic point of articulation: whoever controlled the Roman fort controlled the eastern entrance into the Pennine kingdoms. This strategic centrality makes Catterick a likely spot for a battle. The discovery of a late ninth-century sword at Gilling Beck in 1976 points to consistent military activity in this area and, when considered alongside the nearby earthworks at Scotch Corner and Swaledale, might indicate that Catterick has always been a politically ambiguous and contested region or, at least, exceedingly well demarcated. The conflict in *The Gododdin*, then, might be discussed under this lens. It may have been a battle fought over Catterick and the Aire Gap, pointing towards a concerted effort on behalf of warlords to obtain a Yorkshire-based hegemony. Placing Aeron in Airedale furthers this argument. The legendary Urien is mentioned in praise poems as ruling over both Aeron and Catraeth, along with numerous other territories.[*] Urien was not alone at this battle. We already know the war dogs of Aeron were present, as was Gwallog. Perhaps all these people were defending Catraeth, or attempting to re-secure a lost strategic foothold? Alternatively, Catraeth might just mean 'battle shore'. This would make the location of the conflict unidentifiable, but in reality Catraeth had never been the focus of *The Gododdin* to begin with. It barely appears in the [B] text, which otherwise depicts Picts and Scots as the enemies and across both versions the one constant is that there *is* no constant. Sometimes the antagonists are the 'retinue of *Deor*', other times the nondescript 'mixed hosts of *Lloegyr*'. The events depicted in the poem might be a complete fiction, 'the battle at the battle shore', a lament to an imagined lost realm. A sound geographic identification would be somewhere in Tweeddale based on the other kingdoms mentioned in *The Gododdin* but this has not yet stuck in popular imagination.[57]

---

[*]   Among Urien's arsenal of 'under-kingdoms' are *Yrechwydd* and *Idonn*. Yrechwydd might just mean 'flowing water' and could be placed virtually anywhere. Idonn, on the other hand, is described as 'west of Elfed', therefore probably in Wales. Another place called *Mathry* has been placed in Pembrokeshire. There is not the space in this book to write chapters about the other domains, nor is there the information to fill them, but for the sake of completion they are Brewyn, Pennawc, *Aber Lleu, Gwen Ystrad* or *Gwensteri*, *Llwyfenydd* and Goddeu (meaning 'forest'). Further places are listed as the sites of battles where Urien was present: *Rosedd, Argoed Llwyfain*, and *Arfynydd*. Some of these will be mentioned with more detail in later chapters and only some can be reliably placed, although even then their placements should not be taken as gospel.

For the sake of argument, let us say Catraeth is Catterick. What can archaeology tell us? The Roman fort sits along Dere Street, a vital transport route even in the Viking Age. This road runs beyond into the Castle Hills, dotted by earthworks which might date to the post-Roman period. A landscape of interaction and activity is suggested by various assemblages, revealed over decades of excavations since the 1950s: sherds of pottery urns baked at the nearby settlement of Piercebridge, used for cooking and funerary purposes; shallow pits, drainage dykes, post holes for rectangular buildings and a lone pit-house; pins made of bone and loom weights for weaving and textile work; double-sided combs consistent with a Late Roman provincial style; the corroded remnants of iron knives and scattered spearheads.[58] In 1964 the burial of a high-status fifth-century woman was discovered at RAF Catterick, found alongside copper alloy sleeve clasps, amber beads and a boar's tusk.[59] This individual had been buried with a brooch type most frequently found across Lincolnshire but the origins are unknown. Eight further burials with similar accoutrements were excavated near Bainesse Farm amidst a cluster of abandoned Roman buildings, including juveniles and females buried with glass beads and spears. The rims of pottery urns discovered alongside these specimens are stylistically Roman but have been ascribed an 'Anglian' origin based on their rigidity. Pottery has a long history of being used to identify people groups but really there is nothing stopping the fifth-century Romano-Briton from adopting a north European style of urn-making. These skeletal remains were radiocarbon dated between the third and fifth centuries, earlier than the traditional date of 'Anglian' migration to Yorkshire, so the European flavour of these burials indicates either the presence of early foreign mercenaries or, more likely, everyday cross-cultural awareness.

By Catterick Bridge a few makeshift cist tombs hewn from nearby limestone dot the site. Unlike the Bainesse Farm individuals, who were buried in the foetal position, the people interred within these vessels were cremated and remain only as marks in the mud. Some of the earliest excavation reports from Catterick describe 'Anglo-Saxon' burials all over the place with researchers arguing for a consolidated Germanic-speaking settlement already by the sixth century, indicating that the battle of *The Gododdin* was an *attack* against Catraeth on behalf of the Britons. This line of reasoning was based upon the presence of metalwork and bossed pottery designs consistent with those from Lincolnshire and simply fuels pre-established ethnic dichotomies and a belief that Catterick *is* Catraeth. Among Urien's praise poems are references to him as lord over this hypothetical place, the 'men of Catraeth [rallied] about their prince', but who is to say that Germanic-speaking settlers weren't peaceful allies of the northern British? Who is to say that mixed-marriages between indigenous and migrant groups didn't occur, given the presence of both cist burials and cremations? The similarities between Lincolnshire and Catterick's fifth-century pottery cannot ethnically diagnose these settlers as 'Germanic' either because, as we shall see, Lincolnshire has more evidence than anywhere for being poly-ethnic. Catterick's walls and buildings would have made it strategically important, yes, but the security provided by them also hints at population continuity between the Roman and post-Roman periods. Certainly, by the seventh and eighth centuries, Catterick retained its significance: an army of Northumbrian rebels rallied here in 651 and there were at least two royal marriages over the following decades.

Ultimately, we are left in the dark. Whatever transpired here can only be speculated, with even the textual sources proving difficult to wrangle.

When it comes to early medieval texts, our difficulty in using them often arises from the fact that many have multiple versions suspended throughout time called recensions. *The Anglo-Saxon Chronicle* might be fairly useful in principle but, when you consider the variants, each written in a different location at a different time reflecting different biases, the application of the source becomes more challenging. The *History of the Britons*, written in ninth-century Wales, is a collection of genealogies, histories and parables about a perceived legendary perspective on British origins up to the then-present day. Geoffrey of Monmouth used it as a source for his twelfth-century *History of the Kings of Britain*, which became supremely popular in the Norman world. Geoffrey used *History of the Britons* like a bible, fitting events into a narrative framework, warping what was already a warped history. But that's not all. The original *History* was probably written by a compiler with access to pre-existing chronicles, among them the *Annals of Wales*.[60] This much can be ascertained by the fact that various events are mentioned in both and that the detail is expanded upon in the *History*. Where the *History* mentions otherwise unknown events, however, it can be reasonably speculated that the compiler was relying on a pre-existing source that no longer exists. Kathleen Hughes once argued that some references to events in the north-west of England were compiled from a now-lost seventh-century 'Northern British' chronicle.[61] This hypothetical annal would have included whatever event inspired *The Gododdin* and, if ever found, might finally solve the mystery of Catraeth.

Cé

Bede didn't think much of the Picts. Why would he, when they were responsible for gutting King Ecgfrith, a Northumbrian imperator whose regime had toppled against their spears in 685? 'Pict' is not a reliable ethnonym but a Roman term revived in the seventh century and applied to most people north and distinct from the kingdom of Bernicia. We cannot trust most comments about the Picts but, unfortunately, all our written sources describing these people are from external perspectives. Despite this, smaller details can be assessed. Bede and later scholars subdivided Pictland into 'southern' and 'northern' zones, divided by the highlands and lowlands and frontiers like Cé.[62]

We can be confident that when Bede writes that the 'southern Picts' had 'their seats within the mountains', he is describing Atholl, based around Schiehallion. The contemporaneous sections of *The Annals of Ulster* only mention two Pictish kingdoms: Atholl is one. They do mention a few sub-kingdoms or districts, called *terrae*. One of them is Circind (or Circin), located between Aberdeen and Forfar, which overlaps with Cé, although the actual location of the latter is tricky to consider. It survives in place names much as Cait does and is remembered in Bennachie, deriving from Gaelic for 'the mountain of the people of Cé'. This would place a massive *terra* around the Cairngorms, stretching to the coast at Fraserburgh. The 'Pictish plain of Cé' is also the focus of two lost Old Irish tales, *The Ravaging of the Plain of Cé, by Galo son of Ferbal* and *The Ravaging of Bennachie*, both about distant dimly-remembered battles.* The Irish-born Colmcille is described as a visitor to the plain in his *Life* where it is depicted as a frontier between powerful neighbours. Here, as with the 'great king of the Tay', Colmcille converted a leader called Artbranan, described as 'chief commander of the warband of the region of Cé'.

What does this tell us? Not much. We know that Cé was located in the north-east of modern Scotland, encompassing Mar and the rivers of Ury, and that it separated territories like Circind from Atholl and more imposing neighbours. As a frontier region, Cé would have held a mixed culture with allegiances swaying this way and that towards a more 'northern' or 'southern' form of expression. But let us not think that these people were in any way limited in their movements; we have already seen how the Atlantic can

---

* Another Old Irish epic, the *Tale of Cano, son of Gartnán*, concerns sixth-century Scotland and the Dál Riata. The Isle of Skye (Scí) is implied to have its own distinct ruling dynasty, too. Maybe it was its own little kingdom.

act as a bridge. Whilst a spurious source, the *Life of St Germanus*, written near Lyon in the late fifth century as a theological teaching tool, describes both Picts and Saxons as regular encounters for any visitor in fifth-century *Britannia*. People roamed.

So, too, did Artbranan's warband. Cé may have had no kings.[63] It was recognised in *The Annals of Ulster* as a *terra*, a division of territory similar to a *regio*, and before it was eventually annexed by larger polities may well have just been a landscape of farmers. Most of Scotland began as disparate nucleations. Not just Cé and Circind, but *Fíb* (Fife) too, recorded in a document from 1150. These were not kingdoms at all, simply divisions of land, although more extravagant histories were applied to them retrospectively. Like Atholl and Cait, both 'Ce' and 'Fife' appear in the *Seven Children of Cruithne* as founding territories of Pictavia, enhancing their heritage from frontier farmers to legendary kinglets. Also appearing is 'Fidach', which if ever a distinct polity, may have been centred around Rhynie. If we were to look for a similar 'core' for Cé, then the peaks of Bennachie seem like a safe bet.

Standing atop Mither Tap, one of those peaks, the views afforded to the intrepid hiker are a thing of majesty, well worth the sweat and sore feet making the climb. The boundless expanse of western Scotland stretches as far as the eye can see, affording unparalleled vistas. This high up, the presumed centre of Cé mirrors Sugar Loaf in the heart of Brycheiniog, a granite tor dominating the skyline where an observer can see all the valleys, routeways, tracks and roads. First excavated in the late nineteenth century by Christian Maclagan, Mither Tap boasts a collapsed double wall and blocked well which would have been vital between the seventh to ninth centuries when the site was occupied. If we could turn back time, the walls would un-tumble themselves, the well would spring to life and activity would resume at this frontier fortress. Pottery, metalwork, mammal and fish remains dot the roundhouses and citadel crowning the precipice, a milieu of everyday life, not solely military. Well-fortified and positioned atop a barren stretch of impenetrable mountains, the residents of Mither Tap would have sat comfortably for long periods, although probably only inhabiting the area in times of desperation. If Atholl became embedded in the landscape as a cardinal direction, then Cé became remembered as a march. Presumably, Cé's first ruler was an outsider, which begs the question: who founded Mither Tap? Was it an outpost of another realm? An intrusive pustule atop an unblemished peak? Or does it mark the core of a territory built upon sworn oaths, communal feasts and mountainside raiding?

Judging by the scarce mentions in Old Irish poems, Mither Tap and Bennachie saw frequent military activity, but was this defensive or offensive? A possible paved road connects the outpost to some of the other peaks like Rushmill Burn, marked along its way by features like the Nether Maiden rock. This is the proposed 'Maiden Causeway' and, most probably, the route taken by the builders of Mither Tap's fort, whoever lthey were. Further routeways can be guessed at by the distribution of Christian cross-slabs and symbol stones across Donside, Aberdeenshire, which sadly only hint at landscapes of activity.

Questions linger over Cé like pregnant clouds above Scotland's leaden skies. What did its people think? Did they recognise that they were in a 'middle space' between northern and southern zones of influence, or did they think they were the centre of the world? A short gap in the distribution of early medieval silver

chains between the Forth and the Mounth indicates that this middle space was also marginalised in exchange networks, but surely not uninhabited.

Frontier regions are difficult to assess because they rely on the traditional view that borders are linear and sharply defined. Consult any map of 'Dark Age Britain' and it will render kingdoms with dotted lines indicating where one met another, as if they were tectonic plates. In reality, while linear frontiers certainly did exist, the areas *between* kingdoms often consisted of 'frontier zones', like Cé. At one end of a frontier was one kingdom and on the other was another: somewhere in the middle was a variable landscape and residents whose allegiance shifted depending on *where* across the frontier they were situated. Whilst only a brief mention, we get the impression from the *Life of St Columba* that Cé was home to horse-riding troop leaders and patrolling warbands. Was Artbranan an independent nomad who scavenged the land or had he been hired to watch over the boundary? There is some precedence for equestrian units in Pictland as early medieval sculptures from Argyll to Caithness display figures on horseback. The most notable example is the Hilton of Cadboll stone, but other pieces of stonework from Dunblane to Govan illustrate the regalia of a riding elite.

The best way to view Cé and other frontier zones lies not in Scotland but in Drypool, near Hull, the birthplace of the Venn diagram. If we imagine each territory as a name on a map and at the centre of individual spheres, then the outermost edges of these spheres would overlap with others. Some spheres, like Bernicia, would stretch for miles over Scotland and Yorkshire, whereas others like the Brahingas would be relatively contained to Hertfordshire. Cé's sphere of influence is within a middle overlapping section of a Venn diagram, discoloured and central. These borders were not hard, but fluid.

A relevant parallel can be found in ninth-century León and Catalan, Spain. There, law codes from earlier periods were preserved in legal texts and inscribed on sun-baked clay tablets: one of the most frequent topics of dispute involved territorial boundaries. When farmers could not agree where their land ended and their neighbours began, judges demanded proof of the border's existence; they looked for markers in the landscape such as standing stones or fences to indicate that such a border could even be acknowledged.[64] Where markers did not exist, Leonese law codes indicate that judges perambulated the land to establish them. Early medieval borders came in multiple forms; there were political ones invisible to the farmer and local ones reinforced by landmarks and folk memory. The hillfort at Mither Tap denoted just one of many 'boundary points' strewn across this liminal space.

Cé quite literally falls somewhere in the middle of this.

ℭEREDIGION

At Glanfred, near Llandre and Cardigan Bay, sit the tell-tale humps and bumps of a buried earthwork. This was a sub-triangular enclosure, a double-ditched enclave home to metalworking and cereal production located near an old church within an even older field called *cae'r odyn* ('kiln field'). This was the workplace of a ninth-century blacksmith like those on the Brough of Birsay, as revealed through the dating of some discarded slag, and it was not alone as an area of ore processing in Ceredigion, surrounded by lead production sites dating to the Roman Period and Iron Age.[65] The re-occupation of all these forges is indicated by the ninth-century date of the Glanfred site; some were even re-purposed as farms in the fifth and sixth centuries. Here, on the periphery of provincial rule, foreign occupation and the Roman 'collapse' was simply an interlude. The 'Romans' in the preceding period were just the people already present. *They hadn't left.* For the artisans and their apprentices toiling away at Glanfred, Hen Gaer and Odyn Fach, changes in the wind mattered more than changes in administration.

And greater changes would come, felt across most of the world from Constantinople to China, North America to Wales. In 536 a different kind of flame engulfed the north, lit not by the blacksmiths of Ceredigion but the tectonic forces of the very planet those forges sat upon.

Crises shape communities. They either break under pressure, leading to individuals re-negotiating their identities, or they unite. The Early Medieval Period was no stranger to crises. Some were political, others related to famine and disease and yet others were geological. Several disasters occurred between the fourth and eleventh centuries and many are described in the *Annals of Wales*, the *Chronicle of the Princes*, *The Annals of Ulster* and similar sources from the Irish Sea littoral. Natural events and abnormalities are classified within these pages as *mirabilia* - a catch-all term lumping together everything from outbreaks to eruptions, comets to cattle plagues. The utilisation of *mirabilia* between these chronicles represents a shared historiographical style; they may derive from a lost common source.

These *mirabilia* come in all shapes and sizes and are usually described very nonchalantly, demanding explanation. For example, in the entry for 447, the *Annals of Wales* state that there was a 'day as dark as night'. In 676 'a star of marvellous brightness was seen shining throughout the whole world.' In 689 'the rain turned to blood in Britain and in Ireland.' This last entry might be explained by a real, although rare, occurrence where sand from the Sahara is vacuumed up by stormy weather and then deposited elsewhere, mixing with rain and shrouding all in dark ochre. That some of these *mirabilia* can be explained by genuine phenomena is down to the efforts of Erik Grigg who systematically investigated them alongside known historical celestial and climatological events.[66] Grigg revealed that some *mirabilia* were not only fictitious but wrongly dated: the 'obscured' sun in 624 is two years early; an earthquake on the Isle of Man is in the wrong place; a mention of a comet was probably a glimpse of the northern lights. Are we to blame the chroniclers for these mistakes? Were they simply relying on third-hand information passed between monks from Ulster to Ceredigion?

The most bizarre of all these *mirabilia* occurred in 896: 'Vermin fell down from the air, like moles with two teeth; which devoured everything; they were banished with fasting and prayer.' Any number of explanations have been offered for this 'mole rain': the creatures could be voles, whose numbers can multiply rapidly over mating season. It is possible that a population of voles was sucked up by a hurricane and then dropped out of the sky elsewhere, as rarely happens with frogs and fish. The 'moles' might be a distorted reference to locusts or a proliferation of a well-worn Classical literary motif that rodents were spontaneously generated 'black matter' and not natural animals.[67] What are we to make of these flying fiends? This entry might be fabricated, a fictitious disaster that united the scripture-obsessed monks of the Irish Sea. Perhaps it was an allegorical plague to explain the benefits of religious devotion: the vermin were literally 'banished with fasting and prayer.' The attributed date is exactly in the middle of the Viking Age, so it is possible that the 'vermin' are raiding armies, described as an unnatural pestilence that could only be defeated through supplication. The turmoil of the ninth-century Irish Sea led to many crises; Scandinavian enclaves infested the northern coasts of Wales, where Ceredigion once stood independent and proud.

For 537 the *Annals of Wales* describe 'death in Britain and Ireland', perhaps the most damaging and real of all *mirabilia*. A series of major volcanic eruptions occurred somewhere in the northern hemisphere in 536, as revealed through tree-ring and ice-core dating. This event has been termed the 'Dust Veil' and its impact on the British Isles was varied.[68, 69] A drop in temperature, followed by years of failed harvests, followed by the spread of famine and the later outbreak of the Justinian Plague. For Wales and Ceredigion, people looked to God for answers. It was once suggested that Gildas, our ever-annoyed cleric, wrote his polemic under the shadow of the Dust Veil, blaming the ailing weather on incompetent leaders and foreign *Saxones*,[70] but it is now understood such references to apocalyptic weather are biblical allusions.

But the Dust Veil was not the only natural disaster to affect Cardigan Bay. A much later source and indeed the oldest cartographical render of the British Isles, the Gough Map, made between 1280 and 1340, is our key to understanding further. Only the vaguest outline of Wales is identifiable on the heavily-stylised render, along with three islands in the mouth of Cardigan Bay. Only one of these islands remains: Bardsey, just shy of the Llŷn Peninsula. The identity of the other two has been attributed to inaccuracies on the cartographer's part, but the Gough Map is exceedingly detailed in all other areas, from the locations of rivers to the distances between major cities; it also correlates descriptions in Ptolemy's second-century *Geography*. These elliptical islands existed; a southern promontory adjacent to Aberystwyth and a northern one near Barmouth. So where did they go?

St George's Channel consists of silty clay and sunken sands. Prehistoric stumps and the remnants of submerged trees have been washed ashore in northern and western Wales throughout history and so the likelihood is that this region was once not a sea at all but a very low-lying stretch of salt-marsh and quicksand, like Doggerland.* A legendary 'Welsh Atlantis' associated with Cardigan Bay is already known throughout local folklore, this being Cantre'r Gwaelod. In some of the earliest mentions, a figure called Gwyddno is associated with the place – it was his 'harbour' – mentioned alongside other 'Men of the North' in Middle Welsh triads. This king and kingdom are fictional but the historicity here comes not from Gwyddno but the terrain itself.

The fate of Cantre'r Gwaelod was first revealed in a stanza from the thirteenth-century *Black Book of Carmarthen*, translated by Rachel Bromwich: 'Stand forth, Seithenin, and look upon the fury of the sea; it has covered *Maes Gwyddneu.*' Seithenin was the fictitious keeper of the floodgates of Gwyddno's kingdom. Falling asleep at the job, the tide rushed in to claim all. Merely a fable, it is possible that this story is attached to a folk memory of a real place. A late-thirteenth-century Latin triad from the Exeter Cathedral Library MS 3514 refers to a 'kingdom of Helig' that was also submerged between Ceredigion and Bardsey Island, a separate myth but reflecting the same motif. The *Mabinogion*, a fanciful collection of Welsh folklore, contains a story about a king leading an army on foot between Wales and Ireland, fording only two rivers. It is possible that there was a tidally-locked fen environment connecting parts of Ireland to Cardigan Bay which slowly sank into the sea over centuries.[71] By the time Gildas was writing, this lost land may have lingered or, perhaps, all these tales were simply a response to visible Neolithic stumps. Like the 'mole rain', they were a pious explanation of a slow natural phenomenon.

Moving away from the water, in the north of Pembrokeshire is the presumed prehistoric tumulus of Felindre Farchog, positioned on an ancient parish boundary separating Nevern from Coed Cadw. Interred within the mound, which may have functioned as an assembly point in our period, were twenty-one burials dated between the fifth and seventh centuries.[72] Like the Blair Atholl Man, four of these individuals had been buried in long-cist graves but only one of them with any artefacts: a single glass bead. Their dimensions vary. Some of the graves are tiny, perhaps for juveniles, others are long, others still were unmeasurable. The acidic soil of Felindre Farchog has eroded all evidence of bones and teeth, but what has remained is a sense of continuity between a pre-Roman landscape feature and the burial customs of these proto-Christians of central Wales.

Identity within early medieval Wales is difficult to dissect. Even mentioning 'Wales' clouds the reader's mind with a specific peninsula of the British Isles, divided from 'the English' to the east.[73, 74] Between the fifth and eleventh centuries a Welsh identity *did* form in opposition to an English one, but different terms were

---

* The tidal lowland that stretched between England, Ireland, the Low Countries, and Denmark eight thousand years ago.

used. 'Britannia' has been used throughout this book to refer to the old Roman province, but to ninth-century writers, such as Asser, *Britannia* simply meant the conjoined areas where Celtic-speakers lived.[75] *Britannia* could be Wales, yes, but also most of north-west England, Scotland and Brittany. A territory in north-west Spain called *Britonia* is even hinted at in other sources. These realms are distinct but connected by sea and language. This is what Asser recognised, anyway, but what about the people themselves? What did the bereaved of Felindre Farchog think of their heritage and identity?

Like the names listed in the *Seven Children of Cruithne*, Wales also has a founding figure, Cunedda, who split the land between his sons: Ceredig created Ceredigion. The compiler of the *History of the Britons* recognised this, by his day an inherited legend, and states that Cunedda 'expelled the Scots with much slaughter from those countries, and they never returned again to inhabit them'. This story places the Irish on the Welsh peninsula prior to the advent of the Britons and pits them against one another. This is improbable for, as demonstrated with Brycheiniog, both peoples existed simultaneously and shared a great deal through cross-pollination. On that note the name of the Llŷn Peninsula might derive from the Irish group called the Laigin. Still, there *were* recognisable distinctions between Britain and Ireland, at least to outsiders. In the mid-fifth century, the writer Prosper of Aquitaine referred to the two as the 'Roman' and 'barbarian' islands respectively, indicating that his continental audiences held similar views.[76, 77] So, too, did Corbalengus, 'an Ordovician'. He (or his epigrapher) viewed himself as a member of the *Ordovices*, a Latinised Roman name for a local tribe. The mountainous core of Wales and the proximity of the Irish Sea and the Severn facilitated the conditions under which several group identities formed in contrast with one another – little kingdoms. There are fewer epigraphic inscriptions in the south than the north while, along the English marches, material of a 'Mercian' character starts to emerge. Ceredigion is sandwiched somewhere in the middle of 'Roman' and 'Irish' material identities and had opposing kingdoms to its west and north, the former a continuation of the tribal group of the *Demetae* and the latter argued to be an Irish or Manx colony. We will visit both of these kingdoms later.

For now, let us say farewell to Ceredigion.

The unassuming village of Cwmystwyth has been tucked away in these mountains for generations, its inhabitants sharing a history with the ground beneath their feet. In fact, the whole of central Wales is criss-crossed with intersecting hydrothermal ore veins, used since at least the Bronze Age. Lead was the principal metal smelted at the early medieval site of Banc Tynddol, Cwmystwyth, where burning boles were tended by blackened hands.[78] Scattered dates from pieces of scorched charcoal indicate consistent re-use of this plateau over prolonged periods; the smelters were not crafting anything but processing raw material, perhaps to then distribute to the blacksmiths at Glanfred. This was high quality lead, indicated by the lack of slag. Who led the smelting efforts and for what purpose is completely unknown until the twelfth century when the site became an industrious hub. Indeed, any figures of importance from the past of Ceredigion are a mystery, especially divorced from legend. An inscription found at Llanllyr records the gifting of land to 'Madonmnuac', perhaps one and the same as the Irish saint Modomnóc. Irish ecclesiastical communities active in Ceredigion are hinted at by the excavations of enclosed farmsteads at Llawhaden, in Pembrokeshire, which resemble those on Ireland's south-eastern seaboard. Change personifies Ceredigion: Irish visitors but also new methods of expressing connections with pre-Roman ancestors, as shown by Corbalengus. Whatever its origins, Ceredigion's independence faded in the late ninth century when it became merged with a frontier land called Ystrad Tywi, reborn as the over-kingdom of Seisyllwg amidst an uptick in viking activity.

With all that Gildasian moaning, *mirabilia* and the sad quiet fate of Cantre'r Gwaelod, it can be easy to focus on the negatives. A frayed thread connects the geological processes that caused the volcanic eruptions of 536 to the same ones that forged subterranean lead deposits beneath Cwmystwyth and from there to the blacksmiths at Glanfred, but this is a desperate attempt at storytelling. Some of these little kingdoms can only be viewed as snapshots that tease brilliance. A ninth-century compiler, discussing his list of the wonders of Britain, had this to say about Ceredigion, certainly a positive note to end on:

> There is a mountain called Crug Mawr, and [a] tomb on top of it, and whoever comes to the tomb and lies beside it, however short he is, the tomb is found to be the same length as the man. If he be a short man then the tomb is found to be as long as the man, and if he be a long tall man, even if he were four cubits long, the tomb is found to be as long as the man. And every traveller who is weary, if he kneels three times before it, he will never be worried by weariness again to the day of his death, even if he will go by himself to the ends of the earth.

CILTERNSÆTNA

The territory of the Cilternsætna is first recorded in the *Tribal Hidage* at 4,000 hides. It seems fitting now to afford this document some more detail. A date of creation for the earliest version of the *Hidage* has been proposed by N.J. Higham for 624-625, based on the names of polities and the absence of others which existed in subsequent decades.[79] This would make the *Hidage* a Northumbrian document, created during the reign of King Edwin to impose tribute upon newly acquired southern kingdoms, although it is worth reiterating that a year-of-creation has still not been agreed upon. Several other hidage lists were made that are now lost to us; Bede hints that Anglesey (960), Thanet (600), and the Isle of Man (300) had been similarly assessed, though most if not all of these valuations had clearly been reached via biblical numerology, and may have not reflected anything real. More agreeable is that within the *Hidage* is a second punitive list, focused on territories located in the fens near Peterborough and Oxfordshire. It is this list which includes the Cilternsætna.

Almost immediately we have a comparison to make with the Arosætna; both territories share the same suffix. The Cilternsætna were based around the Chiltern Hills, the chalk downlands that extend throughout southern and eastern England which emerge as escarpments in Oxfordshire. They rise above the Thames floodplain, creating a suitable passageway north-east to south-west or vice versa. There is a reason why so many human-made trackways converge here. Like Schiehallion, these hills functioned both as a beacon and crossroads. The Ridgeway and Icknield Way intersect the Chilterns, following the well-drained gentle descent or the high dry ground of the scarp, dotted by hillforts and monuments like the Uffington White Horse. The routes and the ground they carve through have retained importance since the Bronze Age.

Researchers of the Chilterns have largely focused their attention on the pre-Roman Iron Age from which scores of pottery wares have been identified. The earliest forms have been found at speculative settlements, granaries and storage pits at Totternhoe, Puddlehill, Ivinghoe Beacon and Terrick, their motifs demonstrating links to the continent, as do the associated metalwork finds. A possible timber-faced rampart might have existed at Ivinghoe, where loom weights and spindle-whorls indicate textile production. Later and finer wares from Adwell, Ellesborough and Pitstone further demonstrate overseas stylistic traits. The hillforts of Boddington and West Wycombe also date from this phase of occupation as industry and population increased across the surrounding lowlands. Occupation only intensified with the later addition of ditched enclosures and further storage pits around Puddlehill and an extensive earthwork running beyond Bradenham. By 110 BCE, this landscape was primed to interact with Rome.[80]

Importantly, none of these sites disappeared. As with the Brahingas to the east, the Chilterns were pockmarked with history long before the Early Medieval Period. Ridge-and-furrow farming was taking place here from at least the fifth century. Working backwards from thirteenth-century records and the *Domesday Book*, we can ascertain that the many cultivated forests across the Chilterns originally extended outwards from farming nuclei, many of which were early medieval settlements lying beneath modern townships. Attacking the Cilternsætna through research requires pincer movements, understanding the hills as they were in the preceding Iron Age and then in the High Medieval Period. Physically attacking the Cilternsætna would have been difficult, too, although military activity did occur here. A very dubious entry for 571 in *The Anglo-Saxon Chronicle* references a battle 'with the Britons at Bedford' where King Cuthwulf of the West Saxons captured 'Limbury, Aylesbury, Benson and Eynsham'. These four towns make up a total of 4,000 hides in the tenth-century *Burghal Hidage*, the amount listed for the Cilternsætna in the *Tribal*. It is probable that these four were the manorial centres of the *regio,* but the 571 entry is suspicious because the earliest years of the *Chronicle* were written retrospectively to reflect contemporary claims. Limbury, Aylesbury, Benson and Eynsham were all lost to Mercia in 779 when 'Offa took the town'. A desire to reclaim West Saxon territory may have led the compiler to assert that these manors had *always* been owned by Wessex and so a fictional battle was invented in the distant past.

But what of the Cilternsætna themselves? Both inside and outside the old Roman walls of St Albans' there is an emerging body of evidence for late fourth- and fifth-century activity: pipes and sewers were maintained, small barns and granaries were established and a small Christian community may have persevered, burying treasures and trinkets to the eponymous saint.[81, 82] *Verulamium*, still a major site, was allegedly visited by the continental Bishop Germanus in 429 when he journeyed to the British Isles to combat the growth of Pelagianism. Colchester, nearby, also displays evidence for Late Roman activity, a hoarded coin deposit here, a re-plastered fifth-century church wall there. It is the rural hinterland site of Baldock that should be afforded more attention, however.[83] Here, as at Braughing, is an Iron Age centre that morphed into a Roman site that was further malformed into an 'Anglo-Saxon' settlement with significant continuity between all of these arbitrary periods. First established sometime in the first century BCE, the Baldock site grew to become a wealthy rural villa and was redeveloped through to the early fifth century; a timber gateway was established along a major thoroughfare linking the Icknield Way to Braughing, suggesting that the spread of goods and people was being actively monitored across the Chilterns. As with Braughing, Baldock's sphere of influence and interaction shrank in the fourth century but this did not have an adverse effect on the residents. Unlike those internationally-linked Iron Age sites atop the Chilterns, no pottery whatsoever was found in the Late and post-Roman layers of Baldock. Goods stopped flowing *into* the town, but they continued to be produced; locally made fabric is known from fifth-century contexts. The fact that the Icknield Way was still in use from both Baldock *and* Braughing hints at trading networks taking on more local and insular guises; the routes remained vital, but for shorter journeys.

There is, then, both rural and urban evidence for significant continuity around these hills and hinterlands. The rich soils gave settlers plenty of harvest, supporting their local needs, even following the temporary breakdown of international trade. St Albans' archaeological layers signify a significantly shrunken and renegotiated use of the *civitas*, from a sprawling metropolitan hubbub to a marginal but spiritually vital central place. Colchester is the same and Baldock is a perfect example of the types of small settlements that survived throughout the 'Dark Ages', relatively unaffected by the socio-economic impacts that have wrongly painted this period as a time of chaos.

This period was, instead, a time of prosperity for the Chilterns and their surroundings, especially the aforementioned manorial centres. At Aylesbury, following the line of Akeman Street, pit-houses and rectangular halls have been found dispersed over what were once extensive rural landholdings, so extensive that they became the site of a later minster. Sheep, goats and cats roamed these farms, as did frogs. A number of 'wet pits' have been found at a site along Walton Road, distinct from the already present midden pits so familiar to archaeologists; these holes are believed to have been dug to access local clay deposits which were then distributed out of the settlement as pottery and later re-used as waterlogged rubbish dumps. Picture yourself knee-deep in sticky, clammy clay at seventh-century Aylesbury. Close your eyes and listen to the *ribbit-ribbit* of wildlife, feel the warm sun on your skin or rain on the nape of your neck, hear the turn of the potter's wheel and the bleating of sheep, smell the soaked mud or the roast lamb cooked on a spit with rosemary twigs. These hypothetical moments were once daily.[84] It is important to picture them, drowned under desk-loads of data.

The Walton Road farmsteads were probably a peripheral hinterland to the 'core site' on the other side of Akeman Street in Aylesbury-proper. This was much more extensive, occupied consistently into the eleventh century, home to almost a dozen post-built halls and pit-houses. By the ninth century both these areas were encircled by drainage ditches and defensive embankments, in line with population shifts and subsequent approaches to land divisions across England; Aylesbury did become a *burh*, after all, and a mint. A coin of Edward the Confessor (1042-1066) was discovered during building works along Bourbon Street. The story with Eynsham is much the same, although we have different forms of evidence to dissect. This site was less secular and more spiritual, becoming an important abbey and ecclesiastical centre from the tenth century, if not earlier. It is remembered as the home of the most prolific Old English writer ever, Ælfric. Perhaps uniquely amongst his counterparts, he was adamant to avoid posthumous scribal errors and manipulations of his works (of which there are many) and was said to have left scrupulous instructions to ensure their safekeeping on his deathbed in 1010. Ælfric of Eynsham actually hailed from further south so his presence along the edges of the Chilterns was only transient. Still, he would have observed them from his abbey window,

preaching against Danish invasions or writing about whale-hunting techniques under the pale shadow of the Uffington White Horse.

We, like the Cilternsætna, must thank the potential of the Chiltern Hills. Like bookends to our period of study, the Iron Age and High Medieval evidence expresses the benefit of high vantage points, reliable farmland and well-connected roads. Where Ceredigion was best revealed through the theme of change, the evidence from the Chilterns indicates continuity. Be it at Baldock or Aylesbury, individuals old and new consistently worked the land from the fifth century before spearheading it to new heights come the ninth. Our knowledge of the Cilternsætna ends amongst descriptions of peripheral West Saxon territories. Clearly, they thought this land was worth developing. So, too, did their forebears, all of them.

CRAVEN

It is surprising how much can be said about Craven considering it is not mentioned anywhere until 1086 in the *Domesday Book*. Even then, it remains enigmatic. We are given the names of 125 villages and towns strewn across Yorkshire, Lancashire, Westmorland and Cumbria, all ending in the suffix '-in-*Cravescire*'. From this list, a vague map can be outlined but whether this reflects an earlier polity is difficult to say. Why, then, is there even a belief that Craven *was* a kingdom if we have zero documentary evidence for its existence?

The answers lie in etymology and archaeology. This mystery begins with Craven's name. Two roots have been proposed for this extant toponym that survives in the Yorkshire Dales, both of which descend from ancient pre-Roman Celtic languages. The first is *craf-* from 'garlic', a plant introduced during the Roman Period, associated with tales of Saint David who allegedly advised his warriors to wear it in battle to ward off the Saxons. The second proposed root is *crafu-*, from 'to scrape', which hypothetically became rendered as **crav-ona* for 'the scraped place of stones' and then into Craven. Both wild garlic and scarred rock characterise the Yorkshire Dales, particularly in the south, so either etymology is possible.[85] They could have become embedded in folk memory as a descriptor for a unique territory. Limestone slumbers beneath Craven's surface, occasionally exposed like the bones of a dead goliath; the prominent rises of Pen-y-ghent, Ingleborough and Whernside remain on postcards for a reason, their silhouettes distinct, their majesty ancient, raw. At West Marton a limestone scar bursts through the soil and, while quarried in modern times, would have been extremely prominent in the Early Medieval Period. It may well have functioned as an assembly point, like Iceland's Thingvellir. Tenth-century land divisions called 'wapentakes' converge around this feature, including one called Staincliffe ('stone cliff'); this may be a description of the same geological features that inspired the name 'Craven', just in a different language.[86] Given that Staincliffe was an important wapentake within the Yorkshire Dales, it may well have been the judicial centre of Craven.

But the centre of what? The Yorkshire Dales are, to this day, marked by drystone walls, long hikes, imposing mountains and labyrinthine cave systems, as well as farmers a-plenty. Of all the sites investigated in the Dales, most are farmsteads with zero evidence of high-status material culture or social stratification. Such a thing is hard to quantify and the Dales might have just been a *regio* belonging to another kingdom but, if we are to isolate this region, we are treated with a litany of well-published excavations.[87, 88, 89, 90]

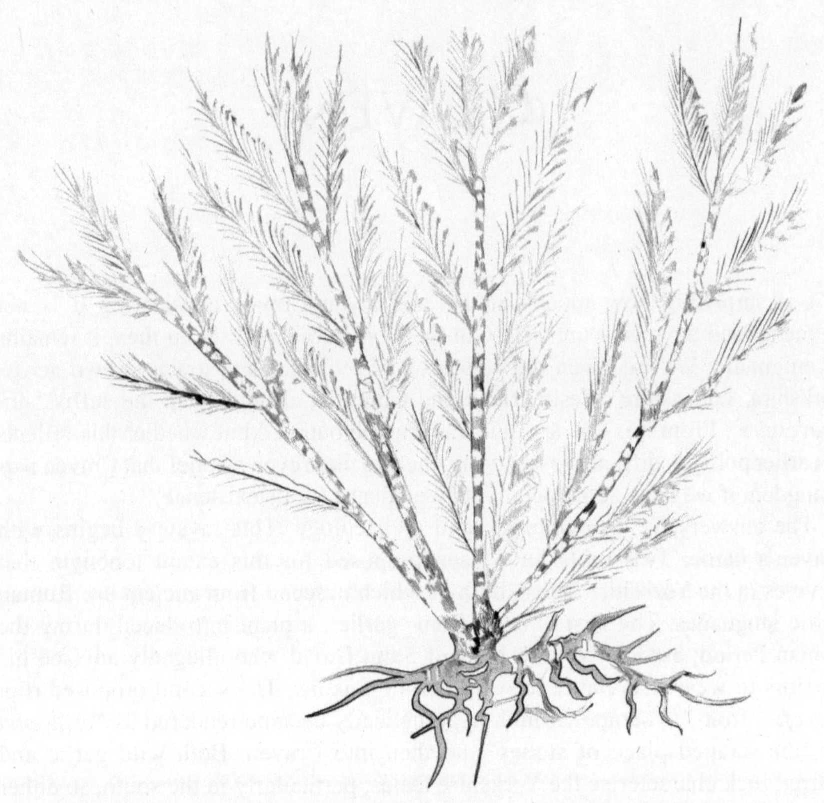

One of the remedies from the Old English Herbarium *(Cotton MS Vitellius C.iii, f. 58v) instructs patients to rub together turnip, fennel, sage, southernwood and wild garlic into a clarified honey to prevent boils. Another mixture creates a protection against elves and 'the people with whom the devil has intercourse'.*

At Gayle Lane, near Hawes, a ditch and field system were found dated between 870-890 and similar, though earlier, earthworks are known near Skipton at Hawkbank Field. Skipton was once known as 'sheep town' ('sceap-tūn'), named in a northern Old English dialect. Whoever dwelt at the shieling found at Selside also farmed sheep; so, too, did the farmers at Clapdale and Southerscales where a mixture of packed earth and limestone slabs cover the floors. People smelted and worked iron at the ninth-century site of Brows Pasture in Chapel-le-Dale whilst their contemporaries at Austwick marked the entrances to their huts with raw haematite, perhaps in a ritualised 'closing' ceremony. Based on radiocarbon dates, the earliest of these sites was inhabited in the seventh century but, interestingly, most seem to have been occupied only episodically. The arable land limits long-term viability and so many of these nucleations were occupied with generational gaps, as observed at Southerscales. All of the sites belong to an 'upland building tradition' where stone walls, rubble infills, turf roofs and rounded corners dominate.[91] There is nothing in the Dales to impress early medieval architects (although a potential *burh* beneath

Burton-in-Lonsdale might) but, as far as pastoralism goes, these lands couldn't be richer.

Under the earth skeletal remains dated between 600-780 are known from Scoska Cave, Foxholes Cave, Chapel House Wood, Arncliffe and Selside, as well as two burials from the old Roman fort at Bainbridge. A copper-alloy tap fastener from Combs Scar Cave, two iron knives from a limestone pavement at Feizor, a strap-end from Smearsett Cave, debased ninth-century Frankish coins from Attermire Cave[92] and a bone comb and silver pin from Victoria Cave: are these ritual deposits in dark liminal spaces or were these caves settled just like the above farmsteads? While it can be tempting to treat these sites and remains as isolated, we must remember the river Ribble as a vital transport route to Morecambe Bay; the haematite lumps from Austwick have been traced to southern Cumberland. It is no wonder that a rectilinear longhouse was established along these banks in the mid-ninth century. Land ownership in Craven may have been determined by natural landmarks, with farmers acting as their own rulers. The seventh-century laws of King Ine of Wessex, preserved in King Ælfred's ninth-century laws, state:

> If free peasants have a common meadow or other land divided into shares to fence, and some have fenced their portion and some have not, and if cattle eat up their common crops or grass, those who are responsible for the gap are to go and pay the others, who have fenced their part, compensation for the damage that has been done there.

Individuals in Craven may have owned their pastures but who, if at all, lorded over them is a complete mystery. Revealing details about the Dales requires parallels.

Similarities abound between Craven and Brycheiniog. Both of these realms are characterised by zones of agricultural activity contained within lowland valleys and uplands dominated by cattle-ranchers and hermits. A central body of water most likely formed the core for Brycheiniog's surplus and the same is plausible for Craven. Surrounded by limestone escarpments and watched over by diving peregrines is the iridescent Malham Tarn which sits in a dramatic landscape alongside Gordale Scar and Malham Cove. Near the tarn is a small structure excavated by Arthur Raistrick in the 1950s; like Ty Illtud by Llangorse, this is another possible hermitage by a lake.[93] Malham was also contested as wool-rearing land in the High Medieval Period; charters between Fountains and Bolton Abbey record spats and territorial disputes. As perhaps *the* most fertile area of the Dales, Malham Tarn could well have been the core of Craven.

Contemporary documents reveal an important landowner from the pre-Conquest Dales, Thorfinn 'of Craven', who governed a vast estate stretching from Bordley to Settle. Again, Thorfinn's lands were sought after, eventually being acquired by Fountains Abbey. Hebden, in Wharfedale, also teases early medieval origins through its thirteenth-century clauses; boundary markers like cairns, marshes and iron veins described using Old English words, reflecting the limits of a large ninth-century farm.[94] As late as 1220 further details are revealed about Craven's past. On the flanks of Ingleborough is a natural limestone depression noted as *Spechscaflade* which has been speculated by Yvonne Luke to derive from Old English for 'speech staff stream'. This feature may have been used as a corral in a manner not dissimilar to Yeavering's grandstand. As with Malham Tarn and Marton Scar, this is another possible assembly point, a 'core' of Craven.

Beyond the bounds of the Early Medieval Period our only evidence for this kingdom is a series of snapshots, some linguistic, others archaeological, all up to interpretation.

Between Kettlewell and Buckden, in the field known as *borrans* ('cairns'), two burials were discovered in 1997, a male and female, neither with any grave goods. Thirty postholes were recorded alongside these remains as well as speculative earthworks near Starbotton in a once well-organised landscape locked between the Roman forts at Ilkley and Bainbridge. Dated to the seventh century, aged between her thirties and forties, with evidence for having been pregnant at least once, the female skeleton was nicknamed 'Olwen' by students at the local school. With reverence, empathy and wonder, reflecting the transient nature of historical funerary rites, Olwen became a source of inspiration for poems, artwork and crafts made by the schoolchildren.[95] She was later re-buried with these grave goods, a fitting assortment for a well-remembered resident of a forgotten kingdom. A few of the children even read their excerpts aloud as her epitaph. Merely a snapshot, trapped in a time capsule. All that remains.

ꟼÁL RIATA

When Scandinavians settled the coasts and islands of Scotland in the late eighth and ninth centuries, they established their farmsteads across landscapes already inhabited. In some cases, native sites were re-occupied or torn down and used for repairs. Because of this, it can be difficult to tell the difference between Norse and native farmsteads, especially shielings. Shielings are small buildings, usually positioned on the very limit of a farm, used for seasonal tasks like monitoring the grazing of animals in the outfield. They are nevertheless central to subsistence. The manure produced by animals in the outfield directly supplements the crops grown in the infield, creating a balance of arable and pastoral farming. Because of their usefulness, they are found all over the northern British Isles.

Shielings were central to survival across Atlantic Scotland and the Irish Sea and are thus well represented not just archaeologically but in place names too. For Old Irish and Gaelic speakers, shieling toponyms usually include *ærgi-* or *àirigh-*; for Old Norse, *-sætr*. These toponyms can be placed on a map to determine where a Norse or Gaelic linguistic influence was strongest.[96] Paradoxically, many Scandinavian shielings have *ærgi-* names, indicating that Norse speakers were re-inhabiting native sites or that the natives had become part of a Scandinavian-Gaelic melting pot. Indeed, it is due to pirates and settlement in the ninth century that the sea kingdom of Dál Riata drowned in the deep, succumbing to new naval warriors: *vikingar*.[*]

Irish documents are useful for rounding off this section on shielings, an agropastoral element intrinsic to the dominance of this once-mighty sea kingdom. Eighth-century Irish laws provide context for how shielings and cattle were valued economically. First is the differentiation given to 'milking' (*milch*) and 'dry' cows; a *milch* was worth two dry cows and reached its maximum value of 0.06lb of silver after six years, usually after producing three calves (*bó threlóeg*). Male cattle held little value to either farmer or *áirge* (the collective term for the herd and dairy) but were still kept around for mating purposes, especially youngsters (*colpthach firenn*).[†] There was a focus on dairy for Irish farmsteads which would shift following

---

[*] 'Vikings'. Scandinavian raiders would have been referred to as vikingr (s.) or vikingar (pl.). By the tenth century, the Irish Sea and Atlantic Scotland were dominated by these people, Pictland and Dál Riata face-down in the water.

[†] This term describes two-year old bulls, the median mating age.

Scandinavian settlement. From the ninth century, agropastoralism took precedence but the verdant islands remained ever-important to life on the waves.

Dál Riata was a thalassocracy, a 'sea kingdom', making it unique on our list. Despite this, the grazing of land animals was important for its economy as the silver provided by a single *milch* allowed tribute and taxation to flow. Multiply the value of a *milch* by tenfold, a hundredfold, a thousandfold and the richness of Dál Riata is revealed. These were not buccaneers holed up in watery enclaves, but a royal dynasty stretching from north-east Ireland to Galloway.

Dál Riata's origins, however, are steeped in the sea mists of myth. The name first appears in *The Annals of Ulster* in the mid-eighth century but let us not think of 'Dál Riata' as a concrete entity. In Old Irish, *dál-* means 'people', *cenél-* means 'kindred' - Dál Riata, then, becomes 'the people of Riata', but this establishes another mystery. The *Life of St Columba*, an earlier source, mentions the 'Corcu Réti' along the Irish Sea coast and it has been argued that this is an earlier name since *corcu-* also means 'people' and, in 741, the 'Dal Réti' are recorded fighting the Picts in *The Annals of Ulster*, demonstrating an intermediate form of the name. Réti might originate from the Old Irish verb *riad-* which describes an 'act of riding: a steed, a journey, a career'. Thus, Dál Riata becomes 'the people who ride', not necessarily a kingdom but a united tribal confederation extending over water. Their association with horses is peculiar but can be disentangled. In compiling his *Geography*, the second-century astronomer Ptolemy mentioned the *Epidii*, meaning 'horses', who lived across the Hebrides, Kintyre and Argyll. Kintyre, although rendered as 'Fidnach', appears in *The Annals of Ulster* for the year 617 where it is described as 'in riaddai'. Later, between the sixth and ninth centuries, the foundational pseudo-figure of Eochu Riata appears in references to Dál Riata's origins. Both mentions are linked: *-Riata* was a genealogical descriptor to distinguish those who claimed descent from the *Epidii*, thus affirming claims to the land. Eochu is an invented figure, an element from a useable past which suited contemporary perceptions.[97]

All this theorising can be simplified by observing how kingship worked in Ireland. Territories were organised by legendary ancestry and groups were not geographically bound. The Dál Riata, like the tenth-century Dál gCais of south-west Ireland, were just another 'people', except that their territory extended over water. Dál Riata even included various sub-lineages, including the Cenél Loairn who controlled an island chain between Argyll, Morvern, Mull and Colonsay with a core at either Dun Ollaigh or Dunadd in Scotland. The Cenél Loairn existed within the wider bracket term of 'Dál Riata' and various kings of the Cenél Loairn were themselves kings of Dál Riata; it was an 'over-kingdom' uniting disparate groups over the Hebrides and Galloway. Each sub-lineage would have a legendary ancestor, like Loarn mac Eirc for the Cenél Loairn. There was also the Cenél nGabráin and the Cenél nÓengusa, each wielding dominion over different parts of western Scotland. These kin groups were collectively known as 'the Dál Riata', evidently a maritime network, but one with a land-based legendary origin across Ireland and Scotland to affirm internal lineages. Most of this information can be extrapolated from the *History of the Men of Scotland*, a tenth-century Old Irish text from the MS H.2.7, compiled in the fourteenth century which lists divisions within Dál Riata and the military contingents belonging to each lineage. One can imagine the rich farmsteads of the Hebrides paying tribute to these pirate kings. This same document even records a naval battle between rival Riatan cohorts. One of these, the Cenél (or Crich) Comgaill, may have split from the Cenél nGabráin to establish a foothold across Cowal and Bute. Airgíalla, an Irish over-kingdom, is also mentioned as a client territory of the Cenél Loairn. Dál Riata's politicking mirrors what has been already mentioned throughout this book, territorial disputes and dynastic rivalries, but at sea.

The *History* preserves how Dál Riata may have looked in the seventh century. By the eighth, their power had started to wane.

Memories of this sea kingdom are found in the most intriguing place: not in Irish or Scottish verse, but in the Icelandic Sagas. Compiled in the thirteenth century, but based on earlier oral accounts, they recount how warriors from Norway conquered the Irish Sea and founded a dynasty that flourished across the North Atlantic. Many characters have Gaelic nicknames or are associated with an Irish or Pictish heritage; Þórunn who married the grandson of an Irish king, Helgi *beolán* and Aleif *faelán* with their Gaelic epithets, Auð's Pict-servant Erpr, the Columban devout Orlyg Hrappsson and the Hebridean conqueror Kjetill Flatnose. Kjetill might be the same as Caitill Find who appears in *The Annals of Ulster* leading a Norse-Gaelic army in the mid-ninth century, something Kjetill later became known for. These Icelandic

traditions place a Norse-Gaelic kingdom across the Irish Sea in this same period, more or less exactly when Dál Riata fades from contemporary records, suggesting that the insular lineages were replaced by foreign ones who maintained a distant link with a Gaelic past.

Dál Riata, despite being built by legend and coracle and consisting of multiple individually powerful pedigrees, succumbed to a new rival upon the same waters that had once facilitated its creation. And the shielings that had once fuelled their coastal dominance became known by new names. Dál Riata's transformation into the later tenth-century Norse 'kingdom of the Isles' did not happen overnight but it did happen.[98] We collectively put so much stock on Viking Age seamanship that we forget, when it comes to the Irish Sea, those longships were following well-trodden whale roads, carved by the people who rode.

Deira

The city of Hull looms over the river Humber, the mandible of central-eastern England and the gateway for many overseas voyages. Long before this shipping town was expanded in the thirteenth century, the northern shores of the Humber were littered with beach markets and trading points. It was one of these, *Petuaria* (Brough), which became the nexus of Roman trade along the river; it was Hull before Hull. *Petuaria* was established as a fort and later grew into a *civitas* for the regional tribe of the Parisi, surrounded by countryside villas like the ones at Brantingham and Pocklington. By the late fourth century *Petuaria*'s waters were silting, desiccating both the beaches and their trade,[*] although the Humber would remain ever central to the dominion of Deira.

Deira is the southern half of Northumbria, situated between the Humber and the river Tees. Like Bernicia, it emerged as a Celtic-speaking territory (known as **Daru* or *Deor*) before being anglicised in the fifth or sixth centuries and, like Bernicia, was the birthplace of several perennial figures of early medieval England. A Roman road knits Brough to Newcastle, passing through the vital stronghold at *Eboracum* (York) well-positioned at a confluence of the rivers Ouse and Foss. Both rivers and roads connected the Roman fortresses of Yorkshire so, while they, like *Petuaria*, faded in economic importance, they remained in the landscape, re-purposed as central places for burgeoning political identities. Deira was chiselled from a collection of previously independent tribal territories, many centred around prehistoric or Roman monuments such as the various fourth-century signal stations along Yorkshire's coast. At Ravenscar there are even inscriptions describing the employment and habitation of mercenaries. It was these mercenaries, *foederati* gathered from northern Europe, who became mythologised as the foundational figures of Deira despite its insular roots.

The earliest recorded king is Ælla, mentioned in both Bede's *Ecclesiastical History* and *The Anglo-Saxon Chronicle*, although he is a composite, knitting together several figures. It is difficult to identify a 'core site' within the kingdom for it is overshadowed in Bede's works in favour of Bernicia and much of Deiran history is simply 'Northumbrian history'. A Deiran, Edwin (617-632), eventually became the total monarch over Northumbria and, after his reign, there were a few

---

[*] Recent carbon-14 isotopic dating suggests Brough persisted in some degree into the fifth or sixth centuries. My thanks to Peter Halkon for this tentative update.

bouts of civil strife between Deiran sub-kings and their Bernician superiors. Still, while Bernicia had the fort at Bamburgh or the palatial complex at Yeavering, no royal palace has yet been identified across Deira. Instead, economic and political routes seem to have converged on a trading centre. Not Brough, but York.

Sitting in York's Museum Gardens, what remains of St Mary's Abbey and the Multangular Tower cleave through the greenery. Over a thousand years of history separate these ruins, the former disestablished by King Henry VIII, the latter worn down by time.

> Wondrous is this wall-stone, fractured by *wyrd*;[*]
> the city has crumbled, the work of giants withers.
> Rooftops in ruin, watch-towers wasted,
> the spoke-gate despoiled, hoarfrost on mortar,
> a shelter from storms cleft and cracked
> eroded with age. Earth's embrace envelops
> the master-crafters forgotten, lost to
> the grave grip of the soil, until a hundred generation
> of people have passed. Much its wall weathered,
> lichen-grey and red-stained, reign after reign,
> stood steadfast through storms; lofty and high,
> yet it fell. Still this remains:
>
> age-old creation, bowed in the earth.

It would be a challenge to name a better Old English poem than *The Ruin*, compiled in the tenth-century *Exeter Book*. Whilst it probably describes the ruins of Bath, the universal lamentation and awe at extant Roman masonry can be applied to many places across England. In Yorkshire, where the Roman presence was intensely militarised, the power of Rome took the shape of strongholds and fortifications, memories of might and the work of giants, like the Multangular Tower. This tower, and the wall it connects to, remained formidable long after the withdrawal of Roman legionaries. Even this long-argued 'end' for *Britannia* is misunderstood. In 410 Emperor Honorius wrote 'letters to the cities in Britain urging them to be on their guard'; this is usually translated as an instruction for the 'Britons to look to their own defences'.[†] This sixth-century record of a fifth-century command is not a declaration of defeat or abandonment but a re-negotiation of order. *Eboracum*, as with *Britannia*, was not deprived of military support, but the guise of that military changed, and this change took place slowly from the late third century. Descendants

---

*   *Wyrd* is usually translated as 'fate', but its real meaning is slightly more prosaic. It means 'what happens'; the passage of time, things, the wind, decay, rot … .

†   Though it might be a reference to Bruttia, Italy.

of the foreign mercenaries employed across Yorkshire's signal stations became the 'guard' of Deira.

By the fifth and sixth centuries excavations across York have revealed layers of loamy soil and refuse. Long argued to be 'dark earth' consistent with decay, these soils could be credible evidence for the re-purposing of urban centres as farmland.[99] Multiple plots were turned over, terracotta tiles torn away to give rise to new growth and post-urban gardens. *Eboracum* had not been abandoned; it had changed. Rising sea levels would have affected the flow of the Ouse, changing the city's character even more as people became more reliant on boats and low tide. At Fishergate, pottery wares from across the North Sea appear in the earliest layers of the site which has been argued to have been a 'colony' of new settlers visiting this old town. In this regard, whilst York was not abandoned it was evidently 're-launched', so to speak, both commercially as a *-wic* in the seventh century and, later, as a religious capital under the Northumbrian church. In 627 King Edwin commissioned York's first church, built in the shadow of the extant Roman *principia*, lost beneath today's Minster.

But it is in the less touristy areas of York where evidence for this enigmatic middle period, stuck between the Roman and Viking Ages, can be uncovered. In the suburb of Acomb, near Severus Hill, the necklace of a high-status seventh-century woman was discovered in 2016.[100] Beads and gold filigree, plain and beaded wire decorating a garnet inset in an assemblage that was once an enamelled cloisonné pendant. Panels that had formed part of this pendant showed signs of repair and 'honeycomb' geometric patterning; it was a cherished piece, caressed on long journeys like the many brooches from Orkney. It is uncertain where this lady or her jewellery originated but some parallels can be found in the Escrick Ring, discovered south of York. Originally believed to date nearer to the foundation of St Mary's Abbey than the fifth century, the Escrick Ring is closest stylistically to Kentish and Merovingian accessories from France. A brooch from Riccall also shares these traits, as do several gold-alloy pendants known from North Lincolnshire and the East Riding. There were secular and ecclesiastical connections between Deira and the continent; the garnets in the Acomb pendant may have hailed from Bohemia and the sapphire from the Escrick Ring from as far away as Sri Lanka. Whoever the wearers of this high-status jewellery were, they represented a demographic shift in Deiran fortunes, the economic and political movements of high-ranking retinues, en route to the 're-launched' York.

The Acomb assemblage was recovered from a suburb that may have once been a royal burial site in the shadow of both *Eboracum* and prehistoric ring ditches at Knapton. Both new visitors and old memories characterise York and Deira. In the clogged sewers of the former *colonia*, intaglio and fragments of fine metalwork washed up to be smelted down by the inhabitants farming within the walls. Statues of Mars and Emperor Constantine sat face-down in the mud; mosaic floors from Toft Green were covered in grime as travellers trampled over them; a depiction of a gorgon slowly eroded as it sat half-submerged in a watercourse. All this paints fifth- and sixth-century York as a place of change, both in the literal sense through water levels and the fact that the city, and Yorkshire, became re-purposed, no longer a militarised frontier but a web of royal commerce and connections.

Also linked to *Eboracum* via surviving roads was Malton, thought to be the fortress of *Derventio*. Excavations have revealed crude stone forges and post-holes dated to the fifth century but then nothing until the appearance of carved crosses in the eighth. Unlike York, Malton *was* seemingly left to rot, no longer serving a purpose.[101] No one individual process occurred across fifth-century Deira; the kingdom was born from individual communities with unique forms of expression. By the eighth century Deiran expression appears to have homogenised; this is when classic 'Northumbrian' stone sculpture and standing crosses dominated, replacing what were previously locally unique monumental investments.[102] Take the Vale of Pickering. At either end of the valley are contrasting burial and structural identities seen through little drifting settlement and cremated remains at West Heslerton and the long-cist burials at Spaunton, Yearsley and Appleton-le-Street. Initially diverse, these funerary expressions became homogenised by the eighth century through a slow acculturation process and the addition of stone crosses. Even just looking at West Heslerton, diversity is obvious. The site is located near a Romano-British 'temple', yet the site plan is closest to continental settlements and DNA evidence is fairly equally split between overseas and insular origins. The settlement phases of West Heslerton have been interpreted as one group inhabiting the same area and rebuilding new structures[103] but it is equally probable that the site was inhabited repeatedly by different people with diverse backgrounds.

Different degrees of social integration reflect what have been called 'conservative' and 'progressive' communities within Deira. Some settlements clung onto the past via prehistoric monuments, Roman sites and long-cist burials for far longer than others, possibly reflecting a dichotomy between foreign and native traditions. Although, it seems in Deira's earliest centuries, there was a deliberate elite strategy of inventing traditions altogether, creating lineages like Ælla's and tying them to re-interpreted barrows and prehistoric graveyards. These expressions would have been different across Yorkshire, eventually becoming regionalised through a process of peer-polity competition where multiple tribal groups settled in one area, married and then later re-invented their heritage as one consistent 'royal dynasty', thus casting Deira out of the bones of myriad unnamed communities.* Yorkshire, as it is now, was diverse. This can also be seen topographically. Generally, there is a mix of gentle uplands and valleys like the Vale of Pickering, the Howardian Hills and the North York Moors, but also flatlands like the Vale of York and the Holderness Plain. Most of these areas are littered with Bronze and Iron Age barrows which were successively re-purposed by subsequent societies, especially following the advent of churches and book-land. Kirk Hammerton's church might be one of the earliest of these Deiran institutions, stylistically closest to examples from North Lincolnshire. Partially constructed from quarried and re-purposed Roman stone, there is a possibility that it was built atop a prominent natural rise or henge-like feature in the marshes north of York, commanding the landscape. A gold aestel (finger pointer) was also found nearby, one of only a handful discovered across the country, dating to the reign of King Ælfred, highlighting the site's scholarly importance. The discussions surrounding Kirk Hammerton's potential henge crystalise the contrasting ways in which early medieval societies interpreted the world around them. Landscapes can be appreciated and interpreted on multiple levels, through both spiritual and secular eyes; one person's 'profane' could be another's 'sacred', and vice versa. Religious homogeneity following the Christianisation of Deiran nobles would have hastened this process of landscape re-interpretation, as seen at the pre-Christian 'temple' at *Gōdmundingaham* (Goodmanham) which was destroyed in the seventh century and replaced by a church.

Indeed, at Goodmanham, all archaeological and textual evidence points to a royal shrine newly established by the late-sixth or early-seventh century, although the surrounding landscape is dominated by pre-existing Bronze and Iron Age barrows. Elsewhere in Yorkshire, these prehistoric monuments were re-used as secondary burial grounds, new corpses cut into the 'sacred' soil. For the people

---

* Pickering, between York and Whitby, seemingly derives from *Pīceringas* ('the dependants of Picer'), as one example.

at Goodmanham, though, the barrows were evidently 'mundane'. At nearby Sancton a similar contrast was occurring. Between the fifth and sixth centuries this pottery production centre appears to have held zero ties to the copious Bronze Age mounds surrounding it. Instead, material identities and artistic affiliations extended eastward towards Saxony and Friesland. *Pottery isn't people*, but the consistency of Sancton-ware pottery and various North Sea wares, like those from Fishergate, point to trade and stylistic sharing along the North Sea rim. Indeed, Holderness (known perhaps as *Emmertland*) would have been a vast tidal wetland with seawater extending as far as North Froddingham. Sailors would have maximised their use of these coasts, feeling closer ties not to landlocked prehistoric monuments but to the North Sea; this much is suggested by Frankish pottery and Rhenish quernstones from Yorkshire graves. However, also in Holderness, seventy unadorned crouched burials discovered at Etton in 1866 indicate substantial insular populations. Christopher Loveluck has gone so far as to explain these differences by arguing that there were two economies within early Deira, one connected to the North Sea centred around Driffield and another west of the Hull Beck, focused on pre-existing tribal identities like Craven.[104]

Driffield *is* one of the few sites we could realistically expect to find a 'royal site' akin to Yeavering. On 14 December 705 the [D] and [E] variants of *The Anglo-Saxon Chronicle* record the death of King Aldfrið of Northumbria here and, four centuries later, the *Domesday Book* marked it as one of the richest estates in the county. Driffield was probably a Bernician landholding and this same origin is suggested for the minsters at Beverley and Watton, established in the late seventh century by monks from Whitby. There is even a *frið* stool at Beverley, used in judicial assemblies. *Frið* is an Old English term for 'legal order' so reveals that Beverley may have played an important role in seventh- and eighth-century assemblies. Two nearby burials from Cottam dated between 725 and 745 reflect the continued habitation of the area although, interestingly, these remains were interred within a prehistoric burial ground. Despite the nearby Christian institutions, some form of pagan funerary practice was being revisited at Cottam, perhaps reflecting a 'conservative' community, or an independent Deiran one.

If Beverley was a 'progressive' Bernician institution, then there may well have been pockets of resistance. According to Bede, John, Beverley's saint, hailed from Whitby and many monuments across Filey, Hackness, Easby, Levisham and York seem also to have been fashioned from Whitby stone. Considering stone could have been readily quarried from Deiran sites, as seen at Kirk Hammerton, the proliferation of Whitby material may indicate a purposeful Bernician-Deiran stone trade where elites invested in this new homogenised form of expression. A 'Northumbrian' identity and ideology constructed from Bernician stone re-planted into Deiran soil as the problematic weeds of the past were exorcised. In 659 Bede writes that a sub-king of Deira had once commissioned a minster at Lastingham although the establishment is framed in a way to mark this as an affront; St Cedd first purified 'the site of the monastery from the taint of earlier crimes'. Reading between the lines, the Deiran elite were just as capable of investing in Christian monuments as their northern superiors but this appears to have been shunned. It was either Bernician stone or no stone at all.

Where there was once diversity and independence, between the re-purposed Romanised landscapes of the Vale of Pickering, the North Sea trade of *Emmertland* or the re-used prehistoric monuments of the Yorkshire Wolds, there was now Bernician, Northumbrian, consistency. Deira became remembered simply as 'a bit of Northumbria'.

Yorkshire has never been isolated. Even for our period, goods and people were travelling from all over to visit 'God's country', as seen with pottery, quernstones and the beads from the Acomb assemblage. One of the beads was decorated in a multi-layered annular twist pattern, an extremely delicate glass-working technique known only by a few finds across England.[105] Their limited distribution represents the work of a single artisan, making a 'bulk batch' while journeying across the Isles, perhaps commissioned by the Acomb lady to jazz up her accoutrements, putting her friends to shame.

These ubiquitous and often unremarkable beads crystalise early medieval interconnectedness. Over 200,000 beads made their way to and fro the North Sea between the fifth and ninth centuries, originating everywhere from the Baltic to the Syro-Palestinian coastline, Iraq to India and beyond. Mette Langbroek's analyses indicate that six per cent of beads between the sixth and seventh-centuries originated from outside Europe, some from as far away as Mali, Thailand, Kazakhstan, Croatia and Zanzibar, distributed outwards from Sicily.[106] Long before the Viking Age the world was connected via persistent trade routes. Deira was one of many, many stops along the way and a very important one, although it is in the Viking Age that we must end this chapter. In the late ninth century the 'kingdom of *Jórvík*' became established between the Tees and the Humber, centred around York. Not a new political entity, but a re-negotiated version of Deira, a memory of independence that had been re-born through political strife.

That indomitable Yorkshire spirit.

ĐUMNONIA

From the shores of Yorkshire to the Isles of Scilly, Dumnonia once peered over warmer and brighter seas, stretching from Land's End to Wiltshire, encompassing everything from the chalk downlands of Dorset to the idyllic estuaries of the Tamar. Mostly based around Cornwall and Devon, Dumnonia was a Celtic-speaking polity that emerged in the Late Roman Period and lasted almost half a millennium before being eroded by coastal processes and West Saxon conquests. It is a difficult kingdom to untangle, overshadowed by romanticisation and literary constructs like King Arthur and characters from twelfth-century hagiographies. Still, beneath these layers, there is a foundation of genuine independence, a Brythonic base still visible in vestigial archaeology like inscribed stones and pottery sherds at Tintagel. The real Dumnonia tells its story not through the knights of Camelot, but through land charters and tin ingots, cemeteries and pollen kernels. It is a story worth telling.

Sea levels are highly variable and periodic: like little kingdoms they rise and fall. In our period parts of the British Isles were surrounded by low-lying atolls and floodplains like Cantre'r Gwaelod and *Emmertland*, now lost. The Isles of Scilly once benefitted from this lower sea level, too, joined by land bridges and shallow crossings, perhaps a single landmass known as *Ennor*. Centrally positioned by the English Channel, *Ennor* formed only one cog in a monstrous exchange network which imported pottery from North Africa and Italy and exported tin to the continent. This network was connected to the Mediterranean and Atlantic Scotland. Indeed, the entire west coast of England seems to have been a thoroughfare for similar goods and people, connecting the Hebrides to Cornwall through the Irish Sea and from there to Bordeaux and the Bay of Biscay. No wonder there were 'British' populations in Brittany and Galicia according to Asser. These places are all within reasonable proximity and Cornwall seems to have been at the centre of it all. Fragments of North African pottery are occasionally found in excavations in Cumbria and elsewhere along the west coast but these quantities are dwarfed by the assemblages discovered here in the south, at sites like Tintagel.

To shoo the Excalibur out of the room, Tintagel was not the stomping ground of King Arthur but you can see why someone would think that. It is a well-defended promontory with evidence of continued habitation throughout a period of history once thought to be nothing but darkness. Finds from the site all point towards a concentrated elite residence plugged into a highly profitable overseas market, exercising domestic and international power. A northern equivalent to this site can be found at Rhynie, in Scotland where, as at Tintagel, there is fourth- to sixth-century evidence of international trade between Britain and the Mediterranean: dazzling jewellery, imported oils, the litter of powerful trade-lords.[107] Tintagel was also a tin-producing hotspot, compensating for the shortfalls of exporters like the Iberian Peninsula, and has been argued to have a structural layout similar to Mediterranean sites like Laconia, its design explicitly inspired by overseas traders and elites. Importantly, a distinction must be made here that the residents of Tintagel were not just bringing foreign and Roman exports *into* Britain but were connecting Britain *to* Rome through ideas of social and architectural organisation.[108] By mirroring Mediterranean styles and investing repeatedly in pottery from Ravenna and glass from Egypt, the magnates at Tintagel were placing Dumnonia on Rome's doorstep, bringing *Britannia* back into the orbit of Empire. This is the same logic exercised by the magnates who buried their dead at Sutton Hoo or at Prittlewell, Essex; suggestions of Rome through grave goods; liminal lords in an aged *Britannia* who still felt themselves servile or connected to the distant Emperor. Both versions of the overseas *Gallic Chronicle*, from 452 and 511, imply that Britain was still culturally and socially very much 'Roman' well into the mid-fifth century, with references to a functioning provincial system, especially in the south.

King Arthur did not live in these provinces but powerful fifth-century magnates did, such as the individual inscribed on the Fowey Stone, or Constantine, 'the tyrant whelp of the filthy lioness', scorned by Gildas. These people are more historical than Arthur but are also shrouded in ambiguity; the real evidence of Dumnonia's origins comes from layers of salt-washed soil. Cornwall and Devon received less Roman coinage than elsewhere in Britain, although a greater distribution of Gaulish and Aquitanian pottery dating between the first and eighth centuries. This represents economic continuity. Between the Roman invasion and West Saxon conquests, Cornwall and Devon were consistently engaged with international trade and had never relied on the Roman stamp of villas, roads and *colonia*. Therefore, when *Britannia* suffered economic shortfalls, the Lizard Peninsula remained unaffected, for it had never been plugged into that crumbling machine, instead benefitting from independent trade networks. Mediterranean pottery has been discovered in abundance at St Michael's Mount, as one example. Also, the *Life of St John the Almsgiver* mentions Britons exchanging tin for corn with continental traders. Fifth- and sixth-century coins from Constantinople appear in Ilchester's archaeological layers and, on the Scillies, more Mediterranean pottery is known from the site of Halmay Down. This site crystallises the continuity of Dumnonia for it is a courtyard of sixth-century buildings clustered around first-century Iron Age structures; many extant prehistoric monuments, like the ones at Halmay Down, became re-purposed as new settlements. These changes are also expressed through cemetery evidence. The Roman towns of Ilchester, Dorchester and Exeter all show signs of fifth-century habitation but it wasn't until the seventh when they became 're-launched' as minsters, much like York. Before this, burials were widely distributed and display a mixture of Christian and pagan funerary rites.[109] At Ilchester, severed heads, feet and a dog are known from fourth- and fifth-century layers; contemporaneous Exeter seems to have been predominantly Christian and 'Romanised', whilst Roman cemeteries in Dorchester were bizarrely re-fortified by timber palisades. Former towns, these ruins were on Dumnonia's edge and became ritualised and re-used by subsequent generations. Elsewhere, villas and pre-Roman sites were re-inhabited as at Keynsham, King's Weston and Whittington. South Cadbury hillfort saw the creation of additional timber ramparts and international trade between the fifth and seventh centuries, too. Iron Age sites like Cannington and Maiden Castle were also re-purposed. High Peak, teetering on clifftops, was probably re-fortified in this period but much evidence has been lost to coastal erosion. Why these areas were re-inhabited and re-purposed when so much of Dumnonia appears to have been unaffected by the decline of *Britannia* further demonstrates that there is no one process of development even within these little kingdoms, let alone Britain.* Maybe some regional tyrants of Dumnonia took advantage of political disparity, whereas others didn't even recognise that anything had happened at all.

In the east of the Lizard Peninsula settlement distribution appears to have been much denser than in the west and settlement generally appears to have been varied. Whilst we talk of early medieval Cornwall as 'Celtic-speaking', it bears a concentration of pit-houses, often seen as archetypically 'Anglo-Saxon', dated between the fourth and fifth centuries. Considering so much international commerce reached the peninsula, we should expect some diversity in building types and language. About fifty inscribed monoliths dot Cornwall and Devon, many displaying links with those in Wales, also inscribed with ogham script. While linked with the Mediterranean, the south-west was also part of that aforementioned Irish Sea littoral. This symbolic convergence can be seen through the various chi-rho inscriptions seen on Cornish standing stones. This is a widespread Christian symbol and its specific derivations in fifth- to seventh-century Cornish epigraphy link the peninsula to southern Europe and also hint at an as-yet-undiscovered monastic core, like the one known at Beacon Hill on the island of Lundy. The influence of continental saint Germanus is felt in various southern Cornish churches and, generally, the religious landscape of the kingdom appears to have consisted of a network of independent reliquary sites rather than monasteries. It is possible that it wasn't until the ninth century when Dumnonia gained its first churches. The earlier toponymic element *-merthyr* from Old Cornish hints instead at 'martyr sites' and an eremitical landscape of saintly dedications, Germanus among them. The *Life of St Samson* places Christian missionaries in north Cornwall eradicating a heathen site at Trigg and the *Life of St Paul Aurelian* hints at monastic crossover between Brittany and the south-west. Other Christian inscriptions connect Dumnonia to a Welsh world. At St Cleer a standing cross commemorates 'King Dongarth of the West Welsh' who was drowned in the late ninth century. Dongarth was the last recorded king of Dumnonia. Before his time older inscriptions across Devon and Cornwall commemorate 'Dobunuss, son of Enabarr', 'Ingenuus' and 'Ulcagnus'.

---

* In 1994 it was suggested by K. R. Dark that Cornwall originated as its own distinct polity by the ninth century, separate from Dumnonia, but born from a small sub-unit of the kingdom.

*Traditions surrounding Arthur's sword Excalibur, the wizard
Merlin and the elements recognisable to us today were
popularised in the centuries following Geoffrey of
Monmouth's influential* History of the Kings of Britain. *
Depicted above is an illustration from one of Howard
Pyle's works (1853 – 1911), highlighting our enduring
obsession with Arthuriana.*

A stone on Lundy dated to 480 CE describes an
unnamed individual as '_____ of the best one', which
is a Latin phrase normally relegated to the continent,
again displaying those long-distance Dumnonian
links.

With links in mind, some of these standing
stones were positioned along roads whereas others
were moved into churchyards reflecting later West
Saxon minster establishments. With kings in mind, we must
look to Gildas. He makes a special effort to demonise the
tyrannus of Dumnonia, Constantine, colouring our modern
perceptions of this translucent ruler. 'Tyrant' technically
means usurper but being a usurper does not necessarily make
someone a bad ruler, just illegitimate. The fact Dumnonia
persisted as a territory for so long would at least demonstrate
the effectiveness of its leaders, whatever their names and
regardless of the insults Gildas threw their way. The
specifics of his rants bear a look; Constantine and his
south-westerly ilk were criticised not for barbarism but
for being pre-occupied with worldly treasures instead of spiritual enlightenment.
These oafs were more 'interest[ed] in sport [than] holy men'; lecherous aristocrats
peering, sneering, over the edge of the English Channel. The sustained presence of
a literate elite in Dumnonia was confirmed by a bilingual inscription dedicated to
one 'Artognou' discovered at Tintagel dated between 650 and 700. Here, the target
of Gildas' vitriol were aristocrats engaged in civil strife, perhaps the forerunners of
Tintagel's later residents.

Further from reality, we have Geoffrey of Monmouth's re-imagined royalty of
Dumnonia. Tintagel appears in Geoffrey's works, re-purposed as the beating heart
of an artificial past crafted out of manipulated Cornish traditions. Arthur is at the
centre of this, usually placed at Glastonbury, in Wales or here at Tintagel. In this
way, the legendary history of Cornwall is interwoven with a Welsh one; Gildas
also connected the two when he was writing in the sixth century, lumping them
together as wretched sinful domains, re-negotiating his perception of a 'British'
identity. Following the Norman invasion of Wales, there was a scholarly desire to
collate what were deemed individual and remote histories; this is the origin of the
manuscript containing *The Gododdin*. But, beyond that, the resulting spiritual and
secular literature generated a pseudo-history for western Britain, a history to be

proud of, overflowing with people like Arthur, Iseult and Tristan, superimposed onto the silent halls of the real post-Roman kings who once ruled here. These two perceptions of the past exist simultaneously across Cornwall and Devon, operating as two layers of the same world.

Despite being compiled in the late ninth century, variants of *The Anglo-Saxon Chronicle* record territorial gains along Dumnonia's eastern borders from the eighth century onwards. The diminishing independence of the south-west, eroding under the West Saxon yoke, Dumnonian victories were obscured and underplayed. Most of these *Chronicle* entries were based upon older land charters, many of which still survive, and paint a depressing picture for the kingdom. During King Cenwalh's time (642-672), pre-existing monastic communities in the Glastonbury marshes were swept aside in favour of new establishments; in 739 King Æthelheard granted land in Crediton, Devon, to create a new monastery;* King Ælfred's will shows significant east Cornish land under West Saxon control and, between 872 and 888, the estate 'of Stratton in *Triconscire*' (Trigg) was gifted to his son Eadward. Most of these land grants were appropriations of pre-existing Dumnonian territories.

As with Dál Riata, we get glimpses of Dumnonia's twilight through Icelandic sagas. The *Saga of Olaf Tryggvason* describes monks on south-westerly islands, raided en route to Spain. The monks on Lundy, once sheltered and supported by international networks, were now at their mercy. The *Life of St Judoc* and other hagiographies frequently connect Cornwall to Brittany, indicating constant travel between the two which is also supported by Scandinavian intrusions and West Saxon governmental inclusions. Both Britons and Bretons (from Brittany) were folded into the councils of Wessex in the ninth century. Dumnonia, and that British dream, was dead. It was killed through land grabs and boundary clauses, buried under peace treaties and paperwork[110] as its memory became romanticised, a false Dumnonia re-born in the tenth century and given new life through Arthuriana.

---

* This charter was amended in the tenth or eleventh centuries with an additional boundary clause which mentions wolves and dangerous pitfalls, along with places called 'Cain's acre' and 'Grendel's pit', describing prehistoric barrows, marshes and dark forests along the hundredal border. The Crediton charter may not even reflect anything real but, instead, the idealised version of a parish: a central church, a ring of intensely farmed self-sufficient plots and then a liminal frontier zone encircling all.

ⅅUNUTINGA

> Then St Wilfrid the bishop ... read out clearly a list of the lands which the kings, for the good of their souls, had previously ... presented to him, with the agreements and over the signatures of the bishops and all the chief men, and also a list of the consecrated places in various parts which the British clergy had deserted when fleeing from the hostile sword wielded by the warriors of our own nation. ... these are the names of the regions: round *Rippel* and *Ingaedyne*, and in *regione Dunutinga* and *Incaetlaevum* and other places.

In the reign of King Ecgfrith of Northumbria, towards the end of the seventh century, the illustrious Bishop Wilfrid was granted lands on behalf of the church, ever-expanding his burgeoning diocese amidst a backdrop of conquests against northern British kingdoms. One thing unites all of these gifts: they all appear to be in or around the Yorkshire Dales. Therefore, they are all within the reasonable bounds of Craven. Craven, as already assessed, was a wide area of valleys and uplands settled by farmers and flocks. It was fertile and perfect for Christian hermits. Translated from the original Latin, *Rippel* refers to lands around the Ribble. *Ingaedyne* has been placed at Otley but *Incaetlaevum* ('wild-cat hill') is slightly more nebulous, possibly the Forest of Bowland Catlow.[111] Finally, there is the *regio* of the Dunutingas, an administrative unit belonging to the 'people of **Dunut*'; this has been argued to encompass Dentdale and to have been centred around or within the vicinity of the prominent peak of Ingleborough. David Johnson has argued for a wider *regio* encompassing Sedbergh, Garsdale and the Howgill Fells, whilst Stephen Walker believes the core to have been Whernside.[112] What we can hypothesise about Dunutinga could fill an entire book, let alone a chapter. It was a Brythonic polity, deemed sizeable and autonomous enough to be a *regio*, and may have been conquered by Northumbria in the seventh century. It might even be an alternate name for Craven, given the similar geography. Importantly, 'Craven' is mentioned nowhere in these land grants, perhaps relegated as one of the many unnamed 'other places'.

We must start with the name: *-ingas-* is Old English for 'the people of', so it being the name of a *regio* firmly within the 'British' Pennines is noteworthy. Was Dunutinga an anglicised name for a place known by a different local term? Or was it a Germanic-speaking polity whose legendary lineage began with a 'Celtic' character called **Dunut*? There are parallels elsewhere in England for both possibilities. The character of Dynod the Stout, son of Pabo, is a solid enough candidate for **Dunut*.

His historicity is doubtful, marrying the semi-fictitious Gwallog's daughter in the thirteenth-century *Descent of the Saints*. As a legendary anchor, however, Dynod may have been recognised by a post-Roman community and embedded into folk memory. Papcastle, in Cumbria, might derive from 'Pabo's fort' and there are the nearby toponyms of Cardunneth and Powdonnet which preserve the name of his son. Cumbria and the Yorkshire Dales provided the circumstances for an abundance of post-Roman polities to form: the terrain consists overwhelmingly of 'core' and 'marginal' territories in quick succession, the lowlands and uplands acting as heartlands and borders for tiny rural communities. Each dale may have been the base for a small territory, each named after a semi-fictional ancestor. Dunutinga may be one of these micro-polities. Overlord Urien allegedly had a network of such 'under-kingdoms'. We get a glimpse of these through the names of Wilfrid's *regiones*.

Equally interesting to consider is the Dunutingas' status in the late seventh century when these grants were made. Wilfrid's *Life*, written in the eighth, mentions that the 'British clergy had deserted when fleeing from the hostile sword' which many have taken to be evidence of Northumbrian expansion under King Ecgfrith. For the Pennine kingdoms, their independence ran dry under a growing Northumbrian imperium; that much is believed, anyway. The actual evidence for a 'Northumbria' that stretched from Lancashire to Yorkshire is challenging and not without biases. Bede mentions that people in King Edwin's time could walk safely from coast to coast and there is no shortage of retrospective romanticisation for the reign of his successor Oswald. It was under Ecgfrith (670–685 CE) that Northumbria was at its largest, but it was a lordship surrounded by frontier zones, not linear boundaries. All this is to say that, while the Yorkshire Dales and Cumbria may have been viewed as 'Northumbrian' from the perspective of Wilfrid's hagiographer, they were probably semi-autonomous client territories. The fact that a Northumbrian king *could* grant a bishop land in a foreign territory is interesting but does not mean that the territory was conquered.

The silence is more revealing. Of all the Northumbrian land grants from the seventh century, only a small handful are situated west of the Pennines: Cartmel, Carlisle, *Ingaedyne*, Dunutinga and *Rippel*. This may indicate that there was a significant power in opposition to Northumbria which kept territorial gains at bay. These speculative 'micro-polities' across Yorkshire and Cumbria are similar in concept to early medieval Irish kingdoms which were tiny and could be 'moved' to other locations to re-affirm land grabs and conflicts. This complicated political maze might have been mirrored in the north-west, preventing an easy 'one-and-done' Northumbrian victory, but rather facilitating wars of attrition where little kingdom after little kingdom would have to be knocked down. It is plausible that the many north-western British polities operated under an over-kingdom which was in turn beneath the clientship of Northumbria, although not crushed by it. Layers upon layers of status and power.

All this is guesswork. Perhaps the land grants simply reflect Wilfrid's own desire to expand his circles rather than any royal interests. But why seek land in Dunutinga? Aside from the profitable pastures, Dentdale is well placed for

connections along the river Ribble, both east and west, and as an entrance into Cumbria. As with Craven, it is easy to see why these areas were homes to dozens of farmsteads. What made these disparate units feel part of a wider territorial entity is difficult to say, however. If Ingleborough was the core of the Dunutingas, as has been argued, then it is worth investigating.

Ingleborough is one of the Yorkshire Three Peaks, a prominent stone seat amongst a skyline crowded with beautiful vistas. Clouds struggle to rise above it, shrouding it in mist even on sunny days. From most corners of the Dales one can see the unique silhouette. Long considered a hillfort, the archaeological evidence atop the mountain (a small broken embankment, possible roundhouses and ring cairns) have changed perceptions. Ingleborough is now considered a complex multi-period site with evidence spanning between the Bronze Age and Roman Period.[113] Whilst not a hillfort, Ingleborough would have still been a noteworthy landmark to base a group identity around. The massif is dripping in defining archaeological and geological features. The limestone pavement is surrounded by cairn-fields and stone settings, as are the slopes, not to mention the *Spechscaflade* arena. Oddly shaped stones wedged into grikes are difficult to date but their placement alongside known Neolithic, Bronze and Iron Age cairns points to a landscape of memory and interaction; some stone settings appear to 'link' distant cairns, whilst others may have served as petrosomatoglyphs: animalistic totems. The mountain may have also functioned in this manner, as an immutable monument to the prehistoric dead spread across generations. This would not have ended come the Early Medieval Period. David Johnson has proposed that the etymology of Ingleborough stems not from the obvious '*burh* of the English' but, instead, **Caer yr Aengli* for 'citadel of the angels'. This theory emerges from several extinct toponyms that litter Ingleborough's massif: the names of streams and wells connected to St Anthony (250-350 CE). A hill in Pembrokeshire, called Carn Ingli, has an identical etymology, except unlike early medieval Pembrokeshire, the Yorkshire Dales were anglicised, so the creolisation from **Caer yr Aengli* to Ingleborough took place, but the name may mean the same thing.

On the topic of names, it may well be that Dunutingas means 'people of the hill', named after Ingleborough. This is the same etymology behind the pre-Roman tribe of the Brigantes, who were suppressed across Yorkshire through the construction of forts. The Yorkshire Dales are enclosed by such structures but two in particular have relevance for our period: *Virosidum* (Bainbridge) and *Oleanaco* (Ilkley). Both are mentioned in the fifth-century military document known as the *List of Offices*, which recounts the size and strength of military contingents across several provinces, including *Britannia*. This document also places a 'leader of the Britons' at *Derventio* (Malton). *Oleanaco* was stationed with a subsidiary *praefectus* whilst *Virosidum* was garrisoned by the sixth cohort of the *Nervii* from Gaul. So, between 395 and 425 (when the *List* was compiled) at least two significant contingents may have been based in the Yorkshire Dales, having a centralising effect.

Whether Dunutinga serves as a unique regional identity or merely an example of the countless micro-polities that existed across the Yorkshire Dales and Cumbria is up for debate. One thing remains clear: these valleys are a tremendously under-researched area. Multiple strands of interdisciplinary evidence reveal the place as a blender for cultures, languages and group identities. There is no better place to look for little kingdoms.

ᴆYFED

One thing connecting all these locations is paths. We make them wherever we go, leaving our footmarks as we carve through the landscape. We go over, under or around things; other times we build bridges, causeways, barriers. We build paths between major centres, roads to ferry goods, walkways to avoid obstacles. None of these kingdoms existed alone; they were each connected to their immediate neighbours via paths, both physical and metaphorical, and travel was relatively unabated.

Sections of one such path, a timber walkway, were excavated from Borth Bog at Llangynfelyn, in northern Ceredigion, dated between 900-1020 CE.[114] Oak and alder panels had been laid atop wooden rails and pegs purposefully sunken into

the tidal swamp and later extended with additional logs between 1080 to 1120, according to radio-carbon dating. This was a small site, too, located amongst a vast coastal marsh stretching under the silhouette of a nearby Roman ruin, linking nameless settlements to one another. Given that the walkway was extended after the Anglo-Norman invasions of Wales, this thoroughfare probably remained important regardless of who was in charge. And this was only one segment. Certainly, the Llangynfelyn walkway extended farther westwards, spanning the shorelines of the sunken Cantre'r Gwaelod, not a barren marsh but a landscape of activity. If travellers kept walking to Caerfai Bay in Pembrokeshire, where similar peaty remains have been observed, they would have entered the old kingdom of Dyfed.

Longer, stormier paths can be followed from Dyfed's earliest days to Ireland. *The Expulsion of the Déisi,* a seventh-century narrative found in various fifteenth-century fragments, places Irish immigrants in Dyfed, led by Eochaid, son of Artchorp. These two figures also appear in Dyfed's similarly shattered genealogy, so they have some vague basis as valid heroic anchors. Déisi comes from the Old Irish *déis-* meaning 'vassal' so the whole fiction is weaving an underdog narrative: the brave emigres of Eochaid fled the Uí Liatháin of Munster and forged a new kingdom for themselves, away from oppression. Dyfed's genealogy takes the fiction even further, listing Emperor Constantine I as progenitor. The *Expulsion* and Dyfed's genealogy were compiled at different times, reflecting different attitudes about Dyfed's origins and the strategic blood ties that bound its contemporary rulers to the past. Dated to the fifth century, a multi-lingually-inscribed stone from Castell Dwyran bearing 'Voteporix' emulates the stylings of Late Roman guardsmen,* and countless ogham inscriptions have been well-recognised in this book already, many from Pembrokeshire.[115] Whether Dyfed's origins were Irish or Roman, this little kingdom was a well-trodden crossroads.

Paths *within* Dyfed connected residents of individual sub-territories to one another. The Welsh term 'cantref' denotes land and legal divisions and most Welsh kingdoms had several cantrefi. They are similar to English hundreds. There were seven in Dyfed, each with an individual bishop, that once may have all been independent territories before being enveloped into a greater realm. The same thing eventually happened to Dyfed in the tenth century, swallowed into the wider regional territory of Deheubarth ('the southern part' of Wales) along with Ceredigion and Seisyllwg. Brycheiniog met this fate too, along with the borderland of Ystrad Tywi. Paths linked all these places together just as they did Scotland and England. In the late ninth century the last rulers of Dyfed are recorded seeking allegiance with Ælfred the Great due to increased viking activity and the political

---

* 'Voteporix' means 'imperial protector' but was probably not understood or used to mean the same thing in fifth-century Wales. Here, unlike in the Palatine Schools of Ravenna, where it was a title once bestowed upon promising youngsters, it may have been read as 'defender', 'city guardian', or something along those lines. My thanks to Donato Sitaro for these words of wisdom.

ambitions of a neighbouring Welsh monarch, Rhodri Mawr. Dyfed's twilight is relatively undignified, then, but it remained an integral part of Deheubarth well into the twelfth century, highlighting the geographic importance of Pembrokeshire. In the Roman Period, this much was recognised, for Gaulish and Mediterranean pottery made its way to the eroded fourth-century promontory fort at Porth-y-Rhaw in abundance. Sailing paths connected Dyfed to Dumnonia and beyond.

Dyfed's routes also dug down. Amongst the Bronze Age mounds of Mynydd y Betws, people buried their dead by the western edge of the Brecon Beacons. This is a suspected funerary landscape where paths were imagined, connecting the fifth-and-sixth-century dead with their eldritch precursors. The same happened at Brownslade Barrow, a Bronze Age mound re-cut with fifth-century burials. Other Demetian* cemeteries are equally interesting. Near-contemporary skeletal remains found at St Patrick's Chapel, in Whitesands, display a broad mix of biological sex and long-cist internments.[116] Interestingly, white quartz stones were placed atop most of the remains, a unique burial rite associated *only* with this site in Pembrokeshire but known elsewhere across burials from Lindisfarne and Brittany; it was a Christian rite associated with spiritual redemption.[117] At West Angle Bay, three cemetery groups were discovered on the rapidly receding shoreline, one of which was enclosed, the walls having once sheltered the dead from bracing winds. Enclosed cemeteries typically date to the eighth century or later; this one was found alongside two earlier un-enclosed cemeteries, displaying continuity and respect for the dead. The contemporary *Irish Collection of Canon Laws* even states that 'holy places' ought to be surrounded by two or three sacred enclosures.[118] Continuity can also be observed on the sands of St Bride's Haven where another cemetery displays evidence of over thirty burials, interred with half-shattered stone slabs, argued by the excavators as an expression of a unique regional identity within the cantref of Rhos in south Dyfed. This unique funerary identity persisted from the eighth to the twelfth centuries whilst, at Port Clew, between the sixth and eleventh, people from east Wales came to Dyfed and died, buried alongside winkle shells and defensive earthworks. More cemeteries await excavation along the arched coastline of Pembrokeshire, forgotten beneath sand, silt and sea.

But these cemeteries had never been forgotten in the Early Medieval Period. Many, like Port Clew and West Angle Bay, were re-fortified and re-purposed; several burials appear to have been built over or dug into as ditches and defensive banks were constructed. Whether the dead were Irish, Roman or Welsh, they were treated as Demetian. At Maenclochog a small, fortified residence was occupied between the ninth and twelfth centuries. On the eve of Pembrokeshire's conquest in 1093 the residents of Maenclochog blocked the paths and sat waiting, defended. Like the Llangynfelyn trackway, they stuck in the mud.

---

* Meaning people from Dyfed. People from Gwynedd were 'Venedotian'.

EAST ANGLIA

Sutton Hoo dominates conversations about East Anglia and the famous ship burial overshadows conversations about Sutton Hoo. There is more to both this site and this kingdom, but to interrogate further requires digging beyond that lone barrow standing proud over the North Sea, the entombed magnate acting as overwatch.

To begin with, when the longship which eventually became buried under the Sutton Hoo mound first sighted the shores of England it would have observed a different coastline. The same geological and tidal processes that gave East Yorkshire a wider span also affected East Anglia. What are now the famous canals were once alluvium swamps, dotted by beach markets and frequented by pirates. The landmass itself was slightly larger, although flatter and boggier.

Hauled onto the hillock, the Sutton Hoo ship and its former crew, dragging their vessel to its final resting place alongside their fallen ruler, would have trudged through extant field systems by the river Deben. Iron Age farmers had worked these lands, subdividing plots and fields co-axially, sharing the same geographic orientation for miles and miles. And they all seem to converge overlooking the Deben's mouth. It was here, in the first decades of the seventh century, where the ship was buried. But it was not the first to slumber at Sutton Hoo.

In the years prior, the bloodied remains of sheep, horses, cattle and men were buried according to the pre-organised field plots, arranged from the corners inwards. The earliest burials, dated to 590, were sheltered by crumbling stone walls, whereas the later ones, closer to 620, were buried in the open. Even a horse-and-rider burial is known, where man and steed went into the dirt together, elaborately decorated with extravagant military accoutrements like gilded mounts, stirrups and brooches. This is the same 'macho' style the Sutton Hoo Man would be buried in, stylistically closest to Frankish 'warrior graves' and Baltic-Scandinavian ship burials. A burial from Lakenheath, Suffolk, is very similar. After all, the famous Sutton Hoo helmet's cosiest parallel is not from England but Sweden. Its owner looked eastwards over the North Sea, the same sea his ancestors or unrelated idols travelled over to first reach East Anglia. But these expressions of martial identity are also deeply Roman, deeply Imperial and indicative more of a generic 'mercenary identity' than anything ethnic or geographic, and their spatial relation to the native field plots demonstrates respectful insular ties. Sutton Hoo was already a place of sacred potency before a longship was interred here. Perhaps the coastline those sailors saw, around the

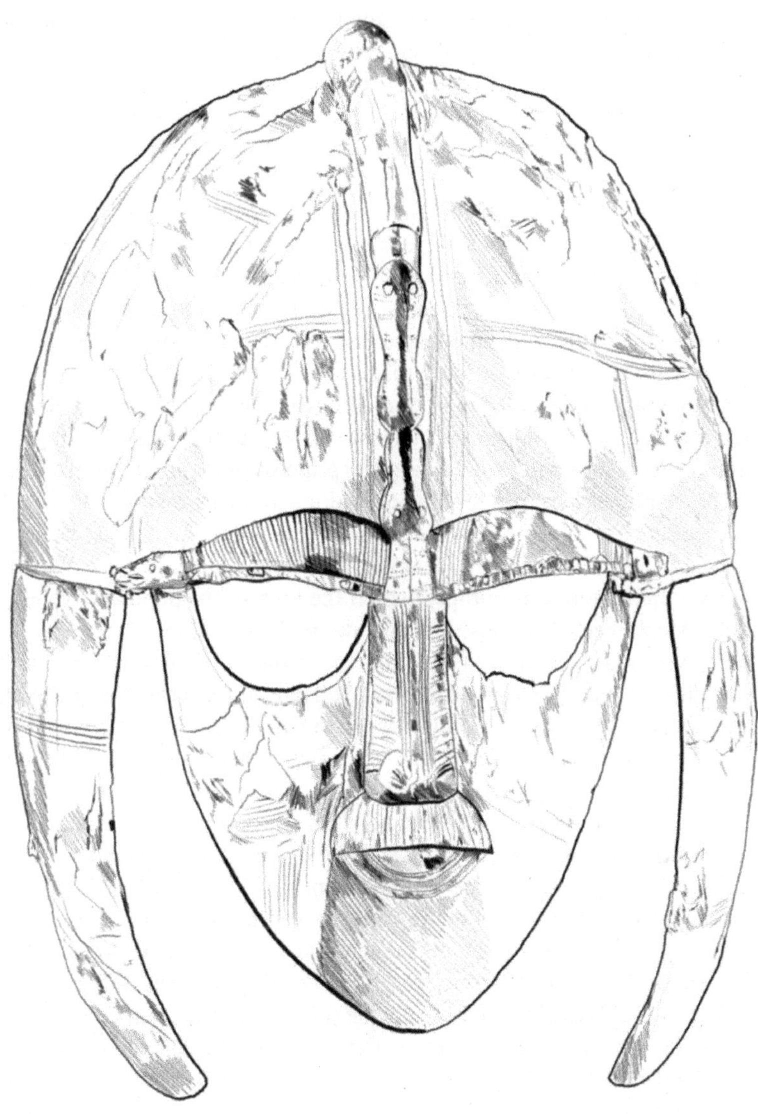

mouth of the river Deben, was even lit with funeral pyres before they arrived, smoke billowing from low hills that would one day become their graves.

The ship burial represents the apogee of Sutton Hoo. From those first field-corner-burials to the Man himself, the style only became more and more ostentatious, further linking this community with various North Sea and continental styles. When the embers of the Sutton Hoo ship turned cold and grey, this landscape had breathed its death rattle. Only a few similar burials are known from subsequent decades, some including bronze hanging bowls, although they pale in comparison to the big one.

A full century later, the entire burial ground appears to have been re-purposed. Long gone were the days of elaborate cremations and multi-day feasts to celebrate pagan prowess. Sutton Hoo was re-negotiated as a haunted liminal space, no longer a centre of activity but a superstitious seaside sanctum.[119] Skeletal remains from the eighth century onwards display marks consistent with executions. When East Anglia converted to Christianity, places like Sutton Hoo, once proudly displaying a pagan past, fell under new governance and new attitudes towards interments, history and the dead. Execution victims were buried here, home now to tumbleweeds instead of traders and onlookers amongst the forgotten, and forbidden, remains of their pre-Christian ancestors. The nearest royal *vill* at Rendlesham, also, appears to have morphed from a piratical enclave into a Christian landholding, associated forevermore with the dynasty of the Wuffingas.

Do the identity and ties of the Sutton Hoo Man matter? Would he have been remembered once the burial ground became an execution zone? Writing in the sixth century, Procopius connected a king and princess of the *Anglii* with a Rhenish tribe.[120] He described a marriage alliance and an overseas invasion in which an Anglian princess led 'four hundred ships' over the North Sea against her enemy. If real, such a fleet was probably launched from East Anglia, for the Wuffingas' origins surely lie in northern Europe, even if the bulk of the populace were of the same native stock who tilled those Deben-side field plots.

Goods, ideas and blood flowed into East Anglia through 'gateway communities' like the royally-overseen *emporium* at Ipswich. Here, at Buttermarket, excavations revealed burials styled in a Scandinavian manner, with corpses neatly laid in dug-out log boats and others styled similarly to burials known from Belgium and the Netherlands; another grave was even adorned with military regalia identical to examples from Armentières in France.[121] In the late seventh century, when Sutton Hoo faded out of importance, East Anglia took on a new role as a gateway community, allowing North Sea people and wares to move unfettered. The Sutton Hoo Man might seem unique but he was only one of thousands of visitors, traders, settlers and sailors who would be encountered in East Anglia. If we imagine the North Sea as the 'land' and rim territories like East Anglia, Kent, Belgium, Jutland and Norway as the 'shore', then these connections are rendered even clearer. This was all one community, a nexus. Be it the Anglian invasion of the Rhine, the Frankish swordsman buried at Buttermarket or the Sutton Hoo horse-and-rider, the North Sea was their core.

East Anglia owes its origins to the North Sea, but also its end. Water flows both ways. These were the waves that facilitated the outbreak of viking activity. East Anglia could have never prospered without the North Sea, yet it died because of it. The funeral pyres of the seventh century and the burning monasteries of the ninth serve as its bookends.

EIRCH & KINTIS

Let us move away from discussing funerals and look instead towards the lifeblood of little kingdoms: rivers. The ecologist's 'river and wold' model of polity formation[122] proposes that communities cluster around river valleys and watersheds, balancing access to upland, marsh and lowland terrain as part of a process of habitat selection, determined and influenced by population density, proximity to other groups and ease-of-access to well-drained soils.* However, on other occasions, rivers serve not as territorial cores but as boundaries; they provide the easiest immediate subsistence and access to trade, but also neatly divide pockets of dry land. Many tiny territories of the Early Medieval Period vanished; the ghost of a *regio* by name of Hroðingas remains fossilised in the river Roding in Essex, for instance. Others can be found tucked away in smaller valleys still, sandwiched between real geography and saintly tales on moth-bitten manuscripts.

The *regio* of Aechse, from the *Life of St Cuthbert*, is one example, but equally small units are known from elsewhere in the same hagiography and similar stories. Later in the narrative, Cuthbert heals the wife of someone who is described as hailing from a *regio* called 'Kintis', and in the *Life of St Wilfrid*, Wilfrid's newly acquired bodyguards all arrive from unnamed northern British territories. Another unidentifiable place is mentioned in only one poem about the legendary Urien, called 'Eirch'. Unlike with Aechse, which can be reasonably deduced to be one and the same as the Roman *Aesica*, sadly similar lines of thought cannot be followed for this beguiling realm.

'All of Eirch' is linked with another polity, called *Llwyfenydd*, in the poetic corpus, for which Stephen Walker makes a strong argument being located at Brougham, Cumbria, based on the discovery of a post-Roman settlement and the etymology of the river Lyvennet.[123] If we take the literature at face value, Urien, as '*Llwyfenydd*'s true lord', would have governed both. If *Llwyfenydd* lies in Brougham then it would stand to reason that Eirch is nearby, but where specifically is anyone's guess and it would do us well to exercise caution, as should aficionados of the similarly murky 'Rheged'.

In his dedicated book, Andrew Fleming hypothesised that both Arkengarthdale and neighbouring Swaledale were micro-polities between 450 and 750 CE, based

---

* In scientific terms this argument works, but fails to acknowledge factors like tenured serfdom, distant overlordship or personal identity. Someone might live along the riverbanks of the Hroðingas but feel as if they were 'Kentish'. Territory and belonging can be ephemeral and completely confined to boundaries of the mind.

on the relative dating of a defensive earthwork between the villages of Grinton and Fremington.[124] This timespan often serves as a neat gap to populate with speculative little kingdoms. Fleming's desire to find one nestled within Swaledale is comforted by the likelihood that such a territory did exist. The earthwork alone doesn't prove anything, especially because it was more recently re-assessed and found to be pre-Roman,[125] but the valley borders, the repeated use of '-in-Swaledale' as a toponymic suffix and the proximity of Swaledale and Arkengarthdale to other known or speculated micro-polities might. Wensleydale, once called Yoredale, is often argued to be associated with Urien and Pen-y-ghent in Ribblesdale is etymologically similar to Pennygant Hill, Roxburgh, which derives from Old Welsh for 'edge of the march'. Marches and marks, borders and barriers, rivers and wolds.

In 954 Eirikr of York, usually called Erik Bloodaxe, was killed near Arkengarthdale on Stainmore, his eyes pecked atop the grey wolds.* A few earlier weapon-laden burials are recognised from Wensleydale at East Witton, Leyburn and Wensley and three separate antiquarian accounts describe 'several pieces of iron armour, together with several battle axes' unearthed near Crakepot by Haverdale and Swaledale in 1846. The 'buckle of a sword belt ... belonged to some of the followers of the Young Pretender' was the leading theory, that there may have been 'a skirmish in this district'.[126] The undated spoils of petty warlords? We are left scrambling for answers.

As for Kintis, it belongs to Kentdale, in Cumbria, which is an area also recognised for a large quantity of small valley-based territories. There are no hillforts here, nor in the Yorkshire Dales, despite their frequency elsewhere in the United Kingdom. There are many known just north of the Solway, for example, like Trusty's Hill. The reason for their absence across Cumbria and the Dales might be a symptom of the areas' particularly fragmented nature, socio-political divisions facilitated by the ups-and-downs of rivers and wolds. There would be no need to make hillforts, central strongpoints used for taxation and tribute, if there was no single large territory to itinerate. Rather, there were lots of tiny ones, valley-based *regiones*, little even by the standards of little kingdoms. Kintis is described in the *Life of St Cuthbert* as being under the control of someone called Aldfrith, otherwise unidentified. The name itself holds the British Latin suffix *-is/es* meaning 'the people of ____', so *Kint* describes either a mutual figure or landscape feature, like the river Kent. Later in the *Life*, Cuthbert gains an estate at *Suthgedling* which is probably today's Gilling East. Gilling West, on the other hand, is described as *Ingetlingum* by Bede in reference to an earlier monastic land grant.[127] Both estates may have arisen from a group called something along the lines of *Gētlingas*.

When relegated to their suspected counties, Kintis, *Llwyfenydd*, Dunutinga and Craven all appear distinct, but looking beyond such modern divisions affords us a vast interconnected web of farming nucleations, which span beyond and between any administrative districts. As mentioned in the chapter on Dunutinga, these valleys may

---

* The [A] version of *The Anglo-Saxon Chronicle* refers to Westmorland as 'Westmoringaland' ('the land of the folk of the western borders') in an entry for 966. It had probably been a frontier zone for several centuries.

have all been subservient to an overlord, not dissimilar to the Welsh cantref system. Given that Craven is afforded 125 place names in the *Domesday Book*, it is possible (though unprovable) that it was the 'over-kingdom' above them all.

More definite is that all these territories, as evidenced by toponyms and the persistence of the thirteenth-century Cumbric dialect were Brythonic or Celtic-speaking. In short, they were the insular territories allied with, or subservient to, Northumbria; they were the lands Wilfrid's well-travelled warriors hailed from, each one of them probably owned a farmstead somewhere in Kintis, others in Yoredale and so on. But let us not oversimplify this complicated territorial web. The means that people like Wilfrid's warriors would have had to ascend the social ladder may have mirrored Irish disputes, where rung after rung of rank and status had to be climbed on the ladder to achieving overkingship. Documents like the *Tribal Hidage* are only a snapshot of hierarchies: they contain but a glimpse of a continuing and ever-fluid process of peer-polity competition, the hidage values of each *regio* temporary, the 'Young Pretender' and Wilfrid's *praefectii* locked in power struggles, their rivers and wolds in flux. Like the *Tribal Hidage*, this whole book can only ever serve as a snapshot of these realms.

ELMET(s)

There were at least three places across the United Kingdom once named 'Elmet'. Each requires a visit and our first lies in Wales. Here, at Llanaelhaearn, there lies an old, inscribed stone. 'Aliortus the Elmetian lives here'. This inscription is found in the north, usually dated to the seventh century. To the south, in the old kingdom of Dyfed, there is another reference. We have already explored the cantref system but these little Welsh kingdoms can be subdivided further. Each cantref typically contains between two and three sub-regions called commotes; Dyfed's cantref of Gwarthaf had eight and one was called Elfed.

Etymologically similar to Elmet, this word might be an Old Welsh translation of the same Brythonic root, deriving from *el-* and *-met* ('many' and 'reaping'), a linguistic boast about either slaughter or farming. The most famous Elmet was a neighbour to Craven and Deira, located in West Yorkshire near Leeds and Garforth, sandwiched between the Pennines and the Vale of York. We can actually be slightly more precise about this placement, given the toponymic suffixes of several villages to the east of Leeds. This geographic spread is the equivalent size of many *regiones* already covered and the *Tribal Hidage* values Elmet at 600 hides, the same as Spalde, Arosætna and the Isle of Wight. A small, moderate polity with the same name as another area in Wales. Aliortus the Elmetian, so far away on the Llŷn Peninsula, may have wandered west to visit the monks of Llanaelhaearn, or maybe he was a resident from another Elmet altogether. The fortunes of Brythonic populations in West Yorkshire and Wales were intertwined, connected through language and history. Whilst not a hero of the Old North, Aliortus joins the ranks of other suspected Elmetians like Baneful Madog and Gwallog the Lawgiver, who made Aeron tremble.

Elmetians are also visible in the fifth- and sixth-century cemeteries excavated at Garforth,[128] Ferrybridge and Castleford, adorned with beads, but their voices are silent. Far louder are literature and legends. Preserved in the *Triads of the Islands of Britain*, Gwallog is described as one of the 'three pillars of battle', alongside Cynfawr and Arthur, as a 'bull ruler', a 'battle protector'.[129] He also appears at the battle at Catraeth and, in tenth-century poems from the *Book of Taliesin*, is described as the 'judge over Elvet', 'who made armies feeble'.[130] The *Book* is a fifteenth-century collection of earlier poems which are usually attributed to a sole sixth-century bard called Taliesin but it has always been a reach to suggest the descriptions are references to West Yorkshire instead of somewhere near Hadrian's Wall.[131] Taliesin, too, is an enigma. Whether he belongs to reality or legend is a question vast enough to fill this book but, if he was real, his works would originally have been spoken in a Cumbric dialect and then later translated into Old Welsh and from there into Middle Welsh, a process mirroring the *Book of Aneirin*. Whoever initially composed the poems made it clear that Gwallog was someone to be feared: 'they tell me of feats in Pictland' 'and the region of Manaw and [Edinburgh]'. This was a man who 'made provocation for [York]', who quelled his enemies 'at Bathgate ... by Snow Hill ... at *Pen Coed* of the long knives', who fed the 'carrion crows everywhere'. He was a 'warlike king, acrimonious', who 'preferred a pile of the slaughtered to trickery'. 'He who has not seen Gwallog has not seen a real man.'[132]

All this imagined prowess posits Gwallog as a widely-feared warlord, someone who could cause equal havoc in Aeron, Catraeth or Atholl, thus it becomes difficult to associate him with any one Elmet. Madog is another, mentioned in *The Gododdin* as a 'baneful shield-bearing' warrior who 'butchered with blades'. Ceredig, son of Gwallog, is one more, described as the owner of one of the 'Three Lovers' Horses of the Isle of Britain'. His horse was named *Gwelwgan Gohoywgain* meaning 'silver-white, proud and fair'. He was the 'gold-chased shield of the battlefield'. All these imagined Elmetians form an early medieval superhero team, with exaggerated attributes and mighty feats worthy of reverence. Middle Welsh literature is filled with such figures and references to even more unknowable ones; 'the shield of Grugun, its boss was broken before the bull of battle'. But works like *The Gododdin* were never intended to be read as histories. They, like this book, are merely suggestions of historic landscapes, imagined narratives piecing together loose fragments for the purposes of entertainment. A dubious mention of four kings of the Old North teaming up against Theoderic of Bernicia in a 'vigorous' siege is usually proffered as evidence of Gwallog's existence, but the four kings (Gwallog, Urien, Rhydderch and Morcant) are, on the face of it, only referred to as leading individual campaigns against their enemies. They became grouped together in later traditions. Urien, we have already met, the suspected supreme leader of the northern British kingdoms. Rhydderch ruled over Dumbarton Rock, in Scotland, and allegedly owned a flaming sword called *Dyrnwyn*. Morcant, by comparison, is unknown. The *Life of St Kentigern* describes a 'King Morken' who ruled over a kingdom in Scotland while other genealogies describe him as Morcant *Bulc*, meaning 'gap', and later traditions place a King Morcant in Wales, an unknown king of an unknown kingdom.

Connecting all of these 'big names' was a similar language across Yorkshire, Cumbria, Lancashire, Wales and Scotland. Elmet was definitely not playing second fiddle either, with Gwallog afforded almost equal praise to Urien. Be it near Leeds, Dyfed or Edinburgh, these multiple Elmets were imagined as kingdoms of warmongers, who imposed dominion over their neighbours and sent out their legions far and wide to do battle.

But West Yorkshire's Elmet might not have even been a kingdom. Bede only refers to it as a forest. It might well have been a vast woodland located near Leeds and Doncaster.* Or perhaps, it was *only* known as a forest in Bede's time. Over

---

* Extensive woodlands covered a fair bit of Deira. Beverley was referred to as *Inderawudu* ('in the wood of Deira') in the eighth century.

a hundred years prior it might well have been a powerful realm in its own right, remembered by praise-poems and slaughter-filled songs, whispered through the twisting trees and roots of the forest. Memories, remains, and images of memories; nostalgic glimpses of Elmet stranded between reality and fiction. By the tenth century, a boundary clause describing the land around Monk Fryston, South Milford and Sherburn-in-Elmet ignores even the old kingdom's name (S 712).* Whatever was once here was either forgotten completely or purposefully obscured, even if new perimeters sat atop ancient ones; an idealised Elmet buried beneath a new kind of a forest, the unrelenting glass, concrete, and steel jungle of Leeds.

In contrast, the *Annals of Wales* and the *History of the Britons* refer to Elmet as a 'country' but, even then, it isn't afforded the same grand status it gets in the poems (which were written down *after* these annals were compiled and possibly referring to a different Elmet altogether). Elmet's end isn't very dignified, either, with King Edwin of Northumbria occupying it in 616 and expelling its king. Edwin's nephew, who had been 'living in exile under the British king Ceredic', had been poisoned shortly before. This hints at two things. The first is that seventh-century Elmet was already toothless, a client-state of Northumbria, allowing its royalty to be fostered there. The second is that Edwin may very well have had his nephew poisoned on purpose and then used the political assassination as an excuse to conquer Elmet. Elmet's fate, in contrast to Catraeth's, is not one written in bloodshed, war and fire, but political and social machinations.

Linguistic shifts and population movements probably also played a part. When the *Tribal Hidage* was compiled, the realm was referred to as *Elmedsætna*, meaning the 'inhabitants of Elmet'. It is possible this refers not to a pre-existing kingdom but a new administrative territory established on the southern edges of the woodland. A frequent toponymic prefix appears within the bounds of Elmet: *eccles-*, which is an Old English word deriving from Late Spoken British Latin used to designate pre-existing religious communities. *Eccles-* names are understood to reflect religious centres that existed prior to Northumbrian expansion, or perhaps simply parcels of land associated with an extant church somewhere else.[133] Clusters of *eccles-* names around West Yorkshire indicate that there were religious communities within and around Elmet. The fact that this is an Old English toponym also hints that the dominant name to describe these territories was coming from external speakers, describing the tangled undergrowth of greening churches. Furthermore, this indicates that Elmet became remembered by *others*, the remnants of a forlorn forest. Micklefield, Saxton, Clifford, Burton Salmon and Sutton-in-Elmet are all remembered as 'the villages *in Elmet*', distinct from all those villages that were not. These names might not indicate the bounds of a political entity, then, but a geographic region, an area of land that extended towards Hatfield Chase and Doncaster. The Humber Wash probably acted as Elmet's southern border, roughly aligning with Dore and Whitwell and the river Sheaf, which were all at one point

---

* Sherburn-in-Elmet is mentioned in the charter but only as the singular *Sireburnan* (Sherborne).

the southern limit of Northumbria, too. Overlapping kingdoms, overlapping borders. Extant earthworks like Aberford Dyke, Grim's Ditch and Grey Ditch, and suspected hillforts at Barwick-in-Elmet and Carl Wark, all have relationships with Roman roads, suggesting that they, too, may have served as linear limits for southern Elmet.*

On Elmet's northern borders, there appears to be a gap in early place names, not seen in the south. The late-and-great Donald Henson once attributed this to the ever-fluid nature of toponyms. Like the *Tribal Hidage*, they are not static indicators of unmoving populations but representative of that permanently fluctuating relationship between speaker, language and landscape.[134] Perhaps this gap between Elmet and Craven indicates a frontier zone which did not become important until after the eighth century.

---

* Lesser linear dykes connect Sykehouse and Fishlakes, near Doncaster, to these suspected Elmetian boundaries. In 655 the Mercian king Penda fell in battle at a place called Winwæd or *Maes Gai* ('white field'), which might lie along the river Went or in the Humber Wash between Hatfield and Leeds.

Elmet was a significant Northumbrian territorial gain but the lands north of it were of lesser strategic benefit, linked by fewer Roman roads and connections to exchange networks. It might be that ambitions stopped at Elmet, with the innumerable Pennine kingdoms continuing as they were; not conquered, but clients. An assemblage of spearheads, coins, bowl fragments and a sword pommel discovered at Middleham nonetheless places a 'Saxon' artistic style this far north, near Richmond (BM-7C4457), either the burial goods of a mercenary placed beyond Elmet's border, or the victim of Gwallog and Madog's quaking presence and baneful butchery. If Aliortus was from West Yorkshire, then perhaps he was fleeing from these forests as a refugee. And he looked back and remembered. It is tempting to envisage roots working their way snakelike through the fading stonework of Elmet wherever it may be placed. Elmets ended up and down the country just as all kingdoms did, do, and will, a blanket of shaded verdigris swallowing crown, coin and chronicle, grass, moss, mould, blanketing all – a realm enveloped into the Earth's belly. Hues of green will cover all things eventually.

Ted Hughes understood this when he composed his poetic collection *Remains of Elmet* in 1979, describing such monumental memoirs through the landscape. The Aberford Dyke, Grim's Ditch and Calderdale; channelling Taliesin, these were the last ditches 'of Elmet, the last British Celtic kingdom to fall to the Angles'. But this was not Elmet's end. In 2017, Fiona Mozley resurrected the name of the kingdom in her contemplative debut novel. There, Elmet slumbers, simply a name beneath a forest, a glade, a romantic ruin.

ERGYNG

The monarchs of early medieval Welsh kingdoms succeeded to their respective thrones via partible inheritance. If a king with three sons died then all of them would receive equal divisions of his kingdom, effectively creating three smaller kingdoms in the process. This much is preserved in Welsh law codes, anyway. How much it was followed in practice is unknown. These laws were formalised in the tenth century by King Hywel Dda of Deheubarth, although our existing manuscript copies date from the twelfth century or later, having undergone significant regional changes in that time. All this is to preface that the struggle of studying early Welsh kingdoms is that their dimensions and structure change century by century. The histories of Brycheiniog, Ceredigion and Dyfed eventually merge as the history of Deheubarth but then they re-emerge as independent regions later down the line, owing to partible succession. The *Laws of Hywel* are a difficult source to untangle, then, and their mileage varies depending on where specifically the laws are describing.[135] Three redactions exist, each corresponding to a different area of Wales. There is the *Blegwryd*, which covers Deheubarth, the *Iowerth*, which tackles the north of Wales and then the *Cyfnerth* redaction, corresponding with the lands between the Wye and Severn rivers. The *Cyfnerth* is the least developed of the law codes, reflecting the traditional view that these inter-river lands were a nebulous border zone.

Ergyng fares similarly, a shadowy frontier located near Gloucester, right on the edge of modern Wales, encompassing the Forest of Dean. Throughout its history Ergyng was under the thumb of larger kingdoms, its independence parcelled up and re-packaged as a fief to be inherited by fledgling rulers, according to the *Laws of Hywel*. Ergyng may have been independent on two separate occasions between the fifth and seventh centuries but our only attested rulers for this liminal zone hail from an equally dubious source, that ever-irritating *Book of Llandâf*.

The *Book* is a collection of episcopal claims from the twelfth century along with some random hagiographical information and over one hundred land charters. All in all, this manuscript reads illogically; the deals and prices listed for territorial agreements include individual treasures, animals and sums of coins.[136] They reflect a wide variety of half-remembered pieces of information from six centuries of Welsh history. As a result, the *Book* is not the most reliable. It is entertaining, however. One tale about a sixth-century saint includes a passage where his body was tripled so that three separate shrines across Wales could revere his corpse. There is a faint possibility the *Book* contains unfiltered early information, genuine charters and the like which we would then be able to use to discuss the hypothetical boundaries of little kingdoms. This would not be impossible, but unlikely, making disentangling the wheat from the chaff particularly challenging.

On Ergyng, one of its earliest alleged rulers is Peibio *Clafrog*, who appears in the *Book* alongside a story about another saint. Peibio is described as an afflicted king, cursed with an incessant dribble of saliva; his epithet meaning either 'dribbler' or 'leprous'. Returning from a border skirmish, Peibio discovers that his daughter is pregnant and orders her drowning. This fails, so he has his men burn her alive. This also fails and so she gives birth and Peibio, doused with regret, is miraculously cured of his dribbling by his new miracle grandchild. All this is to preface the foundation of the village of Madley, Herefordshire. Peibio bestows the site with a monument. No trace of the monument survives and indeed most of this story is a fable. The only kernel of useful information here is that Peibio's name is similar enough to the names of two sons of Brychan, an equally fictitious ruler we have already encountered. Thus, Peibio connects Ergyng to Brycheiniog.

The second ruler described with any detail is one of his descendants, Gwrfoddw, who may or may not appear in the Arthurian tale *Culhwch and Olwen*. This would connect Ergyng's legendary past not with Ireland but Dumnonia. Indeed, Gwrfoddw's successor is even described by twelfth-century historian William of Malmesbury as a king of 'Damnonia', who owned land near Glastonbury. None of these tales give us much beyond a handful of entertaining nicknames but the interchangeable past of Ergyng's rulers might reflect the ever-fluctuating revanchism this little kingdom felt throughout the sixth and seventh centuries. At one point it was under the whim of Brycheiniog, at other times Dumnonia or Mercia.

This paints Ergyng as a bit of a border-land, a nowhere where nobody was king but, paradoxically, everybody had an equal claim. By the eighth century Mercian expansion collided with the Welsh marches, and it would take only a hundred more years for Herefordshire to fall under their dominion. The village of Wormbridge might very well have been on the border of Ergyng, or perhaps even beyond. It was in this period the name of Ergyng was morphed into its earliest Old English form, *Ircingafeld*, later Archenfield, all possibly derived from the Roman fort of *Ariconium*, near Gloucester.[137] Like Cé, Ergyng became a conflicted crossroads. In the ninth century kings of Mercia were involved in constant skirmishes with viking armies who sailed between Wales and England via the Severn and Wye rivers, cutting into old Ergyng.

By 915, it was under the wing of Wessex when Eadward the Elder, son of Ælfred the Great, paid a ransom fee to a raiding party after they had kidnapped a bishop from Archenfield. This frontier was then viciously reprised with the villainous vikingar killed in the bloodbath. Archenfield was saved but it was nothing but a West Saxon hinterland by this point. Conflict between the Welsh and English frequently occurred along this border; an obscure tenth-century source, the *Ordinance concerning the Dunsæte*, records procedures for dealing with such disputes.[138, 139] The Welsh were listed as the 'hill people' (Dunsæte) and the *Ordinance* relays that they were forbidden to cross over into English territory;

'I desire, then, that in every place the men should pray, lifting up holy hands without anger or argument.' (1 Timothy 2:8) This biblical motif of outstretched hands (called 'orans') was popular in the Late Roman world and thus became embedded in early Christian artwork across Europe.

Ergyng was under the boot, from one perspective at least. By 1086, when the *Domesday Book* was compiled, Archenfield was a shadow on the landscape, a non-place. The surveyors compiling the Herefordshire account wrote only that they did not know anything about the area or its history. We are alike in that respect.

But the *Domesday* surveyors did not have metal detectors. We do, but sadly the evidence strewn across Archenfield and the Forest of Dean is non-diagnostic. An anonymous silver *sceat* here, a spindle-whorl there. A copper-alloy stylus points to a monastic foundation somewhere in Herefordshire, the deposition of the Leominster Hoard suggests viking armies found safe-shelter in this borderland away from West Saxon and Mercian oversight.

The scattered remnants of fifth- and sixth-century cruciform and penannular brooches point to a mixed material culture within Herefordshire and Gloucestershire. One of the cruciform brooches is even emblazoned with a triskele motif. This is a pattern typically associated with early Christian Ireland and Classical Mediterranean cultures, so its presence on a North Sea brooch type is fascinating. Indeed, this brooch (HESH-B90BC0) has no parallels anywhere in the United Kingdom. A gilded fifth-century mount, a south-easterly minted *thrymsa* coin, the fragments of two separate enamelled hanging bowls whose closest parallels are found on the Oseberg ship, a chevron-adorned black glass bead and a 'Jutish' shield boss have all been found along the edges of the Forest of Dean. Similarly styled strap-ends, pins and mounts are also known from across Herefordshire, along with the pommel of a sword dated between 600 and 850 CE, just at the time when Ergyng was flip-flopped between Welsh and Mercian interests. It was in this period that an enigmatic stone carving was made in today's Upton Bishop. The carving is a mysterious piece, chiselled onto red sandstone in an arcade style and has previously been dated to any time between the Roman Period and the thirteenth-century Romanesque revival. Recent arguments place it between the eighth and ninth centuries, making the carving one of the rare tangible artefacts from the edge of Ergyng.[140]

The Upton Bishop sculpture has close parallels with similar examples from Brecknockshire, Caernarvonshire and Glamorganshire, all firmly in Wales, along with details from Irish metalwork. So, whilst the sculpture is most likely a Mercian commission, perhaps attached to a new church, its stylistic origins look westward. Nothing highlights the back-and-forth nature of Ergyng better than this.

ESSEX

> ... there came flowing the flood after the tide;
> joining in the tidal stream. Too long it seemed to him
> until the time when they together with spears join in battle.
> There they on the Pante stream with pride lined the
> banks,
> East Saxon spears and the sea-raider army

In the despondent *Battle of Maldon* poem, compiled after a devastating Danish attack in 991, the identity of the defenders is labelled as not English, nor 'Anglo-Saxon', but as East Saxon, the *Eastseaxena*. Three centuries after their kingdom was disestablished, the East Saxons remained a fierce, stalwart and proud people, who valiantly went to their doom amidst the flood of the Blackwater against the *vikingar* who ravaged their coast.

'Essex' is a useful shorthand for discussing the kingdom of the East Saxons, but the bounds of the modern county do an injustice to the scope and scale of this territory. It encompassed parts of Middlesex, Hertfordshire and Surrey. Really, the entire North Thames Basin might best be considered 'Essex' and, as we shall see, was perhaps home to not one kingdom but many.

After all, this was a wealthy and agriculturally prolific region. By the eighth century rural estates were generating quantities of agricultural surplus unseen since the Roman Period and these supplies were paid to central strong points and *wic*s. We have a few charters and records from Essex detailing such payments; land was gifted to a bishop of London in 704 by King Offa of Essex; his successor Swæfred gifted seventy hides to another bishop by 709; and between 716 and 757 land in Middlesex was parcelled off to Mercian royalists. Many payments describe small *regiones* within Essex, like *Deningei* (Dengie Island) and *Hæmele* (Hemel Hempstead), corresponding to the broad scope of the kingdom and specific individual groupings. Essex emerged in this manner in the fifth and sixth centuries as a collection of folk moots and various patronymic Germanic-speaking societies who all shared a common perceived ancestor and came together via inter-tribal marriages and unions. *Brahingas* (Braughing), *Hroðingas* (Roding)[141] and *Berecingum* (Barking) preserve such sub-territories, clustered around rivers. Importantly, several rivers flow into this basin and bisect the land; each was conceivably the centre of a small unit in ages past. Eventually, this conglomeration came to cover most of the North Thames Basin.

Our earliest major reference to Essex comes from Bede. He wrote that, in 604, shortly after the conversion of the king of Kent, Augustine consecrated his follower

Mellitus as the first bishop of London which, Bede states, was the 'chief city' of the kingdom of Essex. Mellitus' patron was Sæberht, an East Saxon king, although by 616 his three sons had denounced Christianity and exiled the bishop. Like Welsh monarchs, the East Saxon rulers may have also practised partible inheritance. Throughout Bede's *Ecclesiastical History* there are numerous references to the divided territoriality of the North Thames Basin. Between 618 and 623 Seaxred, Seaxbald and Sæward all ruled at once; Sæbbi shared part of his rule with Sigehere between 664 and 688 and was succeeded by two separate rulers, Sigeheard and Swæfred and, later, Sigeheard and Offa. Bede describes Sigehere as only ruling 'part of the nation' and often there were religious disputes between eastern and western areas of Essex. A charter even refers to this same Sigehere as partial ruler over Kent in the seventh century (S 233). Indeed, if Essex originated from a large cluster of previously autonomous units, then these partisan groups make sense. Evidently, in the seventh century, Essex was more of a vague collection of kings than a consolidated kingdom. By the eighth, the western region fell under Mercian oversight. The control of the 'chief city' of London also shifted. In the 630s Kent held dominion; in the 670s Mercia; between 673 and 687 the city was back in Kentish hands until the 690s when there was a Mercian reprisal. London and West Essex were constantly juggled by neighbouring parties. Bede highlights that the kingdom was divided from Kent by the river Thames, but Essex's other boundaries are less clear. A dearth in the distribution of East Anglian Ipswich ware pottery, despite the close proximity to Suffolk, would point to a unique material identity for some East Saxons, a denial of foreign imports. However, a few high-status sites across the kingdom, such as Barking, *do* display such wares en masse; the closely-kept luxuries of marshy elites, a disparity that reflects East Saxon diversity.

It is difficult to find a common thread that ties everything together.[142] At Rivenhall continuity is suggested by the convergent sites of a Roman villa and a post-Roman church and the *Domesday Book* hints at the consistent exploitation of ancient forests and fieldscapes between the fourth and eleventh centuries between Thurrock and Dengie Island. At North Shoebury evidence points to the same co-axial field system remaining in use into the Late Medieval Period. In contrast, other Roman settlements and field systems were torn down in favour of new agriculture; at Gun Hill, Iron Age, Roman and Early Medieval ditches all cut into one another, reflecting re-use of the same land but discontinuity between each phase. Buckles, dress accessories and brooches recovered from across Essex are too hybridised between insular and North Sea styles to claim a specific origin; at Colchester, Mucking and Bradwell, Late Roman bronze buckles point to communities of *foederati* descendants, while fifth-century layers elsewhere hint at the knowing adoption of Merovingian brooch styles. The fact that so many contrasting sequences can exist amongst these clay marshlands indicates that Essex emerged through the gradual unification of foreign and native groups, not the submergence of one in favour of the other. This subtle blend of material expressions can be seen through trends in metal-detected evidence and funerary assemblages. Gallo-Roman quoit-type brooches seem only to appear in female graves whereas cruciform brooches are clustered around the East Coast, reflecting affinities with the North Sea.[143]

Girdle hangers distributed across Germany and the Netherlands, thought to invoke the deity Freyr (or Frēa), see their largest concentration in the Springfield Lyons cemetery in Essex along with multitudes of imported beads. Kentish-style pendants are distributed across the kingdom too, indicating close connections between the two polities. None of these items can be tied to a specific geographic origin as they display an aware grasp of diverse contemporary styles and a social desire to emulate neighbours from Kent to Saxony, France to Frisia. All this is made even more confusing when we consider that many brooches and dress accessories, be they 'Kentish' or 'Frankish', were pinning together dresses styled in the Roman *peplos* manner. Essex was, as it is now, diverse and teeming, but we are not so much talking about the spread of people but the spread of fashion and ideas.

These lands were ripe for settlement; verdant tidal creeks fat with fish and Frisians hemmed in by the Chilterns to the north. Indeed, if there was a pre-existing kingdom present around the Chiltern lowlands, then the mysterious 'Calchfynydd', mentioned in praise poems about the Old North, might be an identification.* But despite the heterogenous material culture, Essex's legendary roots sprout from Saxony. Sæberht's ancestors include the deity Seaxnēat, sword-bearing devil-rearing kin of Wōden. Seaxnēat is an obscure deity, mentioned only in Essex's genealogy† and on the continent in the ninth-century *Old Saxon Baptismal Vow*. This association with a Saxon deity is so oblique to the diverse archaeology of early Essex that it must have been an intentional elite-driven effort to connect the East Saxon royal family with a perceived 'Old Saxon' heritage. After all, Saxony and Essex were both filled with pagans and apostates. These international connections were probably born out of the rich markets of London, 'an *emporium* for many nations who [come] to it by land or sea' according to Bede.

Whilst described as the 'chief city' of Essex, some of the earliest coins minted in the capital depict Kentish rulers, suggesting that London was co-owned, or that Essex had always been a client to much richer and internationally connected potentates. London contracted in size and scale between the third and fourth centuries and, beyond a few examples as at Pudding Lane, no new buildings were constructed beyond the 350s. Indeed, most of the city seems to have been abandoned by 400 CE, an artificial silhouette of a once-great stronghold, sheltered by unmanned walls defending only ghosts. Excavations at the Tower of London, however, revealed a few traces of masonry, lead ingots and coins from the late-fourth and early-fifth centuries, reflecting a transient military presence. A coin of Theodosius (408-450) is also known from the Greater London area. Billingsgate, likewise, bore a fourth-century coin

---

* However, Kelso in Tweeddale is more likely. In the twelfth century, this region was known as *Calkou* ('chalk hill'), ruled over by an itinerant lord at Roxburgh Castle, which may sit atop earlier post-Roman ramparts.

† Quite uniquely, with other genealogies listing Wōden instead. Lindsey's genealogy goes a step further and features several figures *even older* than him, like Frealaf and Finn, though they could have been added on to reach a set total of legendary kings.

hoard excavated in a fifth-century deposit. The scattering of London's inhabitants is also reflected by earthworks at Grim's Ditch, Cray Valley and Brockley Hill, perhaps wrought as new walls to defend new societal divisions. Mucking's earliest layers are contemporary with the abandonment of London.[144, 145] So, too, is evidence for sixth-century 'squatters' in the ruins of Colchester and the cemeteries at Keston, Orpington and Beddington, suspiciously located close to Roman villas.

The London that Bede was describing was not this city, but a decumbent spread of timber dwellings located further along the Thames around Aldwych; *this* was the seventh-century *emporia* juggled between Kent and Essex, home to 'many nations', palaces and beach markets. And here, as at St Albans, the Roman church took root to foster new communities.

It is easy to let London overshadow discussions about Essex's early economy. It was not the sole trading centre. Whilst *Londinium* was slowly abandoned, elsewhere in Essex clusters of Byzantine and Merovingian coins point to an economic blossoming. Many of these issues were clearly valued as items in their own right, rather than as currency, pinned and pierced as pendants and pseudo-brooches as discovered at Fingringhoe and Great Bromley. Later, sites at Tilbury, Barking Abbey, Bradwell and Canvey Island became key entrepôts for the spread of new coins into the kingdom, transferable North Sea silver issues called *sceattas*. These gateway communities were dwarfed by Wicken Bonhunt, a presumed East Saxon royal site situated outside London, where a mass concentration of Ipswich ware (so sparse elsewhere in Essex) was recovered. Current arguments posit that Wicken Bonhunt was a London-adjacent pig farm and butchery, its inhabitants engorged on the foodstuffs, oils and foreign wines housed in Rhenish pottery flooding out of the great conduit of *Lundenwic*.[146] Other groups were forging their own coins; a proliferation of *sceattas* minted in East Anglia hints at inter-kingdom trading but many of these are counterfeit measures from Essex. Genuine coins from Kent, Mercia, Northumbria, Denmark and Quentovic also wound up here. Indeed, Essex was one of the major coin users of the British Isles in the fifth and sixth centuries.

Quentovic, situated along the river Canche near modern Étaples, is as likely a source as any for many coins and the Gallo-Roman and Merovingian stylistic origins of certain East Saxon communities. Excavations at la Fontaine-aux-Linottes revealed over a hundred graves filled with weapons, along with wooden pathways, defensive ditches, buildings and bone-working enclosures.[147] Between the sixth and seventh centuries, the residents of Quentovic were drilling beads and throwing pottery, safe behind their wooden palisades. This was, like London, Fingringhoe and Canvey Island, a gateway community of the North Sea;* the material character

---

* This book is limited to the British Isles but 'little kingdoms' existed all along the North Sea rim. Off the Frisian coast, tidal islands like Texel and Wieringen were recognised as distinct rural divisions in early law codes. *Texla* and *Wiron*, home to Friso-Danish despots of the ninth and tenth centuries, water-lords only a couple of days' sail from their East Saxon neighbours.

of the la Fontaine burials is just as diverse as at Mucking and Springfield Lyons. All evidence points to the English Channel acting as a whale road between the Blackwater Estuary and beyond.

It is therefore impossible to identify a unique 'Essex' identity, because not only did the bounds of the kingdom span blurrily beyond the county dimensions, but the inhabitants were also not producing much if any local crafts. All these beach markets were keen import sites, but exports appear to have been minimal, or at least archaeologically invisible.

Regardless, Essex slowly declined under Mercian pressure in the eighth century. London and its hinterlands were contested time after time as East Saxon kings began to be styled as *duces*, rather than their once-proud title of *reges*. A turgid stylistic shift from the previous sporadic and diverse material identities to an overall Kentish and Carolingian façade preceded the Viking Age which would see Essex artistically Scandinavianised. But still, the inner core of the *Eastseaxena*, the regional identity of Essex, remained. It persisted well after the idea of an English nation was formalised. In the *Battle of Maldon*, the sole defenders of the Blackwater were these stalwart warriors. Regardless of migrations, cultural shifts or fashion trends, the people of Essex remained the people of Essex.

ÆUBONIA

There are many islands in the Irish Sea.

There is Walney, in the mud of Morecambe Bay; there is Merlin's island of Bardsey, home of the twenty-thousand saints; there is the North Bull by Dublin; and there is Ireland's Eye, called *Adros* by Ptolemy. There are the Islands of Fleet in Scotland and those of the Menai Strait; in Cantre'r Gwaelod there is Cardigan Island and the holy pair of Anglesey and Ynys Gybi. There are islands of crabs and puffins; Cribinau and Dova Haw and Lambay and the islands of Saint Tudwal who sailed to Brittany; in the Solway are Hestan and Little Ross.

And standing apart is the highest and largest of them all. The central island of many names. It has been Mona and Mon and Eubonia. It is Manaw, *Ellan Vannin Vag Veen*, the dear little island. The Isle of Man.

Man appears in some form or another in various annals spread across Britain. In 584 a battle is recorded in the *Annals of Wales* and an earthquake a century later. The *History of the Britons* charts a bizarre origin for the place, claiming that three successive waves of Iberian migrants tried and failed to settle parts of the British Isles, succumbing to plague, stormy weather and the towering defenders of a glass citadel. Eventually, a fourth wave settled 'Dalrieta' (Dál Riata) and 'Demetae' (Dyfed), along with 'Eubonia, and other adjacent places', before they were expelled by apocryphal ancestor Cunedda. The Irish *Annals of Tigernach* describe an exodus from 'Euonia' back to the mainland in 576, while other fictions recount the foundation of the island in the sixth century from Scottish migrants led by Neithon, a king from Galloway, and the expulsion of his dynasty by King Edwin of Northumbria in the seventh. Only some of these claims have any basis in reality, reflecting the machinations of chroniclers and politicians. They share one common trait: all value Man's centrality. This is an island that was simultaneously settled by Scottish, Irish and Saxon sailors and then allegedly juggled between Welsh and Northumbrian kings and is located in a sea that has long acted as a vital crossroads. An Irish king ruled here for nearly five years in the sixth century after his father had 'ravaged' it in the preceding decade; a century later, Northumbrian and Irish swords 'raged against Man' according to the odd chronicle entry or poem. Like with Cé, the titles of lost Old Irish texts can elucidate scattered bits of information; one called *The Hosting of Fiachnae*, according to Tim Clarkson, might have described a conflict over the island.[148] In the Viking Age, a Northumbrian king fled here after being deposed and, later, Man became a checkpoint between Dublin and York and a base for piratical Norse-Gaels. This period of Manx history dominates discussions about the island's past and so, to uncover the pre-existing 'kingdom' that may have arisen here, we must dig deeper still.

Buried beneath the island's ephemeral bluffs and windswept sand dunes are two-hundred archaeological sites known as *kiells*. A *kiell* is a small simple church usually dated between the sixth and the twelfth centuries, derived from the Manx-Gaelic word for 'chapel', and many are known from the Irish Sea, including on the Hebrides. The word *kiell* has a long linguistic history, as does Man itself. During the Viking Age, Scandinavian raids and settlement led to the Old Norse language hybridising with the local dialect, forming a common tongue. This was further developed through Scottish mutations after the disestablishment of the Norse Kingdom of Man and the Isles in the late thirteenth century. *Kiell* survived all of these changes, but it is almost entirely alone in that regard. Discovering and discussing the pre-Viking Age history of the Isle of Man is like looking for a needle in a haystack; a lone Irish-styled stylus head, barely larger than a fingernail, found beneath St German's Cathedral in Peel points to an early monastic community. Otherwise, reading through Manx excavation reports and then stopping once they reach the 'Norse period' nets us barely a few sentences about potentially early wood, charcoal and bone fragments, many of which offer only the broadest date-ranges.

Speaking of Peel, some of our most extensive pre-Norse evidence comes from the earliest layers of a walled cemetery found here dated between 650 and 1440. Dozens of burials are known, with over twenty dated before the tenth century, discovered beneath a later *kiell* and rampart. These are all long-cist graves like those from Atholl and Dyfed and their inhabitants suffered from a variety of ailments; two of the skeletons had Schmorl's Nodes, another osteochondritis of the knee and most were afflicted with periodontal disease. Aside from a few bronze fragments, there were no grave goods. This is basically all we know about these early inhabitants of Peel. Much more ink has been spilled discussing the Viking Age remains, including the famous 'Pagan Lady' burial[149] which is one of the richest from outside Scandinavia, found alongside goose-wing feathers, an iron distaff, an ammonite and a beaded necklace. She was a wealthy and spiritually connected woman and, despite being buried in the tenth century, was adorned with trappings *already old* by her time. The beads were over three-hundred years old before they were worn around her neck. Many of them are made of re-used Roman glass and others hint at Irish manufacture through their soda-lime-silica make-up. Were they heirlooms? Were they local or foreign imports? Were they cherished by the Pagan Lady, or simply taken from a former Manx inhabitant? The Lady's grave goods, and indeed her high status amongst the wider remains, might reflect societal hierarchies which were already present on the Isle of Man before Norse occupation. We have already seen how a pre-existing Irish Sea polity can become conquered and merged into a Norse-Gaelic one with the Dál Riata. It is not a leap to suggest the same thing happened on Man; invaders inheriting a kingdom. Indeed, there is no gap between the use of the Peel cemetery between the pre- and proper-Viking Age, suggesting continuity, not conquest.

Contemporary human remains were discovered beneath Rushen Abbey, dated between 910 and 950. This is just a few decades after Scandinavians had dominated Man and so can be used as a relative to compare remains which were recovered from deeper layers. Such finds include a complex series of stone settings on the site of a presumed early monastic settlement; boulders had been quarried and hewn to create walls and makeshift dams; the periodic flooding of southern Man managed by the locals. Rushen Abbey is a twelfth-century establishment but there is precedent for it having been built atop a pre-existing site, which was in the tenth century re-purposed as a cemetery for Norse settlers.[150] Furthermore, earlier burials are even known from Rushen dated between 650 and 700, excavated alongside several curvilinear ditches. It is highly likely these finds are just a small selection of a much larger as-yet-undiscovered seventh-century cemetery.

Rushen is first recorded as *Russin* in the *Chronicles of Mann* and a satisfactory etymology has never been proposed. It predates the Norse period as a linguistic fossil, much like *kiell*. Parallels can be found in Rossan Bay, Ardrossan, Rhossan and Rossington across the British Isles where the *ross-/rhos-* element describes 'heath-land', providing a brief glimpse of the island's climate. More rainfall hits Man than most other places across the British Isles and much of that rain then sits in the boggy soils that make up most of the landmass. Otherwise, Man is unvarying, with only a few dips and peaks including the central summit of Snaefell, from which all kingdoms can be seen. In the north the Isle flattens into the Point of Ayre before the waves start to break. Contrary to popular belief, the 'Isle' is not singular; it shares these waters with a few satellites. The Calf of Man is the most prominent, a good swim off the 'cow's' foot in the south, whilst others like St Michael and St Patrick's are attached via causeways. Many of these were once hermitages. Smaller islets like Chicken Rock, St Mary's Isle and Kitterland may have been, too, and highlight the dangers of the Irish Sea and the hidden reefs that would have scarred unguided keels. Langness Peninsula, in the south, was once an island in prehistory but by our time was attached to Man as a long promontory – its name, in Old Norse, means as much. Nearly all place names on the Isle are Norse, but a few non-Norse toponyms are hinted at in earlier sources, like the *Chronicles*. The 1098 entry describes *insula Sancti Patricii* for St Patrick's Isle, which indicates a Goidelic-Latin origin for the place, something like **Inis Patraic*, named after the famous saint of Ireland. It was certainly inhabited early enough; a cluster of Iron Age huts, kilns, hearths and walls underlie a later cemetery, along with hard-fired clay dated even earlier. Continuous permanent occupation of St Patrick's Isle, and Man generally, is hinted at by pottery and post-holes known all over. There may have been warring tribal groups clustered in the north, south and middle of Man, battling over tiny territories – earthworks, dykes and hillforts at South Barrule, Cronk Sumark and our aforementioned islet hint as much.[151] An inscription from Ballaqueeney which reads 'Bivaidonas, a son of the tribe of Cunava' might even name a group identity *within* the island. On the other hand, twenty-two Late Iron Age and Roman Period promontory forts on the Manx coastline point towards an altogether different form of warfare, the raiding of pirates, a sailor's bane in the fourth and fifth centuries. These sites predate the Viking Age but prove that Man's position in the Irish Sea has always made it a haven for free-booters.

One such pirate may have been Maughold, the patron saint of Man and, as modern tradition has it, a reformed raider who drifted to the island in penance, dying in the late-fifth-century. A major community sprung up in memory of Maughold if the eponymous village in north-east Man is anything to go by. Excavations here unearthed a Neolithic chambered tomb and several satellite *kiells*; the tomb may have even been Maughold's abode for several years, or the home of better attested monks like Avitus. The accommodation of others is hinted at by the *kiells* and nearby stone monuments. Most pre-Viking Age sites on this island take this form; ephemeral and eremitical groups sheltered in transient lodgings, communal hermitages for pirates and pilgrims.

Memories of these early Manx communities are found in the diaspora of Christian sculpture that blossomed out of the island in the tenth and eleventh centuries. These intertwined standing crosses and grave markers were born from Norse-Manx hybridity and, despite being 'Viking', many display artistic motifs reminiscent of Irish and Ionan Christianity. The 'twin-link' style was adopted by Scandinavians, as one example, and there are other crosses, slates and stones, which are clearly earlier. Sun-symbols depicting triskele and swastika motifs probably also predate the Viking Age. Slate slabs from Peel and Lezayre are crudely carved with checkerboard marks, an early version of the strategy-game 'Nine Men's Merrells'. Such a game would have passed the time for these communities. Underneath Norse sites are faint traces of these locals. At The Braaid, two rectilinear Norse buildings overlay a pre-existing roundhouse; the famous ship burial at Balladoole is set atop a *kiell* and rampart; a cross shaft in Kirk Michael records the marriage between a Scandinavian and a Manx bride.

Whether they became remembered through stone inscriptions or simply assimilated through marriage into the families of their new overlords, the pre-Norse Manx are an enigma. Archaeology cannot tell us what they thought of themselves or their world. We can only fill in blanks. All of the evidence for Eubonia or Ynys Manaw or Maon comes either from biased sources or lies beneath much more extravagant archaeological layers. This little kingdom met its end in the Viking Age, but we have no idea where it originated. Was it an Irish enclave, a Dál-Riatan spin-off? Or was it founded by Welsh or Northumbrian dynasts? A Manx shaft inscribed with 'Cross of Gwriad' dated to the eighth century creates a tangible link between this island and a Welsh kingdom we will visit later. Llanbedrgoch, on Anglesey, whilst best known for its Viking Age archaeology, was also probably a pre-existing trading point between Man and Wales. On Anglesey, amidst rising Scandinavian invasions, Welsh king Rhodri Mawr claimed ancestry from Eubonia.

True or not, the islanders became known by a new name.

Possibly pre-dating the Viking Age, this inscribed cross from Maughold demonstrates a high degree of literary and religious sophistication, courtesy of the inhabitants. It is also superficially similar to the Kirkmadrine stones, Galloway.

FÆRPINGAS

One of the most famous sentences in the English language was written in the *regio* of the Færpingas. In the mid-twentieth century, a philologist at Oxford was marking essay papers on a hot summer's day in his home on Northmoor Road, and after sifting through manuscript after manuscript, rejoiced to see a blank page. The professor was so overjoyed at discovering this gap in his workload that he even contemplated awarding the student five extra marks. Instead, he scribbled 'in a hole in the ground there lived a Hobbit'.

Before he was an author, J. R. R. Tolkien was best known for studying Old English. The likes of *Beowulf* and *The Wanderer* filled his mind with lament and wonder, inspiring characters like Theoden and Aragorn and populating his Middle Earth with enduring elements like orcs, wargs, Gollum and Smaug. *The Lord Of The Rings* draws from a deep well of early medieval fact and fiction and Tolkien used his own studies and the world around him as his ink and quill. In Tolkien's earlier *Farmer Giles of Ham*, a little king of a little kingdom gets wrapped up in many of the mortal struggles we have already discussed in this book. Writing in western Oxfordshire, Tolkien had no shortage of muses.[152]

The Færpingas are recorded in the *Tribal Hidage* and by Bede, allowing us to locate them. Alongside *Sudergeona* (Surrey) and *Elgē* (Ely), Bede mentions the place of 'Infeppingum' whilst describing the Irish monk Diuma. Following the death of King Penda in 655, Oswiu of Northumbria sought to install a client king in Mercia and sent his monks to act as ordained prelates. One such was the Irishman Diuma, who attempted to broker a marriage between Oswiu's daughter and Penda's son. Diuma died before he could fulfil his mission and was buried in 'the country of the Middle Angles in Infeppingum'. The *Tribal Hidage* ratifies this identification: 'Færpingas in *Middelenglum*' assessed at 300 hides. From the eleventh century, a third document helps us to place Diuma and, thus, the Færpingas. This is the *On the Resting Places of Saints*[153] which records the sites of their corporeal remains, among them Diuma, who is placed at *Ceorlincburh*: Charlbury. This was on the edge of Mercian territory in west Oxfordshire. The burial of Diuma here hints that Charlbury was a spiritual centre of the Færpingas and, indeed, excavations beneath the extant Norman church have revealed a void and traces of earlier walls. Though undatable, they might be the remains of a seventh-century Irish monastery, the final resting place of Oswiu's monk.

Oxfordshire is drenched in history, visible to all who wander through. A Neolithic chambered tomb known locally as the 'Hoar Stone' guards the northern entrance to the shire. Here, at Enstone, one would not be alone in thinking of

Treebeard, the gnarled Ent from *The Two Towers*. Tolkien would have certainly studied the rock; the root of the word 'Hoar' comes from an Old English phrase 'se harne stan' which typically describes boundaries between the physical and supernatural worlds. Similar phrases appear in a collection of anonymous tenth-century homilies, preserved in the Scheide Library MS 17. One even refers to a specific 'hoary stone' which marked the domain of wargs and water-monsters*.[154] Was the Ent of Enstone imagined as a bulwark against such basilisks? Fawler, nearby, is also mentioned in a tenth-century charter as a boundary marker and an Iron Age hillfort at Knollbury may have functioned in a similar manner. Visitors approaching Færping territory might have changed their minds upon reaching the Hoar Stone. Neolithic and Bronze Age tombs were sometimes associated with malignant forces or deities in the Early Medieval Period; a famous example is Wayland's Smithy, a Neolithic long barrow also from Oxfordshire, recognised as the resting place and unknowable forge of a legendary blacksmith. Tolkien also studied Fawler, unearthing its Old English etymology from *Beowulf*, where the phrase 'on fagne flor' appears in relation to the tessellated pathway of the golden hall of Heorot. Fawler derives from a similar root phrase meaning 'variegated

---

* For 1066, the [D] version of *The Anglo-Saxon Chronicle* states that Harold Godwinson's forces clashed with the Normans at the '*haran* apple-tree', hypothesised to be a reference to a peculiarly shaped and lichen-covered stump. Odd shaped trees occasionally earmarked the spots of battles. In 616 or 617, Bawtry ('the ball-shaped tree') was the site of a major skirmish.

floor', probably describing the Roman villa just up the road at North Leighton. The extant mosaic would have impressed travellers and, when *Beowulf* was compiled, a reservoir of fanciful décor and objets d'art were used as templates. There would have been no such mosaic in Denmark or Friesland, where *Beowulf* is set, but such beautiful works of artistry served as examples. The ideal hall of Heorot, depicted in the poem, was one with a mosaic walkway, even if such a hall never existed.

When taken together, these place names and prehistoric structures paint Færping land as ancient and adorned. The Hoar Stone and Fawler may both have functioned as the perimeters of this *regio*, the mosaic at North Leighton and Charlbury monastery as its heartlands. But what of the people? What of the Færpingas themselves?

In the early twentieth century, whilst Tolkien had just started to think about Middle Earth and began his translation of *Beowulf*, the scholar Edward Thurlow Leeds documented the results of a series of excavations at Chadlington.[155] This was a barrow mound peppered with Bronze and Iron Age cremation urns, set beneath a grandiose communal seventh- and eighth-century cemetery. Sixteen graves were recovered belonging to men and women armed with iron knives, along with the fragmentary remains of many more. On the nearby road to North Leighton, a seax, a set of iron shears and two more knives were also found; eight further burials to add to the cemetery's sixteen. Out of all these remains, two stand out for their grave goods: a female burial accompanied by a bronze workbox filled with gold thread and another found with an extremely lavishly decorated singular bead. Perfectly spherical and adorned with tiny gold foils, 'the Chadlington bead is a masterpiece of Anglo-Saxon work' reported Leeds.

Aside from a possible pit-house at Spelsbury, these burials are all that remain of the Færpingas. The distribution of grave goods and biological sex suggests a small Christian community, perhaps pilgrims, huddled together not far from Diuma's tomb. The home of one of England's greatest authors and the birthplace of Sir Winston Churchill, was barely an insignificant Mercian *regio*. More recent isotopic analyses of a cemetery at Berinsfield would suggest most of the Færpingas were also local.[156] Travelling along the variegated path of monks and kings, one wanders into their silent, shadowed domain.

> Where have the horses gone? Where are the riders? Where is the
>   giver of gold?
> Where are the seats of the feast? Where are the joys of the hall?[157]

Fortriu

Lurking in the shadows of all previous chapters on Scotland has been the formidable Pictish kingdom of Fortriu. It was a northern neighbour to Atholl, a conqueror of Cait and Cé and a nemesis of Dál Riata. Fortriu's history dominates Pictish history because they are one and the same. Both the Verturiones, Latin for 'people from Fortriu', and the Picts were the 'barbarians' to Bede, echoing the Roman opinion that the bounds of Scotland were *barbaricum*. The names 'Pict' and 'barbarian' are interwoven throughout history, since the days of Claudius all the way until another *imperium* started to bloom in the eighth century. The story of Pictland is the story of Fortriu and so; to best dissect early medieval Scotland, we must tackle its most famous names.

But let us not view Scotland as monolithically 'Pictish'. Different linguistic and cultural groups called the place their home and each had a vital role to play in Scottish history. The Picts are but one who rose to dominance between the third and ninth centuries but, as we have already seen, they were joined by Gaels and Bernicians, Britons, Colmcille's Ionan monks and possibly even Gauls. The Shetlanders to the far north may not have even been Picts: indeed, there is reason to believe they were viewed as the *barbaricum* of Pictland; whosoever was most 'north' was the most 'barbaric'.[158] In the Roman Period most of Scotland was painted with this brush. To be 'barbarian' was to be 'other' to Rome and this 'other' was fissiparous: the Maiatai, Calidones, Damnonii, Venicones and Votadini were all different tribes mentioned by second-century writers. Tacitus said they had 'red hair and large limbs'. Some were true 'barbarians' whereas others were slightly more Romanised; the Antonine Wall represents a need to divide between these categories and Hadrian's Wall itself functioned not as a prohibitor to movement but a station from which to monitor comings-and-goings. The fact that it was built in the first place indicates that Scotland's residents were important to Rome. A coin issued in 155 CE was found between the two walls, reflecting cross-border trade between the Romans and their 'barbarians' in Ayrshire, which may at the time have been referred to as 'Outer Brigantia': it was not a peripheral backwater, but a northern extension of an economic limit. The origin of the Picts is a back-and-forth between perceptions and definitions. Judging by the distribution of Roman goods in Scotland, society itself was probably divided hierarchically; there was an upper class that received international goods as luxury imports, a middle class that benefitted but could dip in-and-out of the exchange network, but the vast majority of the 'Picts' were locally-bound farmers, unchanged between the second and fifth centuries. But definitions evolve. By the fifth century the previously diverse Scottish tribes were homogenised into only a few Latinised groupings such as the Dicalidones and Verturiones. It was the latter who would give rise to the hegemony of Fortriu, a Pictish kingdom like no other, whose very presence in British history overshadows its neighbours. As we have seen with several English and Welsh kingdoms, Fortriu emerged from a similar Roman Period entity which strengthened its foothold over generations of protection rackets and tribute-taking to develop from a cluster of ancestrally-linked farmsteads and hill-forts into a true image of royalty, modelled on Rome and pre-existing Iron Age systems. By the seventh century a 'Pictish' identity was knowingly constructed and used by rulers of Fortriu who then spread it across the rest of Scotland. Thus, a term that had initially meant 'barbarian' became re-purposed free from Roman oversight: the *reges Pictorum* of the eighth centuries were no longer 'barbarian kings'; they were just kings.

And they had many kingdoms. In the *Life of St Columba* several territories are mentioned alongside the protagonists' journey across Scotland, including Cé, the *Orcades* (Orkney)* and the land of the 'Miathi' (the Maiatai). The Votadini also persevered as a tribal entity into the seventh century. Bede described Colmcille's journey as 'among the northern Picts', differentiating between territories he perceived as differently Christianised, again remodelling that Roman idea of 'us and them'. The Picts were no longer *all* barbarians but the 'northern Picts' were certainly different enough, in Bede's eyes, to their southern kin. Bede rationalised that Colmcille was the reason for their turn to Christianity but the importance of the Ionan mission across northern Scotland has been exaggerated in propaganda perpetuated by sponsors and hagiographies. There were probably pockets of Christianity already within Scotland by the time of these missions and other Pictish kings converted for separate reasons, influenced by different monks altogether. Earlier missionaries and Gaulish preachers may have played a role.

By Bede's time, however, Pictland was as ardent a Christian powerhouse as Bernicia. Excavations led by Martin Carver at the site of Portmahomack tell us what the annals do not: the centralised importance of this coastal monastery and the aware religious tapestry Pictish royals were weaving.[159] Portmahomack's occupants re-used local stones to access freshwater and dam pools, to align buildings and pave roads, to make foundations for smithies and wax workshops, vellum tanneries and writing rooms. This industrious school was established in the sixth century but, by the seventh and eighth, it received massive financial investment from Irish and Ionan monastic centres spread across Atlantic Scotland and became an important core of the Tarbat peninsula. When it was burned down a hundred years later by Scandinavian raiders the site was not abandoned but rebuilt as a series of farms and workshops. Created independently but funded through Colmcille's monastic prowess and institutions, Portmahomack was a Pictish beacon sponsored by local royals and faraway worlds of learning.

Further *regiones* within Pictland can be inferred from the *Life of St Cuthbert*. One called Niduera, believed to be in Fife, is mentioned alongside Northumbrian nobles. In the *Life of St Wilfrid*, the titular character is imprisoned and later freed from *Dynbær*

---

* Writing in the eleventh century, Adam of Bremen called it *Blascona* after the *civitas* of Birsay.

(Dunbar) in 680 following a Northumbrian conquest of a *provincia Pictorum* which included parts of *Fīb*, Abercorn and Lothian. Bede later described a 'brave subject king' of Northumbria who defended this *provincia* and his overlord's ambitions by fighting against the Picts. This client-kingdom, possibly Niduera, was lost to the enemy, who 'recovered their own land which the English had held'. This passage hints at partisan relations *within* Scotland and an Anglo-Pictish nation, Northumbrian colonists on the southern perimeter of Pictland attempting to make inroads against Fortriu. Indeed, the powerhouses of seventh-century Britain included Pictland and, by the eighth, both Mercia and Fortriu were on the rise together, contemporaneously seen as two equally powerful kingdoms ruling over different halves. It was this imperium, a Verturian and Pictish imperium, which rose to fill the vacuum left behind by Rome. Bede bought into Roman historical terms when he described the 'southern Pictish zone' (Atholl) as being dominated by the 'northerners' (Fortriu) in the late seventh century. Atholl, and the Northumbrian section of Scotland, were conquered.

But what was Fortriu? Based around Moray and Easter Ross, the Verturiones originated from a tribal entity and slowly conquered and integrated their neighbours until they became the dominant powerhouse of northern and eastern Scotland. Their presence in hagiographies and annals is normally synonymous with descriptions of 'Pictland' unless specific kingdoms, such as Atholl, are mentioned. Fortriu's largely undocumented rise between the third and eighth centuries undoubtedly swallowed the histories of many other little kingdoms. Then there are names and off-hand descriptions of other places in Irish poems, such as Circhenn or Cīrech ('crest-headed'), where the *Annals of Tigernach* record a battle in 596. This territory, perhaps synonymous with Cé, was probably based around Angus and the Mearns. Then there is Brechin, Forfarshire, which carries the same etymology as Brycheiniog and Fothreve, Fife, from *vo-treb-* for 'small town'. There are also suggestions of overseas origins for Moray, as seminal Scottish toponymist William J. Watson believed the name to stem from Gaulish *Morini* for 'sea-board folk'. Between the Cairngorms and the Grampians is Báideanach, 'the drowned land', the 'bracken land' of Rannoch and the 'cattle forest' of *būkan-siða* near Formartine. Not to mention Kinneddar, bearing a Gaelic-Pictish etymology which suggests it was the 'end of a district', some kind of upland parallel to the Old English *-sæte* divisions. All these realms were overshadowed en route towards homogeneity, kings of Fortriu remodelling themselves on Northumbrian monarchs, and thus Roman emperors, playing the role of 'overking' just as Bernicia and Deira did for all their once-significant neighbours. In the *Life of St Columba* divisions between the Verturiones and their subordinates are still nevertheless explored. The Drumalban mountain range is described as the gateway between the Gaelic and Pictish worlds, between Fortriu and Dál Riata and either Dunadd or Dunollie is listed as the 'chief place of the *regio* of Argyll', synonymous with the territory of the Cenél Loairn. The constant frontier interactions between Northumbria, Dál Riata and Pictland created a back-and-forth of influence and inspiration. Power centres exchanged hands frequently. Dunnottar, Stirling and Dundurn were once all capitals of respective territories but, as with Craig Phadraig and Burghead, became lumped together as a network of king-sites and Verturian strongholds.

By the fifteenth century Abernathy was viewed as one of these core sites; the compiler of the *Scotichronicon* even remarked that 'it had been the principal royal and episcopal seat of the whole Pictish kingdom'.[160] The *provincia Pictorum* became Fortriu as Fortriu became Pictland, just as the idea of 'England' overtook the many disparate groups across the central British Isles. And with different degrees of expansion and assimilation, the names of these Pictish kingdoms became interchangeable. By 716 Irish annals started to use 'Atholl' instead of 'Argyll' to refer to 'the bit of Scotland that wasn't Fortriu'; the kingdom grew so large that the light of other territories bent around it. The mountains of Drumalban became *the* separator between Fortriu and 'everything else', the new Hadrian's Wall dividing 'us and them'.

Not long after, an imposing Pictish king, Óengus, conquered Argyll and obtained the greatest degree of consolidation and expansion Fortriu would ever know. This was the true Pictish imperium. According to the legendary poet Gruibne, 'Good [was] the day when Óengus took Alba, ... he brought battle to seats, with boards, with feet and hands, and with broad shields', and so, by conquering 'the bit of Scotland that wasn't Fortriu', Óengus effectively took control over *all* Scotland in the eyes of chroniclers.[161] 'The Pictish plain of Fortrenn' is even listed as the first place to fall under Óengus' dominion, implying that, to take Scotland, Fortriu had to come first.

It is difficult to say from where Óengus originated. Irish sources name him as a descendant of the insular Eóganachta, but their legendary progenitor is 'Cairbre the little Pict' and traditions associate Óengus with Circind and the Mearns. The Eóganachta are connected with a place called 'Mag Gerginn'[162] which is yet another realm under Fortriu's shadow.* In fact, upon taking Fortriu in the early eighth century, Óengus became forevermore connected with it. Óengus' dominion was a Verturian dominion because dominion over Pictland *was* dominion over Fortriu. It was Óengus who bested Talorcan and wrestled the 'northern pass' from his hands; Atholl fell and Fortriu rose. Amidst these wars a fleet from 'Fortreanoibh' (either Fothreve or

---

* Nicholas Evans makes a compelling case that Mag Gerginn and Circind are the same place, an important lowland territory between Strathearn and the Mearns.

Fortriu) is mentioned as bolstering the naval contingent of sea skirmishes between Dál Riata and Fortriu and, in 729, the *Annals of Tigernach* record the wrecking of over a hundred Pictish ships near Fraserburgh. *The Annals of Ulster* record this 'war between the Picts and Dál Riata' and, by 741, Gruibne indicates that the latter's ruling dynasties were all but extinguished, their half of Scotland conquered. Óengus himself eventually died in battle 'between the Picts themselves' in Circind, according to the *Annals of Tigernach*, and 'the plain of *Cyīl* (Kyle)' was swiftly stolen by an enterprising Northumbrian dynast shortly after. The see-saw of power had flipped in the eighth century, thanks to Óengus. Instead of a Northumbrian lordship and Picts on the periphery, Pictland had become *the* central kingdom which Northumbria scavenged, and it was all thanks to Fortriu. Multiple Pictish kings seem to have existed at any one time, with Óengus' eighth-century wars acting as one of the only occasions when any sort of formal overlordship was attempted, mirroring Oswald and Oswiu's regimes a century prior. Óengus was trying to unify Pictland and we even see a symptom of this in Bede's desire to divide the Picts into northern and southern contingents, describing fractious political entities. By 782 these tropes had become embedded in discussions and perspectives on Pictland. A Pictish king is described as 'king of the Picts on this side of the Mounth' implying that the Mounth had also taken on a Humber-esque role in geopolitically dividing kingdoms.

By this stage in the late eighth century Fortriu and Pictland had been embellished with several centuries of well-worn literary motifs, many originating from the days of the Antonine Wall. The 'painted barbarians', no matter how false an image, became cemented in popular culture. Even today, we view the Picts as blue brutes on the edge of the world. So much scholarly ink has been spilled on these peoples throughout history, even in seventh-century Spain when Isidore of Seville remarked that 'we [should not] omit the Picts, whose name is taken from their bodies, because an artisan, with the tiny point of a pin and the juice squeezed from a native plant, tricks them out with scars to serve as identifying marks and their nobility are distinguished by their tattooed limbs'.[163] Wrongly depicted or not, the fact that *so many* words are spent discussing the Picts in continental, Northumbrian and hagiographical sources imply that Pictland really was important. It was as intrinsic to the British Isles as Wessex. Fortriu mattered. The archaeological wealth from Portmahomack reveals as much but so, too, does the eighth-century *Miracles of Bishop Nynia* poem which remarks that 'of all their talent among far flung nations' the Picts 'had many monasteries ... which flourish now with choirs of monks, worshipping Christ truly and serving the monastic rule'.[164]

But despite these occasional pieces of praise, the Picts had been labelled as *barbarians* in the Roman Period and long has that paint stuck to their limbs. To Gildas, the Picts were relentless sea-raiders and so it is perhaps ironic that Fortriu's end came from different pirates altogether. The same literary motifs that were thrown at Scandinavians in the Viking Age are a direct continuation from remarks made against the Picts in the late eighth century; the 'heathen [practices]' that had been adopted by the nobility in Northumbria, blamed as the cause for the 793 Lindisfarne raid, were not an emulation of Norwegian or Danish customs but, more believably, the trappings of an Anglo-Pictish secular class. Neither barbarian nor Roman, but something new. We should not omit them.

GIFLE & HICCE

Sandwiched between the Cilternsætna and Essex are two polities valued at 300 hides each in the *Tribal Hidage*. This is the home of the Brahingas, the Wæclingas and the Gifle and Hicce.

Lending their names to the Ivel Valley and Hitchin Wood respectively, Gifle and Hicce are located in the river-lands of Hertfordshire and Bedfordshire, centred around Bigglesworth, Eyeworth, Hinxworth and Yielden, along with Wain Wood, Sperberry Hill, Flexmore and Bendish. A few of these toponyms denote specific agricultural practices. Bendish derives from 'bean enclosure' whilst Flexmore was a 'marsh to grow flax'. Yielden, on what is believed to be the border of the Gifle's territory, was likely a swine-rearing shieling near the extensive Bruneswald forest, located over fifty miles from the 'core' territory near Bigglesworth. Whilst wild and managed woodlands once dominated these lands the Wain Wood is alone in its apparent spiritual significance. In the seventeenth century scores of Quakers blessed the hornbeams and wild cherries here, but this was not the first time people chanted from the dells. The Wain Wood is mentioned in the fourteenth century as *Wenygndene*, meaning 'valley of the heathen worshippers', and there is also the extinct toponym of Waylay, recorded as *Welei* or 'heathen clearing' in the *Domesday Book*. Whilst diminished today, these pagan roots once spread between Hitchin and Hatfield.

Both of these unassuming modern towns obscure their presumed early medieval importance: Hatfield has long been suggested as the site of several eighth-century synods, and, on 24 September 672, the first council of the entire English church was held somewhere in Hertfordshire; many later synods were then held at an unidentified location called 'Clofesho' nearby. Following the etymology, *cleófa*- for 'cleft' and *-hóh* for 'spur', Clifford Offer offers a strong case for Hitchin.[165] It's a hung jury but somewhere in Mercia is the best bet.

At *Clofesho* the fate of the English church was decided. Monks were to no longer 'wander from place to place' and were forever assigned to their individual monasteries unless they had 'letters of dimissory from their own abbot'; they were to be content 'with the hospitality offered them', forbidden from exercising any 'priestly functions' should they ever be on the road, according to Bede. These councils led to the creation of more dioceses, as Archbishop Theodore instructed there to be 'more bishops ... as the number of the faithful increases', but no one bishop was to 'claim precedence over another bishop out of ambition'. It was here in Hertfordshire where the opulence and expansion of the church truly began, on the orders of a Greek. Theodore of Tarsus, appointed archbishop of Canterbury at the age of sixty-six, holding the position for another twenty years, was born in what is now Türkiye and began his career in Constantinople, highlighting not just the inter-connectedness of post-Roman Britain but also its international religious importance. 'A man of African birth', Hadrian, according to Bede, was also active in Kent around the same time.

Overseas influence over the Gifle and Hicce is clear through these councils, and the presence of other kingdoms can be seen in land charters.[166] The East Saxon border *regio* of *Hæmele* would have overlapped with southern Hicce and Gifle itself appears to have been divided between northern and southern areas, judging from the toponyms of Northill and Southill (recorded as *Nortgiuele* and *Sudgiuele* in 1086). Along with East Saxon influence, a Mercian presence has been proposed given the place name Offley on the edge of the Hicce. According to Matthew Paris, writing in the thirteenth century, this village was the resting place of one of the most powerful English kings, Offa of Mercia. This has yet to be proved but a tenth-century will certainly lists it as 'Offa's clearing' (S 1497), along with instructions for a nobleman to provide 'feasting provisions to the Hiccan', although this could be for an East Anglian king with the same name who granted territory on the edge of the Hicce between 704 and 706 (S 80).

There has been interest in digging up the history of the Gifle and Hicce since the eighteenth century, ever since the first pottery urns were recovered from the cemetery at Sandy, Bedfordshire.[167] Alternatively described as 'Roman' and 'Anglo-Saxon' over the centuries, the growing assemblage of stamped and incised pottery from this site has been dated artistically to the early fifth century, representing a premature cluster of North Sea cultural influence in an otherwise very insular area. We have already seen the evidence for Late Roman continuity at nearby Aylesbury and Baldock, for instance. Generally, the Sandy pottery demonstrates Belgic influence, made more apparent given the discovery of three fourth-century Gallo-Roman bronze bowls nearby.

Whatever lives were lived at Sandy are now as ephemeral and unknowable as the pagans of the Wain Wood or the flax-farmers of Flexmore. Only the bilingual bickering monks at *Clofesho* could hope to tell us more about the Gifle and Hicce. If only we could place them on a map.

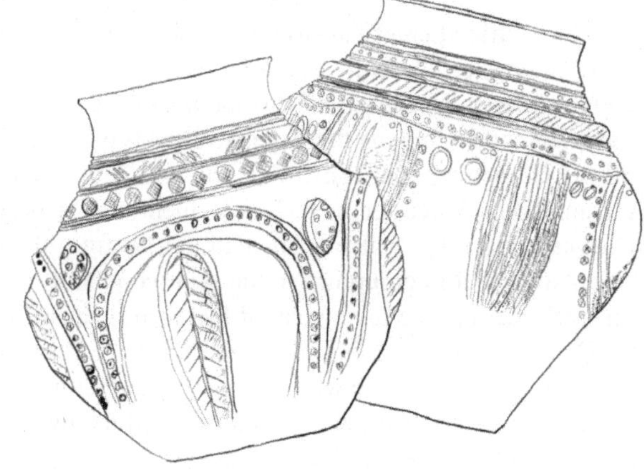

Illustrations of some of the third-to-fifth century pottery from Sandy, Bedfordshire, based on the originals drawn by David H. Kennett in 1970.

GILLINGAS

Gillingas (693-703), Gilling (1243), Yellynge (1307), Elyng (1553);[168] Ealing has been known by many names since it was first gifted to Bishop Wealdhere of London in the late-seventh or early-eighth century by a Mercian king, valued at ten hides for the benefit of the burgeoning inner-city monastery (S 1783). There was never a Roman fort by Brentford on the northern banks of the Thames, yet, amongst the wet clay, Samian ware burial urns and pottery sherds were deposited along with a Macedonian coin from the second century BCE. In the shadow of *Londinium* the 'folk of Gilla' established a small settlement by Ealing's Western International Market, where in 2001 a ditch-and-bank system connected with midden heaps and a pit-house were discovered.[169] They farmed rye, maslin and wheat, the crops which dominated Ealing's fields well into the eighteenth century. The settlers eventually became enveloped by the manorial estates of London's monastic community. In the Roman Period, Ealing was a peripheral nucleus engaged in a symbiotic relationship with the nearby fort, its inhabitants, fishers and farmers, linked by the well-paved route between Silchester and London, trading with other farmsteads, rowing in dug-out boats like the one recovered from Walthamstow, dated between 675-685.[170] New routes were carved through the forests in subsequent centuries; Uxbridge Road dates to the Early Medieval Period, recorded as a 'public way' between 716 and 757. This road was endowed with new monasteries, minsters and churches from the eighth century onwards, a symptom of the councils of *Clofesho* and the growth of London as a Christian capital.

In 830 Southall and Norwood, vital forests for timber, used for the creation of yet more churches, fell under the ownership of the Archbishop of Canterbury (S 1414). Little attempt has been made to identify the residences of the Gillingas across Ealing, at Southall, Norwood or Hayes, but they were here, felling trees, catching fish and paying taxes to monks on the edge of London. And they had many neighbours, among them the Geddingas of Yeading, the Mimmas of Shenley and the Gumeningas of Harrow on the Hill, atop their high-rise heathen temple. A grant from Worcester in 857 even mentions 'a profitable little estate' called '*Ceolmundingchaga* which is situated not far from the west gate [of London]' (S 208). All were folk groupings in the vast woodlands of London's hinterlands. We can smell them in the loamy oak of lost forests, hear them in the lapping water of the Thames, in the bleating of sheep and the call of kingfishers along the river. They are even observable with all their contradictory Romano-Saxon grave goods at the Thames-side hamlet community at Mucking, but our windows into early medieval London are few and far between.

In 1386, an alliterative poem was written in Middle English alongside the payment of high honours to the memory and merits of Saint Eorcenwald in St Paul's Cathedral. Eorcenwald hailed from either East Saxon or Lindsey royalty and was bishop of London between 675 and 693. In his tenure he allegedly travelled London's outskirts in a cart, preaching to the wild men of the northern forests. Almost seven hundred years after his death, Eorcenwald was remembered by an anonymous Northwest Midlands author in the Alliterative Revival tradition, soaked in Old English rhythm and Irish hagiographical motifs, juxtaposed with even older figures like Brutus, Gregory the Great and Emperor Trajan.[171]

In the poem Eorcenwald tears down a pagan temple and expels the idolatrous Britons from the inner city, replacing shrines to Apollo, Jupiter and Mahomet with St Peter, Jesus and Mary Magdalene. London soon became the New Troy, 'the metropolis and the master town', and, during substantial construction work, a vaulted eldritch tomb, decorated with twisted and gilded gargoyles, was unearthed

from the deep. Eorcenwald, away at the minster in Barking, galloped back to the city to speak with this most revered corpse, still alive after all these years, much to the citizens' bewilderment. This was a descendant of Adam, a forgotten king from thousands of years ago. Thus, the poem casts a fourteenth-century memory of the Early Medieval Period, using pre-Roman legendary history inherited from Geoffrey of Monmouth's fictitious embellishments.

Convincing the corpse to be baptised, the unblemished sovereign finally crumbles into dust. The gilded gargoyles disintegrate and Eorcenwald's righteous work is completed. London's bells chime thereafter.

Saint Erkenwald, a bizarre yet entertaining poem, is a tantalising gaze into High Medieval perceptions of our study period, memories and fables attached to London's history. While it is even less tangible than the invisible polities of the Gillingas and Geddingas, it nevertheless hails from a similar historical milieu. If the city's bells did chime after Eorcenwald's undead escapade, then the Greater London wildfolk would have heard them.

GODODDIN

Before they sallied to Catraeth to meet their enemy, the ill-fated warriors of *The Gododdin* were 'nurtured on wine and mead' for an entire year, feasting and frolicking and mustering their strength in the stronghold of Din Eidyn. This chapter will serve as a bookend to early medieval Scotland as we tackle one of the most elusive and confusing territories of them all.

Assessing the Gododdin is a difficult task, depending on the discipline. In the eponymous poem, they represent an alliance of many kingdoms who toppled against the bloodied swords of their enemy in the 'theatre of battle'. Etymologically, 'Gododdin' derives from the Votadini, a Roman Period entity located between the Hadrianic and Antonine walls, around Edinburgh. Through the internecine developments of the first and sixth centuries this tribal confederation carved a small polity for themselves along the Firth of Forth just as other proto-kingdoms of Scotland were forming. The power centres of the Gododdin can only be guessed at but Dunbar, Inveresk and Edinburgh seem likely; these locations are often differentiated from Pictish strongholds, as the abodes of 'Britons', in traditions surrounding the Old North. Gododdin was a Celtic-speaking kingdom, different enough to the lords of Bernicia but also to their counterparts beyond the Forth, an awkward 'middle sibling' between Angles and Picts. An additional sub-kingdom of the Gododdin is even suggested by the name 'Manau Guotodin' which appears in the same poems. Long has this tricky territory been confused with Manaw (the Isle of Man) although modern estimates place it around Clackmannanshire or Slamannan, Falkirk. These are just guesses, however, for the earliest mentions of Manau may as well be just allusions to the vague north. After all, to talk about Gododdin *is* to do a lot of guessing.

In the *History of the Britons*, Welsh king Cunedda is said to have originated from Manau Gododdin and, later in the narrative, King Oswiu of Northumbria is forced to offer restitutions and royal dignities from 'as far as Manau' to shirk the Mercian king Penda when he besieges him somewhere along the Firth of Forth. *The Annals of Ulster* describe a defeat of the Picts at the 'field of Manau' in 711, which *The Anglo-Saxon Chronicle* verify as taking place between the rivers Avon and Carron. Centred around Edinburgh, the territory of the Gododdin could have encompassed smaller realms like Manau, Niduera and *Fíb* during its unwritten history and Edinburgh itself may once have been an independent region known as *Eidyn* before it became the centre of something larger. Castle Rock, which dominates the city's skyline to this day, has been inhabited since the Bronze Age and may very well hold scattered remnants of the Gododdin's mead hall where the 'three score' warriors supped 'for a year according to noble custom' before their campaign. *Eidyn* is remembered in Middle Welsh poetic traditions as the northernmost frontier of the Britons although its specific placement in Edinburgh remains inconclusive. Carriden, a few miles west, preserves *Caer Eidyn* which also means 'stronghold of *Eidyn*'. With this in mind, this sub-territory could either be a single fortress or a larger frontier zone separating the Gododdin Britons from their Pictish neighbours.

As we have already seen, Scotland was never monocultural. The Pictish identity, for one, was knowingly manipulated outwards from the Moray Firth from the sixth and seventh centuries and the wide distribution of Pictish symbols, hieroglyphic animal totems and melted Roman silverwork attests to this. The Gododdin represent a slightly different artefactual and artistic makeup and are referred to differently in textual sources. The compiler of the *History of the Britons* remarked that the Firth of Forth was the 'Frisian shore', probably due to the quantity of maritime goods that entered the estuary. We can imagine sentinels atop Castle Rock monitoring the comings and goings of these outlanders on Lothian soil. Even the name of Lothian is debated. It may hail from *Lugudūniānā* for 'country of the fortress of Lugus', a three-headed Gaulish equivalent to the god Mercury, or from the 'dark stream' of Lothian Burn which flows through the region. Either is possible, as watercourses and natural features often adopt the guises of deities in folklore. Gaulish influence in Pictland is already implied by the name of a seventh-century king, Tarachin, whose name hails from a mixture of Roman and Gaulish religious syncretism, evoking Jupiter-Taranis, a multicultural thunder god.

All this evidence is dense and hard to interpret, much like the poem itself. The broadest take is that it depicts leaders from a cluster of likeminded warbands assembling at Edinburgh until they were beckoned to battle. But even their destination has alternative explanations. In a recent partial translation of the text, Alexander Falileyev has demonstrated that a few lines refer to the 'weak borders' of the Gododdin.[172] A royal Welsh 'bull of an army' was killed along the 'borderland of Gododdin', which might be somewhere in Ayrshire or further north. Much of the language and phrasing of *The Gododdin* was imbibed from Latin learning, however, so quite a lot of it sounds dramatic because it is designed to. Lines referring to a vague 'theatre of war' or 'battle shore' appear in texts that predate the poem and are used in similar contexts, knowingly heightening events without giving too much detail.

Regardless, the main conflicts of early medieval Scotland were not between 'Britons and Angles' but between the old Roman provinces and the emerging extramural precursors to modern Scotland. The Gododdin were sandwiched between these developments, but we must not forget that a significant part of Scottish history is Northumbrian history. In 638 a Northumbrian army was responsible for besieging 'Etin', recorded in *The Annals of Ulster*, which they held for some time after; Cuthbert grew up at a place called 'Hruringaham' near Edinburgh. Bede mentions 'the town of Giudi' in a topographical survey of the Firth of Forth, proposed by Nick Aitchison as a reference to Stirling[173] and, in 655, Mercian and Northumbrian swords clashed here or at Inveresk as part of an inter-generational war. In contrast, Old Irish tractates describe 'Iudeu' as part of Pictland.

The lands between the Forth and the Tees were a melting pot of different royal and regional influences; pressure-points like Dunblane, along the Allan, would have been thundered with foot-traffic from all manner of directions, and as late as 934, the *Annals of Clonmacnoise* describe King Æthelstan of England spoiling 'the kingdom of Edinburgh' as part of his wider campaigns against Alba. After he died in 939, the stronghold of *Eidyn* was captured by the Scots and held thereafter.

But why so much fighting, real or fictitious, over Castle Rock? The initial Iron Age settlement found beneath Edinburgh Castle consists only of a small broch and the walls of a hillfort which, while situated in a geographically valuable area, are dwarfed by the nearby hillfort at Traprain Law.[174, 175] Over ten times the size, Traprain Law was an unassailable promontory but, despite being re-fortified in the fifth century, was abandoned soon after, reflecting wider trends relating to population shifts and the use of land that we will explore in the next chapter. Castle Rock remained inhabited, however, and was valuable but not necessarily the crowning precipice of the Gododdin. However, it took on such a guise in later

literary traditions. *What Man Is The Gatekeeper?*, an incomplete Old Welsh poem from the thirteenth century, invokes King Arthur and his knights to defend '*Eidyn* at the border' against dog-headed invaders.[176] One of the Welsh Triads includes another character placed on the 'border of *Eidyn*' and, from *The Gododdin*, Clyddno Eidyn is associated with the place, who allegedly possessed a legendary halter which could summon and control any horse in Britain.

'From yonder Sea of Iodeo, battle-bold ... Brave Bubon, mightiest in battle's mire'; it is interesting that the Firth of Forth, Edinburgh and Stirling all became 'border points' in literature, doubly interesting that the enemies beyond the border are all from the far north as opposed to the English. An imposed dichotomy between the Gododdin and Pictland emerges, perhaps concerning the slow degradation of the 'Pictish' identity in the ninth century and the growth of the fledgling Scottish state.

Emulating Rome through his very name, Constantín (862-877) was one of the last kings in Scotland to be styled *rex Pictorum*, his successors preferring *rex Alban* instead. They were no longer Pictish kings but Scottish ones. Endless debates about the ethnic and linguistic origin of the Picts and how they connect to modern Scotland perhaps miss the point. The very idea of Scotland, much like England, was manipulated through the worked histories of several little kingdoms of variable linguistic and cultural heritage, Gododdin among them.[177] Early medieval Scotland was a bustling, busy realm. The lowlands and highlands would have been active landscapes. Stock was reared, herds were managed and moved; hides were tanned, soaked in piss and left out to dry; cherry stones found in waterlogged remains at Dundurn alongside leather shoes highlight the mundane diets and fashions of the laity.[178] Bees were farmed, their wax used to seal thatch and their honey to flavour the mead of *The Gododdin*. It was at Dundurn, in 683, that another battle occurred according to *The Annals of Ulster*, this time between Picts and Gaels. Elsewhere, much closer to Edinburgh, a large Christian community harboured a presence around an inscribed stone known as the Cat Stane, where the city's airport now sits. An inscribed stone from nearby Peebles also points toward Christian communities in the fifth and sixth centuries, long before Colmcille would start his missions. These endeavours, launched by monks from Iona, were deeply rooted in Irish Christian beliefs, further highlighting Scotland's multifaceted nature.

By 900 'Pictavia' ceased to be used to describe Scotland, replaced by 'Alba'. Eighteen years later 'Pict' would be written on foreign parchment for the very last time; they are never mentioned again. Instead, the mixed linguistic, cultural and ethnic makeup of Scotland became homogenised by Constantín and the upper class into a 'Scottish' identity through the slow metamorphosis of Pictland into Alba. The Picts never became extinct, nor did the warriors of Gododdin but they both transformed, leaving behind a fascinating legacy. From the inscribed boars and bulls of Dunadd and Burghead to the Dundurn shoes and the poetic guardians who sat waiting by Edinburgh and Stirling, Scotland contributed much to the early medieval artistic corpus, regardless of whether its origins were Irish, Pictish, Brythonic, Northumbrian or all four and many, many more still.

GWENT

From Scotland to Wales, the British Isles have more marvels to share. Despite its dull name, some are contained within the Dublin manuscript MS 23 E 25. It was on these pages that an anonymous compiler rewrote sections of the *History of the Britons* in early Middle Irish in twelfth-century Scotland.[179] There are many differences between this version and the earlier manuscripts, but broadly their focus is the same: a pseudo-legendary retelling of one version of Britain's past together with a collection of interesting places.* In 'a valley in *Aengus* ... shouting is heard every Monday night ... . it is not known who makes the noise' is a choice example, describing a supernatural cave in Forfarshire. Another slightly less bizarre cave is found 'in the district of *Guent*, having wind constantly blowing out of it'. Imagined and imaginative, these caves were separated by hundreds of miles, but people travelled between Scotland, Wales and Ireland all the time. In the south, near Cardiff, such folk travelled to visit the impressive hillfort of Dinas Powys or to seek solitude and preach the word of God. The development of the church has as much to reveal about Gwent as any pseudo-mythical hurricane chasm.

For example, the creation and gifting of stone crosses, several of which have been found at the monastic site of Llantwit Major, including the famous Samson Pillar. This cross, and another wheeled example, were dedicated to separate kings of Gwent and Glywysing, a neighbouring polity. The patronage of these monarchs, and their dedications, embedded them into the financial history of the monastery. All over modern Glamorgan are heavily rounded angular cross shafts, demonstrating influences from as far afield as Ireland and Northumbria. There is faint evidence of early wooden churches at Llanelen, Gower and the island of Burry Holms which were also partly funded by secular lords, tying themselves to spiritual communities. These wooden structures were rebuilt in stone to be larger and more accommodating. Reflecting the burgeoning nature of congregations, the fragments of two supporting pillars for a carved stone screen, grooved for wood fittings, are even known from Llanelen.[180] These would have separated the interior of the church into the tenth and eleventh centuries when monastic reforms across Gwent elevated the status of the clergy. Often, as Gwent's churches were

---

* The original *History of the Britons* also contains a section highlighting *mirabilia* and other 'marvels' of Britain but this is probably an independent text that was later stitched onto the existing manuscript.

rebuilt in stone, their earlier wooden forms became subsidiary burial chapels, as at St Illytud's. At Margam another stone cross depicts a monk carrying a book satchel, highlighting the importance placed on learning and scripture by artisans. A further Llantwit Major inscription is even laid out like a handwritten wax tablet: 'Here [Bodvoc] lies, son of Cattegern'. From a Mynydd Margam cross, this might even name one of these religious investors. This stone, and others from Clwydi Banwen and Cefn Gelli-Gaer, were situated on or within enclosed prehistoric barrows, dominating the spiritual horizon. It is important to place these sites not just within the observable countryside but also the unseen religious landscape that connected them. Wales contains a small distribution of eighth-century church handbells, used by wandering monks to summon crowds which may have served as the foci for 'micro-churches', not structures but small ephemeral communities which worshipped God in the open.[181] New ways of reflecting on the spread of Christianity are necessary to draw out more from such obscure kingdoms;[182] similar bells are known from Austwick, in Craven, although their use here might have been for sheepherding. The multi-faceted nature of farmlands does not exclude them from also being religious landscapes. The Old English word for cattle, *feoh*, also means 'wealth' and, in the eleventh century, Ælfric of Eynsham remarked that cows were holy animals. To be *feoh-spilling*

A cow as depicted in the Bodleian Library, MS Ashmole 1511, f. 30v.

('wealth-strong') may have also described religious devotion. After all, cows were important for the development of parchment.

The expression of belief is a spectrum. On one end you have the ninth-century Welsh farmer too busy with everyday labour to make it to church and, on the other, you have bishops like the ardent Dyfrig, associated with Gwent and Ergyng, but their versions of Christianity are both valid. The high status of the church in southern Wales might reflect that this was a more Romanised area of the country; Caerwent and Caerleon were vitally placed, and the greatest distribution of forts is along the southern coast stretching to Dyfed, linked by milestones. Very early saints, like Julius and Aaron, have also long been connected with Gwent. Mentioned by Gildas as 'citizens of the city of the legions' (possibly Caerleon), these proto-martyrs were among the first in Britain to gain cult status, contemporary with Alban of *Verulamium*-fame, possibly martyred as early as 290 CE.* Constant references to Julius and Aaron as late as 1429 connect them to a specific church in Caerleon, reflecting a tradition associating them with the city. As two of the earliest mentioned Christians in British history, the evidence of their cultic impact and posthumous reputation is sadly too thin to speculate further. More certain is that the nearby toponym Mathern (from *merthyr-Tewdrig*) commemorates a different form of high-status person altogether, like a king, while elsewhere holy wells can be teased out from the names of dedications to other saints. Stone-lined cairns littering the Gower Peninsula, whilst Neolithic in origin, were also once hermitages for the many monks of Gwent and Glywysing and, near Swansea at Church Hill, Penmaen, Roman artefacts lying atop post-Roman ditches suggest the presence of a well-defended coastal chapel, guarded against pirates.

That we can hypothesise this much about the ecclesiastical dimensions of Gwent and Glywysing is because of the evidence for their secular societies. The distinctive hill-fort at Dinas Powys, Cardiff, is but one example of the trendy early medieval 're-occupied Iron Age promontory'. Partially abandoned in the Roman Period, sites like Dinas Powys (and even in France and Spain, hill-forts like le Roc de Pampelune and El Castillón) were re-fortified between the fifth and seventh centuries as mechanisms of power and social ties were re-organised between elite centres and rural satellites, landscape use evolving to reflect demographic changes.[183, 184] This transition between state-backed external military complexes and smaller, local and internal ones meant that old Iron Age hill-forts became the focus for new elite and exchange networks and for demonstrations of status through material and ideological means. The five hearths, four earthen banks, drainage gullies, discarded spear ferrules, knives, combs and glass and pottery fragments from southern France and the Mediterranean recovered from excavations depict Dinas Powys' short-lived leaders as local 'big men' in all their glory. Initial project

---

* Although the name 'Alban' is possibly from two centuries later, an invention to personify the perceived downfall of the British church. 'Alban' means 'Briton'.

lead Leslie Alcock once suggested that Dinas Powys was the central strongpoint of Glywysing whilst Andy Seaman has argued for it being the base of a separate smaller kingdom altogether, based in the Cardiff Basin. Furthermore, similarities in the distribution of the aforementioned pottery across Glamorgan and north-east Somerset might even suggest a trans-estuarine polity straddling the Severn much like our Deiran potters by the river Humber. The seventh century was when Dinas Powys was abandoned, two centuries later than Scotland's Traprain Law, but reflecting that same short-lived re-purposing of Iron Age structures. Established no earlier than the sixth century, Dinas Powys' inhabitants laboured extensively for about a hundred years and then the site fell out of use, much as it had once before. Llavithyn, a westerly hill-fort, and the nearby monastic site at Llandough were linked to Dinas Powys through ridgeway tracks and earthworks along the rivers Taff and Tay but this entire landscape changed when the central hill-fort was abandoned. Why?

Grounded slightly more in observable history than the flooding of Cantre'r Gwaelod, were disasters affecting seventh-century Gwent, including plagues and bouts of famine. Corn-drying kilns abandoned around the same time as Dinas Powys are known across south-west Wales at various spots, including at Bayvil in Dyfed. These kilns had multiple purposes, not just for drying bushels but also parchment. The declines of these kilns can also be seen in contemporary examples from Ireland as bubonic, pneumonic and septicaemic resurgences of the Justinian Plague caused irregular pandemics across the British Isles. From the 540s onwards such outbreaks were not uncommon. Whilst often used as didactic allegories, as in *On the Ruin*, the reality is that plagues and pandemics, such as smallpox, did affect the British Isles. An erroneously dated and pseudo-apocryphal death of a Welsh king is attributed to plague in 682 and a strand of *Yersinia pestis* is known from the cemetery at Edix Hill, Cambridgeshire. It would have been from international entrepôts like Dinas Powys and Tintagel that the brunt of overseas infection was first felt. An extensive Roman *mansio* layered with limestone walls dominated the island port of Barry between the first and second centuries and, in one of the rooms, there was food debris dated between 600 and 860. This extensive facility, complete with a basement, was probably a luxury 'post house' for sailors travelling along the Bristol Channel.[185] It, too, would have acted as a gateway for disease and was abandoned at a time similar to Dinas Powys.

Nor should we underestimate the effects of climate change and increased rainfall, leading to submerged crops and failed harvests. Hill-forts and their satellites can be seen to have been abandoned or re-purposed all across England, Wales and Scotland for our period of study, reflecting either sudden disasters or the gradual population changes that affected communal feasting, petty chiefdoms and peripatetic warlords, all things associated with promontory forts. The spread of the church across Gwent and Glywysing was a major contributor; this area contains the highest number of documented church sites in all Wales.

Lots of churches imply lots of believers. Within the crumbled walls of seventh-century Caerwent nearly two hundred people were interred in unadorned graves and, at Caerleon, isolated burials overlaying Roman buildings suggest an altogether different form of interment, murder victims tucked away in dark corners. Both towns demonstrate evidence of Christian activity and Late Roman proto-urban continuity. In a recent dissertation Marco Leardini speculated that both Caerleon and Caerwent were hubbubs for back-and-forth social interaction between foreign legionaries, officials and natives. These were not the imposing forts of Rome, stamping out locals, but havens for a precious union of international and insular hybridity.[186] The fact that both places retained some degree of importance in the post-Roman period further highlights this and the role the church played in uniting people of diverse heritage. So, too, do an array of curvilinear enclosures recorded across Glamorgan and Gwent, some as early as the third century. Basseleg, near Newport, preserves the Latin 'basilica', suggesting a very early Roman church and Grangefield on the Gwent Levels is recorded as *Lontre Tunbwlch* (possibly Old Irish for 'church house') in a boundary clause from the *Book of Llandâf*. The Welsh-Latin *mystwyr* (from 'monasterium') can be seen at Pontyminster Farm and *radur* (from Latin 'oratorium') is known from Radyr, Cardiff. Like the handbells, holy wells and the wind-blowing dell, these toponyms reflect different stages on that broad spectrum of Christian expression.

In the eighth and ninth centuries it would be these very same sites that contributed to the downfall of Gwent and its neighbours. A Welsh holy-water sprinkler was found in an eighth-century grave in Norway and a twelfth-century censer from Penmaen is recognised at Bearsden, near Viborg in Denmark.[187] Stretching between the Early and Late Viking Age, these finds represent the loot of Scandinavian raiders performing hit-and-run attacks on Wales' south coast. From the date of the sprinkler, it is even possible that these raids predate the 793 Lindisfarne attack but, otherwise, they reflect the double-edged sword that was the rich and powerful church of Gwent. The payments that contributed standing crosses and stone chapels, bejewelled book satchels and reliquaries, tempted sea wolves like food left on a windowsill. From 850 onwards Wales became a frequent victim of Hiberno-Norse raiders and settlers from Ireland and, even in the eleventh century, when Gwent regained a small slice of independence, these little kingdoms were harassed and bled by new foes, at first Scandinavian vikingar but then, from 1081, an altogether different evolution of 'north-man', the Normans of William the Bastard.

GWYNEDD

During the reign of Rhodri Mawr (844-878) the kingdom of Gwynedd grew to its largest extent, expanding over the Menai Strait to encompass much of northern Wales, even abutting Chester beyond Offa's and Wat's Dykes. It was in this period that traditions connecting its rulership to the Isle of Man probably originated; the cross of Gwriad over on Eubonia mentions a figure from Gwynedd's genealogy, Rhodri's grandfather. While we use 'Irish Sea' to describe the waterways between Wales, Scotland and Ireland, a ninth-century letter known as the *Bamberg Cryptogram* refers to it as the 'British Sea' when detailing the links between Irish monks and Gwynedd.[188] * This kingdom was never isolated.

A poem written in the margins of *The Annals of Ulster* records Rhodri as 'of Man' despite the fact that he is already written about elsewhere as a king of Gwynedd. The 'British Sea' afforded him rulership over both. We have reason to believe Gwynedd was one of the more expansive Welsh polities, too. The 'Corbalengus' stone from Ceredigion directly references the Ordovices, the tribal entity that later became Gwynedd, perhaps reflecting territorial gains. Other studies link the name to the Irish ethnonym *Féni*.[189] As with Brycheiniog and Ceredigion, links to Ireland are front-and-centre in Gwynedd's early history although, as with Dyfed, there was a visible attempt at 'Romanising' the kingdom's heritage. Another epigraphic inscription, from Penmachno, proudly ties Gwynedd to Late Roman judicial systems: 'Cantiorix lies here. He was a citizen of Gwynedd and a cousin of Maglos the magistrate.' Another refers to 'the time of the consul Justinus', who was active in Lyons, France, in 540, displaying keen interest in international affairs. Such conflicting identities may reflect divisions within Gwynedd and the differing strategic uses of imagined bloodlines to serve contemporary rulers, Rhodri Mawr among them.

In Gildas' time Gwynedd was not yet at its peak, although the five kings that he wantonly slanders have been placed here, at Dyfed, Glywysing, Dumnonia and Ceredigion. These placings are largely incidental, but it is Maglocunus† and Cuneglasus who are usually tied to Gwynedd. The latter was 'one who raises war against men,

---

* Medieval Welsh poems alternatively refer to it as the 'Sea of Man' after the eponymous isle.

† Described as a 'dragon' ruling over an 'island', Maglocunus has long been viewed as one and the same as Maelgwyn of Gwynedd who was allegedly buried on Puffin Island off the coast of Anglesey in the sixth century, after succumbing to plague.

indeed against his own countrymen, as well as against God.' Excavations near Colwyn Bay have unearthed rubble ramparts and towering four-course-high limestone walls, quarried from nearby sources and similar in plan to hill-forts like Dunadd, Argyll. David Longley, lead excavator, proposed the 'bear's den' referred to by Gildas is actually a reference to Cuneglasus' court, perhaps at Dinerth.[190] Another fort at Garn Boduan, on the Llŷn Peninsula, might feature a sixth-century defensive wall adjoined to a pre-existing Iron Age structure, although evidence is scattered. Likewise, there is a network of promontories and Roman watch-towers linking Chester to Gwynedd, via Caer y Twr atop Holyhead, Castell Bryn Gwyn, Dinas Emrys, Pen y Gaer and Tre'r Ceiri, 'the town of the giants'. The diminished lake at Llyn Cerrig Bach, on Anglesey, holds the single largest assemblage of deposited Iron Age material anywhere in Wales, reflecting consistent ritual use of the site from 300 BCE to 100 CE. Writing in the first century, Tacitus complained that there were druids there. As with the aforementioned forts, there is minimal evidence tying this lake to the Early Medieval Period, but the land of Gwynedd sat atop the land of the Ordovices, and a deeper past was clearly communed with through epigraphy and genealogies. There is also less of a need to differentiate between 'Irish' and 'Roman' pasts for these Welsh kingdoms than we first think. Whilst traditionally viewed as isolated and non-Romanised, there is a growing body of archaeological evidence for large quantities of Roman material all across eastern Ireland, notably around Dublin, in County Meath and along the river Shannon. Distribution maps of lead, silver and iron objects, ranging from the functional to the ostentatious, suggest a trickle-down economy of wealthy Irish warlords who emulated their overseas Roman neighbours and then influenced their own subordinates. A multi-stage process of inspiration, encouraged by Roman goods and the status they brought, tied Irish rulers with an imagined Roman past, much as it did for early Welsh and Pictish kings who similarly re-forged and re-distributed Imperial metalwork. In the fourth and fifth centuries, grandiose deposits like the Coleraine Hoard, found over fifty miles from Belfast, suggest not just Irish raids on *Britannia* but the knowing and active recruitment of the Irish into *foederati* contingents, much as happened across the North Sea littoral. The Gaulcross Hoard, discovered in Scotland, is a similar example from the Pictish world. And if these connections were so prominent, then the slow breakdown of Imperial administration across Wales and England would have affected Ireland, cutting off the exchange networks that allowed the Shannon to grow fat from Roman imports. The Irish raiders so often used as a bogeyman in Welsh histories might instead be the wandering elites of a post-Roman Ireland, watching the 'British Sea' for new opportunities.[191]

Much has been written on British epigraphy in this book but let us not view inscribed stones as distinctly 'Welsh' or 'Pictish'. Hundreds of similar grave and territorial markers are known from Brittany, southern France and even Spain, as at Nantes, Lugo and Santiago de Compostela. Whilst Gwynedd was connected to Man and Ireland, it was also part of a broader Atlantic school of stone sculpture, which was, as were those Irish elites, emulating Roman artistry and linking distant places together through similar vocabularies and designs.

Amongst this back-and-forth of peoples, fashions, elites and ideas there would be a need to name and own land, perhaps one of the few enduring points across all

A selection of Romano-British silver objects recovered from the Coleraine Hoard, found in Ballinreesc, County Londonderry, in 1854.

these little kingdoms. Early major divisions of Wales seem to stem from personal or group names, marking that intrinsic link between populations, landscapes and environments.[192] Gwynedd might hail from 'the country of the *Féni*' sat atop the 'country of the Ordovices' but there is also Dyfed ('country of the *Demetae*'), Gwent ('field of the Silures' from *Venta Silurum*) and Tegeingl, Flintshire, from the *Deceangli* tribe. Micro-polities like Tegeingl can be seen through toponyms like Ardudwy, Cawrnwy, Daethwy, Degannwy and Silwy where the *-wy* or *-wg* suffix denotes specific affiliations with rivers or pastoral units. Some of these suffixes are associated with poetic or legendary characters, or otherwise where a name is common across multiple historical figures. However, there are countless toponyms which connect to unknown personal names from even murkier histories: Brynberian ('hill of Berian'), Gorseinon ('marsh of Einon'), Ruabon ('Abon's ascent'), Ynysmarchog ('meadow of the horseman'), and Ponterwyd ('bridge of Orwid'),[193] conjure images of dreamscapes untouched for millennia, quiet, wispy glades hidden from human eyes and festering peaks guarded by vicious, valiant foes, beckoning beasts and beings of yore. On the flipside, many place names in Wales were ascribed completely fictional founders in traditions surrounding Cunedda's children, purely to explain away cartographical discrepancies. Rheinwg is an interesting outlier, mentioned in the [C] recension of the *Annals of Wales* for 795, having been 'laid [to] waste' by King Offa of Mercia. This is our only reference to this kingdom, although the name re-appears in two hagiographies as *Reinuc,* placed somewhere in south Wales. The name means 'Rhain's land' and this figure appears several times across the genealogies of Dyfed and Brycheiniog.[194] By a process of elimination we can infer Rheinwg was a client state or, perhaps, a temporary union of or between the edges of Dyfed and Brycheiniog. It is mentioned in the *Life of St Padarn* alongside Seisyllwg (Ceredigion and Ystrad Tywi) and Morgannwg (Gwent and Glywysing) and so was probably somewhere between those two conglomerates. Smaller kingdoms still, like Dunoding, Buelth, Gwerthrynion, Dogfeiling, Edeirnion and Meirionnydd are also known but there is reason to believe some of these names were simply invented as ammunition in altogether different identity crises.

In the eighth century Bede decried the Britons as a monolithically doomed, failed race, whose lack of fastidiousness in converting the pagan English led to their diminished status in the present. A century later the compiler of the *History of the Britons* clapped back, combating Bede, adopting certain elements and changing others. In the *History*, as in Bede's work, a lot of the narrative about identity and self-consciousness is imagined; the 'English' and 'Welsh' were composites of innumerable people groups, disputing that ever-enduring dichotomy of 'Anglo-Saxons' and 'Celts'. Still, there was literary conflict. The earliest versions of the *History* state that the island 'was once famous for its twenty-eight noble cities' yet the Vatican recension (954 CE) adds five more, along with the kingdom of Buelth and additional border regions within Wales.* Dyfed, Ceredigion, Gwent, Powys and Gwynedd are the homes for these new additions, thus re-phrasing 'British cities' into 'Welsh cities' due to their placements in the five major Welsh kingdoms. Harry Ellerd-Cheers has argued that this represents a congealed version of a pre-existing local consciousness, cemented into writing and upgraded to a national one,[195] the bias of an anonymous compiler using personal Welsh pride to forge a much wider identity. As the idea of England became consolidated through the tenth century so, too, did the idea of Wales. This is broadly contemporary with Hywel Dda's unification of Deheubarth and the expansion of Gwynedd.

But again, as with Scotland, Wales was multicultural. Old Irish, British Latin, Continental Latin, Old Welsh and Old English were all spoken across the lands and, whilst most people were probably not fluently bilingual, epigraphic inscriptions suggest there was a working familiarity between different tongues.[196] Edwin of Northumbria may have spent part of his youth in Gwynedd and his nemesis, Cadwallon, ravaged Yorkshire in 633. Cadwallon's line, allegedly descending from Cunedda, expired in the ninth century to be replaced by Rhodri's ancestors who lifted Gwynedd up to supreme heights. The twelfth-century *History of Gruffudd ap Cynan* asserts the absolute right of Gwynedd's rulers over all Wales. It would not be until Hywel Dda's day in the mid-tenth century that power scales started to shift temporarily southwards and, whilst it retained a fierce independence and power base, Gwynedd, like all these little kingdoms, also became obscured under the shadow of a new identity.

---

* These aren't 'cities' in the modern sense but substantial towns, Roman forts and Iron Age promontories.

GŴYR

nd that identity was Wales.

Whilst it is undeniable that there were several competing polities across Wales, with some it is difficult even to identify tangible histories. Gwynedd, Dyfed and Gwent all appear in chronicles and traditions, Brycheiniog and Ceredigion less so, but when it comes to the Gower Peninsula evidence for a little kingdom is absent. Still, it seems there was one here, from Rhossili to the Black Mountains. The peninsula remains a geographically distinct area to this day, known for its rolling lowlands and rugged natural borders. The boglands of the rivers Tawe and Loughor expectedly functioned as a barrier for the peninsula's north, although paradoxically Gower became known throughout history as a vital coastal waystation across the Bristol Channel, isolated by land, perhaps, but not by sea.

First mentioned as 'Gŵyr' in the *Annals of Wales* for the year 960, it remains unclear if the peninsula was a unique part of another, larger polity (such as Glywysing) or entirely independent. Caroline Bourne has demonstrated via several disciplines that the latter case is more likely although the evidence is fragmentary. Gŵyr is usually mentioned alongside the frontier region of Ystrad Tywi, between Dyfed and Brycheiniog, which has led some to believe it was also considered a 'no man's land'. Through its geography, however, it was connected to many places by sea; the Bristol Channel is a particularly difficult crossing, but the peninsula mitigated that, acting as a checkpoint for sailors. Monastic students from Llantwit Major may have lodged at Gower on their travels from Dumnonia to Gwent and the multiple identified early medieval churches may even have functioned as inns for the night. These churches are normally associated with cattle enclosures, of which many are known from the peninsula, all dated to the fifth and sixth centuries. Consisting of well-fed lowland regions with bursting streams and springs, Gower was primed for industrious cattle rearing which would have generated wealth for the secular elite. As already seen with Gwent and Craven, there is an explicit link between herds and wealth. The Old Welsh term *praidd* refers to both and herd-rich strongholds would have taken on a role as significant centralisers. The vast number of cattle enclosures, and thus cows, even compared to elsewhere in Wales, would have made the Gower Peninsula a key node in the economies of the Bristol Channel and thus desirable to outsiders.[197]

At least one ogham inscription is known from Gŵyr, at Loughor, probably connected to the same Irish influence that affected Dyfed and Brycheiniog. Elsewhere, suspected royal centres of Gŵyr are limited to toponyms and scant

excavations. Stembridge, Crawley Rocks, Parkmill and Bishopston have all been argued to be analogues to Dinas Powys. The churches appear to be situated on the edges of cattle enclosures, suggesting that ownership of *praidd* was tied with power and status. A suspected royal court at Llys Nini exists only toponymically, possibly deriving from a female personal name. In the past, antiquarians even suggested the legendary figure Enynny, Urien's sister, was the inspiration. Such evidence is impossible to quantify but the idea of a powerful female ruler lording it over Gŵyr seems fairly reasonable, just not the specific legendary connection. Even the name 'Gŵyr' has been suggested to link with *Gwŷr y Gogledd* ('Men of the North'), implying that the peninsula was named after this literary tradition but, if 'Gŵyr' just means 'Men', then it could be affiliated with any tightly-knit group, the 'Peninsula Men' for example. Other genealogical tracts and hagiographies link the peninsula to St David, who allegedly converted Gŵyr and founded churches here in the sixth century, and from him to Cunedda. As seen with Gwynedd, connections stemming from Cunedda are fictitious, but it seems increasingly possible that there *were* rulers here in any case to facilitate and fund the development of David's churches. The idea of kings consistently ruling over a very small bit of Wales is not a stretch either;[198] Ergyng existed and there were demonstrably several valley-based entities distinct from Northumbria for several centuries in the north-west. The existence of Gŵyr as a little kingdom might even be a result of partible inheritance and the gradual segmentation of larger polities.

Still, the geography made Gŵyr 'well suited to independence' in Bourne's words.[199] Parallels with Ergyng offer further insights. Both it, Ystrad Tywi and Gŵyr were repeatedly raided; nearly all tenth-century mentions of the latter are in reference to it being 'devastated' by other Welsh rulers and the *Laws of Hywel Dda* suggest this would be quite normal. Yearly warfare was expected and encouraged, but only for six weeks, so a close neighbour, with wealth to spare and rugged borders to cross, was as good a choice as any, especially if time was limited. And raiding was very much the point: monasteries, people, cattle. Repeated cattle-raids on such a *praidd*-strong area would have served not to crush Gŵyr but instead contribute to the wider cyclical economies of Welsh kingdoms. Not just geographically, then, did the Gower Peninsula serve as a key node in trade networks. Guy Halsall has more broadly suggested that early medieval warfare revolved around 'seasons' and 'cycles' of martial display, raiding and violence.[200] Seen in this light, it is no wonder Gŵyr was often considered part of the 'no man's land' of Ystrad Tywi if it was used in the same manner by contemporary rulers. The significance of cattle as objects of wealth and devotion made Gŵyr rich, the geography defended it and frequent cattle-raids would have made the people proud and stalwart, all factors contributing to a unique liminal identity.

And, as seen elsewhere, liminality breeds centrality. Viking Age deposits at Minchin and Culver Hole suggest regular continental exchange and interaction across the peninsula and at Swansea. Just as it had functioned as a stopover for travelling monks, Gŵyr now did the same for Scandinavian merchants. The Normans would find Gower fiercely resistant. In 1136 the *Chronicles of John of Worcester* record the invaders' 'bodies were horribly scattered among the fields and eaten up by wolves' following a brutal slaughter. Was such a fearsome independence historically inherited? A gift through the ages from the proud Peninsula Men?

GYRWAS

'Gyrwas [which means those] who dwell in the fen, or hard by the fen, since a deep bog is called in the Saxon tongue *Gyr*', wrote Hugh Candidus in the twelfth century, perched somewhere in Peterborough Abbey.[201] Dedicated to the history of the place, Hugh is one of our best sources to trace its origins, born out of the mud kingdom of the Gyrwas. Sometime before 1175 Hugh wrote a Latin history of his abbey using a localised version of *The Anglo-Saxon Chronicle* as a major source. Generally, it is believed that Old English was still well understood amongst the monastic circles at Peterborough. These were learned men and, though they lived hard by the fen, were in touch with local politics, wider ecclesiastical matters and England's deep history. In 1139 Hugh washed one of Peterborough's most sheltered relics, the incorruptible right arm of Oswald of Northumbria. This king had died in a marsh long before Hugh's time but here was his silver limb, untarnished. This was the history that Hugh knew, the mystery of the mud.

As with Spalde and the *Billingas* there is good reason to believe the Gyrwas were important enough to the Northumbrian church to warrant moving northwards. Jarrow, where Bede wrote his *Ecclesiastical History*, was called *Ingyruum* in his time, a clear etymological signifier of similar peoples, as seen with Spaldington, Billingham and Lindisfarne. In 653 Bede referred to a local official from Gyrwe succeeding to the see of East Anglia. This was 'Thomas ... of the province of the

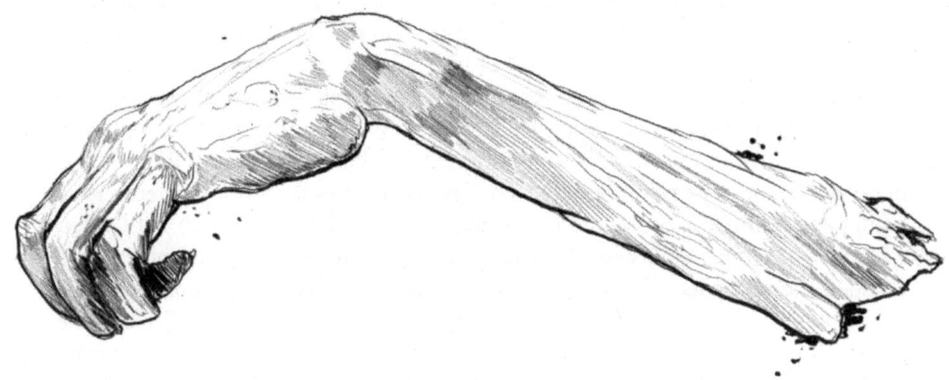

Gyrwas'. In 675 another mud-brother was given a higher station: Archbishop Theodore appointed Sexwulf to be bishop over all Mercians. He was already renowned as 'founder and abbot of the monastery which is called *Medeshamstede* in the country of the Gyrwas'. Described as a recently orphaned foreigner in a Mercian charter (S 68), it is plausible that Sexwulf was a high-ranking minor noble, tied this time not with Northumbria but Mercia. Bede also described how Princess Æthelfryth of East Anglia had been formerly promised to Tondberht, '*princeps* of the southern Gyrwas' before a separate marriage. Æthelfryth is well known for having founded the community at *Elgē* (Ely) which she managed using land given to her by Tondberht in her dowry. Before he died this swamp prince had ensured that there would be elite investment in the Cambridgeshire fen. Unlike Bilmiga and Spalde, then, Bede did not overlook these marshes when compiling his *Ecclesiastical History*. It was because of their perceived isolation, and their liminality, that they became so spiritually important to begin with. Ely, *Medeshamstede* and innumerable hermitages existed in this saltwater between Lincolnshire and East Anglia. Several saints can be placed here: Guthlac, his sister Pega, Cyneburh and Cyneswith, Tibba and the three siblings Tancred, Torhtred and Tova. Like Oswald's arm, even these comparatively minor figures warranted posthumous reverence. Pega's heart was allegedly kept in a reliquary before being smashed by Oliver Cromwell's fanatics in the seventeenth century and Tibba is associated in legend as the patron saint of falcons. Both these important women were recluses in their day, but they posthumously inspired the foundation of churches, an indicator of the wealth that was knowingly invested into the Gyrwas. Pega is remembered in Peakirk ('the church of Pega'), Cyneburh and Cyneswith at Castor and Tibba at Ryhall. Tancred, Torhtred and Tova were allegedly martyred during viking activity at *Ancarig* (Thorney). Aside from Ely, most of these establishments functioned as satellites of *Medeshamstede*, connected to one of the most royally important Christian centres of eastern England. It was from *Medeshamstede* that the flower of Mercian conversion bloomed, spreading as far as Repton, Derbyshire. *Medeshamstede*, in its glory, is one and the same as Peterborough Abbey.

In the Peterborough variant of *The Anglo-Saxon Chronicle*, its origins are connected with the legend of a local spring, *Medeswæl*. Hugh Candidus described it as 'a fair spot … because on the one side it is rich in fenland, and in goodly waters, and on the other it has [an] abundance of ploughlands and woodlands, with many fertile meads and pastures'. It is easy to see why marshes like this were deemed valuable. Over subsequent years of habitation, layers and layers of compressed peat would make the islands of the fen inexhaustible. Even before the Romans industrialised much of this region, Iron Age settlers via the use of salterns were sifting and boiling brine to cure meats and fish, as at Helpringham.[202] At Castor, where two Mercian saints would later reside, Roman engineers and praetorians founded the war palace of a military magistrate, a major palatial complex with eleven mosaic floors and several bathhouses linked by hypocausts.[203] Here, the profuse waters of the fen were not fuelling food preservation but luxury and leisure, until it was abandoned in the fifth century. Two hundred years later, Cyneburh and Cyneswith found God amongst the sulphuric barnacles. The investment in their saintly presence, likewise with the other hermitages, reflects the important secular links that tied the Gyrwas with Mercia, Northumbria and East Anglia. Tondberht and Sexwulf had ancestors who were once independent kings. The fact that both *Medeshamstede* and *Elgē* were founded here demonstrates that the realm still held importance but, also, that there may have been competing interests within it: the *Tribal Hidage* splits the Gyrwas into northern and southern halves. Both local and foreign investment fuelled the development of Ely and Æthelfryth's sister Seaxburh is similar enough to the name of *Medeshamstede*'s founder Sexwulf to suggest that they were related, a minor family on East Anglia's northern limit.

The *Life of St Guthlac* contains a number of useful background details about what life was like for these monks. This 'very black fen of immense size' was awash with hermits and from their hermitages sprang churches, as at Crowland, Lincolnshire. Guthlac built his initial abode in 'a mound of clods built of earth' which had previously been broken into by 'greedy comers to the waste'. This is a description of a re-purposed prehistoric tumulus. Anchor Church Field, around Crowland, is awash with Neolithic and Bronze Age remains which would have been especially visible against the flatter early medieval horizon, when myths were richer. The plentiful barrows would have held an antiquated value, equal-parts revered and sanctified by some, lauded as treasure troves by others. Whilst sometimes feared, prehistoric structures became re-purposed as the foundations of Christian establishments; Guthlac's mound and a Bronze Age henge became Crowland Abbey, their presence in the landscape as mysterious pagan memoirs redefined. The once-liminal monastic hermitages became ecclesiastical centres. High-status pottery and glass fragments and at least two bone combs dated between the sixth and ninth centuries reflect the wealth and goods that would have been bartered across the river Welland between monks and their royal sponsors, funding the spiritual escapades of hermits like Guthlac, Pega, Tibba and Cyneburh.

By consolidating contemporary spiritual and secular power through the re-use of prehistoric material, royalty and the church de-mystified the fen. Whilst they had always been productive, it wasn't until the seventh century when elites saw mound-dotted marshes as opportunities to consolidate their contemporary power. A barrow became not just a barrow but a chance to say 'my ancestor lies there, guarding my border', or the underbed of a Christian establishment. All across these little kingdoms we have seen how folk reshaped versions of the deep past to suit their attitudes. For Hugh Candidus, the history of the Gyrwas was one of holy relics and saintly monks but, for Guthlac, Sexwulf and Æthelfryth, these were uncharted marshes, ready to be tamed.

HÆSTINGAS

In the years following the Battle of Hastings the voices that remembered William's conquest were both raucous and eerily solemn.[204, 205] In one corner, the authors of *The Anglo-Saxon Chronicle* bemoaned the sins of their leaders, framing the Normans as a divine punishment. For those conquerors, however, control over England represented a divine victory against rebels. Norman authors like William of Poitiers and Wace were keen to paint Harold Godwinson as a treacherous leech whilst the compilers of the *Chronicle*, even years after his defeat, still framed his claim as righteous. The Norman victory was a response from God for 'the sins of the nation', no doubt also influenced by Halley's Comet seen above in 1066. Undoubtedly the most open-ended window into this post-battle historiography is the monumental Bayeux Tapestry whose characters and setpieces across nearly seventy metres of cloth can be read in a variety of ways. Here, Godwinson is afforded his just title of *REX* and the events depicted are vague enough so that they can be interpreted according to the viewer's perspective, English or Norman. The tapestry was, and is, a living artefact, influencing authors who then describe the battle it depicted. It was at Hastings where both the real outcome of the battle and later written versions of it reshaped what 'England' meant as a nation, connecting the country through literary traditions to continental Europe. But the origins of Hastings itself are much humbler, a far cry from the watershed moment the battle eventually became, told not through tapestries but toponymy.

Hastings hails from Hæstingas, a group belonging to the common ancestor Hæsta or Hæsten. Events pertaining to their eighth-century activities are mentioned by Symeon of Durham in the twelfth, although the source from which he obtained this information is unknown. Allegedly, the 'people of Hæsta' were crushed by Offa of Mercia in 771 and later fell under the wing of Wessex, although the likelihood is that the Hæstingas had already lost their independence to the South Saxons long before. Nevertheless, they were recorded as a unique territory twice between the 790s and 1011 where they are listed alongside the *Suð-seaxe* and *Suðrige*, other polities. As seen elsewhere, the etymology points to a seventh-century origin but archaeological evidence for the habitation of Hastings is inconclusive. All we have to go on for metal detected finds is, bizarrely, a silver *drachm* minted in Bengal between 850-988 CE (PUBLIC-66D6B7). This is one of only two finds of this type known from southern England, the other being from Surrey (SUR-E12F27) and both are either indicative of modern losses or genuine intercontinental interactions between England and India. Specific details on both coins suggest that they were carried by the same person.

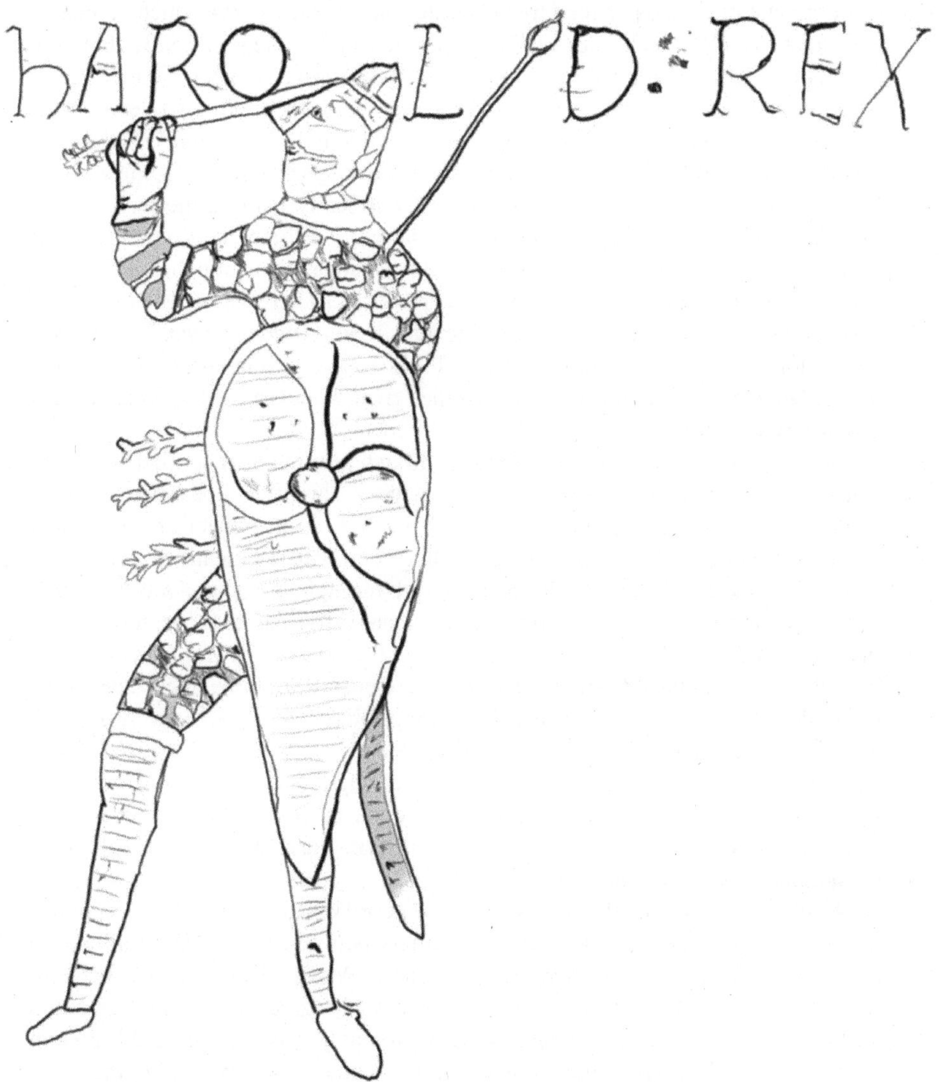

The same trade routes that brought glass and carnelian beads to Deira or elephant ivory to Lincolnshire heralded these rare silver issues. Hastings' sandstone cliffs acted as an important gateway, one of several facing Normandy. Prior to the famous battle, a *burh* was established nearby, given the mention of 'Hæstingaceaster' in 1050. There was a mint here, too, with coins from Edward the Confessor's reign (1042-1066), even emblazoned with 'Hæstingaport'. The Hæstingas were not alone overlooking the English Channel, yet physical evidence for this corner of early medieval England is meagre.

Toponymically, we have more to go on. A charter from 772 (S 108) refers to 'Icel's estate' of Icklesham, *bæxwarena-land* (today's Bexhill-on-Sea, derived from 'people of the box-shaped tree clearing') and *Kæia weorðe* which is today's Kewhurst. Winchelsea also derives from a personal name, like Winece, Birchington, Bullington and Collington, too, and Kewhurst itself means 'Cæga's mound', either a burial or defensive earthwork. Crowhurst, to the north, could also derive from *Crawe*, a corvid-related epithet. There are also Telham, Uckham and Whatlington. This small handful of place names surrounding Hastings provides a fading glimpse of communities and claimants, landowners confidently naming the land around them and embedding ancestors into folk memory. *Anderitum*, the Roman sea-post near Pevensey, became re-purposed as a fictive personal name into the Old English period with forests described as 'the wood of Andred'. There was a need to connect a forgotten history to a recognisable figure, real or not. *Andredes-weald* was said to stretch for over a hundred miles in King Ælfred's time, acting as an impenetrable barrier between Sussex and Kent, called the 'great wood' in the 893 entry of *The Anglo-Saxon Chronicle*.

Both the Pevensey Levels and Romney Marsh also guarded approaches to the lands of the Hæstingas; so, even within the wider realm of the South Saxons, they retained a great deal of individuality. As with the Gyrwas, marshlands played a dual role in defending the Hæstingas and providing them with the means to gain status. Salt, one of the most enduring forms of wealth throughout history, was harvested in great quantities near Cock Marling. Kathleen Tyson has convincingly argued that the modern name is one and the same as the mysterious *Ala Clocha*, listed in a plea case from 1086, deriving from a reference to the fine substance called marl added to salt as a render to rid it of impurities. Udimore Ridge was home to the single greatest quantity of salt pans listed throughout the *Domesday Book*. Control over salt meant control over wealth. Among the many reasons to conquer England, the salt markets of the south surely contributed.[206] Strategically, owning this land would have enhanced the status of the Hæstingas, projecting royal power via dominance of wood and water.

A sub-king of the South Saxons, called Watt or Wattus, may well be one of our few identifiable *Hæstingafolc*, seen in charters between the seventh and eighth centuries alongside another ruler. In a few charters Watt's own scrawls can be seen: 'King Watts agreed and wrote with my own hand' agreeing to land grants and marriages (S 1173). The place name Whatlington may very well place this man in the land of the Hæstingas, either as a local ruler or an outsider. Watt, after the semi-legendary Hæsta, is our only known figure from this salty spur. In 1066 England was conquered by the Normans and whatever vestiges of this little kingdom remained were cut up and re-distributed to new lords like William of Eu. The salt that was once traded north for locally minted issues or across the English Channel for Sasanian coins was commodified even further by continental overlords. Like England itself, this little kingdom fell and as demonstrated, can be remembered in just as many ways as the battle that made Hastings famous.

${H}$ALIWERFOLCLAND

In the ninth century Northumbria was shattered by civil wars and viking armies. Successors emerged here and there; the damp ashes of Bernicia and Deira tried to rekindle themselves, albeit only successfully in the case of the much-diminished former. To some degree, the Pennine kingdoms resisted the advances of invasion for a short while. There was the 'kingdom of *Jórvík*', too, centred around York but to what extent that domain held tangible borders is another story. By far the most interesting of Northumbria's heirs is the liberty of Saint Cuthbert, a *roaming* kingdom ruled over not by kings, but by the chosen folk of a remembered religious community. The 'common people devoted to the man of God': the *Haliwerfolc*.

Beyond a shared territory, one of the most enduring ways to unite a group is a common name. A name creates a label knitting people, both high and low, together which can be used internally and externally to highlight differences and similarities: *us versus them*. The *Haliwerfolc* of Saint Cuthbert appear first in twelfth-century texts and were refusing military commands as late as the fourteenth, but they are much older.[207] The community at Lindisfarne was important enough to be bestowed whole tribal territories, like *Broninis* (possibly Durham)[208] and *Bromic* (Coquetdale, Breamish Valley)[209] and it was between these that the holy nomads wandered.[210] Knowingly created, worked and reworked from the ninth century onwards, resisting the churning linguistic and cultural soup of Anglo-Scandinavian England, the *Haliwerfolc* have a long history originating through opposition to the depredations of viking raids. Cuthbert, the monolithic centre of the *Haliwerfolc*, died in the seventh century and was interred in the monastery on Holy Island. When that monastery was successively pillaged, famously starting in 793, his worshippers removed his remains and carried him with them across northern England. From Lindisfarne to Chester-le-Street and then to Durham, Cuthbert's blackened bones inspired reverence and learning as they moved and, in later texts, legends and parables were brought together to make these adventures more exciting. Cuthbert's corpse and the righteous folk who guarded it became valiant defenders against devilish rascals, a corporate identity built on continuity and common ideas.[211] Raiders who denied Cuthbert's supremacy were struck down by God. Writing in the twelfth century, Symeon of Durham argued that 'a multitude of people from between the river Coquet and the river Tees' were consulted when the decision to finally cease Cuthbert's travels was brought up. Uhtred, a Northumbrian earl, was involved in the decision along with the holy folk themselves. The *Haliwerfolc* are not a traditional polity, but in Symeon's pages they are afforded some kind of governmental structure, bounded lands and authority.[212, 213] They also had wealth enough to justify the parcelling of uniquely owned territories.

Several versions of this source, the *History of St Cuthbert*, depict his people as distinct from Northumbrian armies and ambitions; they were a peripatetic congregation that existed according to their whims. In 1069, when William the Bastard subjected northern England to devastating military reprisals, the memory of Cuthbert held back fire and water in Durham and on Holy Island, saving his people from the Normans. The protective aura of Cuthbert *was* the border of *Haliwerfolcland*, not a pin on a map but a motif within pages and chronicles, a community who obtained political cohesion through their devotion to a long-dead saint. Cuthbert, or imagined versions of him, were simultaneously the ancestral anchor of this territory and the bricks and mortar that held the buildings together, the purse that kept the coins flowing, the food coming in and the defenders loyal. A charter composed between 1116 and 1119 mentions 'all the barons and their friends of Yorkshire, the *Haliwerfolc*, and Northumbria',[214] implying that Cuthbert still held considerable sway after William's harrying. And the name of his people, written here for the first time, bridged what was a longstanding colloquial term with official governmental documentation. Symeon permanently fossilised into charters what was already a powerful group identity in County Durham.

Identities do not exist alone, however. The law of 'us versus them' dictates that, as seen throughout history, communities grow stronger when united against a common enemy. For the case of the *Haliwerfolc*, their enemy writ raw in hagiographies were the vikingar who conquered, settled and farmed northern England around the time Cuthbert's corpse was being juggled from place to place. A conflict for the heart and soul of northern England pitted these enemies against one another. And as memories of the saint made one group identity stronger, the 'viking' identity grew weaker and weaker as ties to the North Sea, longships and Old Norse paganism were unravelled and cut by the scissors of England. An often-overlooked aspect of the term 'Anglo-Scandinavian' is that, over the hundred-or-more years of cultural assimilation between the English and Scandinavians, the 'Scandinavian' element must have diminished in the minds of many former vikingar. Divorced from the intense seafaring culture of ninth-century Norway and Denmark, Scandinavian settlers in England would no longer need to remember cultural lessons about ocean winds, animal migratory patterns, boat-building and clouded beliefs. The core elements that made up their folk identity would be transmuted and, in some cases, eroded over generations. The classic image of a Viking Age boat burial beautifully demonstrates how connections to boats and water could express identity in fluctuating times, seen across Brittany, Man and the Baltic, but not in England. Despite the mass waves of migration from Scandinavia, there have been no boat burials found. Was the identity of these new inhabitants rapidly lost? The explicit conflict between Cuthbert's holy folk and the raiders of the tenth century is fable-like but it is worth considering the ideological implications of this period. As the *Haliwerfolc* became united through death and religion, Scandinavian raiders *lost* their heritage and began to express themselves in new hybridised ways like the Gosforth Cross. In the end, amidst these insecure

identity clashes, it would be Cuthbert, not the 'Vikings', who embedded himself so clearly in County Durham.

> Within that town, as is well known to men,
> There lies the blessed saint, the pious Cuthbert. ...
> Inside the minster ...
> Are relics numberless; there multitudes
> Of miracles take place, as books make known,
> While there God's servant lies and waits for Judgement.

In the last ever Old English poem, *Durham*,[215] written between 1104 and 1109, Cuthbert is immortalised in the walls of his cathedral, his landscape and his holy 'kingdom'.

ᚻEATHFELÐLAND

Everywhere there were dead and dying men drowning in the deep and others scrambling o'er the top of their bodies and you see living ones washing blood from their heads with red water and spears dripping with entrails and you hear screams muffled by reeds bubbling under black bile and you smell the soldiers who soiled themselves or the insides of those who did not get chance and – snapping past – the clip-clop splish-splash of a galloping horse ragged and beaten and crimson splintering o'er the bent end of limewood shields and you hear them squelch underfoot in your cold wet boots – you are missing three toes – and you gasp out of breath and look up and see arrows whizzing past loosed from the frigid hands of village boys and you feel what they feel. They don't want to be here. You don't want to be here. You know kings are near but everyone looks the same now racked and ruined by mud, blood and more mud trampled upwards on everyone's shoes on everyone's rusted mail shirt on everyone's padded helm on everyone's face like those covered in blood running down from the gashes in their heads hit by an overhand axe from o'er the shield wall; one of the men has a hole where his face was; one of the men is trapped under the weight of bodies and bodies and bodies; one of the men lost his nose in another battle years ago but he is there right now reliving it in this moment remembering how pain felt then and how pain feels now; he clutches the pouch his wife gave him that he wore round his neck back when he had a neck. Peering through the rain some seem dumbfounded and some can't remember why they came to this place or which lord was theirs or where their king was or if he is alive still or where their spear got lodged – you fall over and drop your sword and get a mouthful of midges and mildew and malice. Through mud-logged eyes you see blood-slaked marsh-men pulling apart pale viscera and you see thegns dropping shields and sparring swords and clashing and stabbing and gutting and weaving and clubbing and punching – you see shadow-men dragging people into the other-world – men topple onto spears barely lucid with eyes clouded and teeth bared; pressing in now. How long. Jewels and glitter and garnets ripped from still-clutching men as the survivors rally behind a crescent of shields and chants and a God's bone locked in a box mounted on a stick held aloft for them to awe at. One last king slips on something beneath his feet and drops his helmet and you hear men jeer and laugh and then the mist starts to fall and screamers rush in and there is a frenzied joy about it. This king dies with wet slapping noises and his men kneel so that they can till fields for new kings. That old bone in a box drops into the mud next to all the new ones. There are no gods in this bog.

Only dead men.

War on the ground is not political. It is people killing people killing people. For the war bands who marched into battle after battle along Northumbria's southern frontier in the seventh century there were two conflicts at play. There was the explicit immediate skirmish and then the ideological conflict knitting everything together under some form of status-based expansion. While the Early Medieval Period was undoubtedly occasionally violent and prone to sudden changes, it also saw gradual developments and some changes would only affect certain areas. The expansion of Northumbria in the seventh century took several decades but key battles happened only for a few hours. The intention behind most was not to massacre the enemy but instead to subdue or intimidate them so that, when the dust had settled, there were still people left to till the fields for new overlords, thus generating economic growth in freshly conquered territories. If territories were razed to the ground, then what would be the point in capturing them? High-ranking officers and kings may have bled and died, sure, but this was the class that upheld violence; this was their job. The everyday people who made up the bulk of populations in this age were farmers.

In the seventh century, five or six major battles occurred in and around the Hatfield area sandwiched between South Yorkshire, Nottinghamshire and North Lincolnshire.* This was Heathfelðland, a *regio* listed in the *Tribal Hidage* as a sparsely settled waste between Northumbria and Mercia. It was, outside of a few islands, a large expanse of intertidal fenland, connected to the Humber via the rivers Trent, Don and Idle which segmented bogs, swamps and meres, linked to the Ouse and the Vale of York. Not an ideal place for pastoral farming but perfect for fishing, whaling and trading with sailors. These qualities simultaneously made Heathfelðland marginal but focal. To travel along the Roman road of Ermine Street between Northumbria and Mercia was to travel across the edges of Heathfelðland, always travelling *through* the place but never stopping, similar to modern Doncaster. As a frontier zone,[216] Heathfelðland was simultaneously ever under the shifting influences of its neighbours whilst, perhaps paradoxically, expressing a unique 'in-betweener' identity. This can be seen in place names that proudly exude belonging (Finningley, 'folk of the fen'; Winteringham, 'the estate of Winta's people'; Haxey, 'Hakr's Island'; Epworth, 'Eoppa's fort'; Belton 'the enclosure

---

* Much of this chapter (and the one on Lindsey) treads similar water to my first book, *Riddles of the Isle*, so I have expanded upon some prior arguments and approached these marshes and the Flixborough site from different, slightly more disturbing angles.

on dry land'), but also those that imply barrenness (Misson, 'watery plants'; Thornholme, 'thorny island'; Hatfield, 'open heath field').[217] *Meicen*, mentioned in the *Annals of Wales* entry for 631, may have been the place's original name. It was amongst these islets where, in 617, King Æðelfrið of Northumbria was killed; in 632 King Edwin of Northumbria died; in 655 King Penda of Mercia was butchered; and, between 674 and 679,[218] regular frontier raids resulted in the defeat of King Ecgfrith of Northumbria. There is even a possibility that the 642 defeat of Oswald at *Maserfield* occurred on the Isle of Axholme.

In fact, whenever any major or minor event happened across Heathfelðland, the likelihood is that it affected the Isle. This is a liminal land even now and, before industrial drainage, was, as the name suggests, an island (Axholme derives from Old Welsh, English and Norse for 'watery island'). Islands and water meadows like Axholme, Lindholme, Stainforth and Wentbridge were key points of geographic articulation amongst the Humber Wash where Roman roads and river routes criss-crossed and converged. *Danum* (Doncaster) would have also been an immensely busy port town, as evidenced by eleventh-century boat fragments recovered in inner-city excavations. Dwarfing Doncaster, however, indeed dwarfing most other settlements, was the rural productive site at Flixborough. Part-monastery, part-*wic*, part-manufacturer, Flixborough's artefactual and archaeofaunal assemblages present an unbroken chain of occupation from the sixth to the fifteenth centuries.[219] Starting life as a beach market, it became, within a hundred years, a teeming hubbub of butchery and pottery production; within a hundred more a coin-bearing bartering site; and within three-hundred a roughly organised timber settlement paired with a possible monastery at West Halton.[220, 221] There is also a closely situated cemetery at Sawcliffe, pit-houses across Belton and an early church at Winteringham. By the eleventh century, Flixborough is believed to have become a royal whaling outpost; the piles upon piles of porpoise, minke whale and even an orca bone reveal this much.[222] The residents were not opportunistic beach scavengers but expert whale drivers. But why hunt whales? Blubber could be mulched down into oil to light the candles, braziers and torches of monasteries and other establishments while a single large whale contains more than enough food to feed a village. Interestingly, however, Flixborough's inhabitants never built out of whalebone, preferring instead the limbs of the land.

Marshes, like Heathfelðland, were not simply barriers between kingdoms but also borders between *weald* and water, the inhabitants caught somewhere between the land and the sea. Knowledge of the deep in the Early Medieval Period was constricted and constructed, people lacked submarines, so when material *from* this dark blue surfaced, at liminal places like Flixborough's whaling shores, this must have been quite something. Smell the fishy stink of seal and whale carcasses on the beaches of the Humber Wash; hear the waves lap against their eyeless frames, curdling the muddy sands white, murky, red; these ordained behemoths of the unknowable blackness, their world alien to the dry denizens, but now on their doorstep, carved up and used for food and warmth, their bones malformed into ornate vessels and reliquaries. Whilst not used for buildings, whalebone was still highly prized and worked. The Franks Casket, probably made in Whitby, is

inscribed with references *to* the whalebone, which was as central to the stories told across the elaborately carved faces as the carvings themselves. Whales were valued, but in different ways than they are today. The Old English poem *The Order of The World* includes a few lines that rationalise perceptions of the ocean. It was a neutral realm, neither Heaven nor Hell and home to deep ones like whales, sharks and squids; other things, too.[223] The 'Other', unexplainable phenomena and supra-natural entities, seem to have long been associated with marshlands. Even on the Isle of Axholme, the discovery of a Roman Period bog burial in 1747 spooked the locals.[224] A disarticulated Iron Age arm found on Thorne Moor had a similar effect;[225] bloody viscera submerged in peat on the edges of tribal territories, marking the limits between the physical and spiritual realms, a border in more than one sense.

When armies marched against one another along Ermine Street, to kill this king and then that king, the very location of these battles would have been on the minds of soldiers, casting warding signs and muttering quiet prayers against the water-sprites of the mud domain. Years after his death, King Edwin's skull was recovered from a half-drowned shrine known by 'a villager in Heathfelð',[226] and his successor Oswald's remains were similarly heralded. After *his* death, Northumbrian cults writhed in gore; his bones were interred at Bardney in Lincolnshire and his arm became the subject of various miracles. Even the soil his blood touched became holy, despite these obvious pagan undertones. No doubt, in the seventh and eighth centuries, there were enough 'Edwin's skulls' and 'Oswald's arms' to assemble an entire army of skin-grafted kings.

Monarchs, warriors and whales bled together in Heathfelðland, turning this place into a forever-borderland, a nowhere between realities and, yet, despite this, the place where it all happened, the place where England's future was decided in a few key battles and loud, bloody moments.

HWICCE

Entombed in a stone shell in Gloucester Cathedral is Osric, an obscure king of an obscure kingdom, remembered in a chiselled visage made long after the Norman Conquest and long after the annexation of the lands he ruled over, the kingdom of the Hwicce. It is this artificial sarcophagus, carved to resemble the idealised likeness of Osric, which pulls the Hwicce out of shadow into a fictionalised light, but their true memory can still be ascertained through careful reading of charters and economic assessments. These *sound* boring but they aren't always what they seem. Charters are not turgid ambulatory accounts but constructed narratives containing weaponised language and biased viewpoints. They were designed to influence and are a window into contemporary attitudes, arguments and atmospheres, a portal into the everyday lives of Hwiccians whose lives straddled Wessex and Mercia.

Yet their name remains a mystery. 'Hwicce' is a much-discussed word and, as with 'Elmet', was possibly a boastful, generic tribal nickname, something like 'very excellent' from **hywych*, as suggested by Richard Coates.[227] And, as with Elmet, much of what we know from the Hwicce comes from their neighbours. The highly suspect entry from the Wessex-compiled *Anglo-Saxon Chronicle* for 577 CE records the defeat of several 'British kings' in lands corresponding to the kingdom, at Gloucester, Bath and Cirencester. The victorious West Saxons were later pushed back in 584 and, twenty years after, the borders of this heavily contested region took on new importance when Augustine held a conference here between opposing strands of Christianity. This meeting, principally established to convince the native churches to follow the Roman sect, was a failure but evidently this area represented something of a cultural divide. Years later, 'Augustine's Oak' remained a territorial marker.

From the *Hidage* we learn that the Hwicce was assessed at 7,000 hides. It encompassed *a lot* of land, knitting together the Severn and stretching across several former Roman cities and so was highly valued. Dozens of later Mercian charters, compiled after the *Tribal Hidage*, display the year-by-year process by which the Hwicce was slowly subsumed; 20 hides were leased here, 5 over there, 150 somewhere else, mostly to external ecclesiastical institutions. By 1086 the *Domesday Book*'s economic assessments suggest the Hwiccian lands had almost halved in value.* This was a

---

* Calculating the differences in value between the 'hides' of the seventh century and the 'shillings' mentioned in *Domesday Book* is an inexact science, but rough measurements can still be made via careful addition.

piecemeal process of annexation and not entirely one-sided, although, by the ninth century, it seems the Hwicce had gone from a mostly independent *provincia* to a proud-yet-secondary Mercian *regio*. Then it was partially given over to Scandinavians and, later, conquered by Wessex.[228] These external sources still grant us eyes inside. Some grants and land agreements were even *in favour* of the Hwicce, worded in such a way that raises eyebrows. Were Hwiccian kings, like Osric, really secondary to their overlords? 'I, Æthelbald [the king of Mercia] grant to my most respected and very dear associate Æthelric, son of Oshere the former king of the Hwicce, land of 20 hides …' says one charter. Another, that 'Oshere, lesser king of the Hwicce, … conferred into ecclesiastical right with free possession land of 20 hides …' and another where a 'humble bishop of the Hwicce' mentioned land that had been donated *by* Oshere *to* Mercia. Some land was freely given, implying that kings of the Hwicce were respected. Some charters even indicate that there was a historic acknowledgement of former Hwiccian land grants for newer Mercian ones and others detail Mercian grants *to* the Hwicce. Between 777 and 779 the Hwicce was annexed by Mercia and yet a contemporary charter affords the 'sub-king' independent authority. Overall, whilst there are various instances of land being given away, it seems Hwiccian permission was needed for outsiders to build establishments on their soil. It cannot be said, then, that this kingdom crumbled under foreign conquest but rather that the identity of its residents and rulers slowly became 'Mercian' over two centuries of territorial parcelling.

But even then, we get tumbled in terminology. After the Hwicce's independence stalled the territory persisted as a recognisable administrative unit. The diocese of Worcester, founded before 680, was known from then on as *Episcopus Hwicciorum* corresponding to the bounds of the kingdom and by the eighth century memories of the Hwicce enticed Bede. He wrote that a queen 'had been baptised in her own country, [the Hwicce]' long before Wessex and Sussex converted, implying that, whilst Augustine evidently failed, the Hwicce was still Christian, having been independently influenced by other missions. Bede had many reasons to be interested in the realm, given that some of their ruling dynasty was spun from Northumbrian loins. Osric was the grandson of Oswiu whose daughter later married King Æthelred of Mercia. He was a Hwiccian ruler and also a hybrid of two kingdoms, a product of dynastic unity. One of his kin, Oslaf, is even commemorated in today's Oswaldslow and Fladbury is recorded in the *Evesham Chronicle* as having belonged to Osric's mother before 691. He and his brother Oshere are described as 'stepsons' of Æthelred and it was Oshere's own sons who became the last independent Hwiccian kings, their title disappearing after 780 CE. When Mercia fell seventy years later, so, too, did what remained of the Hwicce.

Did people feel it, though? Did Hwiccian soil and Hwiccian salt suddenly become 'Mercian' overnight? To ponder this, we must go back even further, to the fourth century.

Beyond the bounds of Birmingham is a funerary landscape that was used for over three hundred years. This is Wasperton, an infamous cemetery for challenging pre-conceptions about the 'Dark Ages'. Many burials are known from the site, and several have been isotopically traced to reveal their origins; some were local, others hailed from the Cotswolds and near Devon, four were even from the Mediterranean.

There is, too, a mixture of burial rites. In the earliest layers of the cemetery several decapitated skeletons were found with their heads placed alongside hobnails, reflecting wider Imperial military traditions, whilst other burials were orientated into family plots. The latter rite continued into the fifth century, uninterrupted, although later displaying stylistic links to East Anglian groups. Said styles become more accentuated moving into the sixth and seventh centuries, as furnished barrow burials started to dominate the site, taking advantage of the prehistoric tumuli already present. Most important to remember here is that there are no interrupted contexts; generation after generation of Waspertonian changed their funerary practice from a Roman style to an ostentatious barrow-based one.[229] There was migration, sure, but in continuous back-and-forth trickles over about three-to-four-hundred years, rather than in sudden, thrashing waves. Wasperton is situated along the Hwicce's edges where older Iron Age tribes shared borders.

All in all this assemblage emblemises three centuries of shifting identity; it paints the earliest Hwiccians as uninterrupted successors of the Romans who adapted their ways to suit new power structures. Notwithstanding this evidence, the Hwicce had stronger ties in later centuries to Mercia and Wessex. A question looms. Is there an imagined chronological gap between 'Roman' and 'Anglo-Saxon' material? Certainly, at Wasperton, the answer is yes. The dates between the burials are negligible and in many cases overlapping and yet still there is a dichotomy. Part of this has to do with how the Late Roman and the Early 'Anglo-Saxon' Period are studied. The former tends to be lavishly portrayed, with emphases placed on high-status sites and disastrous military campaigns, whereas the latter is dominated by landscape studies, small finds and scant historical records. A perception of a societal collapse from luxury to rural agropastoralism then forms within the zeitgeist. Even if this is reflective of some corners of post-Roman Europe, it does not account for all of them. Look no further than Chedworth.

In about the year 424, the wealthy owners of an extensive thirty-five-roomed villa leaned out of their windows and took in the crisp air of Gloucestershire. The sun warmed the old bricks, laid by engineers three centuries earlier, still standing tall all these years later. It was to be a good day. Two glasses of Greek wine, some olives and an imported cheeseboard later, the owners wandered their halls, breathing in the luxuries of their inheritance. Some of the rooms were elaborately adorned, rich with the splendours of the high life, civic trappings paid for through lavish spending and, in one of them, was a mosaicist, perhaps the last of his kind whose greying hands shakily applied *tessera* after *tessera* to the concrete floor. This was to be a new room, a subdivision of a much larger atrium no longer needed, and it was to be furnished with a red, white and blue mosaic, bordered by double *guilloche* radiations and woven images of flowery knots. There were many mosaics in the villa already, all created in the time of the previous owners. The tradition was to continue. The current residents had the wealth to pay the artisan although they had less to spend it on these days; the world was quieter, but it would pick up again, surely. They muttered a quiet prayer for their children's futures – *things will get better*. When the artisan was finished, the owners were impressed. This was a fine mosaic, serviceable and decorated in a standard unexotic style with only a few mistakes. It paled in comparison to the older examples but that was fine. *That was fine.*

Two centuries later the mosaic sat dusty and pockmarked; chips were taken out of the floor and the underlying stone was re-used. Only the *guilloche* borders remained, a monument to the Romans who lived here in early medieval Gloucestershire.

If the traditional 'end' of Roman Britain is in 410 then Chedworth Villa is an anomaly; it is undeniable that at least one, possibly two, mosaics were made here at least a decade or more after the supposed 'collapse'. A sixth-century fragmentary amphora from Palestine is also known from the site. For the villa's residents, there was no transition between 'Roman' and 'Anglo-Saxon'. For these people change may have been felt slowly looming over the horizon but it was not immediate. Did the owners of Chedworth Villa communicate with their overseas equivalents, like the moneyed Sidonius Apollinaris (430-489) who wrote about the joys of his meadowed estate? There are modern parallels. What do older generations think of the current climate crisis? What about the opulent? Our rapidly heating planet is set to dramatically reshape society in fifty years or less and things may get worse beyond that. These problems will not affect older generations, but they will affect

Haphazard fragments of the fifth-century mosaic from Chedworth Villa, scattered and re-arranged like the ideological remnants of Romanitas. Despite its beauty and function in bordering central designs, the 'guilloche' is one of the more common mosaic motifs and is found all over the Roman Empire.

their children and their children and *their* children. Whilst far less apocalyptic, the view on the ground in fifth-century Gloucestershire may have been similar, a hope that the Empire would return to its glory but an acceptance that, if things changed for the worse, they were a future problem. All kingdoms will fall eventually.

On that dour note, let us return to the Hwicce-proper, now that we have ascertained its multi-geographical origins. Wasperton is not alone in being a bit of a border territory. Really, the entire Hwicce was. It was a buffer between Wessex and Mercia and encompassed the edges or total dimensions of smaller territories like the Husmeræ, Færpingas and Stoppingas. Partially independent, yet always mentioned alongside Mercian overlords, seminal toponymist Margaret Gelling once noted the historical existence of a clear mixed dialectal boundary around Gloucestershire and Oxfordshire. Gloucester itself, although named by Old English speakers, comes from the Latin *Glevum*. It was here where Saxon, Anglian, Latin and Brythonic tongues clashed and churned, making the accent of the Hwicce. So, too, did artistic influences blend; at Broadway, Worcestershire, the 'Saxon' cemetery features insular styles, and Roman coins were found in the purses of sixth-century burials from Stratford-upon-Avon. Long out of circulation, these coins may have still held purpose, either as fragments of the powerful past or as genuine currency to pay struggling mosaicists. Martimow, a field near Radway in Worcestershire, is even mentioned as *mercna mere* in a tenth-century charter, literally 'boundary of the Mercians' (S 773).

Other historical mentions of the Hwicce celebrate what made it distinct. The *mirabilia* section of the *History of the Britons* describes 'the Hot Lake where the Baths of Badon are, in the country of the *Huich*' and also 'the fourth marvel [of Britain, which] consists of wells of salt [that] spring from the earth'. Finally, perhaps, we get a glimpse into why the Hwicce was so desired. The first marvel described here is the extant Roman baths in Bath with which King Osric was associated, but the second is the naturally occurring salt deposits at inland Droitwich, a hugely important resource of the Hwicce, highly sought after by neighbours. As with the Hæstingas, control of salt was control of wealth; it was vital for mundane necessities such as food preservation over long distance journeys. And an inland source of salt? A gold mine. Such a thing could be better protected by geography and standing armies than a brine-marsh by Pevensey.

We are afforded several economic grants detailing Droitwich from 716 to 1000 CE and they reveal that salt was packaged and transported via carts and wagons all the way out of the Hwicce to lands farther afield (S 1446 and S 1534). Importantly, these transactions occurred uninterrupted between the time when the Hwicce was an independent *provincia* and afterwards when it became a *regio* and then, ultimately a collection of shires. A mid-eighth century episcopal lease describes Worcester as the capital of this province and, as late as 855, a separate Mercian charter references the Hwicce as a 'province', muddying the terminologies. There is, then, reason to believe that this unique territory and its identity persisted long after annexation. Why was this? Considering salt was such a valuable resource, and the Hwicce had it in abundance along with useful agricultural land and well-fed watersheds, they may have retained economic importance. Eighth- and tenth-century charters separately refer to Hwiccian swine pastures and coppiced wood used in salt furnaces. Through sustained economic supremacy, the Hwicce kept their identity which was furthermore perpetuated through constant endowments from the Mercian church.[230] At Newent, Gloucestershire, evidence of 'Mercian styled' ninth-century stone sculpture is recognised, similar to the Upton Bishop carving. As with Ergyng, Mercian religious ideals washed over the Hwicce and painted it with a new brush, although the fact that so much footfall occurred here reveals that this 'buffer zone' was nevertheless central.

As late as the eleventh century, the Hwicce's old borders retained their importance. The barrows of Dodda and Blið at Myton, Warwickshire and Bledisloe, Gloucestershire are referred to in charters (S 967 and S 973) and there was another boundary barrow near Lighthorne where, in 1846, skeletal remains and the escutcheons of a bronze hanging bowl were unearthed.[231] In juxtaposition to these sixth-century funerary monuments are the field systems of the Hwicce, inherited from earlier periods much like the Chedworth villa. Otherwise, our knowledge of Hwiccian structures is limited to postholes and the outlines of timber buildings, known at sites like Alveston and Stretton. A quern and a bread oven were also found at Fladbury and parts of a scythe for cutting crops from Bidford.

The agricultural wealth and resources of the Hwicce can be seen through these tools and ovens but, also, the frequent mentions of salt and religious endowments. People wanted to invest in the Hwicce and buy portions of it, because this was highly desirable land. In 1048 'there was an earthquake at many places, at Worcester, Droitwich, ... and elsewhere'. How did this tremor affect distant economies? What tensions emerged after this disaster to the salt trade? Its ability to support a large number of external monastic estates also made the Hwicce's position tenuous, for a crisis could undo that careful balance.

Crises do often appear in charters, with their biases plain to see. In 896 Bishop Wærferth of Worcester brought a land dispute concerning stolen wood at Woodchester, Gloucestershire to a senior meeting (S 1441). The language used in the claim is overwhelmingly violent; the wood was 'robbed', Woodchester was 'plundered' and 'raided', despite the topic being fairly mundane and quickly resolved via perambulation.[232] This minor affair, which only felled a few trees, became overblown in the text to affect *all* of Woodchester and then Gloucestershire and Worcestershire, the former Hwicce. The narrative strategy employed here semantically enlarged the crisis, playing on pre-existing regional divisions between Mercia, Wessex and the Hwicce and the continuing tensions of viking activity across all three. This was the kingdom's legacy; economic prowess and squabbling neighbours, who after generations of financial investment, used the cultural memory of Hwiccian independence through borders, charters and arguments, stacking layers of history upon an already layered frontier, one that had inherited Rome.

These forms of evidence sound boring but they reveal one of the most interesting little kingdoms of them all.

KENT

> 449. This year ... Hengist and Horsa, invited by Vortigern, king of the
> Britons, landed in Britain on the shore which is called *Wippedesfleot*;
> at first in aid of the Britons, but afterwards they fought against them.

Six years later they defeated Vortigern at *Ægelsthrep* and conquered the kingdom of Kent.

That Vortigern and Hengist existed should not be a matter of debate. They *did* exist, as useful literary archetypes at least, but specific details about *when* they did certain actions, their motives, their wider lives and the scale of events are completely unknowable. We should look beyond viewing Kent as the stage for such pseudo-realised heroes and villains and instead celebrate it for what it almost certainly is, the first visible kingdom of early medieval England. This was a land connected to Rome through Canterbury and to Francia over the English Channel and it wasn't until the establishment of the diocese of Lichfield in the seventh century that its international importance faded. Even then, Kent remained a significant and wealthy bridgehead well into the eleventh, separated from its neighbours by the impassable mud of Romney Marsh or the primeval forest of The Weald but connected via Roman roads linking Richborough, Reculver and Canterbury. This was a network of fortlets and footholds, wrought out of the Iron Age domain of the Cantiaci, whose name persisted into the seventh century as the *Cantware*, the 'people of Kent'. Assessed at 15,000 hides in the *Tribal Hidage*, these people shared close affinities with the continent, with the Merovingian courts, but also farther east to Frisia and Jutland and, archaeologically, there was a shared fashion across both sides of the Channel. A letter sent from Frankish King Theudebert (534-548) mentions 'English Jutes' active in Pannonia (Austria, Croatia, Slovakia) and also that he claimed suzerainty over them and their kin in England. This Jutish diaspora is difficult to dissect because it might also be a Kentish one; similar people wearing similar things speaking similar dialects sailing between both sides of the narrow sea. To observe Kent in the sixth century is to do so from the south, from the shores of Merovingian France.

The Merovingians inherited parts of Roman Europe, across modern France and Germany although, from time to time, their territories extended over Burgundy, parts of Spain and, also, The Alps. Slavic and Germanic-speaking tribes along and beyond the river Elbe were also under their overlordship. This was an extensive and well-organised realm and there is reason to believe *Britannia* may have been part of it, from one perspective at least. A sixth-century poem from Venantius Fortunatus records the *Euthiones* (Jutes) alongside the Britons and several of the earliest Kentish law codes share terms with those from Frisia. Frisia, the horizonless wetlands of the Low Countries, was under Merovingian hegemony as early as the seventh century, partially described as a *gau*. This term reflects former or current Frankish territories and so its presence within Kent should raise eyebrows. *Sturige* (Sturry), *Limingae* (Lyminge) and the 'East *gau*' (Eastry) represent subdivisions of the kingdom imposed upon the landscape, possibly reflecting the overlords across the Channel, or the knowing emulation of Merovingian territorial administration which was itself *already* following a Roman legacy. Sturry was even listed in a charter as having particularly 'well-known boundaries' (S 8). Kent, then, was the recipient of a two-stage process of mimicry. The Merovingians have been described as Roman cosplayers, if you like, and Kent was influenced by the Merovingians, but also Frisians and people from Scandinavia.

This is apparent at Westbere, a small village near Sandwich where a cemetery from the fifth century displays clear similarities with Frankish and Frisian material, radiate-headed brooches, biconical pottery, cloisonné jewellery, garnets and gold filigree. The difficulty lies in whether or not this cemetery represents a contingent of Late Roman mercenaries, kitted out in the fabric of military exuberance, or genuine Merovingian and, by extension, Frisian and Jutish visitors.[233] Because there is so much crossover between these material identities, it is difficult to say from which pool Kent emerged. We might best view its origins as the drainage from a post-Roman soup of fine goods and ideas. Many cemeteries, such as Westbere, lie under the centres of Kent's lathes, seven of which existed by the time of the *Domesday Book*. These were Sutton-at-Hone, Aylesford, Mitton Regis, Wye, Canterbury, Lyminge and Eastry. Some are certainly archaic, inspired by the Frankish *gau* system.* Canterbury's territory was the Burhwara's, Lyminge the Limenwara's and Wye the home of the 'wics of the Wi-ware' mentioned in an 858 charter (S 328). Where *-wara* means 'people',† and is sometimes even synonymous with *-sæte*,[234] these names may represent early judicial divisions, 'the people of the *burh*', for instance; further subdivisions can be inferred just by observing Kent's geography. The *ceaster-ware* ('fortress dwellers' of Rochester) are mentioned in 761 (S 266), the *mersc-ware* ('marsh dwellers') in 798 (S 153),‡ the Weowara of The Weald existed by 1066, the *waldwaru* ('forest dwellers') by 1086 and the island of Thanet (*Ruoihm* in the *History of the Britons*) was home to the *Tenet-waru*.

---

* *Elgē* ('eel district', Ely) may have been a *gau* of East Anglia, near the Gyrwas.

† Bede mentions the *Boruhware* as a distinct population within England, presumably one and the same as the Bructuari from the Rhineland. A more obvious example is Hill, Mavesyn and Hamstall Ridware in Staffordshire, deriving from the Old Welsh *rhyd-* for 'ford' and Old English *-wara*.

‡ This charter also refers to two other groups: 'a place called Hafingsæta, on the southern side of the river which is called *Limen*. This [land] is alongside another piece of land called Bobingsæta'. *Caping-sæta* and *Rumining-seta* appear in two other charters, S 1288 and S 21, also referring to places in Kent.

These charters, although from centuries after Kent's origins, reflect how the kingdom was structured, indeed how most kingdoms were structured. Scattered royal villas and palaces surrounded by extensively worked outlands, the free holdings of the workers, distributed between a complicated mosaic of resources, wildscapes and frontiers, with mass trade limited to royally-overseen productive sites. Eastry's earliest royal cemetery, at Finglesham, proudly displays how some of these groups may have formed, through the recycled veneration of ancestors and the monumental investment in funerary landscapes. By solidifying ancestry through barrows and entombed metalwork, the territorial centres of Kent's early lathes became cemented and, through them, a growing sense of a 'Kentish' identity: 'this is our land, bathed in rays of gold.' Other early estates like Gillingham ('the home of Gyla's folk') are mentioned in later charters as 'lands held from manors', hinting at that same process of expansion and overlordship we have thus far seen. But why expand? Ownership of resources underlies the circulation and control of wealth, something the earliest Kentish kings understood. By 689 'iron-bearing lands' near Lyminge were desired (S 12) and there are frequent eighth-century references to salt-works at Lydd and Sampton and wool-rearing pastures on Sheppey, 'the isle of Sheep'.

There is no need for Merovingian overlordship for any of these socio-economic processes to begin, but it is implied. One of the earliest rulers of Kent, Eormenric, has a suspiciously Frankish-sounding name and so do some of his descendants. A short narrative set in Kent, contained within the *History of the Britons*, also hints at obvious overlordship, although its contents are lurid and not entirely concerned with fact.[235] This unconvincing addition also contains one of the earliest references to Vortigern whose name lingers throughout history as a powerful (and lambasted) figure. It was Vortigern who was allegedly responsible for the 'Saxon Conquest' of the fifth century, sealing *Britannia*'s doom. Interesting for our purposes is the idea of Vortigern as sole ruler of large swathes of the country, however, and he wouldn't be the first nor the last to be afforded such status. In the *Life of St Leonor*, a Dumnonian ruler is described as 'chief of the Britons on both sides of the sea', referring to Brittany, and a Roman general is referred to as 'the great king of all the kings of the British nation' in the *History of the Britons*. The idea of supreme rulership stems from Imperium. It can be seen in King Coenwulf of Mercia styling himself as *imperator* in documents from 798, in the *magister militum* depicted on the Repton Stone in Derbyshire and, most obviously, in the term *bretwalda*.

Britain ruler.

While the term first appears in the ninth-century *Anglo-Saxon Chronicle* it is implicit in Bede's work through repeated references to various kings who held 'imperium' over others. It does not mean 'ruler over all Britain' in the modern geographic sense but a recognition of vague supremacy widely wielded over similar territories. The third overlord, according to Bede, was Æðelberht, king of Kent. Certainly, it was Kent and East Anglia (home of the fourth, Rædwald) which were the first English kingdoms to make a dent in the continental consciousness and assemblages like those from Faversham point towards obscene wealth and majesty here on the east coast. Saucer brooches, Merovingian coins, hanging bowls and Frankish bird brooches litter Faversham and, at Buckland, Dover, an unusually high proportion of swords in the burials may reflect even higher status.

Æðelberht was partially responsible for the Christianisation of England. Therefore, he had a hand in bringing parts of Britain *back* into Europe, into the institution of the church and all the secular and worldly gains that came with it. In 597 Æðelberht accepted Augustine's mission into Canterbury but the conversion of Kent probably started long before that. Christianity must have already been welcome for a mission even to be considered. Æðelberht's wife, Bertha, whom he had married a decade before, was Frankish and Christian herself, and even Bede states he converted in 595. Was pillow talk responsible for England's first royal convert? It is undoubtedly more complicated than that. According to Gregory of Tours' *History of the Franks*, Bertha was accompanied by her monk Liudhard and Augustine arrived with a letter from King Theudebert that already stated that 'the English eagerly desired' Christianity. How was this information gathered and then passed to Rome without significant trans-channel contacts? Did Æðelberht submit a request for a conversion mission, perhaps seeking to ratify his elite status alongside his more powerful overseas neighbours? Merovingian kings were different from high-status war leaders, such as those who patrolled Britain in the sixth century. They were more than that: they were monarchs, not chieftains and part of their power came through the institution of the church. By joining the church, by uniting with the Merovingian dynasty, Æðelberht was communing with an altogether higher form of kingship. This was no longer about 'central people' but 'central places' imitating the Roman Empire, binding a ruling dynasty to a specific place (Canterbury) and attempting to cement that personality cult into brick and mortar. Such a transition, from person-focused to institution-focused, would not finish until much later; it was, like the Christianisation of England, far from a simple 'one-and-done' affair. After Æðelberht's death his son required a separate conversion and place names like Thunderfield and Woodnesborough point to the localised veneration of pagan deities across Kent. Presumably, Irish and Welsh forms of Christianity, spreading eastward from the Hwicce, had already affected the kingdom too. If the cemeteries are anything to go by, this was a multi-faceted land of contrasting beliefs and affinities.

By 603 a Kentish apogee had been reached in terms of power and dominance; Æðelberht's kingdom would only decline from there. Only in 664, when Roman Christianity became the sole religion for most of Britain, was his and Augustine's mission finally realised but, by that point, Kent was already on the back foot, soon to be conquered by Mercia. All the while, the peninsula served as a Roman bridgehead, both geographically through the close connections to Francia, but also spiritually through the links that tied Canterbury to Rome and London. An invisible heart pumped blood through the arteries of the English church and it was loudest in Kent. This kingdom and, to a lesser degree, East Anglia were portals to continental aristocracy and Roman bloodlines. An East Anglian dynast, Earcongota, as well as having a Frankish name, became a nun at Farmoutier-en-Brie, along the river Seine. Bede has it that her virtuosity came from a 'golden coin' she carried with her, said to have come from Kent, although the object is probably a metaphor. At

Sibertswold and Barfreston, Kent, Merovingian coins are known from as late as the seventh century, so these connections never ceased. A burial of a child from Namur, Belgium, is even known at Long Whittenham.[236] Probably, the Frankish presence in Kent was restricted to a small handful of powerful weapon-bearing aristocratic families who influenced local politics. Even when Kent fell under Mercian control, squabbles between both Kent and Francia continued as King Offa debated with Charlemagne about the cheese and wool trade. Tolls were in place across the Channel towards the end of his reign, making merchants and officials on either side fat and wealthy if it weren't, of course, for piratical raiders. In 792 Offa decreed that even Kentish churches were obliged to provide support against 'sea-borne pagans' along England's southern seaboard (S 134). Those defences failed for, in 804, Sheppey and Hoo were abandoned following sustained viking activity and Canterbury became a refuge for the nuns of Lyminge. In 811 some of the earliest viking camps were established in north Kent, possibly castaways from the contemporary Danish invasion of Frisia. Perhaps it is ironic that this garden of England, whose roots lay in Europe, was one of the first places to suffer at the hands of international ne'er-do-wells.

But domestic warfare was also occurring. In 798 Offa's successor Coenwulf 'harried as far as the land of [Romney Marsh]' and *his* successor was even styled as 'king of the Mercians and the Kentish-men'. A modern-day coincidence regarding both domestic and international travel has elucidated further information about Kent's past. The exceptional cemetery at Faversham was all but destroyed by railway engineers between 1858 and 1874, but it is through more recent work (the construction of the Channel Line) that the Saltwood and Cuxton cemeteries were discovered – paying for past sins, perhaps. All across Kent, these cemeteries and associated sites reveal more about its earliest histories. Richborough, Lullingstone, Snodland and Milton all possess evidence for very late occupation in the fourth and, possibly, even fifth centuries and Canterbury's masonry and metalwork were still being repaired into the latter. At the mouth of the river Dour, a Roman fort by Dover was inhabited well into the eighth century if midden evidence is anything to go by. Farther north the continued agricultural and residential use of hinterland villas at Bishops Cannings and across the Marlborough Downs is implied through archaeology. Wessex 'captured' this area in the seventh century and the 800 CE mention of the 'Wilsæte', which occupied an administrative flashpoint between Wessex and the Hwicce, implies this represented an extant Roman *civitas*. The continued use of the chapel at Lullingstone, the font at Richborough and a baptismal bath near Teynham also point to the pre-Augustinian continuation of Christianity; the odd chi-rho inscription dotted across Kent says the same. In fact, by 604, not only was Canterbury established as a see but so, too, was Rochester, reflecting pre-existing internal divisions within Kent (Bede refers to the place as *regio Caestruuara*, suggesting it really was a separate, distinct territory). Therefore, neither Canterbury nor Rochester were 'established' as religious centres. They were *re-established*, receiving fresh international backing and funding.[237, 238, 239] Overseas commercial aid is suggested by one reading of Procopius' work, where he recounts an amusing tale of a shipment from Boulogne to an island of 'dead souls' off the coast of *Brittia*. An entertaining suggestion is that the Greek Procopius had mistaken Thanet for the Greek word *thanatos*, 'death'. Thus, the idea of an undead island off the coast of Britain was born. But beneath this fairytale is the mundane detail of trade between Francia and Kent as early as the mid-sixth century. At Sarre, on Thanet, trading weights and a woodworker's plane were found dating just after this period, the tools of an artisan counting his coppers on the edge of England, ready for international buyers. More worthy of note, however, is Procopius' direct mention of 'some of the *Angli*' accompanying Frankish ambassadors to Constantinople in the sixth century 'to establish [Frankish] claim that this island was ruled'. In the eleventh century, continental monk Adam of Bremen wrote that Saxons, from Britain, were granted land by the Franks as payment for mercenary activity in 531 and earlier writers like Gregory of Tours certainly counted Saxons as part of the Merovingian world.[240]

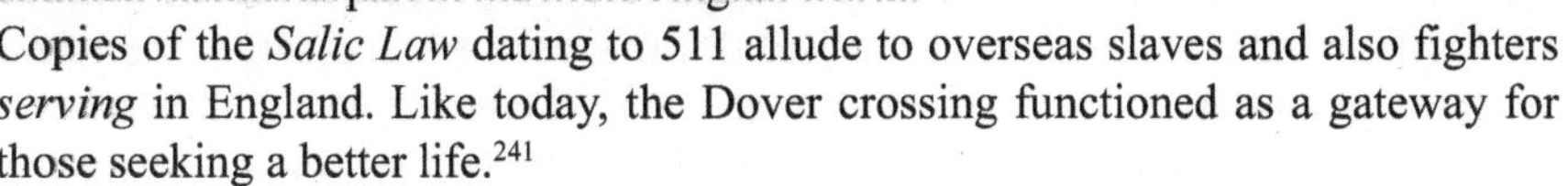

Copies of the *Salic Law* dating to 511 allude to overseas slaves and also fighters *serving* in England. Like today, the Dover crossing functioned as a gateway for those seeking a better life.[241]

Such journeys went both ways and herein lies the problem with ascribing an origin to Kent. Similar material from Faversham appears in France at Vron, Nouvion and Herpes-en-Charente, where it is even fancier, more expensive and in greater abundance. Were Frankish goods and people travelling to Kent or were Kentish people travelling to Francia? And how do the Jutes and Frisians, mentioned by both Bede and Procopius as contributing to the earliest settlements, fit into this? Some material can be seen as distinctly Frankish – for instance, radiate-headed brooches, but the distribution of these is not at all limited to Kent. A brooch identical to one excavated from Mill Hill[242] is known from Kilham, Yorkshire, implying an additional step in the process of emulation and cultural exchange between Rome, Merovingian France, Kent and then Deira.

King Edwin married a Kentish bride in 625, knitting his kingdom's fortunes into Kentish ascendancy just as Kent had tied itself with Francia; radiate-headed brooches may have wound up in Yorkshire through such arranged marriages. Other items, weaving swords, bracteates, gold braids and bow brooches, are more indicative of northern Europe, Kent's Scandinavian heritage. However, these distinctions between 'Kentish', 'Frankish' and 'Jutish' items are missing the mark; these are all different expressions of the same Late and post-Roman material identity, the power and legacy of Rome rendered through different lenses. The 'Jutish' version of Late Roman metalwork can be found most clearly concentrated on Kent's coast, with the 'Frankish' rendition farther inland. Eventually, this all merged to form a 'Kentish' expression which then spread across the rest of eastern England. Even in Kent's genealogy, the Roman term for the Isle of Wight, *Uecta*, appears as a named progenitor; and when Æðelberht's law codes were committed to paper they were borrowing from Merovingian and Roman ideals.

In the pages of the twelfth-century *Tome of Rochester* we have the earliest English legal system. Property rights, including rights over slaves, were emphasised as were regulations against inter-family blood feuds. These laws delineated sharp divisions between the free and unfree, and various stages in-between, from labourers to military officials, nobles to kings, determining at each stage of the socio-economic scale the monetary value of individual ranks. Here is the very foundation of the first kingdom. 'Free women of the keys' are also mentioned, highlighting the important role women played in running households and leading administrative functions, along with the divine right to rule that underpinned the very idea of a king. Placing the position *above* that of a battle leader, descent from Wōden made someone royal. Many royals were buried at Sarre, on the gateway island of Thanet, between 480 and 700 CE in elaborate graves containing coins of both Byzantine emperors and Merovingian kings. The long use of this cemetery highlights those investments in history of which early Kentish rulers were fond, to solidify their rule as eternal. Then there is the evidence from Finglesham, including the famous depiction of the 'Weapon Dancer', emphasising the militaristic side of the aristocracy. Cowrie shells from India across Kent's beaches suggest a well-plugged trade network. In 1066, when William the Bastard touched down at Bulverhythe before the battle of Hastings, his first thoughts were to take Kent. There is even a link here. The Hæstingas are remembered in Hastingleigh, 'forest of the Hæstingas', preserving the far-flung wanderers of *that* territory. The Isle of Oxney, Kentish by 724, was probably disputed between the two.

On the south coast of England, from the Isle of Wight to Sandwich, Canterbury and Reculver, were international communities tapping into a fashionable European economy. Procopius remarked once that 'the Franks planted ... immigrants in the more deserted parts of their own territory'. If 'their territory' included Kent, then such links are made ever clearer. By emulating the Merovingians, and thus Rome, the cultural shell of Latin and European Christendom, housing the yolk of statecraft, commercialisation and supreme rulership, was willingly cracked open in Kent.

And from that first kingdom came all others.

LINDSEY

espite eating up a fair bit of Bede's word count, widespread investigation into the kingdom of Lindsey, centred around North Lincolnshire and Lincoln, waited until the 1980s. From then serious research began into this most beguiling *provincia*, designated as such by Bede himself, placing Lindsey above the petty status of *regio* and affording it more autonomy. Alan Vince opened the floodgates for rivers of research to follow;[243] Kevin Leahy showed the world how overlooked Lindsey had become,[244] and Caitlin Green demonstrated that this 'Anglo-Saxon' kingdom actually had Brythonic origins born from a Roman *colonia*.[245] All these studies show that even a little kingdom can make a big splash. There is too much to talk about with Lindsey, from its links overseas to its independence against Northumbria and Mercia, from its paradoxical genealogy to the folkloric heritage that inspired tales like *Havelok the Dane*.

Lindum Colonia (Lincoln) was one of the foremost centres of *Britannia* but our textual record for the city has a gap of about three centuries. The last mention of **Lindonensium* dates from 314, at the Synod of Arles, where it was listed alongside London and York as an important episcopal see.[*] It wouldn't be until the seventh century that it returned to the page. In that gap Lincolnshire did not fall into disarray but rather the opposite. Archaeological and toponymic evidence suggests it retained some measure of Roman continuity, especially within the city walls where weeds gained only a slight foothold amongst slipped roof tiles and mossy, mildew-covered masonry. The church of St Paul-in-the-Bail was repaired and re-commissioned once or twice between the fifth and eighth centuries and the very name of the city suggests Old English took quite a while longer to become the *lingua franca* than elsewhere.

By back-mutating the word 'Lincoln' into its oldest form of *Lindum Colonia*, Caitlin Green has convincingly argued that there was an interim stage of development, a state *after* the Romans but *before* Germanic speakers renamed the city. This was **Lindēs*, a Brythonic word and the missing link between Lincoln's original Latin name and what it is today.[246] This means that, before Lincoln became an Old English city, the language on the street was predominantly dictated by Latin and Celtic speakers for about two centuries. In other words, *the Romans never left*.

---

[*] Technically, Lincoln itself isn't mentioned, but a place called *Londonensium* is which, given the fact London is already listed twice, is probably a garbled reference to Lincoln.

Etymological studies can seem arcane. For physical evidence that Lincoln persisted as a Late Roman centre, archaeological and metal-detected goods suggest it took until the late fifth century for a stereotypically 'Germanic' artefactual signature to become prevalent across central Lincolnshire where the place names and finds are otherwise 'Celtic'. Beforehand, such goods, tied with North Sea, continental Saxon and Frisian styles, were relatively contained in a twenty-five-kilometre radius around Lincoln, at cemeteries like those at Elsham, Cleatham and South Elkington.[247] These cemeteries are among the largest and most bountiful in the country and the evidence from them, funerary urns, bronze hanging bowls and Frisian-styled combs, can be used to ascertain the diverse geographic origins of Lincolnshire's distant kin. Whilst it is difficult to avoid conventional terms when discussing Lindsey, we should view the kingdom as cosmopolitan, where people from all over Europe and the British Isles intermingled. Sure, the cemetery material surrounding Lincoln might suggest that it wasn't until the sixth century that 'Anglo-Saxons' invaded the core of the county but as stated elsewhere in this book, *pottery isn't people,* and these goods cannot be tied to specific ethnicities. Who is to say that the spread of North Sea ware isn't indicative that, after several generations, the Britons who ruled *Lindum Colonia* changed their conservative views on pottery, metalwork and dress styles and adopted progressive and fashionable European costumes? The cemeteries could also indicate foreign mercenary stations, placed there by a British enclave. Lindsey's transition from *Lindēs* to *Lindsege* ('island of *Lindēs*'), displays the slow evolution of language, fashion and cultural ideas that were bound to happen in a region as desirable as this. Indeed, Lincolnshire is home to the largest quantities of *sceattas* anywhere in the country and the peat-rich marshes that border its edges would have made many a farmer and fisher rich and restless. The fact that Lincoln appears to have persisted as an enclave for so long suggests the area was relatively centralised and that the 'fall' from Roman times to the Early Medieval Period was invisible. On that needlessly periodised note, we should also stop thinking in terms of 'immigration' and more 'migration' when it comes to North Sea folk. Deira, Lindsey, Spalde, Gyrwas, East Anglia, Kent, Essex and the Isle of Wight were all interwoven with the North Sea to the point where they should each be considered peripheral territories of a watery core. People were not simply migrating from Jutland to Lindsey and staying put but going back and forth over the waves and along the way sharing language, ideas, beliefs and goods. Essex's sword god, Seaxnēat, hailed from Saxony and the Swedish helmets that predate Sutton Hoo knowingly emulate Roman motifs.

At the cemetery of Scremby quantities of worked-ivory bag rings have been found that originated from the kingdom of Aksum, Ethiopia. How these goods, manufactured en masse and exported in bulk, made their way to Britain was via middlemen. An elephant hunter worked the tusks and later the products were shipped to the Mediterranean and, from there, northwards to the Basques and Britons in Spain, or along rivers alongside amber and fur to the Baltic Sea and, finally, to England where they adorned the graves of a *nouveau riche* class and their families. A couple are even known from excavations at The Mile, Pocklington, in East Yorkshire,[248] and many more are distributed along the east coast, including at least one found inland at Empingham, Rutland.[249, 250]

The Late Roman military document the *List of Offices* suggests that Lincolnshire was already diverse before 425 CE, listing all manner of continentally-named troops about its borders. 'Pannonians' are even mentioned as being stationed at *Dano* (Doncaster).[251] * Roman *foederati* were international. Let us not forget that Stilicho, a Roman, was of Vandal descent and this was the case for many *generalissimos* and their subordinates. Whilst Stilicho marched across fifth-century Italy, other Vandals were staking their claim to residences across *Britannia*.

In researching his surname, David Windell investigated many toponyms deriving from the personal prefix **Waendel*, itself deriving from 'Vandal'.[252] Usually clustered near riverine routes or Roman roads, Windell suggests that this toponym can be used to plot the distribution of Vandal *foederati* across England. There are ten instances in the south and three close to other toponyms that seem to describe the 'Suebi', a different group from along the Elbe. There are also some Frankish toponyms. But let us not get carried away. The 'Sarmatian' unit stationed at *Bremetecananum* (Ribchester) in 175 CE was still the 'Sarmatian' unit three centuries later, despite probably no longer being Sarmatian at all but rather the distant descendants of a once foreign militia. The ethnicity and historical origins of these contingents were fluid; their genetic descent mattered only to the person doing the compiling. The 'Sarmatians' of fifth-century Ribchester would have been thoroughly local, much like the average 'Vandal'. These ethnonyms only reflect the distant geographic provenance of the *original* garrison, not any sort of rigidly maintained bloodline.

More relevant to Lindsey's early development is the *absence* of Vandal place names. They seem to be clustered wherever there *aren't* Frisian-influenced toponyms, such as Frieston and Friesthorpe in Lincolnshire and East Yorkshire. This is of interest. Were the two groups opposed? North Lincolnshire, Nottinghamshire and South and East Yorkshire have the greatest density of Frisian-influenced place names, suggesting that these areas were particularly connected across the North Sea to the Low Countries. Friesthorpe, near Grimsby, is Old Norse for 'small farm of the Frisians', which indicates that there were still Frisians (or Danes from Frisia) living here in the Viking Age. Lincolnshire is also home to the greatest concentration of Old Norse toponyms altogether, suggesting that Lindsey was, on the whole, very susceptible to Scandinavian linguistic influence. Given that, outside Lincoln, its early history appears to be tied with the North Sea, this is not surprising. An area with a perceived cultural heritage and folk identity that connected with the North Sea would be susceptible to a similar cultural upheaval in the ninth and tenth centuries, far more so than other parts of England. Where others fostered belonging with their

---

* This was the *Praefectus equitum Crispianorum*, a 'cavalry' unit from Crispiana, a site on the banks of the Danube. Stationed nearby at *Morbio* (possibly Scaftworth) were the *Praefectus equitum catafractariorum*, an extremely heavily-armoured equestrian force. A tenth-century administrative district, called Morthen, existed somewhere to the west of these two forts, close to Rotherham. Recent research suggests a Mercian centre lies beneath the Norman motte at today's Laughton-en-le-Morthen. Continuity and consistency!

ideas on 'Vandals' or 'Huns', in Lincolnshire people may have held stronger ties to 'Frisians' but whether or not these names reflect the specific geographic or ethnic group is another question entirely. There are clashing identities at play here. How can we rationalise Lindsey's Celtic-speaking origins with a traditionally 'Germanic' linguistic identity? This little kingdom is far more diverse than it first appears.

Take Tealby. This is a small village also studied by Caitlin Green.[253] Deriving from Old Norse for 'farm of the _____' - well, isn't that the conundrum? A peculiar toponym, Green has suggested it hails from *Taifali*, a label for an Asiatic kin group enveloped into Roman *foederati* contingents in the first century as with the Vandals and Suebi. The *List of Offices* even records a '*Taifali* cavalry' unit stationed in Lincoln and Caistor's Roman walls are believed to have been built from undressed Tealby stone. As with Friesthorpe, the fact that the founding members of a farmstead were still remembered and re-named by Old Norse speakers in the ninth century indicates cultural knowledge of a diverse history. The *List of Offices* also mentions a large number of *bucellarii* stationed near Lincoln which derives from 'hard-tack eaters'

but has been argued to be a distorted reference to Huns in the past. The jury is out on that one, but the Frisians, Taifali, Alamanni, Vandals, Suebi, Jutes, Saxons, Angles and Britons are *in*. They were all in Lincolnshire, fighting and trading, speaking and shouting, loving and dying, turning it from *Lindēs* to Lindsey over centuries of acculturation and appropriation. The way kingdoms grow.

So that well-worn line about Britons needing to 'look to their own defences' bears repeating a final time. If the 'own defences' of Lincolnshire in the fifth century were made up of so many diverse groups, third-or-fourth generation migrants with proud histories, or fresher arrivals, then the character of the people *being defended* would be re-shaped. This is *with* us needlessly subdividing the 'defenders' and the 'defended', too. And this is without mentioning the fluid borders of marshland kingdoms; Lindsey was surrounded by wetlands and bogs, extensions of the North Sea, and such a cultural melting pot would have undoubtedly led to prideful contenders for rulership. Erected at Caenby, near Lincoln, was a massive burial mound along the side of Ermine Street, housing the cobwebbed bones of a stylish warlord.[254] This unnamed magnate, entombed in a tumulus that would have rivalled Sutton Hoo, was buried in a manner like his watery kin and yet on his person were the artistic swirls of local Romano-British art and his helmet, adorned with a foil fragment of the north European 'Weapon Dancer', was inspired by Roman legacies. The Caenby warrior, whoever he was, used the diverse culture around him to forge, warp and wield a powerful military presence; elsewhere in Lincolnshire, penannular brooches and bronze hanging bowls suggest the work of 'Anglo-Britons'. Such a multi-geographical panoply of contemporary North Sea, Brythonic, Merovingian, Byzantine and then older Roman and Iron Age identities can also be seen in the famous Prittlewell burial in Essex and in excavations at Street House, Yorkshire, where dozens of seventh-century individuals were buried with gold filigree pendants amidst the ruins of an Iron Age enclosure. One garnet-inset pendant was decorated with a unique Roman-inspired scallop design and at least two already-ancient tribal coins from the Iron Age had been pierced and worn as necklaces.[255] Artefacts and markers of identity can also be appreciated in multiple ways by different people, influenced by factors one might not first consider; recent research by Ashley Rickman suggests even light levels could redefine the shape, form and impact of a piece of ornamental decoration.[256]

It was a legacy like this, of a boastful and ardent kingdom that looked to distant horizons, which allowed Lindsey to pester Northumbria and Mercia where many battles were fought along its seventh-century frontier. Lindsey became remembered for so many reasons; its fens were reworked into the homes of Grendel, the Lincoln Imp, and the Haxey Hood, as folklore embellished the 'thin places' those swamps were cursed to become. Its Old Norse heritage took centre-stage in the thirteenth century where 'British kings' were said to rule over Lincoln, proudly displayed on Grimsby's town seal. Lindsey's religious importance, as one of the first post-Roman centres converted to Christianity, linked it with Rome, Lindisfarne and Bernicia and made it a main player in Bede's work. Now, Lindsey is remembered as one of the more prominent little kingdoms of England and only time will tell how future studies will acknowledge, research and use its diverse origins.

LOIDIS

Leeds has dominated discussions of Elmet for too long, especially when it seems clear that the latter extended southwards, closer to Doncaster and Sheffield. In 632, shortly before the battle between King Edwin and Cadwallon at Heathfelðland, the latter's eighth-century *Eulogy* describes Cadwallon urging Britons to 'meet in Elmet'. Elmet and Heathfelðland were close; this same poem labels 'fierce' Gwallog responsible for the 'great and renowned mortality of Catraeth'. They may have even shared a common border along the wetlands of Calderdale. Here, unusual toponyms like Todmorden, Mytholmroyd and Thunerton denote early North Sea acculturation; Thunerton might even mean 'Þunor's town', an English equivalent to the Old Norse god Þórr. There is also Ferry Fryston and New Fryston, formerly Water Fryston, near Wakefield which hint at a Frisian presence. These place names might hail from the sixth or seventh centuries when sailors made inroads through Heathfelðland towards Leeds whereas other toponyms around the river Calder date slightly later. A cluster of regionally specific Old English toponyms are scattered across the Agbrigg and Morley wapentakes to Elmet's south; *-waella* for spring (instead of *-walla*), *-rod* for clearing, *-pihtel* for croft, *-wang* for meadow, *-alor* for alder and *-scep* for sheep (instead of the Northumbrian *-scip*). It has been proposed that these hail from a Mercian dialect, perhaps the 'settlers of Elmet' mentioned in the *Tribal Hidage*. A tenth-century reference to one *Loidam Civitatem* in the *Life of St Cathróe* also suggests that Leeds functioned as an important crossing point between Cumbrian and Danish-occupied territory.

On the topic of toponyms, whilst Elmet's all describe villages being *in*

The largest object from the West Yorkshire Hoard, this lozenge-shaped ring with a garnet inset dates to the eleventh century, although it was found alongside earlier material, including a fragmented piece of jewellery from the seventh. Perhaps the hoard reflects the routine spoils of inter-generational profiteers along the river Aire or a tradition of votive deposition.

Elmet as an important descriptor, to the west of Leeds the Old English toponyms of Walsden, Walshaw, Walton, West Bretton, Bretland and Cumberworth all describe 'foreigners' from the Old English *wealh-*. Foreign from only one perspective, mind. There is also Ledsham and Ledston and Leeds itself which derive from the Brythonic *Lōdēses* ('the people of the river Lāt'). So, we have Old English names indicating a notably 'foreign' presence and then Brythonic names which describe a native group, all scattered near the bustling northern city of Leeds. Burghshire, centred on nearby Aldborough, also preserves the surviving post-Roman remnants of the Brigantes.*

Bede thought Elmet and Loidis were two separate places. After the suspected monastery of *Campodonum* was burned by Cadwallon in 633 he states that the altar remained 'in the wood of Elmet' whilst the structure itself was rebuilt 'in the *regio* known as *Loidis*'. *Campodonum* might be best placed somewhere near Grim's Ditch and *Danum* (Doncaster) but any spot between Manchester and Tadcaster is possible. More precise, however, is Loidis' placement, roughly corresponding with the city and its environs. Loidis may have been only a sub-region *within* Elmet or the secular capital *of* Elmet, especially if Elmet was the name of a woodland and became enhanced in later poems. Let us not forget there are other Elmets.

Loidis is the only British *regio* mentioned by Bede, offering a superb parallel to the many small speculative Pennine kingdoms. How many existed and for how long? Bede was, as mentioned, writing in the eighth century and yet he still described Loidis as a *regio*, whereas Elmet appears to have faded by then, remembered only for its fallen leaves and fallen kings. Leeds, nevertheless, was an important former Roman town although diminished.[257] In 2008 a hoard was discovered nearby, buried in a hole that had been re-opened multiple times between the seventh and tenth centuries. The *Frys-* suffixes of New and Ferry Fryston hint at North Sea marshland activity seen already throughout Lindsey and it is telling that a seventh-century cloisonné fragment from this hoard displays continental origins, similar to the Escrick Ring. *Sceattas* minted in London, East Anglia and Frisia made their way to seventh-century Leeds, along with a silver-gilt cross

---

* This is the Claro wapentake, centred either on Aldborough (an extant Roman municipal centre and the base from which Cadwallon raided Deira in 633) or Coneythorpe near Claro Hill (which means 'king's farm' in Old Norse). This hill, recorded in 1894 as being covered in earthworks and burial mounds, now sits shamelessly beneath the A1 but was once the meeting point of a small territorial division similar to Craven's West Marton. This territory, usually called Burghshire after the *Domesday Book* hundred, encompassed Knaresborough, Harrogate, Spofforth and Wetherby, among others, and was owned by 'the greatest of the English thanes in the north' according to Symeon of Durham. Viking Age material like imitation dirhams, a re-purposed Iron Age ring from Knaresborough, and the Vale of York hoard suggest a resurgence in the importance of this regional division and its heritage in the tenth century. Sadly, Burghshire is a little kingdom relegated entirely to one footnote but sits neatly alongside Loidis, Elmet and *Eoferwic* as a former Deiran territory.

pendant and a peculiar mount emblazoned with a triskele motif. This find has only a few parallels, including a notable enamelled mount from Lincolnshire. These metal-detected trinkets point to substantial cross-cultural contact between Saxons, Britons and Frisians in Loidis. This former Roman city may have been attracting merchants and thieves from far and wide.

Clearly, in the seventh century, Northumbrian nobles under King Edwin deemed it pertinent to construct a royal dwelling just outside the city, an important secular complex later turned to ash by a vengeful Briton, reflecting the fast-flowing nature of the rivers of time.

Magonsæte & Wreocensæte

The 'Great' and 'Wrekin inhabitants', two settlements atop the border between Mercia and Wales, observing omnidirectional movement over the limit of Offa's Dyke. Although, as with most of these little kingdoms, things aren't always as they seem. The *-sæte* suffix remains debated. What exactly does it mean?

Historical geographer Della Hooke hypothesised that it designated pre-existing Celtic-speaking polities overtaken by Mercia and turned into frontier outposts.[258] For the Wreocensæte this would have been the Cornovii, centred on Wroxeter and the Wrekin, and for the Magonsæte this was either Kentchester (known in Latin as *Magnae*) or the Maund Group of churches based in Herefordshire. We know more about the former, for the Magonsæte are obscured by another name, or perhaps another territory altogether. It would be too easy if they were listed in the *Tribal Hidage*. Instead, directly after the mention of the Wreocensæte (at 7,000 hides), we have the 'Westerna'. Whether this is a separate name for the Magonsæte or a reference to a separate location remains unknown. Whilst we can tentatively place the Magonsæte in either Shropshire or Herefordshire, it is difficult to pinpoint what is meant by a term that essentially means 'westerners'. Indeed, that may be the point. Considering that a few *-sæte* territories appear on the Welsh border, it might be that 'Westerna' was a generic term for the taxation of the *Wealas*: the Britons of Wales, a political identity put to print, a punitive hidage value placed upon the rulers of Gwynedd or Ergyng or elsewhere.

The *Tribal Hidage* does not mention the Magonsæte, but they do appear elsewhere. The 'Magon-' element probably derives from the Roman market centre of *Magnae* or *Magnis*, Kentchester, referred to in the *Antonine Itinerary* and the *Ravenna Cosmography*. This was a fairly substantial town, home to a public spring and religious temple, and archaeological investigations have revealed earthen banks last used in the early sixth century. Not an overwhelmingly important place in the Roman Period, *Magnae* may have become re-defined in subsequent years as populations shifted and socio-economic spheres of influence contracted. It seems likely that this was the centre of whatever territory made up the Magonsæte although later the territorial core became associated with Worcester in the twelfth century and, later, Shrewsbury. This is partly due to the fact that both the Magonsæte and Wreocensæte became combined through the shirring system; the northern half of the former and the southern half of the latter were adjoined to create Shropshire, first mentioned by name in 1006. Interestingly, Shrewsbury is commonly thought to have been the royal court of another completely different Welsh kingdom whose ashes we will soon sift, so the likelihood that these two

-*sæte* territories were mangled from the meat of older realms is probable. In all likelihood, both the Magonsæte and Wreocensæte were satellite folk groupings led by Mercian outriders. They were probably formed at the same time and had similar allegiances and enemies.

In terms of artefact distribution, Shropshire's greatest concentrations occur in both the Magonsæte and Wreocensæte's halves of the county around the junction of the rivers Teme and Corve and the Severn and Tern respectively.[259] Here was the most inter-polity transit and interaction. A seventh-century cemetery at Bromfield, Ludlow, was in its day crowded by over twenty Bronze Age barrows. There are fewer now, disgracefully ploughed and flattened to make way for a golf course but records of the artefacts found within remain, a spearhead, a knife and a belt buckle.[260] Later, in the tenth century, a stone cross was mounted at the site although it cannot be conclusively said if the original burials here were Christian or pagan. The grave goods reveal little of the occupants' status, only that they were sent to the afterlife with military trappings. Also, the existence of two possible border forts at Baschurch and Lydbury North reveal less about the Magonsæte specifically and more about the general militarisation of the Mercian border.

In the eighth century, Offa, the king of Mercia (757-796), created his famous dyke and cemented this borderland forevermore. At over a hundred kilometres long, this bank-and-ditch earthwork is the longest ancient monument in Britain, although not static. At some places along its length, Offa's Dyke is afforded additional banks and ditches, sometimes counterscarps, and moves in relation to certain landscape features, rising to meet hills and extending east or west to avoid valleys; there is a huge westward bend near Perrystone, for example. The dyke was never a linear structure dispassionately dropped onto the ground but a living monument whose function changed at different points along its length. Importantly, this frontier existed *before* the creation of Offa's Dyke; it was simply the 'hard border' that sat in the middle of a much softer cultural perimeter, and, like all frontiers, it was not just a barrier but a bridge. On either side of Offa's Dyke were opposing identities which became re-defined after the creation of the earthwork. Perhaps it ran through previously open terrain, creating new clashes where previously there were none. Perhaps in other places it knitted territories together, acting as a common enemy. The dyke was more symbolic than functional and its enduring presence in the landscape afforded it great importance in subsequent centuries to the point where Offa's Dyke enhanced Offa's reputation. As memories of the Mercian king became greater so, too, did the status of his earthwork.

'There was in Mercia in fairly recent times a certain vigorous king called Offa, who terrified all the neighbouring kings and provinces around him, and who had a great dyke built between Wales and Mercia from sea to sea', says Ælfred's biographer, Asser, and, while it doesn't quite stretch 'from sea to sea', the symbolism of Offa's Dyke was apparent a century later. It not only functioned as a gateway but also a partition: on one side was Wales, an identity that emerged through competition and, on the other, were polities like the Magonsæte and Wreocensæte, artificial identities positioned as border sitters.

To call such polities artificial is not to disparage them. People led colourful lives here just like everywhere else. At Wroxeter limited excavations have revealed questionable evidence that the former Roman *civitas* was persistently occupied well into the seventh century.[261, 262] Theories as to why have ranged from the genuine continuity of inhabitants and subsequent generations or the conquest of a new ruling party commandeering the ruins. Undoubtedly, people in Late Roman Wroxeter were living an *almost* urban life. A fifth-century tombstone dedicated to 'Cunorix, son of Maqui Coline' indicates the movement of Irish elites in the vicinity and several light wooden structures may have been constructed in the shadow of the former Roman basilica, but a lack of dateable finds has thrown doubt on initial claims. Similar evidence is known from fifth-century Leicester. Whilst the buildings and occupants of these cities changed function, they did not disappear; these re-defined streets and structures are the footprints left behind by post-urban rulers, 'big men' in charge of surplus, distribution and the means of production. Contemporary with them is the Whitley Grange bathhouse, Shropshire, where crumbling masonry was used as foundations and sill beams for later architecture which, in some cases, emulated the forms and designs of Antiquity whilst still being executed in new north European-influenced ways. Thus, the blending of classic and fresh, conservative and progressive, here in the heart of the Wreocensæte. But even this name suggests that the 'Wrekin sitters' were *new* to this land. Archaeologically, all evidence suggests that the Cornovii remained here for two, maybe three, centuries after Wroxeter declined.

The same situation is possible for the Magonsæte. In 1101 monks allegedly discovered the bones of local Saint Mildburh in Shropshire. Seeing an opportunity, the site became an international pilgrim hotspot and, later, Wenlock Priory. Amidst the interest attracted to see Mildburh's bones, much ink was spilt investigating and crafting tales associated with her life. It is in texts like these that we learn of some of the earliest Shropshire-based kings, including Mildburh's father Merewalh, listed as *Westan-Hecanorum rex* ('King of the Western Hecani'). This is yet another name of difficult veracity. Long thought to just be a synonym of 'Magonsæte', thus making Merewalh one of their kings, the links are tenuous.[263] All we know is that Herefordshire and Shropshire were home to numerous tribal identities and successors to Roman divisions which later became homogenised under the terms Magonsæte and Wreocensæte. The Hecani are just another ghost. In 680 the dioceses of Lichfield and Hereford were established which probably centralised several of the more fissiparous affiliations already present, effectively cementing the Magonsæte and Wreocensæte as overarching names for former confederations. Smaller groups in the same area can even be seen in charters and scant references in the *Domesday Book*, like the Meresæte in north Shropshire,[264] the Rhiwsæte outside Wroxeter, the Temersæte of the river Teme and the Hahlsæte of Ludlow. Seventh-century polities were unique and intensely-defined, especially along their territorial borders. It is within these borderlands where resource-driven interactions, exchanges and conflicts occurred most frequently. Welsh triads refer to victorious soldiers from Gwynedd beating back their enemies along the Wye and, in 760, a battle is recorded between Ergyng and the Magonsæte, as two examples, but even as late as 1016 the 'Magesæte' are mentioned as a distinct unit fighting alongside the ealdorman of Mercia. By the eleventh century this term may have just meant 'Welsh border folk', as with the Dunsæte referred to in the *Ordinance*. This source also mentions the Wentsæte which could be another name for Gwent or another 'settlement' altogether.

Other borders were social. In the seventh century King Ine of Wessex first put to parchment the terms *Englisc* and *Wealas*, affording the latter less socio-economic status and value and forever delineating barriers between the two groups where, more often than not, there were bridges. Mercian border forts at Broseley, Burwarton and Burford were both bridges *and* barriers for interactions between Wales and England as, too, were certain individuals. Merewalh, king of the Western Hecani, was allegedly buried at Repton and his son Merchelm's name means 'Mercian helm'. This minor dynasty was associated with Mercia, despite Merewalh being an 'illustrious Welshman'. The kingdom was a facilitator of cross-cultural interaction. It is ironic, then, that Mercia, with so many borderlands, eventually became one in totality during the Viking Age when it functioned as a long march separating the *Englisc*, *Wealas* and Danes.

MEONWARA

Ever interested in ethnicity, Bede conceived that it was Jutes who settled the Meon Valley, giving rise to the Meonware ('Meon people') who lived in the *provincia Meanuarorum*. At only twenty kilometres in length, extending from the South Downs to the sea, the river Meon flits past clusters of quaint villages tucked away in Hampshire and may represent the core of an early political territory whose existence faded long before Bede read his first book.

In the Roman Period mercenaries from Jutland worked, lived, settled and died in *Britannia*, bringing with them their families from overseas and embedding themselves in local customs and cultures, contributing to the swirling milieu that makes our island so flavourful to this day. Areas of early Jutish linguistic influence can be inferred through the toponymic element **Yte-* or **Ite-* from 'Jute', to be seen at places like Bishopstoke, first recorded as *Yting-stoce,* and the 'province of *Iutarum* in the New Forest' mentioned in the twelfth century. Such folk influenced the British Isles from the first century onwards, seen also through the concentration of great square-headed brooches from Kent and the Isle of Wight, an ostensibly 'Jutish' artefact type, but one with roots in the same Roman mercenary culture that affected Britain. The point is that it is tricky to say concisely where Jutes and other groups settled, even when we know they were present. The very notion of concisely defined ethnic groups which we can track on maps using large arrows owes its origin to Roman authors who invented terms like 'Germanic' to homogenise vast population groups.[265] Then, when such 'Germanic' groups became front-line mercenaries and were installed elsewhere, they brought with them their cultures and added to the already heterogeneous Roman military assemblage of ideas and art styles, creating a blender. To confuse matters further, the name of the river Meon comes from a Celtic or perhaps even older word meaning 'dampness'.

Other toponyms along either side of the river are more easily identified, such as Watton ('Wada's valley'), Middlington ('village of the middle folk') and Swanmore ('swan's pool'). There is also Exton, recorded in 940 as *East Seaxnatune* or 'town of the East Saxons' (S 463), and no fewer than three charters dated between 826 and 956 refer to Droxford in association with the old Meonwara realm (S 276, S 446 and S 600). Said documents refer to holy wells, river bends and heathen burial grounds as directional anchors, marking out the old limits of Bede's *provincia*. In 1900 and 1974 over fifty burials were found here which line up suspiciously well with the locations of the 'heathen burial

grounds' mentioned in the charters.[266] Droxford, then, was another key cog in the kingdom of the Meonwara.

But who were their kings and where did they come from? That is always the big question: assessing the geographic origins of founding figures and the settlements they may have ruled. Iron spearheads, shield bosses, rings and loops tell us little about Droxford's early inhabitants. The same applies to knives, tangs, stray beads and adzes. A pottery urn decorated with intertwined knots and a penannular brooch would suggest quite the opposite to Bede: that these warriors sallied from the Irish Sea but, as aforementioned, the Roman military melting pot brewed a stew of international ideas and motifs. The 'Jutes' of Meonwara were no more Jutish than they were Irish, Brythonic or Pictish. These grave goods suggest a mixture of identities some even being buried with Roman coins. Undoubtedly the most famous thing to emerge from the valley's soils is the Meonstoke façade, the wall of a fourth-century aisled Roman building re-purposed in later years as the floor of a timber structure.[267] * How, then, to trace these peoples? In Droxford and at Meonstoke we may be looking at Late Romans or their immediate descendants carving out a fledgling territory along the river or re-defining a Roman *pagus* (rural division) into something new.† They may have hailed from all over the Empire, but they came to rest on the limits of the Meon, possibly between the borders of two former provinces or *civitates*.

Beyond these bounds lay *Hamwih* at the mouth of the Solent. This was the vast trading site that became Southampton. As at Droxford, excavations here have revealed an overwhelming quantity of material.[268] Towards the north-west margins of the site, people were packed in like cattle, elbowing for space in the teeming markets whereas, at the southern end along Chapel Road, suggestions have been made that it was a comparatively rural district for monks and artisans. Here were the crafters making their goods to be sold in the more boisterous and bustling northern quarter. Alternatively, we might be looking at two ends of the socio-economic scale: the cramped tenements of the lower class and the luxurious open courtyards of the secular and spiritual elite. *Sceattas*, ingots and alloys were smelted here out of iron and copper imports, turned into knife blades and barrel-locks, buckles and keys and, elsewhere, pins, pendants and strap-ends. The discovery of polishing stones and innumerable spindle whorls also suggest that *Hamwih* played a key role in the overseas textile industry; perhaps these items were traded alongside Epping timber and Pevensey salt for international goods, Rhenish quernstones, pottery from north-east Ireland and wheel-thrown ware from Dorestad. An eighth-century hagiography describes the place as a shipping port to Brittany and Francia.

All of this evidence post-dates Droxford and the establishment of the Meonwara, as accurately as we can be, by quite a few centuries. Up the Solent from *Hamwih*, however, was the river Meon and along its banks were odd traces of the Jutes that may or may not have existed here. But what Bede meant by 'Jute' was undoubtedly different to earlier uses of the term and it would not be the only thing Bede would discuss in his *Ecclesiastical History*.

---

* Exciting, but not as unique as it sounds. Excavations at 1-9 Micklegate, York, revealed burials and buildings carved around and atop extant Roman walls between 609-662. One of the skeletons recovered was isotopically traced to the Yorkshire Dales.

† Scant references in charters and *Domesday Book* suggest the presence of *regiones* within this 'Jutish province', such as *Andeferas* and *Cleras*, centred around Andover and Nothing Hill respectively, and an administrative group called the Hylthingas near Southampton. A forged eleventh-century charter (S 360) might describe another early river-based territory, *Micheldever*.

MIDDLE ANGLES & MIDDLE SAXONS

To be in the 'middle' of something implies an existence related to other places. Middleham lies in the centre of Wensleydale, Middlewich was the salt-trading town between Northwich and Nantwich and Middlesbrough is the *burh* equidistant to the religious centres at Whitby and Durham. With that in mind, the separate polities of the Middle Angles and Middle Saxons were both 'in the middle' of other realms, suggesting that they must be late names, emerging *after* whatever it was that they found themselves between. The Middle Angles receive a whole chapter in Bede's *Ecclesiastical History* where he describes them as 'the Angles of the Midland country' led by 'Prince Peada, the son of King Penda'. In 653 Peada was elevated to the position of lesser king over this region and baptised in an attempt to marry the daughter of King Oswiu of Northumbria. 'The nation which he governed' was also Christianised by four monks from afar and, when Penda died in 655, Oswiu 'succeeded him in the throne' and made one of his monks 'bishop of the Midland Angles, as also of the Mercians'. We have already met this monk, Diuma, in the woodlands of the Færpingas.

Territories like the Færpingas, Gyrwas, Spalde and so on were all Middle Anglian, representing a contested region between East Anglia, Essex, Lindsey and Mercia. The fen basin around Cambridgeshire sees the bulk of mentions in the *Tribal Hidage* which might suggest the various territories were all the original names of groups that were later homogenised under the blanket term *Middelenglum*. This idea of Penda and his son creating the kingdom of the Middle Angles might also be an origin myth promulgated by the Mercian church and then through Bede's work as part of an overlordship tradition. Both the Middle Angles and the Middle Saxons are mentioned overwhelmingly wherever Mercian interest is concerned, so it seems plausible that 'Middle Anglia' was just a collection of areas that fell under Mercian governance and became networked together for the ease of spiritual and secular administration. There was never an independent Middle Anglia. From the seventh century onwards, it can be seen across England that larger kingdoms buried smaller ones under ideas of sub-kingship. Later in this same century a Mercian king invaded the northern edge of Lindsey and is described as leading thirty *duces regii* ('smaller rulers') into battle, the petty kings of Middle Anglia.

With the *Tribal Hidage* we get but a fleeting glance at these communities *before* they were artificially conjoined, before their identity got boiled down to being 'in-between' their neighbours.

A 'province which is named *Middleseaxan*' first appears alongside a reference to Mercia through a charter describing land at *Tuican-hom* (Twickenham) for the

Compiled in 1626, Sir Henry Spelman's 'Archaeological Glossary' contains a number of embellished, edited and abridged terms copied from older manuscripts. His version of the [B] recension of the Tribal Hidage cannot be relied upon for accurate spellings and pronunciations but does display neatly the overall list of territories, many 'in Middle Anglia'.

year 704 (S 65) where King Swæfred of Essex granted a bishop 'a certain portion of land' with the permission of King Æthelred of Mercia. Much as parts of Essex fell under the Mercian shadow so, too, did the Middle Saxons. Both *Middleseaxan* and *Middelenglum* are relatively late territories that were created or, at the very least, named by Mercia although the realms they consisted of certainly existed beforehand. The Gumeningas and other groups in the Greater London area are described as being 'in the Middle Saxon province' in a charter from 767 and, from the reign of Edward the Confessor (1042-1066), the Stæningahaga are also named (S 1142). Whilst the idea of *Middleseaxan* is a seventh-century creation, the individual components had earlier origins.

1. *Myrcna continet* 30000 Hidas,
2. *Woken-setna* 7000 hid.
3. *Westerna* 7000 hid.
4. *Pec-setna* 1200 hid.
5. *Elmed-setna* 600 hid.
6. *Lindes-farona* 7000 hid.
7. *Suth-Gyrwa* 600 hid.
8. *North-Girwa* 600 hid.
9. *East-Wixna* 300 hid.
10. *West-Wixna* 600 hid.
11. *Spalda* 600 hid.
12. *Wigesta* 900 hid.
13. *Herefinna* 1200 hid.
14. *Sweordora* 300 hid.
15. *Eyfla* 300 hid.
16. *Wicca* 300 hid.
17. *Wight-gora* 600 hid.
18. *Nox gaga* 5000 hid.
19. *Oht gaga* 2000 hid.
20. *Hwynca* 7000 hid.
21. *Ciltern-sema* 4000 hid.
22. *Hendrica* 3000 hid.
23. *Unecung-ga* 1200 hid.
24. *Arofeatna* 600 hid.
25. *Fearfinga* 300 hid.
26. *Belmiga* 600 hid.
27. *Witherigga* 600 hid.
28. *East-willa* 600 hid.
29. *West-willa* 600 hid.
30. *East-Engle* 30000 hid.
31. *East-sexena* 7000 hid.
32. *Cant-warena* 15000 hid.
33. *Suth-sexena* 7000 hid.
34. *West-sexena* 100000 hid.

And just because the Middle Saxons were labelled by Mercia alongside the gradual erosion of East Saxon leadership does not mean that the area was peripheral. The very fact that it was valued by Mercia suggests quite the opposite. London was firmly in *Middleseaxan* and at least ten synods were held in Chelsea between 785 and 816, pointing to both economic and spiritual importance. Later Wessex also started juggling the territory, by association through its desires to hold London and it is always possible that the city retained a unique character even within the province.

At its foundation, kingship in the Early Medieval Period was localised. Who was to boss around the 'king' of the Gumeningas if no overlord ever showed up in person? Above him, however, were sub-regional and regional overkings who facilitated greater economic and transit links and thus political and financial stability. During the Viking Age, such links were temporarily severed and there is good reason to believe the idea of the 'petty kingdom' re-emerged as London and, by extension, *Middleseaxan* became a consolidated region of warlords hard-pressed by Wessex and both Mercia and the Middle Angles' territory regressed into the loose confederation of tribes from whence they came.[269] It is in this period that we get a mention of another petty territory, the 'tribe called Gaini' (Gainsborough), from the *Life of King Ælfred* and it is from Old Norse that the Isle of Axholme was finally named.[270] In and around Deira at least three Scandinavian kings ruled separate divisions at the same time between 895 and 905 (Knútr, Sigfrøðr and Harðaknútr). Such intensely small units existed up and down the country and, if anything should be made clear in this book, it is that no matter how extensive the regime, or how large the kingdom, or how wealthy the state, local affinities persist.

⌒Pecsætan

Some kingdoms can be used as mirrors. In the Peak District we have a mountainous polity which may have become economically central through its resource-rich mines, an agriculturally fractured realm, with a few belts of rich farmland separated by ill-drained soils, a parallel to Craven.

The 'Peak sitters' are listed in the *Tribal Hidage* at 1,200 hides, about two Elmets' worth, which coincidentally was one of their immediate neighbours. Heathfelðland was another, separated by a thin frontier around the hundred of Scarsdale, Derbyshire. Calver Cross Dyke has been argued to be another perimeter for the Pecsætan's southern bounds with the majority of their defences stemming from natural geography. The Peak District is vast and hides bleakness in its beauty, precipitous drops over the edges of natural crags, scarred moors and winding gorges. In some places marginal, its agricultural potential is dispersed and so, too, were settlements with occupants spread out across disparate farmsteads and rural enclosures. We know much more about the Pecsætan than we do Craven, which allows us to draw certain comparisons.

Both regions may have held convergent identities, upland herders and farmhands whose interactions with outside polities were based around the trade of ores and foodstuffs. There is also a lack of burial evidence in the Peak District which does not automatically mean the area was desolate. Rather, like Brycheiniog and Dunutinga, this was a zone of transient interaction. Some months were busy, as when the crops were due in *haerfestmonath* (September), but, when the winter chill set in, the Peak District, like Craven, was quiet, perhaps punctuated only by the echoing din of miners below. Neither were wastelands. An Old English synonym for such, *weglaest*, also means a 'wayless place', a junction leading to nowhere or, perhaps, only downwards.

Evidence for early medieval mining is dim but we can infer that attitudes towards the underground were mostly negative. Influenced by pre-Christian beliefs, poems like *The Wife's Lament* depict the loamy earth as a realm of twisting roots, toothy caverns and jagged gateways to the other world, yet also the natural birthplace (and deathplace) of all things.[271] *Soul & Body II*, from the tenth-century *Exeter Book*, describes the human body as 'a foul thing of earth'. The howling cave in Gwent screeched as banshee-like as the one in Forfarshire, amplifying the voices of subterranean spectres. In a shadowy thicket beneath the looming spine of Mam Tor lies Derbyshire's Odin Mine, a name sure to conjure up images of the under-gods. Direct connections between this certainly ancient shaft and the pagan deity remain debated but the Peak District *does* have an extended history of lead mining. Romans extracted *galena* (raw lead sulphate) from this region and the *Ravenna Cosmography* even mentions two local sites, *Lutudarum* (Wirksworth) and *Derbentione* (Little Chester). First mentioned in a hunting dispute from 1280, the *Oden* opencast may have been harvested in earlier centuries, given that other areas certainly were by the ninth. Roman lead pigs are known from Carsington reservoir, too, dating to the fourth. In Craven, Roman mining efforts were confined to Wharfedale and the east of Malham,[272] with some speculative iron leaching noticed near Kettlewell[273] and, as with the Pecsætan, it remains unclear if such activities persisted afterwards. If they did, then iron and silver may have been highly sought, viewed as an inherited industry of the Empire.[274] Ores of the highest purity occur in deposits between Cumberland and South Wales with slightly more contaminated veins known from Lincolnshire, Northamptonshire and West Sussex.

And whilst lead was certainly valuable, harvesting it presented considerable risks. Cave-ins and floods would have been frequent, and the natural poison generated by the ore taints the very ground above. Would such toils be worth it?

N.J. Higham has suggested that the Pecsætan were a consolidated tribal unit with origins in the pre-Roman Iron Age, hailing from the group who gave their name to Roman *Lutudarum* and that the existence of the Pecsætan implies significant continuity with previous Roman *pagi*.[275] This sees parallels with other -*sæte* territories and archaeological evidence within the Peak District would reasonably suggest that there was minimal upheaval within the Early Medieval Period. Neither do historical documents regularly refer to the place: *Peac lond* is cited in the [A] version of *The Anglo-Saxon Chronicle* for the year 920 and a charter from forty years later refers to the wider administrative area as the '*pago*' of *Pecsæt* (S 712a). By the time of the *Domesday Book* the wapentake of Hamenstan, near Bakewell, has been theorised to have become a central place but much of this analysis has to be guesswork. Yes, the network of Roman forts and roads in the Peak District *could* be evidence of a centralised lead-mining industry. Yes, the consistency in finds of Derbyshire ware pottery *could* indicate economic and political saliency throughout the seventh and eighth centuries. And yes, the dearth of Old Norse-influenced toponyms *could* point to the existence of a tightly knit regional identity that resisted settlement.[276] However, all this could simply be evidence of a Craven-like situation where individual valleys and gullies became home to small rural nucleations with very local spheres of interaction. This type of realm would never really be on anyone's radar outside of agricultural taxation purposes or for lead or silver extraction in this case.

As with Lindsey, if Pecsætan *was* a contested region it would have been juggled between Mercia and Northumbria. It certainly became part of Mercia in the late seventh century but whether it had any kind of independence beforehand is difficult to say. Geographically, the Pecsætan occupied a vital spot near Elmet and Heathfelðland which would suggest it was also predominantly Celtic-speaking and may have been viewed as an extension of the latter's frontier-status, although yet again -*sæte* is an Old English term. Evidence for regional expression is surely topped by the Benty Grange Helmet, a nationally important piece of elite regalia pulled from a barrow mound in 1848. Composed of iron bands covered by plates of

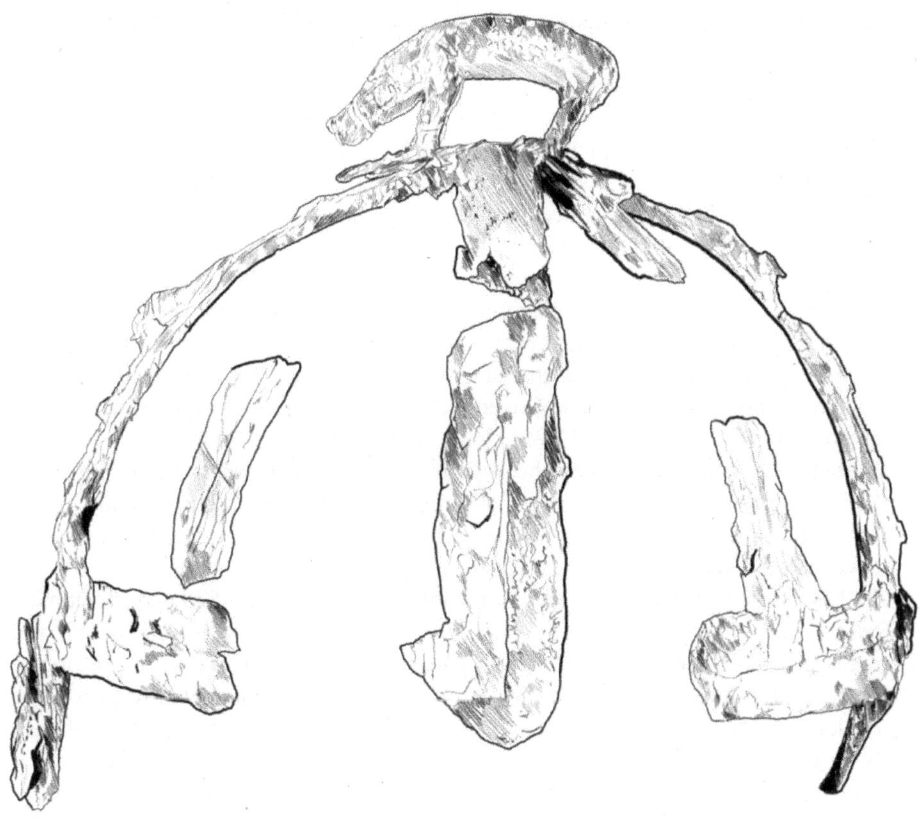

polished horn, this magnificent helm would have topped the head of an imposing warlord and was itself crowned with a plumed bronze boar figurine. A bristled mane, whistling in the winds, echoing the crimson crests of Rome.

The eternal debate between burials like this being evidence of migrant chieftains or locals taking up new traditions will not be solved by the Pecsætan, but the Benty Grange Helmet dates to the late seventh century when Christian iconography started to more overtly influence the styles of armour and weaponry. Viewed from the top, the helmet is scored by a cross motif, its wearer a warrior of God.

And war would find its way to Derbyshire. Dore and the Whitwell Gap were important borderlands for Mercia, mentioned in 829 and 942 CE as key gateways between kingdoms. These were, at times, the south-westerly limit of Northumbria, placing the Pecsætan right on their doorstep, even though in earlier years Bede regarded the river Idle as 'the limits of the Mercian peoples'. Certainly, Northumbrian iconography influenced the Peak District. A regionally unique school of stone sculpture with an emphasis on figural scenes, such as those depicted on the Winkworth Slab, is known in abundance, contrasting with the surrounding areas which otherwise emphasise abstract designs. If this *was* Northumbrian-influenced, then it might represent a southerly extension of that aforementioned Bernician artistic milieu, so dominant already in Deira. Alternatively, these sculptures could be insular, reflective not of foreign influence but deep-rooted traditions; it has also been suggested they are Mercian in origin. The field systems of the Pecsætan seem to have continued from the co-axial layouts of the Iron Age and, deeper still, there seems to have been an observed emphasis on springs and wells as holy sites, rather than churches. Buxton's etymology suggests it derives from a regionally renowned 'rocking stone', a peculiar natural feature caused when wind perfectly tilts a boulder in a see-saw motion and Bakewell was referred to as 'Beadeca's spring' in *The Anglo-Saxon Chronicle*. Less famous than Bath's 'hot baths' was the similar *Aquae Arnemetiae*, the bubbling, belching water beneath Buxton. A dearth of churches and an otherwise high frequency of natural features like these may reveal ties that bound the Pecsætan not to the heavens above but those below. Lud's Church, although named in the sixteenth century, is a series of exposed faultlines and mudstone fractures which would have made a perfect venue for hilltop rituals. Indeed, local affinities may have been distinguished by such peaks: the 'White' and 'Dark' Peaks are locally defined by differing underlying soil and sediment types. Very similar to the Dales, this contrast between fertile and marginal lands would have influenced both settlement distribution and travel.

Much like Craven, the Pecsætan probably met their undignified end sometime before the compilation of the *Domesday Book*, lost through the shirring system, if not earlier. Still, at places like the black gates of Lud's Church, we get suggestions of the subterranean shadows that linger below and, if we cannot coalesce enough evidence to appreciate the Pecsætan as an individual polity, then perhaps there is benefit in contrasting it with other realms. Here, in the Peak District, we have a chance to postulate more about Craven's role in Northumbria's expansionist regime by observing how the Pecsætan changed, or didn't change, between the foundation of *Lutudarum* and the naming of Odin Mine.

Pencersæte & Tomsæte

These boundaries belong to *Coftune*. First, the boundary of the *Tomsætan* and the *Pencersætan* before Reht's gate to Wærburh's clearing, then to rush hill by the front part of the ploughed land to the narrowest part of the boggy copse, thence to the spring. From the middle of the valley, then down to the black mere near Ceolferð's marsh and down towards the River *Colle* along the stream to the enclosure at the willows, then to the front part of Heoden's copse, thus to the forked birch tree south of Coenberht's grove. Then, over the marten's ridge and down to the willow mere out towards Hopwood's *wic* then along the fence down by Eamba's hut south to the hoar tree, thence to the crow's brook, Penda's oak tree, and a willow, always alongside the *Twige* so that it comes to Wærmund's house thus round the hill of crows to the confluence. Up by the common land to the middle of the heath-hill and then to the bright stream, the red slough, the boundary brook, and the hart's wallowing place, then near the roe's lair, then to The Great Lime Tree of Byrnhelm and Eadbald and the king. Then, to an ash tree and Creoda's oak and Tīw's swamp, thence across the heath to Babba's clearing and Wylheard's tree along the hollow way, then out over the heath towards the south of Cybbel's enclosure towards the clearing, and again to the heath's spring. Signed in the place which is called in Latin 'at the valley'.

Dating to 849, this boundary clause describes the well-trodden limits of two groups, the Pencersæte and Tomsæte, around Cofton Hackett, Worcestershire (S 1272).[277] Penkridge and the Tame-Blythe Basin seem like strong suggestions for their origins, the former having been consistently inhabited since at least the Bronze Age and described as a 'renowned place' in 958 (S 667). Cofton, however, is listed as early as 780 when it was granted by King Offa of Mercia to the church, so we are already viewing an old system of boundaries (S 117). It is even written as such, dredging up folk memories of crow-pecked mounds, trans-dimensional hoary oaks and revered warriors. 'The Great Lime Tree' is mentioned in a later clause concerning Tardebigge (S 1534) which, incidentally, is the least explainable place name in the country.[278] The Pencersæte and Tomsæte also defy most theories: we know nothing about them save that, by the ninth century, they were still remembered in lands which by then were Mercian but a century

prior would have been Hwiccian; indifferent layers of political nomenclature. Archaeology also offers little help in ascertaining identity, a fifth of a brooch from Penkridge, a filigree gold sheet found near Tamworth. Are these the spoils from unknown territorial skirmishes? Whose sides were remembered in charters but never put to song?

ℭPENGWERN

Other fallen kingdoms tell their stories and there are few as sad as Pengwern's.

'Come outside, maidens, and look at the land of Cynddylan.
The court of Pengwern is a raging fire […]'

Known only from poems, Pengwern's memory hinges on the confidence of compilers, the luck of manuscripts evading destruction and the enduring fame of fallen kings. Mentioned in the *Lament of Cynddylan* and the *Songs of Heledd*, we learn of King Cynddylan of Dogfeiling and Pengwern's righteous reprisal against a monastery in Lichfield and the vengeance that such an act brought upon his court.[279] Whilst dated between the ninth and twelfth centuries, these two elegies describe events from the seventh. In 642 Cynddylan fought at the battle of *Maserfield* against King Oswald of Northumbria and, fourteen years later, raided across borders and struck out against a Mercian establishment near Birmingham. 'Cynddylan, fiery supporter of the marches, mail-wearing, stubborn in battle … before Lichfield they fought, there was gore under ravens and keen attack.' Pengwern was a polity like Aeron, remembered for all the wrong reasons: defeat, loss, despair, but, unlike Aeron, has become almost entirely forgotten.

In response to the raid, it appears that Pengwern was extinguished overnight. It was torched by attackers and, in the space of a few hours, Cyndyllan was killed, his dynasty severed, and all records charred. In the original Old Welsh, the survivors of the attack were said to have sheltered atop *Dinlle Vrecom* from where the former queen and her maidens could see their kingdom wreathed in flame. *Dinlle Vrecom* preserves the Latin *Viroconium* (Wroxeter), the *civitas* capital of the Cornovii, so this passage may refer to the Wrekin but placing Pengwern itself has always been a challenge. Somewhere near Lichfield, sure, so probably in Shropshire along the traditional border. As for Wroxeter and the Wrekin, they are surely the same as the Wreocensæte. Were 'Magonsæte' and 'Wreocensæte' the Old English terms for ashen Pengwern? In the ninth century this area was still regarded as the Mercian district of *Wreocensetun* (S 206). Three hundred years later, whilst ambling on this very spot, Gerald of Wales resurrected Pengwern from near-total obscurity, listing it as one of the 'three capitals of Wales'. It was the capital of Powys[280] which abuts the Wreocensæte, as far as we can tell from vague references to borders, so it is possible that, within this gap, Pengwern once existed, independent and proud, bucolic ruins nestled in a tiny glade. A thirteenth-century poem attributed to the legendary Merlin, called *Apple Trees*, features a single off-hand mention of Pengwern, where 'men drink mead'.[281] Both the Wrekin and the Berth, Shropshire, were Iron Age hill-forts although neither show much if any evidence of being re-inhabited in the Early Medieval Period. If they were, perhaps re-occupation was temporary, transient, the mead-drinking ghosts of Pengwern cowering amongst sunken masonry. Before the foundation of the Wreocensæte and after the fragmentation of the Cornovii's territory, sat Pengwern, in both a geographic and chronological gap.

Traipsing through modern Shrewsbury, the walls from which songs once echoed slumber still and silent. The crunch of the earth underfoot like tattered leaves and crumpled pages might prompt a distant memory. Pengwern collapsed but, by Gerald's time, rose again as the erroneous core of a much larger, more powerful kingdom. He placed it here in Shrewsbury and afforded it the title of capital but the real Pengwern rests elsewhere. Its inhabitants are entombed, its cattle-raiders spent, the ichor of its raging fire cold and damp: snuffed out and, if it wasn't for three poems and an intrepid itinerant, gone entirely. A true lost realm.

POWYS

Mercia's bane, the marcher kingdom.

There is reason to believe that Powys was less of a kingdom and more of a loose confederation of petty territories, much like its nemesis over Offa's Dyke. Standing proud on a Bronze Age mound in the parish of Llantysilio-in-Iâl is a record of this historic rivalry, inscribed on the ninth-century shaft known as the Pillar of Eliseg. We have seen throughout Britain various instances of warlords marking their claims via re-using prehistoric tumuli, but the Pillar is interesting for other reasons. By reading the westernmost inscription, now lost but accurately recorded in 1696, we can travel downwards through Powysian history, but only *one* history. Indeed, the Pillar, as with all chronicles and genealogies, is but a single view of this kingdom's past and excludes more than it includes. It does, however, reveal enough names to be reliably dated to sometime before 854 CE. This was the reign of King Cyngen, whose father is mentioned in the inscription along with a host of older ancestors and their achievements. A lost section of the Pillar probably listed what Cyngen himself had accomplished, contrasting his successes with those of the ancient Eliseg. Such feats were military victories and liberations, all framed against Mercia and the *potestas Anglorum*.

> It was Eliseg who united the inheritance of Powys,
> however through force,
> from the power of the English,
> land with his sword by fire [...]

Whilst Mercia grew stronger and its border polities became more centralised, Powys matched force with force and the erection of the Pillar is but one window into the consolidation of this authority. Perhaps Powys was a disparate collection of under-kingdoms all based around individual valleys, no doubt including ashen Pengwern, whichever groups preceded the Magonsæte and Wreocensæte and the Hecani. The stylistic links between the Pillar and later Mercian Cheshire-based round-shafted crosses also suggest archaic links over Offa's Dyke between what were once independent British territories. Whilst the Pillar describes a centralised kingdom, we need only observe Powys' etymology to pull back the curtain. The name stems from *pagenses* which means 'country folk', itself an evolution from the Latin *pagi*, a Roman administrative term for rural units connected to *civitates*. In this regard, Powys' origins may lie in the hinterlands of Wroxeter and, after the fourth century, it expanded outwards, absorbing smaller tribal entities along the way. The *pagi* of *Britannia* underlie many early medieval settlement groups. These were small tightly-knit resource-bound population centres and many owe their origins to Magnus Maximus and other Late Roman military officials. The continuity of the fifth century was a direct result of the consistency of *pagi*. Maximus, for example, consolidated the groups around Wroxeter and, after his death, amidst the absence of an immediate ruler, these groups remained powerful in their pre-established domains, gradually bloating. It was only in the sixth century when such *pagi* started to wither and wilt, morphing amidst wider social changes into petty kingdoms. Such nomenclature can throw us through a loop but, interestingly, Magnus Maximus himself appears on the Pillar. Thus, Powys became a successor of Rome.

The former Emperor (383-388) also appears in the genealogies of Dyfed, the Isle of Man and the thirteenth-century *Lineage of the Saints*. Several origin myths, such as the arrival of the Déisi who founded Dyfed, may be remembered remnants of Maximus' genuine reforms: the installation of foreign troops on frontier outposts as at Pembrokeshire's recently discovered Roman fortress, or here in Powys. Leslie Alcock suggested Maximus was also responsible for the foundation of a kingdom called *Galwyddel* (Galloway)[282] and Guy Halsall has proposed that Maximus was the *superbus tyrannus* disparaged by Gildas.[283] His legacy is writ raw in early Welsh tradition. The legendary Dunawt is potentially a warped version of Maximus' son Donatus and even more abstract 'descendants' like Coel of Aeron and Guorgust of *Ebrauc* are said to be linked to the long-dead Emperor.* The murky nature of these half-imagined people makes connections problematic, but it is undeniable that, five centuries after his death, Maximus was remembered on the Pillar of Eliseg.

It took until the ninth for Powys to be directly named in a written source although events in surrounding areas can be used to tease out older histories. The battle of Chester in 613 saw the deaths of a few Powysian kings. One 'Solon, ... king of the Britons', mentioned in an Irish account, became remembered in Middle Welsh tradition as Selyf. Perhaps it is better to style such figures as kings *in* Powys for this was a fractious region not beholden to a single reigning overlord. Selyf, for instance, only appears in *some* of the kingdom's genealogies and the Pillar itself presents only an oversimplified view of the realm's history, representing a single dynasty and obscuring all others.[284, 285] Through careful analysis of these bloodlines from unrelated praise poems, D.P. Kirby suggested that doctored Powysian histories knowingly cannibalised other much smaller kingdoms, such as Gwerthrynion which has an almost identical genealogy.[286] The thirteenth-century manuscript containing the eleventh-century *On the Place of Brecheiniauc*

---

* In the *History of the Britons*, York is listed as 'Caer Ebrauc' and has been argued to have been the centre of a small Brythonic kingdom which preceded Deira and Northumbria. Here, neutered urban life *did* persist into the fifth and sixth centuries, governed by the local remnants of a highly bureaucratic and reduced Roman taxation system: of this much we can be sure from York's archaeological record but identifying rulers is a fool's errand.

also implies that Powys originated from various competing royal strands. Rhos, a cantref of Gwynedd, even has its own genealogy with separate kings and was in the distant past an independent kingdom long before becoming annexed. The existence of dozens of similar political entities across what became Powys is a certainty. The *History of the Britons* refers to kings of Buelth and Gwerthrynion, linking their heritage all the way back to Vortigern. These once-independent units were webbed together through forgotten marriages and familial links and, by the ninth century, their histories became homogenised as versions of a Powysian past. There are more: Maelienydd, Elfael, Arwystli, Cedewain and Cynllibiwg. Elfael suffered frequent knocks down the political food chain, from a petty kingdom to a marcher lordship, to a fragment of Powys County Council. Cynllibiwg, known only from the *mirabilia* section adjoined to the *History*, was allegedly the home of a marvellous spring which was always filled with fish; another marvel was located in Buelth, the eternally bound paw-print of King Arthur's dog. An extensive 'middle zone', as recognised by Gerald of Wales, lay somewhere between Brycheiniog and Powys, home to quarrelsome petty rulers. 'The Lands Between' were ruled over by such characters as Elystan the Famous and Iorweth the Long-Troubled, both of whom appear in certain Powysian genealogies, and associated through tradition with a descendant of Roman commander Ambrosius Aurelianus.[*]

Therefore, it might be best to reconsider both Powys and Mercia as rival confederations who subdued minor kingdoms across either side of Offa's Dyke. Imagine specific territorial units harassing one another regularly, rather than a series of pitched battles between two large 'nations'. This situation is undoubtedly the case for Powys' north, a region later known as Y Berfeddwlad ('the middle country'), composed of countless cantrefi. One such, Rhufoniog, is listed as a distinct kingdom in the *Annals of Wales*. Occasionally juggled between their larger neighbours like Powys and Gwynedd, small polities like Rhufoniog may have fulfilled a role very similar to Ystrad Tywi or Gŵyr as political buffers used for inter-kingdom proxy wars. Dogfeiling and Edeirnion, usually mentioned as the kingdoms of Cunedda's children, are all located along this border, too, as is Tegeingl, all invariably tossed between regimes. For the latter, Mercian dominance seems likely. In 796 King Offa defeated an army at Rhuddlan, another Mercian king died nearby in 821 and, later, it became the site of a *burh*. Like Ergyng, Tegeingl was a frontier region with allegiances swaying this way and that. In 822 a more direct military seizure is suggested by the *Annals of Wales* when 'the fortress of Degannwy [was] destroyed by the English, and they drew the kingdom into their control'. That a follow-up invasion occurred in 853 suggests that this Mercian victory against Powys was short-lived.

It is in this context that we should place the Pillar of Eliseg, erected over the imagined grave of someone like Vortigern or Magnus Maximus, to oppose Mercian victories against Tegeingl and Ergyng, proclaiming over the marcher hills that 'we

---

[*] This region is Rhwng Gwy a Hafren, Welsh for 'Between Wye & Severn'.

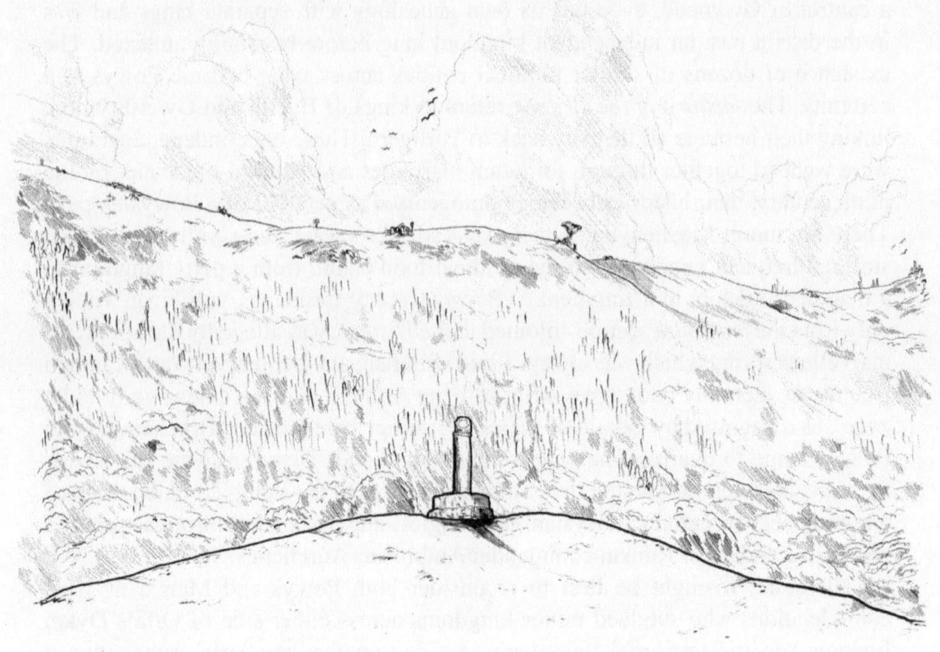

Powysian kings are strong and have mighty ancestry! Forefathers, one and all! Bear witness!'. But rigid identity is exactly the type to become brittle and fracture, unmalleable and sluggish compared to more pragmatic notions of self. Not long after Powys was annexed by Gwynedd.

But it was not dead. In the twelfth century a version of the Powysian realm was re-born through dynast Maredudd ap Bleddyn which his son Madog later expanded. This Neo-Powys was described during his reign as extending from Chester to Pumlumon, all the way to Meirionnydd (another former kingdom). The extent of this supposed realm then grew even larger, becoming associated with Ceredigion but such expansiveness was not to last. After he died in 1160, chaos ensued and the same micro-polities that once made up Powys were scavenged by Gwynedd and Deheubarth, like vultures on a corpse. Powys itself segmented into the short-lived lordships of Wenwynwyn and Fadog in the south and north, rebelling against Gwynedd in 1277.[287] By this point there were more castles than grains of sand in Wales, wrought out of raw stone like Chepstow or Clearwell. These often-moated fortresses served as the bricks and mortar in re-cementing a resistant Welsh identity.

In his reign Madog was knowingly tapping into a distant past and even named one of his sons Elise after the eponymous pillar. It is from Madog's courts where interest in the poetic traditions of Old Wales was kindled, spawning the manuscripts containing all the triads and tales we have been consulting thus far. The Welsh Marches have always been a bit of a stopping ground. Folded hills conceal threats across the Shrewsbury Plain and Lower Wye Valley. A continuity of border communities is inferred since at least the Late Neolithic, influenced by geography, watersheds and self-fulfilling cycles of perpetuation. Such terrain would become the breeding ground for ostentatious territorial displays, such as the Bronze Age Mold cape and later hillforts like Old Oswestry, Moel y Gaer and the Wrekin. It was here where the Roman Empire deemed it necessary to build substantial bases, as at Buckton and Chester and supply depots like Leintwardine. Chester even bears evidence for undergoing significant repairs in the late fourth century. Roads which linked these fortresses through the Marches, like those between Penkridge and Chester, or Gloucester and Caerleon, would have become pressure points in the Roman Period and thereafter, facilitating rapid movement over borders. Large walled towns, such as Wroxeter, Kentchester and Caerwent, then emerged to accommodate the dispersed Iron Age tribes who had once dwelt between these limits.[288] Indeed, they were built precisely to re-organise hillfort communes: Wroxeter re-centralised the Cornovii; Kentchester is associated with the Decangi (possibly the *Deceangli* of Tegeingl) and Caerwent with the Silures. These towns scattered Iron Age tribes and re-organised their trade and social networks through the meatgrinder of Roman administration. When that administrative machine retracted towards the end of the fifth century, the towns' inhabitants dispersed and the old hill-forts became re-occupied.

Associated with Powys through church dedications, the continental saint Germanus is recorded in an anti-Pelagian text as visiting *Britannia* twice during this period, declaring that the island was still 'most wealthy' with a retained administrative system and organised military. By the sixth century most former Roman towns and their occupants had expanded outwards; it is here that the origin of the 'country folk' begins, a proto-Powys that emerged from several fractious Late Roman and post-urban groups occupying the Marches. Burial mounds along the border indicate a mad dash to name monuments: Wolferlow, Peplow, Purslow, Whittingslow, Onslow, where *-low* means 'barrow' and not to mention the Pillar itself. Was Eliseg's monument, then, not raised to combat Mercian expansionism at all, but to thwart the ascension of other sub-kingdoms of the country folk? Other kings in Powys?

As with the Romans before them, English castles along the Marches further fragmented communities and led to the desertion or shrinkage of many border villages. The country folk once again became country-bound. It is from these tattered scraps of Powys that we must leave Wales behind, having only briefly covered its vast diaspora of peoples and polities, more than deserving of a book of their own.

RHEGED?

No name tempts early medievalists quite like Rheged. A paper on the topic is like a van full of sweets or a free iPhone in your spam folder. It is a chance to hear something new about this most beguiling, most irritating, most difficult of 'kingdoms', one whose very placement, name and ruler have been the subject of rigorous academic scrutiny for over a century. The intention here is not to add further layers of dispute but to place the idea of Rheged alongside what has already been discussed, the valleys of the north-west.

What can we safely assume? West of the Pennines the natural geography and Roman roads facilitated the development of innumerable small and self-sufficient farming nucleations. Not kingdoms, these farmsteads were close to the Irish Sea and therefore may have been influenced more by the development of power and kingship in Ireland than any English models. Saying that, we cannot be certain because most of our sources are poems[289] which throw around terms like spears on a battlefield. Rheged, for example, is typically listed alongside the place called 'Goddeu' which suggests both were viewed as 'bountiful forests'. Not even territories, just landscapes. Rheged might not even be that important but just another half-imagined realm handpicked from an arsenal including Aeron, *Pennawc, Brewyn,* Catraeth and *Arfynydd*. Men of Rheged fought at a place called 'Argoed' according to one of dozens of poems about the famous Urien. His name has cropped up here and there in this book and, whilst probably a real figure, we cannot know where he was based, largely because we cannot work out where his kingdom was. A similar territory called *Arfderydd* has been argued to be Arthuret, Cumbria, based on sound etymological grounds[290] and this place is described in the same traditions that lament frequently about Rheged. Were they neighbours? And how do we know that Rheged deserves more importance than *Arfderydd*? The hybridised *Rheged-Arfynydd*, 'Rheged of the Mountains', even appears in another poem. The word may stem from Old Welsh *rhy-ged* for 'one of great gifts'. Was it an expanding, generic label that encompassed miscellaneous areas?

> You are a poet working on a praise-piece for your expectant lord, whose sweated skin still steams, fresh from battle. Around you are a labyrinth of valleys each home to squabbling kings and their kingdoms, the cacophony of their booming voices deafening in the mead hall: an assortment of names to choose from, and your king, Urien, is the mightiest of them all. So you go through the list, one by

"

one, deliberately choosing which sounds best connected to the most recent syllable, simile, or metaphor. 'Rheged' – yeah, that works.

These 'stock names' might have been picked to add flavour to pseudo-histories. Urien's reputation was certainly enhanced over the years, a 'raucous cattle-raider' always surrounded by herds. This meant wealth, lots of it. Urien had an abundance of booty from border strife and used it to pay poets and to keep his warriors loyal. When he died the luck and generosity of subsequent rulers would be compared directly and, frequently, against him. Therefore, Urien's memory persisted, 'Rheged, beyond the sea'. Given that the kingdom is so closely tied with the man himself, it cannot have remained too impressive once he passed. In 634 Oswiu of Northumbria married his great-granddaughter Rheinmelth, sealing the polity's end.* This time there was nothing to praise, partly because Rheinmelth appears in Bede's work which, whilst not always true, is at least reliable. Urien, on the other hand, is a component of an oral tradition where bards like Taliesin and Aneirin committed to memory sprawling collections of figures, places and events which were later cemented into text and organised in such a way that implied they were *always* ordered. In reality the poems we have now are just the surviving versions, fossilised, diminishing the creativity and impromptu sporadic nature of the original format. These surviving manuscripts have gone on to influence all scholarship about Urien, Rheged and the Old North. *The Gododdin*, although it mentions Aeron, Catraeth and *Eidyn* omits both Rheged and its master. Were they irrelevant? This would be at odds with other works but where there is a gap people seek to fill it with Rheged. '[The Solway Firth placement] has been repeated so often that its origin as an unproven hypothesis is barely remembered today', as Tim Clarkson rightly remarks in a refreshingly sceptical 2010 publication. This kind of logic is what has perpetuated Rheged's situation; where there is a blank spot on the 'Dark Ages Map' it *must* be Rheged. However, our only reference to the realm's location is in a twelfth-century tale which describes a character riding 'day and night all the way from Maelienydd to the land of Rheged' to reach *Caer Lliwelydd* (Carlisle). Given that Maelienydd is in Radnorshire and Carlisle in Cumbria, we have almost four-hundred kilometres to place the kingdom. But maybe Rheged wasn't a kingdom after all.

Was 'Rheged' a group name, like the Dál Riata? This would neatly parallel the Irish kingdoms because archaeologically this region is quite lacking in high-status sites, the type that would serve as palaces for Urien.[291] Whithorn and the Mote of Mark, both north of the Solway, are some of the only exceptions. The former was

---

* Rheinmelth is described as the granddaughter of Rhun, who is elsewhere labelled a son of Urien. This Rhun and that one could easily be different people however, making Rheinmelth the progeny of another kingdom. In a poem connected to Gwallog 'the war-bands of Rhun and Nudd and Nwython' are described as being driven back somewhere near Stirling.

a religious centre and the latter an expansive workshop and both share evidence of international interaction. Outside these locations, exotic material generally decreases further eastwards into Cumbria. Even along the extant forts of Hadrian's Wall, such as Birdoswald, which remained occupied into the sixth century, material is sparse.[292] Carlisle, too, is lacking in high-status evidence from before the eighth century.* We have textual references *about* Cumbria, but these only mention mundane places like *Dacor* (Dacre), *Deruuentionis* (Derwent) and Kintis, far from the exuberance of Rheged. With its meres, shallows and riptides, did the Solway Firth function as a fringe, rather than a maritime hubbub? Therefore, did 'Rheged' mean anywhere in particular? Was it a metaphor for an idealised land, a realm of shadow placed nebulously between Wales and Scotland, two areas linked through literature and legend?

Between Dumfriesshire and Galloway is the excavated fortress of Trusty's Hill, affording a grand view of The Fleet from a perfect strategic position. Despite a detailed excavation report, debates persist about which kingdom this elite residence belonged to.[293] Was it Aeron? Was it Dál Riata? Was it Rheged? Part of this discussion concerns the presence of Pictish symbols carved into a rock outside the fort's gate, very similar to those known from Dunadd and Edinburgh. Do they immortalise Verturian agents on their southern border? Or are they reflective of a much broader artistic tradition associated with warriorhood and seamanship? In the twelfth-century *Life of St Kentigern*, the grave of a king is marked by symbol-carved stones, echoing those seen here. Maybe the fortress straddled all worlds, an entrepôt betwixt Pictland, Gaeldom and the Old North.

Bordered by rubble walls and earthen banks, the summit's ramparts cover nearly five-hundred square metres, segmented into terraces up and down the slopes. Grooves and cut-marks suggest these plateaus were connected by suspended timber platforms. They would eventually rot and collapse. In the fort's wake, stonework and trees were burned. Charcoal fragments and iron residue indicate that Trusty's Hill fell amidst a firestorm. Was this the end of the unnamed kingdom? A broad date range spanning the sixth and eighth centuries has been given for the vitrified material, suggesting that the place was abandoned not long after. There is minimal evidence for any repair work. After three centuries of occupation, Trusty's Hill was torched and left to fester. Fire and flames, forged in battle, but this was only the latest inferno to grace the site. The immense amount of metalworking material, everything from furnished brooches to crude iron files, stone crucibles, raw lead ingots and slag fragments, suggests that Trusty's Hill was home to a prosperous smithing industry. A single sandstone slab, perfectly flat on one side, and nicked on the other, may have been the anvil that thousands of hammers beat against here in the Boreland Hills. Hot metal on rock, cooled in the salt spray of The Fleet.

---

* But a mention of a seemingly independent Brythonic leader called Waga, in the *Life of St Cuthbert*, suggests there existed some local authority here, along with a functioning Roman fountain and aqueduct.

Elsewhere, cattle were slaughtered and their bones used for fuel and so, too, were willow and oak. Cut into planks, hazel may have been twisted into wattle structures and seaweed used to create lye or soap. This belching mound would have been busy, noisy, stinking. Then quiet, but never silent. After it was abandoned, there are signs that Trusty's Hill was still visited, possibly serving as a pseudo-legendary monument across the Solway. The Pictish symbols carved by the gateway, despite being similar to others like the Burghead bulls, are typologically unique. Close in form to psalter depictions of sea monsters, Classical motifs can be appreciated in the sinewy draconic creature. Was it a limbless symbol of aggression? Was it revered? Hated, even?

Pictish beasts, unlike those from Scandinavian artwork, are never depicted in defeat but always in grace. A rock-cut basin filled with water sits alongside the symbol as does another at the similarly-inscribed gates of Dunadd. Such ritualised doorways were used in kingly ceremonies, again with parallels in Ireland. When Ptolemy compiled his *Geography*, he made sure to mark a 'royal site' on the edge of Galloway. Was Trusty's Hill the site of such a ruler? Battered atop a stormy shore, the symbols and basin may even have been carved *after* the fort was burned when it became a smouldering empty monument.

From sites like this and the Mote of Mark, the shining metalwork of early medieval Scotland was forged and distributed, trickling down the high table of boozing warriors like water through stone all the way from Bernicia to Cait. Garnets, recovered on site, may have been imported from Bohemia but, elsewhere, the lead and iron seems to have been locally mined. And much like metal, cultural and artistic affinities were mulched and melded here at Trusty's Hill, layered and beaten into something new, twisting strands of Roman, Irish, Pictish and North Sea material together. The creation of goods, loud, scorching, reeking, would have been an act of theatre in itself, as religious and artistic connotations were forged, and

identities were stacked. But was this identity 'Rheged'? Are Trusty's Hill and the Mote of Mark the princely centres of Urien's kingdom? Do their final soot-covered contexts mark his pallid grave? We can never know.

In 603 'an immense and mighty army' led by King Áedán mac Gabráin of Dál Riata was defeated near Drumelzier in the Tweed Valley, sealing southern Scotland under Northumbrian shoes.[294] Over a hundred years later, an Anglo-Pictish bishop was active at Whithorn. Scattered across nearby Nithsdale are dozens of unique hybridised sculptures and stone crosses stranded between Mercian, Bernician, Pictish, and Gaelic styles, like at Boatford and Thornhill, the mark of a new dominion upon southern Scotland or perhaps the opposite: the creation of stabilising monuments amidst inter-regional chaos here in the scarred gorges.[295] Largely, Nithsdale is nameless in the Early Medieval Period. Edward Moore has demonstrated that a regionally cohesive Pictish-influenced identity was formed here, first recorded as *Strat Nith* in 1124, but this too, is no Rheged.[296] There was also a minor gold-working smithy at Tynron Doon, active during the same period as Trusty's Hill. Because other hillforts, such as Dunadd, Castle Rock, Dumbarton Rock and Bamburgh, can be so easily tied to specific kingdoms, Trusty's Hill sits as an outlier. It *must* have been the base of a powerful elite whose influence stretched far and wide, but the big question lingers. Was this elite Urien and was his kingdom Rheged?

People will bicker about this forevermore, but the truth is that there is currently not enough evidence to support anything conclusive. This is Urien's legacy, whose feats and significance were well-understood centuries after he supposedly lived and, even if Rheged was born from myth, surely most can 'agree: he sweeps aside enemies; he deserves the image: Lightning Destroyer'.

RŌTALAND

Before the county system had been formalised, England was mostly divided by hundreds, each with a central place. County towns abolished these, becoming regional capitals in the eleventh century. Typically, a county is named after its major town: Lincolnshire has Lincoln, Nottinghamshire has Nottingham, Leicestershire has Leicester. Amidst all these is the oddity of Rutland which, apart from a brief sojourn in Leicestershire between 1974 and 1997, has remained an independent county without a conventionally named centre for over a thousand years. The theories about why this is will take us back through time, far from the 1994 Local Government Commission to the eleventh century and even earlier, into the Bronze Age.

Recorded as *Roteland* in the *Domesday Book*, containing around fifty settlements and six partial hundreds, this East Midlands realm abounds in rich forests and pastureland and, while the central body of water is a modern reservoir, there is no reason to believe this wasn't a well-fed and fertile region way back when. *Rōtaland*, named sometime in the sixth or seventh centuries, evokes a tightly-knit kin group that became baked into land charters and folk memory, much like the Brahingas. These fecund lands were a bountiful prize for Rōta to own. The modern bounds appear to be relatively archaic, unchanged since at least the tenth century. Rutland is bordered by high ground to the west dotted with Bronze Age barrows. As already demonstrated elsewhere, prehistoric tumuli were often re-purposed as territorial markers in the Early Medieval Period. This almost definitely happened here: imagined ancestors acting as sentinels.

But what did they guard? In 2016 the fragments of a large copper alloy bowl with openwork foot rings were discovered in an extant Bronze Age mound (LEIC-47AE03). Once suspended from hooked chains, this sixth-century vessel had been re-interred into a prehistoric tomb alongside a plain gold triangular belt buckle and boss which the bowl enclosed. Remarkably similar to a high-status sixth-century burial assortment known from Prittlewell, Essex, this small yet unique assemblage represents the grave of a *Rōtaland* ruler, an Early Medieval raddleman.* It was purposefully placed within an even older monument to deify

---

* Inhabitants of Rutland are sometimes referred to as 'Raddlemen' or 'Ruddles', allegedly stemming from the red-ochre soil of their home territory. Eric Idle, Sir-Robin-the-Not-Quite-so-Brave-as-Sir-Lancelot, played in a band called *The Rutles* inspired by Rutland.

the status of its new inhabitant, carving familial bonds through the morasses of deep time. Elsewhere, four *sceattas* minted across England and the Low Countries were discovered by detectorists, along with several cruciform and long brooches, girdle hangers and pins distributed all over Rutland. All of these finds, spread across the parishes of Whissendine, Belton-in-Rutland and Glaston, can be dated between 450 and 700 CE. Of particular interest is the partially broken fragment of a single copper alloy linked pin, folded by ploughing. This pin was styled with anthropomorphic intertwined vine-like motifs usually ascribed to a 'Mercian' style. After all, *Rōtaland* did fall within the bounds of Mercia. Before 2010 a spacer plate inscribed with runic script was also discovered (LEIC-3EBE93), appearing to spell out the personal name 'Ceolburg'. This plate may have once held up the dress of a local lady; did she cherish this accoutrement, marking it with her name?

The inscription is reminiscent of one dynasty of Mercian royalty, among them Ceolred and Ceolwulf. Indeed, by the ninth century, Ceolwulf II became the last recorded independent Mercian king to hold any jurisdiction over the East Midlands, losing it to viking armies. There is an interesting although tenuous link here, suggesting that *Rōtaland* was a royal landholding. It certainly seems to have become one by the tenth century.

Amidst Scandinavian invasions, Ælfred the Great's sister, Æthelswyth, married into the Mercian royal line and posthumously his daughter Æthelflæd became known as the 'lady of the Mercians'. Both women benefitted from a Mercian tradition of queenly importance and succession; their names appear on charters and land grants, and, by 1066, Queen Edith of England was listed as *Roteland*'s sole landholder. Edith Weston, by Rutland Water, is named after her. Charles Pythian-Adams keenly suggested that *Rōtaland*, through marriages to Mercia, became a West Saxon territory in the ninth century and was held by dowager queens into the eleventh.[297] Subsequent research has followed this theory. *Rōtaland* was a known and recognisable territory within the East Midlands, representing a much older

system of land organisation which remained distinct even amidst county and shire reforms.[298] There is even an argument to be made that 'Rōta's land' was *already* a consolidated tribal unit by the sixth century, if not earlier, given that its boundaries all seem to avoid Roman structures and are equally lined with barrows, suggesting that it is an archaic territory of the Iron Age. Rutland's northern neighbour Melton, previously known as *Framland*, once looked similar and, while its modern bounds are larger than Rutland's, Bob Trubshaw has demonstrated that both were the same size before Norman expansions.[299] These areas may have originated as Iron Age entities, so unique that they became remembered, in some form or another, centuries and centuries later.

Rōta and Franni's lands are certainly distinct. There is a surprising dearth of Old Norse-influenced toponyms across the former, especially considering that Rutland abuts Nottinghamshire, Leicestershire and Lincolnshire, three of the most linguistically Scandinavianised areas in England. This lack of Old Norse place names implies that Rutland was held onto as a royal territory whilst the rest of Mercia was overtaken by foreign armies and settlers. The stalwart defenders may have stood their ground from Fliteriss Park ('disputed brushwood region'), Burley ('forest by the fort') or Twitch Hill ('look-out point'), all enclosing Hambleton, Rutland's core. Franni's Land may have been guarded by occupants of the Burrough-on-the-Hill fort if it was still active beyond the fourth century. Even if it wasn't, like Rutland's barrow mounds, the ruins may have taken on new meaning as watchful wardens, defending these Leicester-adjacent landholdings. At Glaston the occupants were buried in an inhumation cemetery where Edward Thurlow Leeds discovered gilded square-headed brooches, amber beads and 'Celto-Saxon' material in 1950.[300] Glaston is one of the few Old Norse toponyms in Rutland, alongside Normanton. By the mid-tenth century, Anglo-Scandinavian relations in the Danelaw had harmonised, so it is from this period these place names probably date.

Glaðr joins Rōta, Franni and even Sir Robin as an early medieval raddleman but it is the women who gave Rutland its ancient importance. Edith, Æthelflæd, Æthelswyth and maybe even Ceolburg held onto Rōta's land like it was their own. Like it was a cherished belonging, carved with its owner's name.

SOMERSÆTE

Owning land was, and is, important. Anyone fortunate enough to transition from the rental to the homeowner's market surely knows this. The act of having your home leased to you by an unseen overlord is a sinister, irritating feeling, made doubly annoying with the tendency of landlords to be avaricious layabouts. In the ninth century the *Sumortūnsæte* fell under the dominion of Wessex, but it wasn't until the reign of King Ælfred that they were named as the 'people of Somerton', the settlement which gives this *regio* its title. It may have held a different name beforehand, coined by Old Cornish speakers before being re-worked in Old English to something like **Glestingas*, after *Glestingaburg* (Glastonbury), which was once a hermitage. Glastonbury Tor is well regarded as a pagan hotspot with evidence of sixth-century metalworking and butchering activity at the site, as well as a timber building and, later, rock-cut monastic cells.[301] Most of Somerset's spiritual history, however, takes the form of not a single massif but an array of low-lying riverside monasteries situated on chalk hillocks. Indeed, most of the sources that describe Somersæte mention religious endowments.

This was a small region strangled, both geographically and politically, between Dumnonia and Wessex. The aforementioned distribution of monasteries is mirrored by the distribution of West Saxon churches across Wiltshire and Dorset and, even as late as the fifteenth century, tithing documents and dedications from Cornwall suggest a relatively de-centralised society with only a few ecclesiastical and secular elites. Somerset was viewed as an extension of the same landscape, organised in the same way. These sparse settlements hint at the frequent re-organisation of land management and ownership and we have already seen how Dumnonia was nibbled down by decades of West Saxon overreach. Somersæte, right on its eastern edge, was among the first of these subsidiary realms to fall under new boots. The name alone, which is Old English, is a striking contrast to Cornwall. Well, almost. **Kornu-wealh* features an Old English suffix, but *-wealh* usually denotes 'Britons', 'whelps', even 'Romans'. We have already seen it used east of Loidis to denote a different linguistic identity. Somerset, on the other hand, is like Arosætna, the 'inhabitants of Somerton'. Both areas wear their linguistic influences on their sleeves. It was probably in the seventh century when Somerset and Cornwall gained titles like their modern names, the former becoming 'book-land' for the burgeoning West Saxon church. Newly conquered Somersæte settled by new 'sitters', not gifted to dynasts or squabbling kings but permanently handed over to clergymen. They were the latest landlords. Other names within Somerset hail from the subsequent fragmentation of these new estates as the territory was divided further between thegns and minor lords to act as a judicial buffer zone between Wessex and Dumnonia. These are the *-ington* names where *-tūn* denotes a slightly later enclosed settlement, such as Wellington and Woolavington. Sherborne, also, was a major West Saxon bishopric.

Importantly, the West Saxon landlords of Somerset were not engaging with the Dumnonians in only one way for their own benefit. An important ninth-century bishop and King Ælfred's biographer, Asser, was a major figure in Wessex despite hailing from Wales. Not only does Asser's high status in the court suggest that there was mutual trust between the *wealas* and Wessex but also that they were not barred from rising through society. The church united them with the Saxons just as it knitted Somersæte together. Many West Saxon minsters, as at Keynsham and Banwell, appear to have been built atop pre-existing communities. Whether this reflects new 'sitters' entirely or merely a continuation of, or a partnership with, the inhabitants is difficult to discern. On that same note, the cemetery evidence from Camerton suggests that the town was continually occupied between the fourth and seventh centuries. Again, there is no evidence whatsoever of conflict but rather the mutual exchange of landlords. And, as with Glastonbury, these were multi-faceted locations. Carhampton, Gillingham and Ramsbury were all exporting worked iron and metal goods and at Cannington a burial ground spans fourth- to eighth-century contexts, its entombed inhabitants including Romans, pagans and Christians. There were scribes, smiths and churchmen wandering and working across Somerset, Dumnonians, all of them, until they became 'West Saxons'. Cheddar, a major 'West Saxon' site, includes Romano-British pottery. The identities of who owned the palace and who lived there are different. Interesting within this context is the recently re-assessed assemblage from Hardown Hill, Dorset.[302] This collection of eight spearheads, an axehead, knife, shield boss, perforated flint pebble and a brooch is overtly tied to North Sea affinities yet found far to the west of all known similar material from sixth-century England. Oddly, one of the spearheads was inscribed with a fish-like symbol, a watchful totemic animal to bring the wielder good

Either acting as a maker's mark or a now-forgotten folkloric element, the 'fish' symbol on the Hardown Hill spearhead joins the Trusty's Hill serpent and the Burghead Bulls as unknowable animalistic logos of personality. Illustration modelled on Vera Evison's original drawing from 1968.

luck. Clearly, they had the opposite for this assemblage tells a story of defeat. Dorset even hails from a similar name, *Dornsætan*. Are these the weapons of an intruder or a fashionable local? Is a distinction important?

An edited 722 entry in *The Anglo-Saxon Chronicle* describes how Queen Æthelburh of Wessex ordered the demolition of a fortified residence at Taunton which had been built by her husband. This already implies that at least eastern Somerset was 'West Saxon' by the late seventh century. Nearby lands were certainly being parcelled off and subdivided at the same time. To the north a Mercian charter from 736 describes how King Æthelbald granted ten hides of land to his 'venerable companion' for the foundation of a minster in the land 'that in ancient times was named Husmeræ' (S 89). It is believed that this is the ancient name of a *regio* or *provincia* (both terms are used) located along the river Stour near Kidderminster; they are alternatively called the *Wiogorna*. Whilst far from Somerset, archaic lands being re-defined through the establishment of new borders and parishes is a remarkable parallel. Steven Bassett, arguing for the existence of a *regio* at Wootton Wawen near Birmingham,[303] rightfully makes the case that many tenth- and eleventh-century parishes have the same dimensions as earlier territories, their names changed, their inhabitants newly overseen. The 'territory which is anciently called Stoppingas' from another one of Æthelbald's grants became a minster and the locals suffered a new landlord (S 94). Did their identities change during this process of socio-economic renegotiation? Likewise, did the Husmeræ, or the *Sumortūnsǣte*, feel a change to their notion of self when they were transferred like goods?

Self-identity in general is fraught throughout Old English texts, especially these West Saxon land charters. Here, at unstable points of contact along the Dumnonian border, boundary clauses rely on vague, abstract descriptions of land features. In essence, they use metaphors and kennings in place of more practical descriptors: a copse becomes a 'vixen's dike', paralleling genuine Old English riddles. But a boundary clause, essentially an economic and legal document, shouldn't be trying to confuse its reader, or should it? Like communications with letting agents, these charters are vague *because* that ambiguity allows them to be used to stake wider claims. The Pencersæte and Tomsæte charter already demonstrates that, to best understand borders, the reader *already* needed to know what they looked like and their local history. In a Somersæte context this would work for West Saxon officials who created, upheld and promulgated these borders. For the Dumnonians, brought up in a different literary environment, these charters may have been needlessly obtuse. Asser, straddling both worlds and a member of the ecclesiastical class, was well learned, the laity less so. It is possible these boundary clauses were made to be purposefully confusing. The borders they describe were fluid, relying on the manipulated memories of biased perambulators. These remembered borders could then be abused to encroach upon further territory. When that memory was lost, the borders themselves would fall into disarray. These 'pressure points' would become areas of tension, where self-identity was in flux:[304] 'This is my land!' 'No! Its mine!'. In 846 King Æthelwulf granted land in Devon and, a decade later, one of his sons even used these continued regional divisions to plot against his father in a minor rebellion. Asser, recounting a highly moralised version of the event forty years later, may have downplayed the immediate impact of this short-lived revolt on the frontier sites of Taunton and Cheddar.[305] All this makes us ask what Asser, a Wessex-dwelling Briton, thought of his allegiances.

The most enduring boundaries were geographic ones, rivers, mountain ranges, fens. Paradoxically, the Severn watershed appears to have acted like the Humber; it was *not* a barrier but a bridge between Gwent, Ergyng, the Hwicce and the Somersæte. Cybi, a sixth-century saint, is associated with both Wales and Cornwall. The *Life of St Kenelm*'s narrative includes only locations from this area and, in the 1980s, drainage work around Glastonbury recovered a seventh-century Byzantine censer; a similar artefactual signature, also including Gaulish pottery, is known from finds across Gwent and Glywysing. On both sides of the Bristol Channel people were bartering, buying and selling the same things.

Two other saints, Botolph and Rumwold, are universally associated with boundaries. Rumwold's *Life* implies familial boundaries between petty lords during his childhood whilst churches dedicated to Botolph are typically located *on* natural boundaries such as Edge Hill between Rutland and Leicestershire. Botolph's connection with borders is self-fulfilling.[306] He is associated with boundaries because his churches are usually situated on them *because* he is associated with them to begin with. Identity, caught between kingdoms, arguably at its most enduring.

A final charter, from 971, details how King Eadgar of England granted privileges to Glastonbury. 'The islands of *Bekeria*, called Little Ireland' is described as being situated amongst the Glastonbury marshes (S 783). This was a new Hibernian religious institution. Not evidence of an Irish diaspora but a specific monastic group tied through nomenclature to Ireland. The *Life of St Patrick* mentions 'Bec Ériu' (Beggery Island, Wexford) which is probably the original establishment that inspired this one; one of Brychan's legendary twenty-four sons is described as residing 'in *Cornwallia*'. Via palaeography, the study of handwriting styles to date and trace manuscripts, Colleen Curran even suggests that many, if not all, Breton manuscripts in ninth-and-tenth-century England made their way to the country *through* Glastonbury, their Caroline miniscule style influenced in turn by Francia and then Brittany.[307] Ultimately, then, Somerset became home to artificial identities, monasteries that appropriated and used different cultures. One wonders what the locals thought between the seventh and tenth centuries, renting their home from landlord after landlord. One hopes they were at least better than ours.

SUSSEX

*S*uthsaxa is a kingdom of contradictions. It was a 'Saxon' realm yet housed an internal Brythonic polity; it is described as a bloodstained wilderness despite the fact that Christians were already here before the 'first' conversion; it has one of the longest seaboards but few trading centres. How did this geographically central region evade consolidation for so long? How did external perceptions overshadow reality? And was there ever really a 'king' of the South Saxons at all?

Written accounts like the *Life of St Wilfrid* paint Sussex as dripping in pagan debauchery as late as the eighth century but this otherness was not entirely invented. Geography played a part. Sussex is segmented by river valleys that run north-to-south with thick forests that once limited movement from east to west.[308] The South Downs, the Weald and the rivers Arun and Rother were natural guardians, physically obscuring outside views. Rumours and theories about the inhabitants may have run wild; a tale of Wilfrid avoiding 'spells' cast by South Saxon wizards became embedded in eighth-century popular culture, thus reinforcing misconceptions. Even so, many of the earliest residents seem to have been genuinely confined, separated from one another as tightly defined blocks around the Ouse and Cuckmere and sheltered from the otherwise busy West Saxons and Kentishmen. Despite this, we *do* hear of some local individuals like King Watt and the *duces regii* active in Wealden in the seventh century; and other South Saxon sub-kings appear in charters from 710 to 772. As with the East and West Saxons, the term designated a loose area of land home to numerous elites, not an organised hegemony. Deira also seems to have emerged this way before being dominated by a single dynasty. And where you find inter-polity competition, you find dramatic social expression.

At the hillfort of Thundersbarrow, elites between the fifth and eighth centuries buried their dead alongside prehistoric antecedents. They re-labelled this mound as the crypt of Þunor the storm god and made this grave theirs. At Rotherfield a similar Iron Age structure was re-purposed and re-occupied. Many groups, indigenous or otherwise, lit their torches beneath the silhouettes of those who came before, defining themselves by their geography and history.[309] By associating themselves with monoliths and monuments, small communities declared their presence amongst local resources and competitors. Before the Early Medieval Period, scattered pottery in the Roman villa at Beddingham suggests that new conquerors were already staking their claim; after, a thirteenth-century ambulist was still recording 'stone barrows' along the edge of the county. From their posts southern ghosts maintained their ceaseless cordon. At places like Burpham Peppering and Pipering they even watched the sea.

A posthumous presence along coastal headlands imposed an identity over the waves, alerting sailors that the South Saxon lands were home to competitive kings, so many that Sussex persisted as a fissiparous realm long after its neighbours had centralised. By the time Mercia and Wessex were more or less distinct, Sussex was the opposite, fragmented like Powys and dependent on geographical axes of communication. In fact, even by the Conquest, the establishment of Sussex's rapes suggest the persistence of segmented territories ruled over by squabblers.

But why were they squabbling? There is evidence for a small trading place at Pagham, due to the presence of locally made pottery and eighth-century *sceattas* found alongside a cobbled road, but this was no *Hamwih*. At Bishopstone, around sixty buildings were erected over several centuries of farming and feasting, yet this was no town and there were no palaces like Cheddar or Yeavering. At Bullock Down, near Eastbourne, co-axial field systems were intensively cultivated, yet trade was limited; people may have exported over the English Channel and the Weald, but this land had no entrepôts and few imports. Presumably, fields were worked, and barley was grown, coasts were fished, and eels were eaten, forests were hunted, and deer were caught, but it seems to have all been for local economies. At Botolphs, in the Adur Valley, a whale washed up in the sixth century and was immediately butchered but, unlike at Flixborough, this was a chance event, and no industry ever prospered. In Ashdown Forest, iron-working is suggested by stray finds of ninth-century charcoal and slag and a bloomery furnace dated 315-785 is known at Mayfield but these were no Ceredigion forges. Was a South Saxon smith repairing longships and forging weapons to wage inter-valley wars? More likely, given the dearth of iron objects in Sussex burials, ingots were sent elsewhere to Kentish overlords.

Launched from *Bucgan-ora* (Bognor Regis), did ships carry swords and spears to other kingdoms? Or was travel restricted to mundane affairs, like the trade of fish and timber? Travelling along Sussex's coast would have afforded a sailor the ability to visit numerous small beach markets whilst the landbound ambulist would have struggled with the same 'dense forests and rocky coasts' Wilfrid's hagiographer bemoaned. This inner disparity affected everything from political unity to economic expansion, but it also saved the realm from easy conquest. Having already covered the Hæstingas, other obvious 'kingdoms' within Sussex can be found to the west. Even at Bognor Regis, a proud heritage was recognised. An Iron Age hero was offered to the earth alongside sword, shield and spear before the Romans arrived, placed alongside pottery and an elaborate ceremonial helmet in a farm at North Bersted. 'Beorgan's stead' was then built atop his mound before 680 CE and, as his bones crumbled, they fertilised the cereals grown by the new landowner in a striking parallel to the Corieltauvi coin re-use at Street House mentioned earlier.[310]

Further westward, new research by Michael Shapland suggests the existence of *another* inter-Sussex polity. South of Chichester, Selsey juts into the English Channel connected by a thin causeway. It was possibly an important Iron Age trading site and, by the seventh century, worth about 87 hides. The strained fate of a Brythonic kingdom was decided here, argues Shapland,[311] piecing together the things *not* said by historical records and, where present, relevant archaeological material. A lump under

When John Speed published his map of 'The theatre of the empire of Great Britaine: presenting an exact geography of the kingdomes of England, Scotland, Ireland ...' in 1612, he depicted King Ælla of Sussex as an ardent conqueror, neatly ruling a consolidated polity coterminous with the modern county. It seems clear now that Sussex, like Essex, was home to not one king but multiple; three distinct territories that became erroneously remembered as 'South Saxon' through a mix of contemporary culture and geographic isolation.

Church Norton, a fifth-century stone hall by Marden's Roman villa, long-lost tumuli from Medmerry, this was the landscape where Wilfrid 'converted' King Æthelwealh and his pagans in the seventh century. Selsey was an island at the time – it is even depicted as such on the Gough Map – and shares a similar status as Lindisfarne and Glastonbury as a sea-bound Christian site. It is through comparisons like these that the idea of a kingdom based around Chichester and Selsey originated for both Lindisfarne and Glastonbury were peripheral to immediate power centres. Here, then, is the last paradox of Sussex. Nearby Kingsham may have been the palace of Æthelwealh whose very name means 'king of the Britons'. King of the who? But was this not *Suthsæxa*? How could a British king rule here? And when Bede repeated the tales of Wilfrid's conversion of Sussex, he relegated such details to the background; 'the whole province was ignorant of the name and faith.' But were they? Evidence would suggest otherwise, and he even mentions an Irish monk at Bosham. Taken together, it is possible that there was a comparable polity to Hæstingas here in West Sussex, one with an obscured origin. The closest comparison would be Lindsey, which has an overtly 'Germanic'-seeming genealogy despite its origins as a Romano-British polity.

Clearly, Sussex was more than its name suggests. It was evidently not a *Mad Max*-style wasteland where shipwrecked sailors became the prey of vulturous spellcasters but something more, a status that can only be revealed through careful interdisciplinary work. Michael Shapland's efforts have uncovered the exact type of hidden histories lurking all over the British Isles.

SUÞRIGE

There's a conversation in *Game of Thrones* where two characters from north and south of The Wall debate directions. 'I just don't understand how you southerners do things' says Osha the wildling, from beyond The Wall, 'I'm not a southerner' says Theon Greyjoy, from The North. 'You're from south of The Wall. That makes you a southerner to me.'

In that one line, an individual 'from The North' becomes re-defined as 'south' to something else. The anchor from which his identity is based is moved. North becomes south. The etymology of Surrey ('south region') is a similar tale. It implies that the territory originated as the southern bit of a larger political entity, maybe Middlesex? But it was *north* of the South Saxons and was undoubtedly viewed differently by those people than it would have been by Londoners. Artefacts are scattered across *Sudergeona, Suðrigeon, provincia Surrianorum*. They range from gilded saucer brooches to engraved oval buckle frames, Carolingian zoomorphic mounts to Frisian-minted *sceattas*. From Ireland and Francia wealth was flowing, surfing on the waves of trading parties and mobile nobility. What Surrey was 'south' of depended on the direction of these travellers. London, that unceasing hub of commerce, was its anchor.

Artefacts like the above, very similar to those from West Kent and Essex, have been found by detectorists and archaeologists all over the county. Whilst the 'south region' of London, Surrey was *central* to traders, this much material could not have ended up here as London's off-cuts. At Croydon, Beddington, Ewell and Guildown, finds are especially concentrated in cemeteries, dominated by Late Roman quoit-style belt buckles. Of these, only Croydon continued into the seventh century,[312] the others fading out of importance as they became overshadowed by newer cemeteries at Merrow, Tadworth, Greenwich and Ashtead. This process of cemetery replacement reflects the coalescing of kin groups into larger communities. This happened in seventh-century Lincolnshire and was a key step on the road to the formation of Lindsey. Surrey never became a kingdom, yet it retained individuality. Brythonic origins are also hinted at, given that charters referring to Chertsey label it as both a 'gateway' and 'landing place of the British' (S 1165 and S 1508). An early chi-rho inscribed jet ring recovered at Bagshot[313] also places early Christians here while the toponyms of Penge, Walworth and Leatherhead imply Celtic-speakers. Elsewhere, a *francisca* throwing axe from Croydon, spearheads at Fetcham and thirteen swords at Mitcham imply the spread of staging posts for duelling mercenaries and territorial aggressors.

The fate of these satellite outposts would have depended on the flourishing of London. In the ninth century, when it was lost to viking armies, Croydon was also occupied and at least one coin hoard was buried here. Earlier crises, like the Dust Veil (536) or Justinian Plague (542), would also have influenced the prosperity of the *gau*. Ten *tremisses* minted in Constantinople were deposited in Kingston-upon-Thames during a period of turmoil; why else? Possibly for insurance purposes, as a 'pick-up later' package? Further elements are implied in a lease from 672 to 674, when a bishop was given land by King Friðuwald (S 1165). Friðuwald is mentioned as a lesser king of Mercia, representing 'the province of the men of *Suþrige*'. Similarly named people like the Mercian *princeps* Friðuric, Queen Friðugyth of Wessex and Oxford's patron princess-saint Friðuswith imply that there was a particularly pious, or at least wealthy, family within this southern region whose activities attracted eyes from afar. Royal women often straddled multiple kingdoms, balancing their loyalty between bloodlines as mothers, wives, daughters and patrons, an unenvious and mostly unrewarding role but incredibly important. In the 680s King Cædwalla of Wessex granted lands at Farnham (S 235) as Surrey changed hands once more but then it fell back under Mercian control alongside Essex, East Anglia and Middlesex in the eighth century. This 'south *gau*' is named identically to Kent's lathes, another superior kingdom. Assigning a character to these units is difficult. They may have been the bases of foreign henchmen or defiant local groups or both. Surrey's hill-fort at Caterham was used as a marker in the Early Medieval Period if the name is anything to go by, deriving from both Old Welsh and English. *Cathair-* ('hill fort') and *-ham* ('estate'): both foreign henchmen *and* defiant local groups named this place.

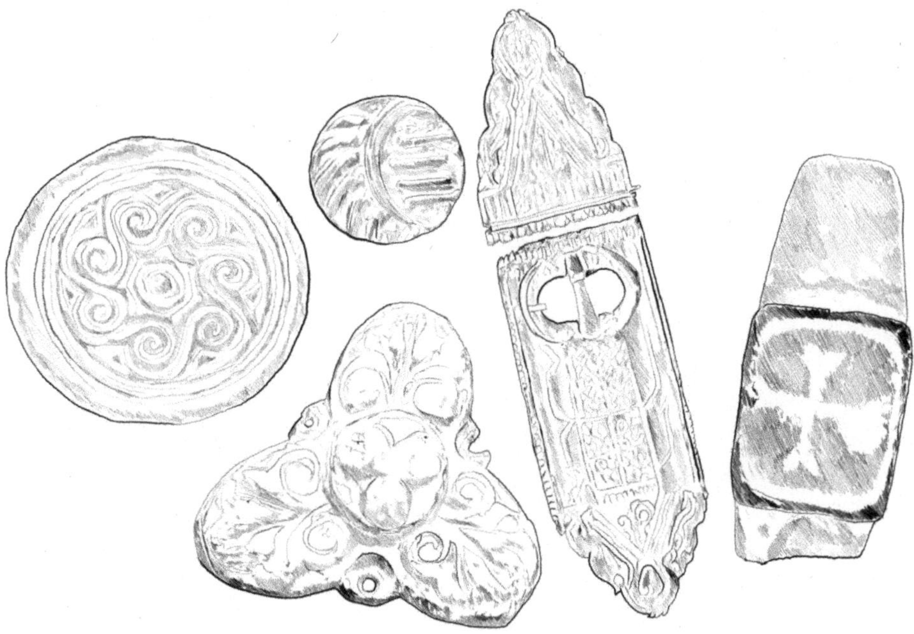

Regardless of their origins, in Surrey's earliest days these speakers came from all directions to occupy geographically and economically central positions, consolidating their roles between London, Kent and Sussex. Woking and Wokingham from the *Woccingas*, Staines from the *Stæningas*, or Godalming, which appears in the eleventh-century copy of King Ælfred's will as *Godelmingum*, were all named after these people. But whether Wocca or Godelm felt they were from the north or south is a matter of perspective.

STRATHCLYDE

Strathclyde sticks out like a sore thumb, Scotland having not been mentioned for several chapters, but it also appears as an outlier in most histories, ignored in favour of traditional narratives about the English and Picts. Strathclyde is something different, a northern British kingdom which survived into the late eleventh century as its neighbours were subsumed into that indomitable new identity of Alba, Scotland. But Strathclyde's story has two halves and can only be told with two names. First, we sail to Alt Clut.

Or perhaps, farther south? If we were to follow the legendary genealogy of the kingdom, preserved in Harley MS 3859, the kings of Alt Clut hailed from *dimor meton,* the 'middle sea' of the Mediterranean.* Such textual mentions are best treated with some caution; the *Life of St Kentigern* connects the realm to Powys and Gwynedd instead. In this story an Irish jester plays in the court of King Rhydderch of Alt Clut who rules over Dumbarton Rock along the Clyde. This volcanic plug is more or less what 'Alt Clut' means, a Brythonic term for 'the Rock of the Clyde' and was Strathclyde's original name. Alt Clut and Strathclyde are the same kingdom, separated by a few centuries and a dozen-or-so miles. In the Viking Age the territorial core of the northern Britons moved from Dumbarton Rock to the ford at Govan, so they were no longer represented by 'the Rock of the Clyde' but 'across the Clyde': *Ystrad-Clut.*

The Clyde connected people on either side but became fossilised in hagiographies as a strange realm, home to otherworlders. Cadog, in his *Life,* challenges an undead giant on these shores, believed to be a distorted reference to the discovery of cetacean fossils. In reality, Strathclyde was no more isolated than anywhere else in Scotland – not at all. These poetic links are fictional, but they indicate the historic ties between Scotland and Wales, many forming part of that 'Men of the North' tradition. In this sense the 'North' was an ambiguously located zone, sometimes exotic and other times familiar, a workable epithet, like Rheged, to be used however poets wished. For example, a literary barrier was constructed 'on the side of the mountain *Bannauc'* marking the inhabitants of Strathclyde differently

---

* In manuscripts, Jerusalem and the Mediterranean were often depicted as central to Old English perceptions of the world. In contrast, many far northern and eastern locations like Libya and Norway became half-imagined, relegated to little kingdoms only fools and angels dared to visit.

to the Picts and Gaels: they were proud Britons.[*] Why else would some of their kings be associated with Brycheiniog, Powys and Gwynedd in genealogies? As late as 1256 charters from Meliden and Llanelwy were mentioning Kentigern, a saint usually associated with Strathclyde, and several centuries earlier a silver penannular brooch similar to those from Shetland was deposited at Pant-y-Saer, Anglesey. Links and literature, real or otherwise, connected Scotland and Wales well into the High Medieval Period.

Rising above the headwaters of the Clyde is the volcanic rock of a mighty kingdom. This fort lashed sea, salt and stone together through timber ramparts spread across both summits and occupied a central position for trade and military networks across western Scotland. The Rock would have been valuable to administrators and, amidst periods of raiding in the third and fourth centuries, well connected across the Irish Sea. It is no wonder that this fortress became known in so many different languages; in Latin it was *Petra Cloithe*, in Gaelic *Ail Cluaide* and the fact that the Brythonic 'Alt Clut' became synonymous with the entire kingdom demonstrates the prominence of this promontory. It was the base from which cargo shipments were launched according to the *Life of St Columba* which describes King Rhydderch as generous with his donations to the Ionan monks. Rhydderch's Alt Clut was a wealthy realm, often in conflict with the Dál Riata, but there is no need to distinguish between 'Irish' and 'Scottish' for these battles. Gaelic speakers had acculturated on both sides of the Irish Sea; Roman references to the *Scoti* pillaging Argyll are not descriptions of mass migration but a linguistic shift observable in pre-existing attackers. It was during the breakdown of administrative rule in the north when independent weapon-bearing warlords, like whoever ruled over Birdoswald, carved out small territories modelled on pre-Roman groups. Alt Clut comes into the picture somewhere around this time, alongside other realms like *Calchfynydd*, Goddeu and others which lack names. Goddeu superficially resembles Cadzow, between Alt Clut and the Gododdin, which is listed as the domain of Rhydderch's queen in the sixteenth-century *Aberdeen Breviary*. At Yarrow Kirk inscriptions discovered in 1803 suggest the presence of other elites: 'In this place lie the illustrious princes Nudus and Dumnoganus ... the sons of Liberalis'.[314] Similar figures appear in genealogies connected to the Old North, perhaps pointing to a dynasty based in Selkirkshire. Another figure called Gwenddolleu, mentioned in similar poems to Urien of Rheged, has been speculated to have ruled over a kingdom based at Carwinley along the river Esk.[315] Such allusions to ephemeral domains are memetic tropes: characters, places and events stranded between memory and fiction, used as mental triggers, allowing orators and poets to cherry-pick references and to tie narratives together. Some of the kingdoms were real and others were not. There is a Pictish group called the 'Naturae' that appear only in the semi-legendary *Miracles of Bishop Nynia*, for instance, and another called the 'Miathi' who were allegedly defeated near Stirling between 595 and 597. If this book has demonstrated anything at all it should be the fact that it is very difficult to tell the difference.

---

[*]   A chap called Llif, mentioned in *The Gododdin*, hailed 'from beyond *Bannauc*'.

Saying that, Alt Clut and by extension Strathclyde, certainly was real. An early king, Coroticus, mentioned in the *Life of St Patrick*, is labelled an 'unjust' ruler and an energetic raider in Ireland. His sons served in a vital warband according to the thirteenth-century *Descent of the Men of the Old North*. Roaming self-sustaining gangs already existed in south Scotland before Roman withdrawal and their continued presence in the sixth century (for example: Artbranan of Cé) suggests nothing really changed. Patrons of insular Christianity were also already present before Irish monks wandered over the narrow sea in the fifth and sixth centuries. One possible donor is the obscure king Barrovadus, mentioned in an inscription from Whithorn and it is worth noting that Patricius himself came from the West Coast *to* Ireland which he called a land of 'barbarians and pagans'. Ninian, another early saint of the north, is probably a fictitious composite but nevertheless demonstrates the importance attributed to Whithorn's past as a centre of early Christianity. It, like Flixborough, was part-monastery part-production centre. Stripping back these hagiographical traditions, we can ascertain that saints like Kentigern were active and welcome in northern courts, presumably practising at Glasgow, Abercorn, Melrose and Hoddom. Some of these are Bernician monasteries but have earlier Brythonic origins. So, too, does Bernicia itself, of course. Certainly, the picture painted by all of the aforementioned northern kingdoms is much more complicated than a simple transition from *Berneich* to Bernicia; these were splintered realms that became consolidated under a Germanic dialect. In the *History of the Britons* the first Anglian king Ida allegedly 'joined *Din Guayroi* to [his kingdom]' suggesting that Bamburgh itself was once the centre of another realm entirely. Like turning over stones in a garden, wherever you look there are more little kingdoms than meet the eye.[316] *

There are also more dynasties to Alt Clut. A successor of Rhydderch, Neithon, considered Coroticus an ancestor whereas later kings did not, possibly highlighting internal divisions across The Clyde. External divisions can be identified through the conflicts between Alt Clut and the Dál Riata, specifically the Cenél Comgaill. A political border separating the two has been suggested along the Cowal Peninsula by Elizabeth Rennie.[317] In 642 a Dál Riatan king, Domnall Brecc, was slain by 'Owain, king of the Britons' somewhere along the river Carron, an event later commemorated in a stanza from *The Gododdin*.

> I saw mighty men who came with the dawn,
> And it was Domnall Brecc's head that the ravens gnawed.

---

* Fiona Campbell-Howes has proposed that two petty kingdoms existed within Fortriu; *Moreb* and *Ros*, centred on Burghead and Inverness respectively. Both of these territories are mentioned in the *Martyrology of Tallaght*, and their broadest outlines can be drawn through the distribution maps of Columban dedications and Class II Pictish stones. Both of these little kingdoms emerged and developed through peer-polity competition as tightly knit ecclesiastical and political divisions, with ideological affinities swaying between 'Pictish' and 'Gaelic'. It is possible that Icelandic sagas record the partial conquest of these territories in the late ninth century.

Whilst probably added to the other verses of the poem at Dumbarton Rock, that King Owain was regarded as ruling over *all* the Britons in Scotland is worth reiterating. Alt Clut at this time was one of the few Brythonic realms left in the north. By the end of this century, Northumbrian overlordship unravelled after the death of King Ecgfrith, giving Alt Clut the room to expand across its formerly conquered neighbours. Bede even writes that 'some part of the British nation' regained their independence, co-existing alongside the 'narrower bounds' of Northumbria for the next few centuries. From this point on 'Briton' became synonymous with 'Alt Clut' so, when Irish annals record subsequent British raids in County Louth and Antrim, we can assume this is the handiwork of the men of the Clyde. Likewise, the Middle Irish *Prophecy of Berchán* poem, which describes a 'king of the Britons of green mantles' defeating a Pictish army, is also probably a reference to Alt Clut.

But all good things must come to an end. The last textual mention of Alt Clut is sandwiched between a re-asserted eighth-century Northumbria and the expansion of Óengus' Pictland. In 756 both kingdoms allied against Alt Clut and the king was forced to capitulate, swearing oaths of surrender at Govan. In January 780 Dumbarton Rock burned, but who lit the fire and for what reason we do not know. The next time we hear about the kingdom, it was by a different name, in a different age.

Strathclyde, 870. A viking army of Irish, Frisians and Scandinavians unleashed themselves upon Dumbarton Rock, conquering the fort and enslaving its ruler. For two years he festered in a Dublin prison, chained and ransomed at exorbitant prices, before being murdered in a manner ill-befitting the king of the Clyde. As for his kinsmen, those who were not enslaved moved their court and kingdom to Govan and it was from here that an artistic explosion erupted in the form of decorated stones and grave covers. Many famous 'hogback' monuments owe their origins to Govan and, thus, the legacy of Alt Clut. They are but one product of the multicultural canvas of Norse, Pictish, Northumbrian, Brythonic and Irish artistry championed by the surviving elites of the tenth-century kingdom which, by this point, was rebranded as Strathclyde.[318]

Contemporary with this renaming was the increasing use of the term 'Alba', which represented an evolution of the classical 'Albion', a unifying label that encompassed Scots, Gaels, Britons and Picts, making it less specific than previous names like 'Pictland'. As Alba rose to importance, *Strat Clut* emerged from its Clyde-based chrysalis. Numerous other names dot tenth- and eleventh-century mentions of the kingdom: Brythonic warriors 'fell upon the towns of the Scandinavians' across Northumbria in the 920s, giving rise to the territory of Cumberland, named after the *Cymry* (Britons). In this same decade, King Eadward of the West Saxons was hailed as overlord of the *Stræcledwealas* and, in the next, 'the land of the Cumbrians' submitted to his successor Æthelstan. At the famous Battle of *Brunanburh* Strathclyde pulled no punches. They were a major player alongside men from Orkney, Wales and Scotland and, despite losing, remained fierce adversaries of the English for decades. In 945 King Edmund launched a punitive raid against 'Cumberland' (meaning Strathclyde); twenty-one years later there was a reprisal against the *Westmoringas* (Westmorland) and later a 'king of the Cumbrians' became connected to the myth of Eadgar's imperial coronation in 973.

Strathclyde suffered a death by a thousand cuts moving into the eleventh century. In 1000 King Æthelred the Ill-Counselled sent a raiding party their way in vengeance for sheltering viking crews and, with 'sufficient ferocity' they were plundered by an earl of Bamburgh in 1038, later suffering a 'violent subjugation' at the hands of the Scots in 1070. Ultimately, in 1107, the 'Cumbrian regions' became just a small corner of Scotland: conquered Strathclyde, Alt Clut, dimly remembered through a dozen different names in a dozen different languages. By the thirteenth century the Brythonic tongue that had first uttered the words of *The Gododdin* faded completely and the Old North was no more, cast into the shadows of lore and legend. This is how we remember the kingdom, no matter its name.

SWEORDORA

In 1679 the wandering Celia Fiennes described an expansive mere in Cambridgeshire as 'three mile broad and six mile long. In the midst is a little island where a great store of wildfowle breed'. This was Whittlesey Mere, playing no small role in highlighting to Celia the many marvels of Britain. In the years following, she took up travelling for travelling's sake, galloping across the country simply to see it all. 'The ground is all wet and marshy but there are several little channels [which] run into it ... by boats people go up to this place'; nor was she alone in traipsing the wilderness which, by her time, was already changing. '[W]hen you enter the mouth of the Mer it looks formidable and it's often very dangerous by reason of sudden winds that will rise like hurricanes', wrote Celia, immortalising a landscape lost forever.[319] Whittlesey was the last of the great swamps to be drained, once a vast bog that encompassed subsidiary fens like Yaxley, Holme and Farcet, today the site of Peterborough's suburbs and innumerable irrigation ditches. Now, the water of Whittlesey emerges only if one digs deep, into Sweordoran soil.

Many things end up in the fen; hopes, dreams, ambitions, Spitfire planes, fourteenth-century silver thuribles and incense dispensers. The latter assemblage was deposited during a time of crisis, the Dissolution of the Monasteries in the 1540s, alongside blocks of quarried stone and the remnants of barges that once ferried goods between Sawtry and Ramsey Abbey. When the mere was drained, the wildfowl, eels and fish that once called this place home all left, the sedge and reed, once dominant, were desiccated. These elements of a prehistoric ecosystem had persisted since the Mesolithic Period and had been manipulated by settlers ever since. The 300 hides ascribed to the Sweordora in the *Tribal Hidage* came from somewhere, the toil of eel-wranglers, egret-catchers, bog-miners. In the 1146 foundation charter of Sawtry Abbey, the mere and a north-western promontory called 'Swere Point' and, behind it, land called 'Swere Hord' were listed. Six centuries later other promontories like Grimeshord and Alderhord, where *-ord* effectively means 'a portion', were still included on maps. Whatever became of 'Swere Hord' is unknown. Nowadays it lies roughly beneath Thorne or Coates: the torpid landscape that named it has been mutated irreversibly and, with it, the Sweordora vanished.

'Sweor-' is an example of folk etymology where the gradual evolution of the Old English *sweora-* (for 'neck') changed into 'sweor' and then 'sweord' and then finally 'Sword Point', a reference to the striking topography of the promontory, piercing the northernmost edge of Whittlesey Mere and providing occupants a natural pier to fish from, shores to haul boats and land to make homely.

At *sweora-ord*, 'the point at the end of the neck of land', settlers pressed cheese, picked their noses and cleaned their ears, all activities observable through the Roman and early medieval finds recovered from Stilton and Peterborough. The shores of Whittlesey would have been constantly active: cold shoes splashing in the black mud, writhing trout and flapping waterfowl snuffed out by frigid farmers. Local clay was baked and used to make funerary pots distributed along the river Nene from kilns like Warsford, Chesterton and Yaxley. In the eighth century at least one *sceat* minted at Domburg made its way to Sawtry. At either end of the North Sea were these wood-panelled fen-side central places. Domburg was a vital node in the trading networks of the Low Countries, walled by sand dunes and sheltered from northerly winds. The 'hurricanes' mentioned by Celia Fiennes were these same winds, give or take a few centuries for, like Domburg, on Zeeland, Whittlesey functioned as an extension of the North Sea, another 'outer rim' bazaar encouraging three-day journeys in either direction.

The twelfth-century *Book of Ely* labels these regions as home to the 'southern Angles living on the great fen on which the island of Ely is situated' and, prior to industrial drainage, the East Anglian fen, much like the Humber Wash, was more water than land. Affinities and allegiances looked east and were, like Dál Riatan fortunes, tied not to shores but seas. The engraved fragments of a sixth-century square-headed brooch from Sawtry and a lozenge from Folksworth, imported from Pas-de-Calais, another gilded example that washed up here from Lincolnshire, are the connective trappings of water folk. Otherwise, unknown, we can infer the names

of former residents like Wynnbeald, Sunmær and an Old Norse 'king' via local toponyms: Wimblington, Somersham and Conington. In the sixteenth century the antiquarian William Camden wrote that the 'exprese remains of an ancient castle' could be seen at Conington which he claimed had been the palace of 'Turkill the Dane', a character who persists in local myth. According to Camden, Cnut the Great (1016-1035) had given Turkill rulership over Whittlesey, commanding him to divide and manage the settlements' access to dry land. By Camden's time the marshes were still rich 'by the commodity of fishing, the plentiful feeding, and the abundance of turfe gotten for fewell' and he wrote, based on information given to him by 'ancient predecessours of good credite', that a noteworthy ditch on the mere's brim separating Whittlesey and Ramsey was called 'Sweresdelf'. The sword-edge of the Sweordora.

These island-dwelling patricians were never trapped by their terrain and would have never drained Whittlesey Mere to rid it of moisture;[320] * they had door-to-door access to a tax-free commercial motorway. A lightly-corroded copper *sceat* minted in southern England is just one piece of evidence for this, an unusual coin which depicts seemingly random squiggles and the outstretched pose of a formless pontificator (CAM-6EB843). Is this the faded visage of a half-remembered Roman antecedent? The abstract depiction of the 'Weapon Dancer'? A character from *Beowulf*, perhaps one of the Finns, Geats or Danes raging so rampant across the North Sea?

They would have thrown axes, like a sixth-century example recovered from Huntingdon; they would have worn long brooches like those known from Peterborough; they would have used, copied and bartered coins like the varied *sceattas* minted in Kent, East Anglia and along the Humber. Picking through the litter of the Sweordora we can see what they wore, what they did and how they did it; we can make judgements about the owner of a Kentish garnet brooch (CAM-274762) or the horse which was once emblazoned with a swirling gilded mount (CAM-758D07). Maybe such things were given as bridal gifts, unions between Heligoland and East Anglia, Frisia and the Gyrwas, *Texla* and Ely. Maybe they are loot from forgotten battles, or the spoils dispensed by swamp kings. People were lovers here, they were children, farmers, fishers, warriors. They were slaves, servants, independent, autonomous, unbothered.

When Whittlesey was drained all of this was lost. We are left now with memories of a patchwork people, re-assembled and re-defined. They, like Celia Fiennes, travelled the world, saw it all and brought pieces of it back home.

---

* They may have installed canals and causeways to ease travel and bolster fisheries but not with the same rigour as later fourteenth-to-seventeenth century irrigative works.

'Teyrnllwg'

In the *History of the Britons* the character Catel Durnluc offers hospitality to a saint on entry into Powys. Praised for his charity, Durnluc is positioned as biblically virtuous, almost as legendary as Brychan and Gwallog as a named vessel for a story set in the distant past. The name 'Durnluc', however, survived for much longer, entering Modern Welsh as 'Teyrnllwg' via genealogical lists. *Teyrn-* ('king') and *-wg* (a territorial suffix) combined to create the idea of a previously unknown kingdom. By the eighteenth century, antiquarian Iolo Morgannwg solidified this idea, lulling subsequent generations into following the trend. Charles Onam, writing in 1921, following on from the work of William Stubbs who proposed 'Teyrnllwg' connected Powys to Rheged, was so bold as to place this lost realm: 'the lands between the Ribble and the Dee [were] originally known as Therynllwg, of which the later Powys was the surviving remnant.' It wouldn't be until the 1960s that the idea of a missing kingdom of 'Teyrnllwg' was refuted but this fascinating middle zone in north-west England, sandwiched between the northern edge of Wales and the Pennines, encompassing today's Manchester, Liverpool and Lancaster, is still ripe for exploration.[321]

'Teyrnllwg' evidently did not exist but it is as good a name for this chapter as any, as we gaze over the candles that were lit in the post-Roman gloom of the north-west. Abutting Craven, Elmet, Kintis and Strathclyde and bounded in parts by the rivers Ribble and Mersey, this region is typically absent from maps of 'Dark Age England', but just because a name can't be placed does not mean these regions were silent.

They were very much the opposite. Pollen analyses from White Moss and the edges of Craven suggest a change in agricultural practices between 480-580 CE, as woodland began to be managed on a relatively intense scale and, while uneven, the sparsely populated regions of Lancashire and Greater Manchester were noisy with the sound of falling trees and braying oxen. Joseph Delaney, author of the criminally underrated *Spooks* series, populated this realm with boggarts, bugganes, ghosts and ghasts. Like Tolkien, Delaney was inspired by a reservoir of older folklore from the Early Medieval Period.

When Wilfrid was granted land here in the seventh century, *iuxta Rippel* was included. Previously suggested to be restricted to the southern Yorkshire Dales, lands 'around the Ribble' could technically encompass the West Lancashire lowlands on either side of the river as far south as Makerfield up to Whalley. The former has been suggested by Denise Kenyon as a hybrid regional name formed through the Old English creolisation of an existing native name, it was probably a small unit centred on Ashton, Ince and Newton. Whalley, however, was a prolific manufacturer and exporter of stone crosses from the ninth century which lines up with what we know of land grants in the north-west. As with Wilfrid's endowments, these pockets of land were gifted to the burgeoning Northumbrian church as part of a patronage system, not evidence of outright conquest but certainly indicative of expansive ecclesiastical governance. *Iuxta Rippel*, then, might have been larger than previously stated. Cartmel 'and all the Britons with it' were also granted to Cuthbert in the 670s. The boundaries and histories of the British kingdoms that lay to the west of the Pennines are not known but this was undoubtedly no vacuum. These lands were inhabited and if these ecclesiastical land grants are anything to go by, *already* sub-divided into easily recognisable units.

Mapping these pockets is difficult but can be done to some extent through place names. The scant traces of concentrations around Wigan, the Fylde, Rossendale Forest and Cheetham suggest late-surviving Brythonic speakers. Some examples include Preese, Great Eccleston, Pendleton and Oldham. These toponyms include archaic elements, mixtures of Old English and Old Welsh words or generic allusions to oldness. Their distribution falls loosely into defined belts, corridors and pockets of less marginal land, suggesting an organised network of communities divided by embayments and lowlands. The Mersey was one such boundary marker although its name originates from Old English. Still, despite the fact that it probably wasn't given this name until the seventh century, we can reasonably assume it, and the surrounding marshes, already functioned as a nether-space. In the Roman Period important crossing points along the Runcorn Gap and between Wilderspool and Warrington certainly suggest that there was a desire to ford this limit. Nico Ditch and Beca Bank, un-dated linear earthworks near Manchester, have also been argued as extensions of these north-westerly borders. Similar to the Aberford Dyke to the east, these ditches may have bounded Craven and Elmet's western outlands and were used as points to monitor trade and transit. A debased Carolingian coin and several Northumbrian issues from Attermire Cave, Settle and the haematite ore from Austwick would suggest that Craven's residents looked westwards towards this region; a suspected market-site at Meols on the Wirral, where Frisian and Northumbrian coins were found, would suggest they looked back eastwards. Other Northumbrian hoards from Ribchester, Lancaster, the Cartmel peninsula and even near Aldport in Manchester indicate frequent trade and wealth; Aldport means 'old market'. The presence of Northumbrian material would imply that Old English speakers eventually dominated this region of England, too, but again the evidence is tricky. A gold finger ring was discovered in Castlefield, perhaps a gift of patronage?[322] Several hybridised toponyms reflecting both Old English and Old Welsh, like Penwortham and Cheetham, would imply a very slow linguistic development, the slow acculturation of Brythonic speakers into Old English might be a symptom of the bit-by-bit process of Northumbrian land annexation in the north-west, to fuel church grants. Even Manchester, despite its characteristically Old English name, is a derivation of the Latin *Mamucium*. In contrast, Celtic place names are conspicuously absent around the Lune Valley except the eponymous river. A Roman Period tribe called the Contrebis may have existed here, later

Illustration from the 'Tract on the First Arrival of the Saxons' (Cotton MS Caligula VIII, ff. 28v-29r) from a late twelfth-century manuscript copy, depicting the royal bloodlines of Wessex, Mercia, Kent, Bernicia and Deira, connected to one another via apocryphal antecedents and the survivors of Noah's flood. The so-called divine provenance of the monolithic 'English'.

replaced by a Germanic-speaking successor kingdom occupying a clearly defined territory near Kirkby Lonsdale.[323] Ultimately, such a hypothesis relies on disparate evidence. Old Norse toponyms like Birkby, near Cartmel, contain the linguistic element *bretar-* ('Briton'), suggesting that even in the tenth century there were conservative pockets of linguistically Celtic communities. The later hundred of Amounderness, although a tenth-century Hiberno-Norse territory, may have been established atop a pre-existing lordship in the Fylde, not dissimilar to the situation suggested for Man and the Lune Valley. Likewise, the Old Norse toponym of Coniston ('king's estate') does not automatically mean that there *weren't* rulers here beforehand, and that Scandinavians didn't simply insert themselves into and overtake local hierarchies.

The whole notion of confined early medieval ethnic divisions has its roots in Bede's work where he grouped the British Isles into five 'peoples', each with their own neatly separated languages, and waxed poetic about the 'Angles, Saxons and Jutes'. He then ascribed moral failings to whole ethnicities, chief among them the Britons, reflecting more about his and the church's views than any racial characteristics. In the second book of his *Ecclesiastical History*, Bede writes that it was prophesied 'that the faithless Britons, who had rejected the offer of eternal salvation, would incur the punishment of temporal destruction'. Indeed, sometime before 616, King Æðelfrið of Northumbria brought such retribution to British monks outside Chester which Bede framed as a deliverance. Scarred post-Roman remains known from Heronbridge, outside the city walls, would certainly suggest that this punishment had more bite than bark.[324] The battle of Chester was re-framed by Bede as a righteous outcome caused by several centuries of British depredations. In reality, it is unclear what prompted Æðelfrið to march into the north-west to wreak havoc but that need for peripatetic warlords to extract booty from their neighbours is as sure as any.

Generally, such material is rare in the north-west, especially in Lancashire. There are a few burials known from Inskip and Hasty Knoll and an isolated North Sea pottery vessel found in Manchester, but these finds usually lack provenance and context. Four pit houses found beneath Deansgate, Manchester, have been argued to be 'Anglo-Saxon' but there is simply no way to ascribe ethnicity to a relatively uniform building style.[325] These cobbled yards and square-built domains are only evidence of squatters dwelling above the extant road where rivulets of watery time cut new inroads through old stone but whatever language they spoke or whatever identity they clung to is unknowable. Did they look forward or back? Of equal dubiousness is a 'boat burial' discovered in 1973 near Quernmore.[326] Shaped like a dugout canoe, two large halves of a wooden coffin were unearthed from sodden peat found to be housing a burial shroud and the acidic remains of hair and toenails. Radiocarbon dated alongside two other boat-shaped burials from the Pennines (at Featherstone and Haltwhistle), this individual was placed in their watery tomb between 500 and 700. Not an actual boat, but carved to resemble one, this bygone observer would have overlooked the Irish Sea from the canoe's resting place, a fitting final view. Whilst the notion of a boat burial atop a high hill parallels the Sutton Hoo Man and, thus, eastern affinities, the form of the coffin is closer to native canoes and rafts. There were also no grave goods that could reasonably be ascribed to a material identity. Like the Deansgate squatters, the 'Quernmore Canoe Burial' is another unknown needlessly ascribed an ethnic origin, mirroring Bede too closely.

The north-west is still a uniquely distinguished area of England, teeming with diverse independent communities. The ever-nearing edges of Liverpool and Manchester have done nothing to quell the local spirits of their respective cities and even areas like Preston, overlooked in favour of Lancaster, have long roots as important priestly centres of English history. In the Viking Age much of the north-west fell under Hiberno-Norse influence and, at risk of repeating lines from previous chapters, it seems clear that the raiders were not carving roads anew but stepping into the shoes of pre-existing settlers. Several large multinucleated settlements bound through social and resource ties existed already, formed out of post-Roman communities that later were transformed and renamed through Old English as the Northumbrian church inflated. Kirkby Lonsdale, sometimes Yorkshire, Lancashire, or Cumbria, is a perfect example of the fluid identities that were flowing and silting in the waters of the north-west. They surely deserve a name.

ŪNDĀLAS

Names are important. Oundle, Northamptonshire has defied satisfactory etymological explanation for decades, affording this unassuming village a not insignificant degree of acclaim within certain circles. If it hadn't been for the confusing name, would Oundle even be remembered?

Said to hail from the Old English term for 'undivided', Oundle is mentioned by several titles across the eighth century and beyond, as *Undolum*, *Undela* and *Undale*, each meaning something like 'the undivided folk', or 'those which have no share'.[327] Bede describes a 'province called *Inundalum*' twice. First, that it contained a monastery 'called *Inhrypum*' and, again, as reference to a people rather than a place (*Undulana mægð*). From *un-* and *-dāl* for 'no share' or 'no division', it might be that the *Undālas gained their name from an external recognition of poor or marginal land; they lived on a 'bad share' or maybe their land resisted divisions by overlords. We have seen throughout this book the enduring names of certain groups; the *Undālas can be placed comfortably alongside the Hwicce and Gyrwas. Theories linger in the undulating ground of Oundle, located on the western banks of the river Nene. Seemingly, this river also failed to divide people, but was there anything here worth dividing?

Along Ashton Road the land conceals Neolithic and Bronze Age ditches, pits and barrows; cropmarks, tracks and palaeochannels carve their way through the fieldscapes. Presumably, there was a substantial cemetery here, as recognised through the discovery of six collared urns in the Victorian Period. These earthworks, and a site near Ashton, became an extensive field system in the Iron Age and then the hinterlands of a Roman villa.[328] Part of a Samian ware cup, some miscellaneous bronze pins, bits of pottery and a few undescribed coins were unearthed here in the nineteenth century. More recently a sixth-century chip-carved cruciform brooch and a possible coin of Magnus Maximus were found within the vicinity of the town; iron slag and offcuts are also recorded from Oundle Wood, perhaps the site of an old smithy. Several dateable features of the Iron Age and later Medieval Periods, like ridge-and-furrow fields and a moat, are recognised from Oundle but early medieval evidence is inconspicuous. If we turn instead to textual sources, such as the eleventh-century *On the Resting Places of the Saints*, we see a different story.

Listed in the first half of the document, which predominantly covers saints buried in Northumbria and Mercia, Cett is placed in *Undola* along the *Nén*. Like this book, *On the Resting Places* is organised somewhat arbitrarily with a few groups of geographically proximal names listed immediately alongside one another and others contradicting previous mentions. The style of the list is influenced by

A manuscript depicting King Æthelstan of the English presenting a gospel book to the community of St Cuthbert at Chester-le-Street, housed in Corpus Christi College, Cambridge (MS 183, ff. 1v).

Roman documents, and it was possibly even written overseas, cementing on to parchment the international fame generated by many of England's earliest saints. Cett is among the most obscure figures on the list. A 'D-lister' of the time and a patron for an obscure group that had long ceased to exist when the document was compiled. A more famous individual, Wilfrid, died in Oundle in 709 and over two centuries later Archbishop Wulfstan was also buried here. Between these two funerals Offa of Mercia held court nearby at *Yrtlingaburg* (Irthlingborough) and a local monastery was apparently burned down according to chronicles but, otherwise, Oundle remained on royal peripheries, consistently inhabited by famous religious individuals. In 963 it was gifted to Peterborough Abbey and in the following decades a small chapel was probably built here if the discovery of a ceremonial bronze plate and some eleventh-century pottery is anything to go by. If not, then Oundle still serves as a great example of saintly territories. Like the boundaries of the *Haliwerfolc*, the successive deaths of three different saints, each one arguably more important than the last, must have crystallised notions of local identity within the town. Visitors may have approached the 'undivided land' and thought of it as Cett's country, Wilfrid's country or Wulfstan's country, similar to how we might associate certain parts of the USA with rockstars. Some saints were universal, their fame so widespread that they defied space entirely, whereas others were regionally focused or even localised. This could also change over time. Cuthbert and, by extension, his holy folk became remembered in Durham even though they had previously wandered elsewhere. As the relics and remains of the saint moved so, too, did the people and the territory associated with them. Were the *Undālas* undivided by their mutual admiration for multiple saints buried on their doorstep? Was their territory defined by their 'bad land', the prehistoric and Roman ditches or more nebulous conceptual markers? These celebrities might not have had any particular bearing on the development of a location, but their posthumous presence informed external and internal notions of self.

With the *Undālas* we get a bottled example of how saints, their bones and their memories informed perceptions of a polity. On a very small scale in Northamptonshire, religious figures played as vital a role as kings and war-bands and, while the evidence they have left behind might not be as tangible as a chip-carved brooch or a usurper's coin, they were clearly one of the few things that resisted division.

UNECUNGA-CA & OTHERS

The *Tribal Hidage* lists several unknown territories which are usually placed in the Cambridgeshire fen. Information about them is either non-existent or entirely speculative. Indeed, even placing some of these polities affords them too much integrity. Take Hendrica, a *regio* valued at 3,500 hides in the earliest version of the *Hidage*, although later subtracted to 3,000. The changes in value may reflect nothing beyond scribal errors or subsequent scribes' attempts to invent some numerical significance. The total value of all the kingdoms in one recension of the *Hidage* is 144,000, which has been argued to be symbolic, so edits to Hendrica's value might just stem from a need to meet an arbitrary whole.

Hendrica is listed after the Cilternsætna which suggests it was located nearby. When taken together the hidage values of the Cilternsætna (4,000) and Hendrica (3,000) add up to 7,000 which has been argued to be a nominal number, the economic assessment denoting a 'secondary kingdom' such as Lindsey. It is worth remembering that Lindsey is listed as 'Lindsey with Heathfelðland', implying that both halves made up the total 7,000, not just Lindsey itself. It is not implausible that the Cilternsætna and Hendrica were two halves of a similar entity. Additionally, tallying up the hidage values of all the miscellaneous Cambridgeshire fen territories, the Spalde, Gyrwas and so on, gives us a total of 6,900, just shy of the 'nominal' value for Lindsey. Suppose this number represents a 'secondary kingdom', which is to be debated. In that case, the numerous territories of the Cambridgeshire fen may have coalesced into a singular entity had conditions allowed.

Our evidence for Hendrica is that it was located near the Chilterns and was valued at around 3,000 hides, the same value as three *burhs* in the tenth century, so reason would suggest it was fairly substantial. Arosætna (600) and the mysterious 'Unecunga-ca' (1,200) are both listed alongside it, suggesting they, too, must be located nearby. A compelling if unprovable explanation for the mystery surrounding both Hendrica and 'Unecunga-ca', why we cannot place them on a map and why no place names correlate their locations, was suggested in 1947 by Josiah Cox Russell. Via palaeography, Russell concluded that both 'Hendrica' and 'Unecunga-ca' were scribal errors and miscommunications of two other polities. He suggested that 'Hendrica' was a perversion of the word 'Sudrica' (Surrey) and 'Unecunga-ca' a perversion of 'Sunninga'. The explanation for these misspellings stemmed from Russell's belief that the *Tribal Hidage* was passed between Kentish and Mercian hands and that the specific regional styles of copiers influenced the later errors in the manuscript.[329] Considering the *Hidage* was probably read out loud and then copied down, later versions of it without the pronunciation alongside may very well have miscommunicated the exact names of polities, especially if they were transcribed hastily.

If the identification with somewhere near Sussex and Wessex is followed and Hendrica and 'Unecunga-ca' represent mistranslations of 'Sudrica' and 'Sunninga', then they bear investigating. *Suþrige* in the tenth-century *Burghal Hidage* was valued at around 3,400 hides, close to the combined value of Hendrica and 'Unecunga-ca'. The *Sunningas* afford us another chance to look beyond simple mathematics, however. Unlike 'Unecunga-ca', which is gibberish, 'Sunninga' correlates with Sonning, Berkshire, which was a lesser centre of the bishopric of Ramsbury from 909 CE; tenth-century stonework can still be seen in St Andrew's Church. The village is located near Reading and Basingstoke, both of which also have early medieval ancestry in the *Rēadingas* and *Basingas*. All three of these *regiones* follow a well-observed trend of hailing from a common ancestor. They are each the 'people of Sunna, Rēada and Basa' respectively, although *rēada-* might alternatively be a topographical descriptor denoting coloured soil. As for the *Basingas*, they are mentioned in passing in the 871 CE entry in *The Anglo-Saxon Chronicle*; Ælfred 'fought against the [viking] host at *Basengum*, and there the Danes won the victory'. Both the [A] and [E] variants of the *Chronicle* mention this and also Reading. Excavations nearby at Cowdery's Down have revealed an assortment of sixteen rectilinear buildings and two pit houses, some with suggestions of raised wooden flooring. This was a substantial central place and, whilst the site lacked in artefacts, could be dated to the sixth and seventh centuries.[330] Founded with tall roofs and mighty support beams, a royal *vill* for local potentates. Conquered by the Great Heathen Army, *Basengum* went on to produce some interesting skeletal remains.

Dated between 776 and 899, a disarticulated cranium of an adolescent female found lit Oakridge, Basingstoke, might represent the victim of grisly facial mutilation. Shallow marks above the individual's teeth and nose would have severed arteries shortly before her death since it appears that her nose was removed, and her forehead cut. That this poor individual suffered so much trauma can be ascertained via osteological analysis, but for what reason is unclear.[331] Her cranium was located near an Iron Age earthwork which probably functioned as a border for the *Basingas* in the eighth and ninth centuries. Was she beheaded *after* being mutilated? Was her head mounted on a boundary pole? Several law codes from the seventh to the eleventh centuries verify mutilation as a practice for shunning thieves and rapists across Wessex, but this instance may have been localised and uniquely cruel. We do not know anything about the individual's life up to that point, but we can make some guesses that her final moments were bloody, loud and perhaps at the mercy of a mob. What were her closing thoughts? This book has concerned itself with overviews of socio-economic territories but the residents of all these realms would have had dreams, ambitions, hopes, fears and childhoods just like this woman. It might well be that she was an outlier, a member of no kin, an outcast or exile and hated for it. Maybe she was viewed as a *nīw-fara*, a stranger, someone who straddled the world between little kingdoms and held no common identity whatsoever; in the words of *Beowulf*, a *mære mearcstapa* ('notorious boundary-walker'). Trespasser. Outsider. Troll. A law code from seventh-century Kent offers a peek into such perceptions

> If a stranger ... who has come from afar strays off the track and neither calls out nor blows a horn, [they] should be taken for a thief, either to be killed or to be redeemed.

Another scribal error suggested by Russell was the Herefinna, valued at 1,200 hides. This palaeographical conundrum may conceal the unmentioned but geographically similar polity of the **Hyrstingas*, based at Hurstingstone Hundred, Huntingdonshire.

The **Hyrstingas* are obscure, but their etymology associates them with forests; they are the 'people of the wooded hill'. The name of the hundred, Hurstingstone, also offers a glimpse at the meeting point of this archaic group, at an old monolith atop a mound. The current 'Hursting Stone', known as the Abbot's Chair, is a twelfth-century fragment of a standing cross but it would have had precursors. It probably replaced a now-lost pagan monument. All of this land was intensely wooded in the Early Medieval Period as can be gleaned from local place names: Yaxley, Sapley, Woolley, Stonely, Abbotsley, Pidley (where *-lēah* means 'forest clearing'). The need for a centrally identifiable place for the 'forest dwellers', to discuss common issues and adjudicate crimes seems obvious, atop a high hill overlooking the dark forest. Whether they were independent or beholden to an overlord from Mercia would have mattered little to the **Hyrstingas*, sheltered as they were by their geography. As they were but a small contingent of the Middle Angles, so, too, were the 'forest dwellers' made up of even smaller unknowable groups.

Found in Suffolk, an eighth-century incomplete copper-alloy pendant inscribed with runes stating 'Budheard the Bilhearding made this' suggests ever-tinier tribes (SF-DC39C5). The **Bilheardingas* or 'people of Bilheard' might have been as small as a family, just a father and his son, a blacksmith and her apprentice. Perhaps Budheard lost his creation on his walk home through the marshes en route to impress his elder.

Place names allow us to speculate, although with caution, about the founders of patchwork England. The Isle of Axholme, North Lincolnshire, is surrounded by a cluster of -*ingas*- toponyms, as one example, like the 'people of Mæssa' at Messingham, the 'heath people' at Rossington or Imma's folk of Immingham. There is also Faldingworth ('enclosure of the animal folders') and Spridlington ('village of the spear people') farther east. In the *Life of St Guthlac*, the protagonist is said to hail from the tribe of the *Guthlacingas* but whether or not this group existed already or if the name was just derived from Guthlac's is unknown. It was probably a play on words: *guth*- from 'war' and -*lac* from 'gift' highlighting Guthlac's prowess before he was a monk and, by extension, the status of his family. Another example would be how the [E] version of *The Anglo-Saxon Chronicle* mentions the *Eforwicingas* or 'people of York'; these appear to be later names applied to pre-existing political or judicial centres. On the other hand, considering the *Basingas*, *Rēadingas* and *Sunningas* are all situated in what would become the heartlands of Wessex, it seems reasonable to postulate that they represent its forerunners. The *Basingas* may have even been part of the Meonwara realm, rubbing shoulders with the *regiones* of *Andeferas*, *Cleras*, and *Micheldever*. Similarly, the *Tribal Hidage* begins with a reference to 'the first *Myrcna* lands' which may reflect that many of these formerly individual -*sæte* territories became what was later known as Mercia. The Middle Angles are also represented by several of the smaller polities. A stray charter from the Hwicce mentions 'the clearing of Eadwold's folk' (*Eadwolding leahe*, S 786) and there was also 'the land with its boundaries which belongs to the *vill* called Wican in the *Sæferne regio*' in Worcestershire, mentioned between 757 and 774 (S 142).

Finally, the *Hidage* records the Noxgaga (5,000) and Ohtgaga (2,000) which have long evaded placements. They are referred to alongside the Isle of Wight but might be either different names or miscommunications of *Rōtaland* and *Framland*, near Leicestershire. Perhaps a placement doesn't even matter. Noxgaga and Ohtgaga represent the enduring quest to identify a common name and place that unites a historic people. In direct contrast to 'Teyrnllwg', here we are not searching for a name for a place but somewhere to place a name. Judging by their hidage assessments, Noxgaga and Ohtgaga were wealthy; the former dwarfs the Cilternsætna by a thousand. The very fact that such significant *regiones* could be mistranscribed, forgotten and then completely obscured through the hundred or so years the *Hidage* was in use really does demonstrate this document's difficult nature. That 'Noxgaga and Ohtgaga' were archaic names even by the time of its creation is a possibility. When the names went out of fashion so, too, did any attempts at identifying their locations. Either this theory or something closer to Russell's suggestion regarding 'Unecunga-ca', that they are complete gibberish resulting from subsequent rewrites of the same document, seems logical. The -*ga* suffix is similar to the Frankish -*gau*, seen already in Ely and Surrey, tentatively placing Noxgaga and Ohtgaga on the south or east coast.

As large as 5,000 hides or as small as a runic inscription, a need to *belong* has persisted throughout history. Even for those who do not the very fact that they don't has defined them.

WEORGORAN & WHAT REMAINS

As with many cities, Worcester began as a well-resourced and strategically located Roman fort, erected atop a pre-existing Iron Age trackway which forded the Severn. Later, people developed the hinterlands, inheriting the masonry, shelter and road network. By 691 this *civitas* was still recognised as belonging to the *uueorgornas*, appearing as *Wigranceastre* in 750. The Severn follows one of its straighter paths past the city, so the proposed etymology of Weorgoran, *vigora* from Gaulish for 'winding river', is difficult to quantify. Maybe it was metaphorical. Here in the city, as with all cities, all manner of winding rivers, both physical and metaphysical, converged to bring and export goods to the world beyond. And Weorgoran encompassed more than just Worcester; 'the woodland clearing of the Weorgoran' is recorded in a Mercian charter and when Æthelflæd 'ordered the *burh* at *Weorgenacesatre* to be built for the protection of all the people' this encompassed all subsidiary estates across a radius of about a day's travel. Worcester's evolution into a *burh* in the tenth century reflects most clearly that Roman inheritance; the burghal network connected southern England via military and economic checkpoints to dissipate the impact of raiders, affording Worcester and other places a greater status as a revised central stronghold. Roman forts became English *burhs*. Placed equidistantly along these winding rivers, Worcester's Severn-side location made it an integral and effective checkpoint, slowing riverine approaches into the Hwicce.

The extent of Hwiccian expansion is a tricky thing, however. Wychwood in western Oxfordshire has long been suggested to have made up the kingdom's borders; 'the wood of the Hwicce' but there is a cluster of similar toponyms as far away as Rutland: three 'woodlands of the Hwicce' (Witchley Heath, Wichley Leys and the *Hwicceslea* hundreds), a 'valley of the Hwicce' (Whissendine)[332] and, just to the south, the 'estate of the Hwicce' (Whiston, Northamptonshire). There is also the 'riverbank of the Hwicce' (Wychnor, Staffordshire). Are these the far-flung outposts of a diminished kingdom? An annexation of *Rōtaland*? How far, truly, can a kingdom and an identity persist when removed from its core?

'Weorgoran' ceased to be used as a group identifier after the eighth century, more often than not replaced by 'Hwicce'. Maybe it was a precursor name or a sub-group within the kingdom. We can never know. The phenomena of smaller, more nebulous territories existing within and between many of the kingdoms covered in this book can only really be approached towards the end of our narrative. At the most intimate, local level, commonality and togetherness persisted around mutual places, the more defended and connected the better. Even when the idea of England was solidified, these tiny neighbourhoods were *still* being called by local names. What remains is a list of the most fascinating which could easily all make up their own book. Winteringham, North Lincolnshire derives from a group who believed they shared a common ancestor that appears in Lindsey's genealogy as Wōden's successor; Repton, a vital Mercian royal holding, started life as 'the hill of the Hrype';* even Mercia was known by many names, like '*Suðanhymbre*' ('south-Humbrians') and '*Suðangli*' ('south Angles').† It likely emerged out of territorial groupings based at Tamworth, Winchcombe and Breedon-on-the-Hill. Similarly, there are the north and south folk of East Anglia, segmented in the seventh or eighth centuries when three separate monarchs reigned over the broads. Later land grants to Sherborne, Dorset refer to a Brythonic community called *Lanprobi* already present, although this evidence is not unchallenged;[333] either the *Iceni* of Boudicca-fame or someone called **Ycel* is commemorated in Suffolk's Icklingham, Beda in Bedfordshire, Cana on Canvey Island, Haca in Hackney and Hæfer in Havering-atte-Bower, both in London. Hering in Harringay, Pada in Paddington, Tota in Tooting, Dene on the Dengie Peninsula, the war god Tīw in Tewin and Welwyn. *Modingahema*: Mottingham. The 'home of the elves' at Alvingham and the 'Goblin's church' of Pucklechurch.‡ The 'spring dwellers' of Wellingore and the Germano-Celtic **Dorcingas* along the river Mole. A *provincia* named after a loop in the Thames, the Horningas, existed somewhere in Berkshire, though they are difficult to place (S 1001). Benna's fortress, at Beningborough, is more obvious. Abingdon in Oxfordshire is apparently named after the Æbbingas, but legends have distorted most attempts at identifying the origin of this Thames-side town; so, too, are the **Wimlincgas* of Womenswold shrouded in ambiguity. Tolkien's Eorlingas have a historical parallel in Arlingham, Gloucestershire and Bede implies that Sunderland, *sundorlande*, originated as a 'special' land within or outside of Bernicia.§ He also

---

* Bede also refers to Ripon as *Hrypsetna*, the name deriving from a common element.

† Charters S 101 (722 - 736) and S 103 (716 - 745) list Æthelbald as 'king of the South Angles' and S 94 (716 - 737) as 'king of Mercia and of the South Angles'. If distinct, *Suðenglum* territory may have encompassed parts of London, Surrey and, possibly, the woodlands north of Essex. To complete all four arms of the compass, a 'North Saxonland' is sketchily recorded in *The Annals of Ulster*'s entry for 918, 'on the banks of the Tyne'. This may specifically refer to the diminished heartlands of the Eadwulfing dynasty that clung onto a vestigial Bernicia, centred on Bamburgh.

‡ From *pūcel* for 'little goblin', perhaps a garbled reference to a fallow deer as hypothesized by Carole Hough. Pucklechurch is first recorded in a tenth-century charter (S 553).

§ Sunderland was not alone as there would have been several 'special' tenurial monastic estates much like it. The estate of Snodland, in Kent, is listed as 'Snoddinglande' in a tenth-century lawsuit, though it is difficult to say if the name was commemorating a specific person in this case. Much and Little Wenlock, Shropshire, may both derive from **Wininicas* ('white enclosed place') referencing the limestone geology of a similarly enclosed ecclesiastical territory.

refers to *Tiovulfingacestir* ('fortress of the folk of Tiowulf') by the Trent where the folk of Lindsey were baptised by Northumbrian hands; either Caistor or Littleborough fit the bill for this untraceable redoubt. Other, more generic territories, are listed in lawsuits and rent-notes from the tenth and eleventh centuries: hints of the Ceastertuninga ('fortress folk'), the Heartingas (somewhere in Sussex), the Camp-sætena (S 911), and the *Wirlingas (probably Worlingworth, East Anglia). An inexhaustible list of minute field or copse-sized communities, where the entire sense of each name is just 'inhabitants of ___', can be teased through the *Bradsetena* (S 1591a), *Cregsetna* (S 331), *Fromesetinga* (S 727), the *Elmesetene* and *Ombersetene* (S 1597), the *Lilsætna* (S 723), *Incsetena* (S 1305), *Cruddesetene* (S 1577), *Ig-setna* (S 340), *Mossetna* (S 201), *Locsetna* (S 1350), *Worðig-saetena* (S 374), and finally the *Beonetsetena* (S 201). Now, most of these *can* be placed on a map, but the names would have been useful probably in very specific, resource-driven administrative decisions only, and it is worth raising questions about the local acceptance and long-standing currency of these external titles. Over in Mercia, Birmingham has one of the more glaring etymologies, from the Beormingas; then there are the 'ridge dwellers' of the Bilsæte in Bilston, Wolverhampton and the 'cave people'[334] of the Snottengas near Nottingham.* The remaining entities unmentioned from the *Tribal Hidage* also deserve a look: Widerigga, the East and West Wixna, their neighbours the East and West Willa, the Wigesta and Wihtgara too. In analysing this document, Chris Baker has attempted to place many of these names by following a clockwise rotation;[335] the Wigesta south of Lincolnshire, the Wixna between Ely and Spalding, the Wihtgara in Bedfordshire and the Widerigga in Buckinghamshire.† With that last one, a charter referring to 'the people of Wiðering' in Cambridgeshire suggests that they should be located elsewhere. Still, these might be two separate Wideriggas, just as we seemingly have several Hwicces and Elmets. The Wixna are remembered in *wixena broc* (Whitsun Brook, Worcestershire), a '*provincia Wisse*' mentioned in the *Life of St Guthlac* and also the river Wissey. The Willa might be preserved in the archaic Well Stream, Cambridgeshire. These territories' western and eastern contingents must have been divided by watercourses. Be they in Buckinghamshire or Cambridgeshire, the Widerigga display the difficult nature of pinpointing these realms. These borders were discrete, known in detail only by some, preserved in distorted form via oral traditions then fossilised as toponyms, local myths, landscape features and manipulated charters. And there are places not even mentioned in the *Hidage* despite being nearby; *Meahala* (Mepal), *Bilsingge* (Beezling Fen), *Beorningas* (Brangehill), *Gruntifen* (Grunty Fen).[336] What about

---

* Referred to as *Tig Guocobauc* ('house of caves') in Asser's *Life of Ælfred* which might be the original Brythonic name for the place, as with *Meicen* for Heathfelðland.

† The Wihtgara are probably the Wihtwara (on the Isle of Wight) but for the sake of argument an alternative suggestion is entertained. It is always possible 'Wihtgara' refers to a separate group.

The brothers Hengist and Horsa as they appear in Sir Edward Parrott's 'Pageant of British History' (1909). Claims that modern studies are 'rewriting history' by dispelling the Anglo-Saxon invasion myth fail to understand that all of history has been rewritten from the start, through various lenses at various points. Written history is there to be challenged to best dissect the past; what happened, when they did, who did what and why.

the Beansæte from Feckenham (S 190), the Grantesæte of Great Chesterford and the Stursæte of the river Stour? What of the Halsæte of Alcester[337] or the wasteland of *Ondred* in Sussex? What about Wroxeter's Rhiwsæte, Scrobsæte and Ercall? The Meallingas of Surrey? The Hæslingas of Cambridgeshire? The administrative districts of Morthen and Balne?* Essex's *Fengge* (Vange); the **Stepelsæte* and **Postsæte* along the Wye? What about Bernicia's early tribal centres of *Gefrin* and *Coria*; did they retain their individuality? These groups are from hagiographies, charters, the *Domesday Book*, even later Medieval tax rolls and forest codes. Some are just toponymic suffixes and guesses based on aerial archaeology; we haven't even reached the legendary or corrupted names from Welsh poetry!

Surely what remains is an admission that we are getting much of this wrong. To return to Worcestershire, in the early thirteenth century, the poet Laȝamon interpolated or invented a territory here, 'Dorchestre-seten', for his *Chronicle of Britain*. There was no singular process by which belonging and group identity were expressed in the post-Roman period. There was no set manner in which territories,

---

* Balne, which may have encompassed the riverlands between the Don and Aire, derives from either Middle English or Latin for 'bathing place'. The hypothesis that it represents a post-Roman territory rests on similar grounds to Burghshire and Elmet.

polities, kingdoms and overlordships developed. There was also no set time; -*sæte* names probably date to the later centuries of the Early Medieval Period with -*ingas* and -*wara* being slightly earlier. One or two even appear to be shorthand for other names entirely; the 'Beardsætena' of Bardney, the 'Badsetena' of Badsey (S 203), the 'Hiisetena' of Iona, the 'Wihtsætan' of Wight, and the 'Bocsætena' of Buckland (S 963). It is highly unlikely the residents of these locations referred to themselves in this way. Regionality and locality had the biggest hand in deciding where people's allegiances lay and how they viewed themselves alongside one another; even *not belonging* was a way to belong to something, some creed, some tenet. All across the disciplines of archaeology, history and linguistics are instances where things and people clash; the stylings of the Caenby warlord, Gildas' references to fire and famine, the faint loans between Germanic and Celtic languages. These crossover moments, periods and processes would have informed people's ideas of self and community but also otherness. They would have been perpetuated through funerary displays, literary traditions, annual cycles of warfare and raiding, the bestowal of wealth and gifts to foster familial loyalty and they would have been disrupted, morphed or reversed through responses to fluctuating economic, social and political fortunes. The battle that ended Pengwern was only one of many. At the core of all of these little kingdoms is more or less the presence of indigenous power. Indigenous in the sense of either 'pure Britons' or third-generation emigres from elsewhere using, adapting or carving out their niches within local power structures. Simply put, territorial power would not be expressed similarly across all of these locations were it not for the consistency of Late-into-post-Roman Britain. There are odd differences, sure, such as the varying poetic traditions between *The Gododdin* and *Beowulf*, but cattle-rustling, ring-giving and celebrating martial prowess in a mead hall remain the same. Even the lost realms of Rheged and the Golden Age Germanic coast hit similar beats, neither serving as historical locations but instead the traces of mutually desired greener grass. When Urien appears in the poem *Arise, Rheged*, he is an outsider, uniting imagined territories all with different names, acting as the idealised overlord. All tiers of socio-political allegiance appear in that text; variations of places we've already covered, like Aeron-*Eidywet*, appear in others. These are all ephemeral, but moving into the seventh century, polities started to stabilise and grow, many in eastern England using the most dominant language and mechanisms of power; Germanic dialects, hidage valuations and Christianity. Following Kent's footsteps, these would be the first kingdoms.

From the farmers and warriors buried at Sutton Hoo to the back-and-forth land parcelling of Sherborne, the evidence suggests power was already localised and insular within Britain, never the sudden gift or imposition of emergent 'Anglo-Saxon' invaders. You could pick more or less anywhere in the British Isles to observe this carefully pieced-together narrative through excavations, textual references and phonetic developments and it would say the same thing in different words.

All of these groups, and many more unmentioned, can be poked and teased out of these forms of evidence and others but, whether or not they used the names we have given them, is a mystery.

WESSEX

It may seem odd to jump from unidentifiable or miniscule folk groupings to *the* premier kingdom. How, in any sense, does Wessex suit this book's *raison d'être*?

To answer that requires moving away from its status in popular culture and the later ninth century. Wessex was a crucible from which the flames of England sprouted but it was not alone in its steadfastness; Bernicia survived the Viking Age as a diminished lordship and Lindsey, despite drowning in Old Norse toponyms, remained a vital borough well into the tenth century. From Wessex and, later Mercia, violent armies conquered the edges of Wales and moved northwards to put down and then annex Danish-occupied lands across England. Mercia, too, fell under West Saxon governance. By the time the Danes next invaded England, it was a unified realm with most former kingdoms converted into earldoms, regional differences, administrative distinctions and allegiances notwithstanding. Wessex became total, all-encompassing; where there were once little kingdoms there was now Wessex and from this admixture came England.

But Wessex itself has pure, undiluted roots, if we stick to the chronicles. Indeed, by Bede's time, 'West Saxon' was a new term, requiring explanation much as 'Northumbrian' did. Beforehand, areas we would now call Wessex (Hampshire, Wiltshire, Berkshire) were the fractious realms of the *Gewissæ*, a tribal identity like the Hwicce, meaning the 'strong' or 'trustworthy' ones. As late as 745, the archaic term *rex Gewissorum* was still used, even though alternatives like *rex Saxonum* eventually replaced it. In this regard, a 'Saxon' and then a '*West* Saxon' identity, was knowingly created and laid over another one. The *Gewissæ* were rebranded. Where they appear in chronicles, dubious as the entries may be, they are associated with slaughtering Britons and winning battles, the glorification of war. Classically opposed in the literature, both Gewissan and Brythonic warlords were a squabbling kaleidoscope of people from different backgrounds and different ideas. It was their union, not division, that formed Wessex.[338] Why else would so many of its earliest kings bear Brythonic names? Cerdic the creator, Cenwalh the coward, Cædwalla the conqueror. As with Lindsey's genealogy, the idea of it as an ethnically and linguistically pure 'Germanic' nation is a consequence of dynastic propaganda; these regnal tracts display Britons like Cædbæd 'Battle-Crow' and Cynegils. There is also Gewis, evidently a fictitious primogenitor created *after* Wessex was consolidated to explain the origin of the *Gewissæ*. This literary genesis of the West Saxons emerging out of a bloody battle where all Britons were either extinguished or enslaved is a myth but a workable one, manipulated and repeated during the reign of King Ine (689-726), as is suggested by his law codes which distinguish between *wealh* and West Saxon. These myths imply more about King Ine's reign and the social politics of his realm than they do his forebears. Above all else they point out the contradictory nature of distinguishing between 'Germanic' and 'Celtic'. The re-use of native barrow mounds and the adoption of Brythonic individuals into genealogies further the idea that these dynasts knew they were multicultural. When Bede wrote about Wessex, he was already imposing these eighth-century fortunes backwards in time; he pictured Ceawlin (560-592) as almost a *bretwalda*. We have no way of knowing these specifics, but this century saw the emergence and expansion of large barrow mounds in what would become Wessex, across Wiltshire and Dorset at Cuddesdon, Taplow and Rodmead Hill. These expressions of monumental status reflect the growth of regional kingship, the dawn of the *Gewissæ*, not at one centralised location but at many, and this process can be seen all over Britain: the inscribed stones of Wales that hint at powerful elites, the square-barrow cemeteries of Pictland, the fissiparous lineages of the Dál Riata. There were several kings of proto-Wessex,* just as there were in Essex and Powys, although, by Cædwalla's reign (685-688), the status and legends attached to him suggest not only that he unified these divisions, but also tied himself to a fictional legendary past, that of Cerdic and Cynric and Ceawlin, to homogenise future dynasties.

Many of these histories are myths and many of these myths are histories, parallel memories like *History of the Britons* in one corner and *The Anglo-Saxon Chronicle* in the other, immortalising different perspectives on the same thing and responding to each other via working legends and weaving tales. There was never a Saxon conquest, for one. The *adventus Saxonum*, the settlement of large groups of Germanic-speaking war-bands across *Britannia*, was a consequence, not a cause, of the gradual decline of state infrastructure and military governance across the Western Empire. The three or more centuries of migration, subsequent territorial upheavals and slow processes of settlement became remembered and immortalised as watershed moments thanks to the scholarship of people like Bede and the oral traditions and codified legends that came before him. Wessex's origin story, seen in this light, is of a little kingdom that was destined for greatness from the moment the strong ones touched the shore.

Archaeology, as it is known to do, muddies the waters. In Patching, West Sussex, sometime after 461, someone buried a vast quantity of Roman gold and silver coins from both *Britannia* and the continent. None had been re-used as relics or jewellery; this was a stockpile of genuine currency, still valued. Was it used to pay mosaicists in Chedworth? Or bribe Irish mercenaries at Bosham? Stamped with the long-dead face of Constantine 'III' (407-410) and the contemporary emperor

---

*   The [E] version of *The Anglo-Saxon Chronicle* recounts how, in 626, King Edwin of Northumbria 'slew five kings' in Wessex whilst on the warpath for one in particular, Cynegils, who had tried to have him assassinated.

Severus III (461-465) the Patching Hoard and its earlier kin in Hoxne, Suffolk, are snapshots at either end of this slow Late Roman decline.[339] Nobody woke up the day after Honorius' decree and thought, 'Well, guess we're in the Early Medieval Period now.' Such processes were glacial and, in some places, overlapping.

Mucking, Essex: where Roman field enclosures and pottery workshops functioned alongside new North Sea-style cemeteries; Piercebridge, Durham: where Roman drains, pipes and buildings were repaired, possibly as late as 450; Rendlesham, Suffolk: a Late Roman central place that became an enclave of pirates from near and far; Barham, nearby: where Merovingian and Frisian coins were dropped by traders on fifth-century soil; Druce Villa, Dorset: where villa-dwelling genteels lingered into the seventh century; Great Chesterford near Colchester; where fifth- to seventh-century people buried their dead with Roman coins in their mouths, paying the putrid ferryman Charon; Empingham, Rutland; where scatters of pottery indicate the continued use of a Roman fieldscape; Spong Hill, Norfolk; where about two decades' worth of vegetation separate the Roman settlement from early fifth-century burials, many containing Roman goods.

These sites represent cultural crossovers, hotspots where old or extant Roman material was re-purposed and re-used by new or old people re-negotiating their affinities, identities and activities amidst an ever-changing world. Wasperton in Warwickshire, Wally Corner in Oxfordshire and Queenford Farm near Dorchester. Worlds that had long been changing throughout the Roman Period that, importantly, never stopped changing. Spong Hill, especially, was a community that changed *with* the times. A hugely important cemetery connected to nearby settlements via waterways, Spong Hill's material allegiances point to Lower Saxony and Frisia – the famous 'Spong Man' jar topper sits atop a throne very similar to an example known from Cuxhaven – but the cremation urns that house its residents' remains were previously used for cooking and the cemetery is surrounded by Romano-British sites. Settlement hybridity. These goods, styles and ideas that flowed over the North Sea are like today's American, German and Japanese imports. Is a rubbish heap filled with crumpled Coke cans evidence of large-scale American immigration? No. It signals a change in fashion, consumerism and diet, influenced by the overseas prestige of a brand. Goods like Spong Hill's burial urns and the Roman material that so often accompany them were two different fashion statements: the latter overtook the former as the next 'in thing'.

And these dichotomies might not have been so obvious. The people travelling between Germany and Frisia were living in a Late and post-Roman world just like the residents of *Britannia*. These are not 'Germanic' or 'Celtic' material affinities but simply differing expressions of a 'Late Roman' one. A choice of fashion, then, and the result of hybridity is something like Wessex. In terms of linguistic differences, the common element between Britons and 'Anglo-Saxons' would have been Rome or versions of a Roman past, a mutual topic. When cultures interact, they borrow and appropriate from one another and transform collectively into something new. Not a Saxon conquest, but an immersion and convergence of expression between conservative and progressive remixes of the same thing, Late Roman and Late Roman. Indeed, by the third and fourth centuries there were people from northern

Europe and the southern continent at the cemetery at Lankhills, Winchester.[340] Isotopic evidence points to a diverse array of residents, the early *Gewissæ*.

'When the strong ones came to these shores, they inherited the thrones of lords', or so smoky mead hall tales claim. Pits, ditches and postholes dated to the fifth century at Netherhampton, Salisbury, express the mundane side of Gewissan origins, the establishment of a new type of building in a site that was continuously inhabited since the Bronze Age.

North of Amesbury and Stonehenge, near Durrington and Figheldean, an eldritch mound known as Barrow Clump slumbers beneath trees on Salisbury Plain, its rest interrupted by the scratching of badgers and the burrowing of rabbits. Snuffling around amidst the dirt and gnawing on the bones of old kings, the beginning of Wessex can be seen here through an extraordinary excavation,[341] and now the womb of kingdoms is home to nought but rodents. A poor end for the strong ones.

After their ancestors had seasonally converged on the same spot of land for generations, eventually Barrow Clump deserved immortalising. It was deemed fit to erect a monument, to set aside the baking of pottery and the knapping of flint to strip back topsoil, to lay turf, to gather and work timber and bone to construct a bell-shaped hump atop the earth. In the Late Neolithic, the first people of Barrow Clump scattered antler fragments over the soil. Over a thousand years later, Bronze Age folk perforated whetstones, worked beads out of coral and drank out of chalk cups. They fletched and carved bird bones to make necklaces, they waited for the broken legs of their relatives to heal, and they pressed their fingernails into beakers

and pots. A fractured femur on one of these skeletons tells of an eventful childhood and a limp-ridden adulthood but community and belonging, care and togetherness. A child buried alongside a fossilised sea urchin reminds us of heirlooms and treasured things and quiet intimate moments or perhaps we are reading too much into these ephemera? Archaeological evidence like this strips back the charters and chronicles and reveals the normal, mundane aspects of life. People like you and I lived here millennia before the idea of Wessex formed.

Horses, coins, pottery and the odd bone or two were deposited atop these layers between the Iron Age and Roman Period as new burials intersected old ones and subsequent generations re-assessed their approach and relationship to this most forlorn mound. Situated in a landscape of similar tumuli, and the famous Stonehenge, Barrow Clump was an anchor through time and a central place for hundreds if not thousands of people across its long history. It was never continuously inhabited but episodically re-occupied every few generations and, on each occasion, the Barrow Clumpers re-defined themselves and thought up new ways to honour the people already buried there. They oriented their deceased about the previously interred, they sited themselves in an imagined otherworld and they made sure to not disrespect the wights.

By the sixth century, when the *Gewissæ* were carving territories and warring with one another, Barrow Clump saw a new period of use along its southern berm, avoiding the central mound which was, by then, already brimming with burials. Almost a hundred people were commemorated here between the sixth and eighth centuries, over half of them alongside furnishings and material goods, fewer than that with weapons. We can read into this data how we like and can craft a story however we please, as Gildas, the Nennian compiler, and subsequent chroniclers all did, inferring from evidence a dramatic narrative. Pick and choose the words to explain the histories of the great square-headed and saucer brooches, the silver straining spoon, the glass, coral, bone, crystal and amber beads, the copper-alloy penannular decor and angular spearheads, the shield bosses, iron board rivets, nails and tang knives laid over people's legs, next to their skulls, atop their pelvis; bow brooches, trumpet brooches, button brooches; iron, copper, bronze; a gilded finger ring, a head-moulded pendant, irregularly shaped melon beads, the fragmentary wire of spear grips, the alder frame of a shield, the curved blades, the microscopic fragments of leather, the bracteate-like designs, the silvering, the foil, the bucket, the bone pins, the horn-gripped sword laid to the left of a man's arm.

Their owners led local lives. Of the isotopic samples, only the earliest four to be buried came from elsewhere, whereas all subsequent individuals displayed westerly origins, from Cornwall or Cumbria, and their biological sex distribution was more or less equal. The women lived longer than the men, who appear to have died between 35 and 45 years of age on average or in late adolescence. They lived different lives; two had *spina bifida*, one had a carious tooth which had been wiggled and bored by someone with vague dental knowledge; many had dislocated hips, fractured femurs, even bony necrosis. One woman had lost the little finger of her right hand when she was a child, decades before she died; another had a chronically inflamed patella and walked with difficulty. These people farmed and lived around livestock. Whilst most ate carb-rich food, one woman's diet was almost all meat. Was she a rich landlady? Sheep fluke and tapeworm could be found across many of the others, typically a sign of the mixing and matching of people in tightly-knit communities, rural and urban sprawls of busybodies. Maybe this community was in uproar when one male suffered a catastrophic blow to the left side of his skull, shattering his jaw and dislodging his eye; maybe they all came together over the slow healing process since he lived for another twenty years with fewer teeth and wonky vision. Another had a cut mandible; more had injured metacarpals from sword fighting. One child had even been beheaded. A punishment? A violent raid? A freak accident?

Maybe they strained shamanistic soups with the silver spoon, maybe they tamed horses with the cheek-ring snaffle, maybe they wore their brooches only for celebrations. The spoon is most similar to finds from Kent and France, the horse bit from Droxford, the brooch from Visigothic Spain. No matter where these styles originated, they were worn, worked and celebrated by the people of Barrow Clump, no matter where they came from, binding their cloaks and *peplos* dresses together using culturally appropriated metalwork. Now faded, microscopic remains of textiles indicate linen, cloth and wool was worn and willow laths were used in the sword's scabbard. The bucket was made of yew. Many of the objects were made long before the people who used them were buried at Barrow Clump and, still, they carried with them Roman coins, ten from the third and fourth centuries, pierced and stitched on to clothing. And they all wore rings on their left hands.

Why did these people live this way? Why did they bury their dead in such an old, venerated place? Were they trying to communicate with the future as with the past; the mound positioned as an immutable monument? Why, if only four of the individuals hailed from overseas, were all subsequent burials accompanied by such overt 'Saxon' furnishings? Why did they all wear rings on their left hands and what did they think of Stonehenge and what about the Roman forts and the Visigothic brooch and the food available to them and the beheaded child and the man with one eye?

And were they Wessex? Are the Barrow Clumpers and the hundreds of cemeteries surrounding them the crucible of Wessex? Was this where Britons changed their fashions to suit the times, spoke new tongues and made themselves culturally Gewissan? The last kingdom of England. No matter the elaborate tales or creation myths or genealogical additions, Wessex was once but a small collection of regional groups just like everywhere else. This little kingdom grew strong and only the strong ones survived.

WIHTWARA

engist and Horsa, Cerdic and Cynric, Port and Ælle, Stuf and Wihtgar.
When King Cædwalla called himself for the first time 'king of the West Saxons' in a charter from 686, he had already conquered the Isle of Wight, wresting it from Mercia and bringing it into the West Saxon fold which had, by then, largely Christianised and centralised around the Thames Valley. Legendary ancestors like Cerdic, Port and Wihtgar emerged shortly after, transcribed onto the vellum sheets of compilers as they re-wrote oral traditions from the previous two centuries. Some have more claim to reality than others but Port and Wihtgar are the Stuf of legend,* the latter implied to be the originator of the Isle's name, here at the very base of Britain overlooking the Channel. As traditions would have it, Port created Portsmouth and Wihtgar the Isle of Wight. However, Portsmouth's etymology originates from its status as a Roman *portus,* and Wight was already known as *Insula Vectis* by the second century. In 296 the usurper Allectus and his Frankish mercenaries were killed in a battle in the fog-strewn Solent and, two centuries later, *Vecta* was overwhelmed by Jutes. You've heard this all before.

Vectis, possibly meaning 'journey', might have a Germanic root which implies there were already such speakers all over southern England by the first century, which is not unlikely. The 'Jutes' were already here. Certainly, according to Bede, when Cædwalla conquered the place he 'destroy[ed] all the inhabitants' and it became a bit of a backwater, although retaining marriage links to both Wessex and Kent. The last independent king of the Isle, also the last pagan king of all England, Aruald, was killed during this massacre. His surviving nephews were then hunted by Cædwalla to *Ad Lapidem* near the New Forest where they were subsequently killed.† Cædwalla then succumbed to wounds sustained during this battle, Aruald's revenge and the wrath of the 'people of Wiht'.

---

* Forgive the pun. When writing Ælfred's *Life,* Asser stated that his mother, Osburh, was descended from the royal line of Stuf and Wihtgar. By convention, during significant conflict with viking armies, this positioned Ælfred as a reformed and virtuous Jute versus his distant Jutish relatives.

† Bede's *Ad Lapidem* has not yet been placed but a location by *Hamwih* seems likely, possibly at an extant Roman milestone or ferry point. Lepe is one of the more enduring suggestions, located within the 'Jutish kingdom' of Ytene.

Found amongst a cluster of a dozen similar mounds are these people, located at cemeteries like Bowcombe and Chessell Down. Upon excavation in the nineteenth century, a vast assortment of spearheads, scabbard and sword remains, iron knives and copper-alloy fasteners were found; 'some of the workmen say they met with an urn' reads one antiquarian's report. As at Barrow Clump, certain practices and rites can be observed through the burial of these loved ones; shields laid gently on chests, pottery delicately placed beside heads, the teeth of dogs and oxen, white snail shells, bird bones and half an iron horseshoe accompanying them to the afterlife.[342, 343] In the centre of the Bowcombe Down burials had been a mighty funeral pyre, only visible now through burnt chalk. It would have shone brightly in its day. So, too, did coins of Marcus Aurelius (161-180), like diamonds in the rough, found alongside scattered Roman roof tiles and amphora fragments, quarried limestone blocks, quoit brooches, oyster shells and red deer antlers, the third- to fifth-century refuse of villas at Brading, Shide and Carisbrooke. Poor imitations of continental garnet disc brooches found in a female grave at Chessell Down suggest that the knowledge and market for expensive material from abroad was present on the Isle of Wight but not the artisans to make them. Even so, the island was a major entrepôt and its importance continued long after it was conquered by Wessex. Gurnard and Carisbrooke have been suggested as vital trading sites for the island and a charter from 826 refers to a meeting point by an old barrow (S 274). We can picture the sea people of Wight debating the influx of new goods, the effect of distant viking raids on trade routes, the high taxes enforced by Louis the Pious.

Falling under the ever-transient and sometimes ephemeral strength of Merovingian overlordship, Wight, like Kent, would have at times resembled a Frankish outland but, at other times, its own unique entity. The dialect and historic language of the isle is a perfect demonstration of this. Carisbrooke, like Caterham, preserves the Old Welsh *caer-* suggesting that there was already a fortress that retained its importance through linguistic shifts. The Solent, likewise, whilst possessing an uncertain etymology, is certainly not a Germanic word. The local insult *cagmag* has several Irish, Gaelic and Celtic precursors, whilst *-combe* (Bowcombe, Gatcombe, Luccombe) for 'valley' probably stems from an Old English and Old Cornish crossover. A form of 'trade talk' developed on Wight,

a polyglot speech criss-crossing between Frankish, Latin, Breton, Gaelic and Germanic tongues, as locals argued, bartered and haggled with visitors of diverse backgrounds. Like Man, Wight was not peripheral but central. The fact that the island was first conquered by Mercia in 661 and again twenty years later by Wessex hints as much. It was desired. The waterways which brought Visigothic *tremisses*, Frisian pottery and western penannular brooches to the island adorned the locals with international furnishings; long-cist burials were discovered in the nineteenth century alongside the overtly pagan barrow mounds and, at Chessell Down, both a man and woman were buried with weapons, bronze hanging bowls and pails from the eastern Mediterranean. These sea people must have felt connected to all these international links at once, sometimes contradictory, other times complimentary. Wight, in its observable archaeology, is a microcosm of the United Kingdom; islands adorned with overseas influences, diverse languages and local responses.

YTENE

This book could only ever end with Ytene. Not only does it come last in the alphabet, but it is also known only from John of Worcester's twelfth-century *Chronicle of Chronicles*, where he wrote that the New Forest was once the site of a Jutish province.[344] That is, more or less, the entire story, synthesising however many riddles we have had to deal with throughout this long list of little kingdoms. Ytene means 'Jutes' and John, following historical tradition, placed them in the New Forest, Hampshire. Here was where Aruald's two nephews fled, seeking kinsmen amidst the ancient trees, frosted heather and gnarled roots before they were gutted by Cædwalla. Whether there was any sort of political or tribal entity here distinct from the Meonwara, Wihtwara and *Gewissæ* who were all nearby is completely unknowable but possible. The distinct topography, the fact that the forest functioned as a gravelled borderland and a shelter for deep-wooded denizens all indicate that, yes, here may have been 'Ytene'.

Any map of early medieval England is destined to situate names without borders in vague places, affording each territory a bit of wriggle room in its exact dimensions. Balancing readability, accuracy and page-size can be the work of madmen. Ytene, despite the fact that we know only of it from John of Worcester, who may have been adapting the work of former scholars Florence of Worcester and Eadmer of Canterbury, crystalises unique local dialects, toponyms and mannerisms that all would have made the New Forest distinctive. This was, as it is now, an ancient, wild wood. The 'foggy and corrupted air' of the place accompanied King William Rufus to his grave when he died here in 1100; did he know then that his was only the latest royal corpse to quench these bloodied soils? Much like the farmlands of West Stow, Suffolk and Burghshire, Yorkshire, the continuous status of these natural domains hints that there was no societal upheaval between the Roman Period and what came after. Be this the province of Jutes or others, the New Forest remained unchanged. It wasn't until the reign of Rufus' father, William the Bastard, when it was given its current name, when many if not all of these little kingdoms became folklore. Local myths and oral traditions are often one of the only ways we can back-date traces of individuality: Danes allegedly drowned off the coast of Bosham after stealing the holy bells of the monastery in the tenth century and Crowle on the Isle of Axholme is still blamed for failing to alert other villages about approaching raiders. I think any exploration of post-Roman territories has to come from such odd, local viewpoints.

Out of this laboratory of expression came a mosaic of kingdoms, big and small, experimenting with new ways of reinforcing status through pre-existing mechanisms, within boundaries defined or otherwise, set on charters or remembered through songs. Not all kingdoms set out to conquer but some did, and other dynasts must have felt their realm would always stand tall, only to see it wither within their lifetimes. They have each left behind contrasting legacies, many explored within this book, but many more excluded due to lack of space. *Little Kingdoms* can only serve as a starting point for more dedicated investigations into the patchwork of polities that once made up England, Wales and Scotland and, in many cases, still do. It is through analysing history on a local scale that we can begin to appreciate the formation of territories on their own terms, individual histories, not to be overseen from a temporally removed eagle's eye position, but from the ground. We have traced the cattle-ranchers of Craven and Dunutinga, the immortalised soldiers of the Gododdin, Rheged and Bernicia; the apocryphal ancestors of Wessex and the anachronistic antecedents of Dyfed and Gwynedd; the waters of Ceredigion, the lead of the Pecsætan, the mud of Heathfelðland, the flames of Pengwern. The farmers of Aechse. Even now there are only embers of what these kingdoms once were, but their stories can be retold through careful interdisciplinary work and a little creativity. At Edwin's *villa regia* of Yeavering the mechanisms of kingship from Roman, Frankish, Kentish, Deiran and Brythonic worlds all combined to forge something new. The status of its interred individuals and magnanimous structures attest to the power of these kings, the ashen layers an epitaph for their impermanence, like the pharaohs of Shelley's *Ozymandias*.[345]

I set out to write this book because I am fascinated by these tiny territories and the melancholic laments they have left behind. Exploring the United Kingdom today, the initiated can still trace the distant memories of these domains and their dynasties; the bend in a river might have once borne busy merchants, a distinctive rock on a high hill may have marked a spiritual borderland, a memorable place name indicates there was once a mighty ancestor here or a belief in one. Memories and perceived heritages are the bricks and mortar of these ephemeral polities; traditions and customs that bound people to places, things, concepts.

The waters of the river Wharfe are permanently connected, in my mind, to my grandparents and uncle, where their ashes are scattered. My grandmother, especially, dedicated her later years to researching our family tree and the many tall tales that have populated the last five hundred years of history, possibly even further. The profound impact she has had on me as I've grown up is instilled in all memories of her and the river Wharfe now contains one. The river is now *her territory, their territory*. If I should ever have to make an ancestral claim to Simon's Seat, I will know they watch over me from the wolds, woods and water. Such a personal thing is merely my interpretation of a place and its history. Undoubtedly, these connections are nothing new and they were forged in the past as they are today. I end this book now, finalising the manuscript in *my territory*, the kingdom which my wife and I have built, with a mind to appreciate these places on their own terms and to acknowledge the impermanence and contradictory nature of our island's many histories.

When England, Wales and Scotland became united in shapes more or less coterminous with what they are today, many of these histories were forgotten.

An equal number were remembered and baked into unique dialects, prideful local histories and folklore. The Isle of Axholme, where I grew up, is only one example but there are parallels all over the British Isles. From this isle to that one will stumble upon little kingdoms. It is up to you what you make of them.

REFERENCES

1. Green, C. (2022). Britain, the Byzantine Empire, and the Concept of an Anglo-Saxon 'Heptarchy': Harun ibn Yahya's Ninth-century Arabic Description of Britain. *Global Perspectives on Early Medieval England.* eds. Jolly, K.L. and Brooks, B.E. Boydell & Brewer.
2. Noble, T.F. ed. (2006). *From Roman provinces to Medieval kingdoms.* London: Routledge.
3. Gelling, M. and Cole, A. (2000). *The landscape of place-names.* Shaun Tyas.
4. Bynon, T. (2016). 'London's name'. *Transactions of the Philological Society.* 114(3), pp.281-97.
5. IJssennagger, N.L. (2017). Central because liminal. *Frisia in a Viking Age North Sea World.* PhD Thesis. University of Groningen.
6. Colgrave, B. ed. (1985). *Two lives of Saint Cuthbert: texts.* Cambridge University Press.
7. Koch, J.T. (1997). *The Gododdin of Aneirin: Text and Context from Dark-Age North Britain.* University of Wales Press.
8. Cynddelw. (12th c.). *Elegy on Einion ab Madog ab Iddon.*
9. Woolf, A. ed. (2013). *Beyond the Gododdin. Dark Age Scotland in Medieval Wales. The Proceedings of a Day Conference held on 19 February 2005.* Fife: The Committee for Dark Age Studies, University of St Andrews.
10. Breeze, A. (2010). 'Yrechwydd and the River Ribble'. *Northern History*, 47(2), pp.319-328.
11. Bromwich, R. and R.B. Jones. eds. (1978) *Studies in old Welsh poetry.* Cardiff: University of Wales Press.
12. Hilton, J.A. (2006). *Anglo-Saxon Attitudes: an introduction to Anglo-Saxonism.* Anglo-Saxon Books.
13. Anderson, B. (2006). *Imagined Communities: Reflections on the Origin and Spread of Nationalism.* Verso Books.
14. Wimmer, A. (2008). 'The Making and Unmaking of Ethnic Boundaries: A Multilevel Process Theory', *The American Journal of Sociology* 113(4), pp.970–1022.
15. Brubaker, R. (2014). 'Beyond Ethnicity', *Ethnic and Racial Studies*, 37(5), pp.804-10.
16. Harland, J. (2021). *Ethnic Identity and the Archaeology of the aduentus Saxonum.* Amsterdam University Press.
17. Oosthuizen, S. (2019). *The Emergence of the English (Past Imperfect).* Arc Humanities Press.

18. Schrijver, P. (2009). 'Celtic influence on Old English: phonological and phonetic evidence'. *English Language & Linguistics*, 13(2), pp.193-211.

19. Hart, C. (1971). 'The tribal hidage'. *Transactions of the Royal Historical Society*, 21, pp.133-57.

20. Baker, J. (2017). 'Old English sǣte and the historical significance of 'folk'names'. *Early Medieval Europe*, 25(4), pp.417-42.

21. Brookes, S. (2020). *Territory formation in Anglo-Saxon England: names, places and districts*. Ediciones Universidad Salamanca.

22. Faith, R. (2009). 'Forces and relations of production in early medieval England'. *Journal of Agrarian Change*. 9(1), pp.23-41.

23. Airt, M. and Niocaill, M. trans. (1983). *The Annals of Ulster to 1131*. CELT.

24. Freeman, P. trans. (2014). *'Muirchú's Life of Saint Patrick', The World of Saint Patrick*. New York: Oxford Academic.

25. Czére, O. *et al.* (2021). 'Multi-isotope analysis of the human skeletal remains from Blair Atholl, Perth and Kinross, Scotland'. Tayside and Fife Archaeological Journal, 27. pp.31-44.

26. Fraser, J.E. (2009). *From Caledonia to Pictland: Scotland to 795*. Edinburgh University Press.

27. Clancy, T.O. (2010). Atholl, Banff, Earn and Elgin: 'New Irelands' in the East Revisited. *Bile ós Chrannaibh: a Festschrift for William Gillies*, eds. McLeod *et al.* pp. 79-102.

28. Sharpe, R. trans. (1995). *Life of St Columba*. Penguin UK.

29. McDonald, A.D. (1985). 'Iona's style of government: the toponymic evidence of Adomnán's Life of Columba'. *Peritia*, 4. pp. 174–86.

30. Henry, P.L. trans. (2006). *Amra Choluim Chille, Dallán's Elegy for Columba*. Ultach Trust.

31. Harvey, A. (2025). 'Three Fallen Kings: On the edge of Northumbria in the Isle of Axholme (617-679)'. *Early Medieval England & Its Neighbours*, 1.

32. Colgrave, B. ed. (1999). *The Ecclesiastical History of the English People*. OUP Oxford.

33. Giles, J. A. ed. (2019). *History of the Britons (Historia Brittonum)*. Good Press.

34. Hudáček, P. (2014). 'Kingdom, Monarchy or State?: On the Topic of Using a Concept of State in the Early Middle Ages'. *Forum Historiae*, 8(2). pp.1-44.

35. Dickinson, T.M. (2004). 'An early Anglo-Saxon cemetery at Quarrington, near Sleaford, Lincolnshire: report on excavations, 2000-2001'. *LHA*. 39.

36. Green, C. (2020). The population groups of Early Anglo-Saxon Lincolnshire. *Britons & Anglo-Saxons. Lincolnshire 400-650*. Lincoln: History of Lincolnshire Committee. pp. 163-210.

37. Colgrave, B. ed. (1985). *Felix's Life of Saint Guthlac: Texts, Translation and Notes*. Cambridge University Press.

38. Dumville, D.N. (1976). 'The Anglian collection of royal genealogies and regnal lists'. *Anglo-Saxon England*, 5, pp.23-50.

39. Leake, J. A. (1967). *The Geats of Beowulf: A Study in the Geographical Mythology of the Middle Ages*. Milwaukee and London: University of Wisconsin Press.

40. Cameron, K. (1976). *The significance of English place-names.* Oxford University Press.

41. Bryant, S.R. (1999). *Settlement and Landscape in the Late Iron Age of Hertfordshire and the Northern Chilterns.* PhD Thesis, University of Sheffield.

42. Burleigh, G. (2015). Burials, ditches and deities: defining the boundaries of Iron Age and Romano-British Baldock. *Archaeology in Hertfordshire: Recent Research.*

43. Thorpe, L. trans. (1973). *The History of the Kings of Britain.* Penguin Classics.

44. Fitzpatrick-Matthews, K.J. (2022). *Britannia in the Ravenna Cosmography: a reassessment.*

45. Cain, G. (2018). *Exploring the Kingdom of Brycheiniog: an integrated archaeological approach in an early medieval landscape.* PhD Thesis, University of Oxford.

46. Lane, A. and Redknap, M. (2020). *Llangorse Crannog: the excavation of an early medieval royal site in the Kingdom of Brycheiniog.*

47. Rennell, R. (2010). 'Islands, islets, experience, and identity in the Outer Hebridean Iron Age'. *Shima: The International Journal of Research into Island Cultures,* 4(1), pp.47-64.

48. J.J. Tierney. ed. (1967). *Dicuil: Liber de Mensura Orbis Terrae.* Dublin.

49. Winterbottom, M. (1978). *Arthurian Period Sources: Gildas v. 7 (History from the sources). The Ruin of Britain.* Phillimore.

50. Laing, L. *et al.* (2014). 'Excavations at the early and later medieval site of Ballachly, Dunbeath, Caithness, 2007-10.' *Proceedings of the Society of Antiquaries of Scotland.* 143. pp. 265-302.

51. Morris, C.D. (2021). *The Birsay Bay Project: Volume 3-The Brough of Birsay, Orkney: Investigations 1954-2014.* Oxbow Books.

52. Morris, C.D. (2023). The Brough of Birsay, Orkney. *The Viking Age in Scotland.* eds. Horne, T., Pierce, E. and Barrowman, R.

53. O'Dell, A.C. *et al.* (1959). The St Ninian's Isle Silver Hoard. *Antiquity,* 33(132), pp.241-68.

54. Forsyth, K. (2020). Protecting a Pict? further thoughts on the inscribed silver chape from St Ninian's Isle, Shetland. *Proceedings of the Society of Antiquaries of Scotland.* 149. pp. 249-76.

55. Watson, W.J. (1926). *The Celtic Placenames of Scotland.* Birlinn Ltd. (2011).

56. Padel, O.J. (1997). 'A New Study of the Gododdin'. *Cambrian Medieval Celtic Studies.* 35. pp.45-55.

57. Clarkson, T. (2012). *The Men of the North: the Britons of southern Scotland.* Birlinn.

58. Wilson, P.R. *et al.* (1996). Early Anglian Catterick and Catraeth. *Medieval Archaeology,* 40(1), pp.1-61.

59. Sherlock, S.J. (2017). 'Excavations at Marne Barracks, Catterick, North Yorkshire, SE 254 970.' *Yorkshire Archaeological Journal.* 89(1), pp.75-98.

60. Remfry, P.M. trans. (2020). *Annales Cambriae: A Translation of Harleian 3859; PRO E.164/1; Cottonian Domitian, A 1; Exeter Cathedral Library MS. 3514 and MS Exchequer DB Neath, PRO E.164/1*. SCS Publishing.

61. Hughes, K. and Dumville, D. (1990). *Celtic Britain in the Early Middle Ages: Studies in Scottish and Welsh Sources*. Rowman & Littlefield Pub Inc.

62. Noble, G. and Evans, N. (2019). *The King in the North: The Pictish Realms of Fortriu and Ce*. Birlinn Ltd.

63. Cook, M. (2012). *New evidence for the activities of Pictish potentates in Aberdeenshire: the hillforts of Strathdon*. Proceedings of the Society of Antiquaries of Scotland. 141. pp.207-29.

64. Collins, R. (1992). *Law, culture and regionalism in early medieval Spain*. Taylor & Francis.

65. Jones, I. *et al.* (2018). Early medieval enclosure at Glanfred, near Llandre, Ceredigion. *Archaeologia Cambrensis*. 167. pp.221-43.

66. Grigg, E. (2009). 'Mole Rain and Other Natural Phenomena in the Welsh Annals: Can Mirabilia Unravel the Textual History of the Annales Cambriae?'. *The Welsh History Review*, 24(4). pp.1-40.

67. Kotva, A. (2024). *Noxia Animalia: Pests, Rats, & Evil in Late Antiquity*. Framing Disaster in Late Antiquity. Leeds International Medieval Congress, 'Crisis'.

68. Gräslund, B. and Price, N. (2012). 'Twilight of the gods? The 'dust veil event' of AD 536 in critical perspective'. *Antiquity*, 86(332), pp.428-43.

69. Gjerpe, L.E. (2021). The 536 Dust Veil Event and the long 6th century. *In Situ Archaeologica*, 15. pp.31-58.

70. Woods, D. (2010). 'Gildas and the Mystery Cloud of 536–7'. *Journal of Theological Studies*, 61(1), pp.226-34.

71. Haslett, S.K. and Willis, D. (2022). 'The 'lost' islands of Cardigan Bay, Wales, UK: insights into the post-glacial evolution of some Celtic coasts of northwest Europe'. *Atlantic Geoscience*, 58, pp.131-46.

72. Casswell, C. *et al.* (2018). 'An early medieval cemetery and circular enclosure at Felindre Farchog, north Pembrokeshire'. *Archaeology in Wales*, 56, pp.100-06.

73. Edwards, N. (2017). Early Medieval Wales: material evidence and identity. *Studia Celtica*, 51, pp.65-87.

74. Thomas, R. (2022). *History and identity in early medieval Wales*. Boydell & Brewer.

75. Charles-Edwards, T.M. (2013). *Reflections on Early Medieval Wales*.

76. Mommsen, T. ed. (1892). *Chronica minora saec. IV, V, VI, VII*. Berlin: Weidmann. pp.341–499.

77. Charles-Edwards, T. M. (1993). Palladius, Prosper, and Leo the Great: mission and primatial authority. *Saint Patrick, AD 493–1993*. eds. Dumville, D.N. and Abrams, L. Woodbridge: Boydell.

78. Anguilano, L. *et al.* (2010). An early medieval lead-smelting bole from Banc Tynddol, Cwmystwyth, Ceredigion. *Historical Metallurgy*, 44(2), pp.85-103.

79. Higham, N.J. (1995). *An English empire: Bede and the early Anglo-Saxon kings*. Manchester University Press.

80. Bryant, S. (2000). *Settlement and Landscape in the Late Iron Age of Hertfordshire and the Northern Chilterns*. PhD Thesis. University of Sheffield.

81. Biddle, M. and Kjølbye-Biddle, B. (2001). 'The Origins of St Albans Abbey: Romano-British Cemetery and Anglo-Saxon Monastery'. *Alban and St Albans: Roman and Medieval Architecture, Art and Archaeology,* (24) pp.45-77.

82. Thornhill, P. (2000). 'The Sub-Roman Cult of St. Alban'. *Mankind Quarterly*, 41(1), p.3.

83. Burleigh, G. (2015). 'Burials, ditches and deities: defining the boundaries of Iron Age and Romano-British Baldock.' *Archaeology in Hertfordshire: Recent Research*.

84. Stone, P. (2011). 'Saxon and medieval activity at Walton Street, Aylesbury'. *Records of Buckinghamshire, 51*. pp.99-129.

85. Rowley, A. R. (2008) 'The name of Craven', *Craven History*.

86. Stephenson, K.B. and Stuart, W. (2003). 'West Marton: at the centre of Craven?' *Craven History*.

87. Johnson, D. (2019). *New Light on the 'Dark Ages' in North Craven. Recent advances in the archaeology of the Yorkshire Dales*. Skipton: Yorkshire Dales Millenium Trust.

88. Johnson, D. (2015). Chapel-le-Dale, North Yorkshire: the making of an upland landscape. *Landscape History*, 36(1), pp.25-45.

89. Johnson, D.S. and Russ, H. (2014). Excavation of a Late Seventh-Century Structure in Upper Ribblesdale. *Yorkshire Archaeological Journal*, 86(1), pp.80-105.

90. Johnson, D. (2017). 'Early Medieval Rural Settlement in North Craven: A Reassessment'. *Contrebis*. 3.

91. Blair, J. (2018). *Building Anglo-Saxon England*. Princeton University Press.

92. Coupland, S. (2024). *After Dorestad: Silver and gold in Carolingian Frisia 850-900*. Fourth Dorestad Congress. 'The Year 1000'.

93. Raistrick, A. and Holmes, P.F. (1961). *Archaeology of Malham Moor*. EW Classey.

94. Beaumont, H. (2004). Hebden Township Boundary, past and present. *Archaeology and Historic Landscapes of the Yorkshire Dales*. pp.69-77. eds. R.F. White and P.R. Wilson.

95. Cale, K.J. (2004). "Was the skeleton lady dead?". *Archaeology and Historic Landscapes of the Yorkshire Dales*. pp.105-10. eds. R.F. White and P.R. Wilson.

96. Foster, R. (2023). Norse Shielings in Scotland: An example of cultural contact. *The Viking Age in Scotland*. eds. Horne, T., Pierce, E. and Barrowman, R. pp.189-96.

97. Ríagáin, R.Ó. (2024). Becoming Dál Riata: A Critical Evaluation of the Emergence of an Early Medieval Insular Polity. *Scottish Historical Review*, 103(1), pp.1-76.

98. Jennings, A. and Kruse, A. (2009). 'From Dál Riata to the" Gall-Ghàidheil"'. *Viking and Medieval Scandinavia*, pp.123-49.

99. Mainman, A. (2019). *Anglian York*. York: Blackthorn Press.

100. Dickinson, T. (2023). The 'Acomb area' Treasure find: fragmented evidence for a seventh-century high-status female burial near York?. *Anglo-Saxon Studies in Archaeology and History 23*. ed. Hamerow, H.

101. Wenham, P. *et al.* (1974). *Derventio (Malton): Roman fort and civilian settlement*. Cameo Books.

102. Dobson, L. (2006). *Landscape, monuments and the construction of social power in early medieval Deira*. PhD Thesis. University of York.

103. Powlesland, D. (2011). West Heslerton: Past, present and future. *Great Excavations*. ed. Schofield, J.

104. Loveluck, C. (2001). 'Early Deira: Archaeological Studies of the East Riding in the Fourth to Ninth Centuries'. *Archaeological Journal.* 158(1). pp.398-9.

105. Heaser, S. (2025). *Anglo-Saxon Beads 400-700 AD: A Visual Guide to Types and Techniques*.

106. Langbroek, M. (2024). *Exploring Dorestad's bead networks*. Fourth Dorestad Congress. 'The Year 1000'.

107. Noble, G. *et al.* (2019). Rhynie: a powerful place. *The King In The North.* pp.58-81. eds. Noble, G. and Evans, N.

108. Turner, S.C. (2006). *Making a Christian Landscape: The Countryside in Early-Medieval Cornwall, Devon and Wessex*.

109. Pearce, S.M. (1978). *The Kingdom of Dumnonia. Studies in History and Tradition in Southwestern Britain A.D. 350–1150.* Padstow: Lodenek Press.

110. Probert, D. (2010). 'New light on Aldhelm's letter to King Gerent of Dumnonia'. Aldhelm and Sherborne: *Essays to celebrate the founding of the bishopric*, pp.110-28.

111. Jones, G.R.J. (1995). 'Some Donations to Bishop Wilfrid in Northern England'. *Northern History*, 31(1), pp.22-38.

112. Walker, S.M. (2022). *Socio-political change in the English county of Cumbria: 400-700*. PhD Thesis. University of Birmingham.

113. Johnson, D. (2008). *Ingleborough: Landscape & History*. Palatine Books.

114. Hughes, E. (2005). 'An early medieval trackway at Llangynfelyn, Ceredigion'. *IFA Yearbook and Directory*, 5, pp.22-3.

115. Redknap, M. (2009). 'A Corpus Of Early Medieval Inscribed Stones And Stone Sculpture In Wales, 1: Breconshire, Glamorgan, Monmouthshire, Radnorshire, And Geographically Contiguous Areas Of Herefordshire And Shropshire'. *Speculum*, 84(4).

116. Groom, P. *et al.* (2011). 'Two early medieval cemeteries in Pembrokeshire: Brownslade Barrow and West Angle Bay'. *Archaeologia Cambrensis*, 160, pp.133-203.

117. Giot, P. *et al.* (2003). *The British Settlement of Brittany: The First Bretons in Armorica*. The History Press.

118. Wasserschleben, H. (1874). *The Irish canon laws*.

119. Carver, M. (2011). What were they Thinking? Intellectual Territories in Anglo-Saxon England. *The Oxford Handbook of Anglo-Saxon Archaeology.* pp.914-47. ed. Hinton, D.A.

120. Thompson, E.A. (1980). 'Procopius on Brittia and Britannia'. *The Classical Quarterly*, 30(2), pp.498-507.

121. Scull, C.J. (2011). 'Foreign identities in burials at seventh-century English 'emporia''. *Studies in early Anglo-Saxon art and archaeology: papers in honour of Martin G. Welch*. pp.82-7.

122. Krebs, C.J. (1994). *Ecology*. New York: HarperCollins. pp.61–74.

123. Tove, O. *et al.* (1996). 'A Post-Roman Settlement at Fremington, near Brougham'. *Transect through Time: The Archaeological Landscape of the Shell Northwestern Ethylene Pipeline*. eds. Lambert, J. *et al.*

124. Fleming, A. (2010). *Swaledale: Valley of the Wild River*. Windgather Press.

125. Ainsworth, S. *et al.* (2015), 'Swaledale's 'Early Medieval Kingdom' revisited', *Landscapes* 16:1, 3-17.

126. Whellan, T. (1859). *History and Topography of the City of York and the North Riding of Yorkshire*, 2.

127. Pickles, T. (2009). 'Locating Ingetlingum and Suthgedling: Gilling West and Gilling East.' *Northern History*, 46(2). pp.313-25.

128. Richardson, J. (2023). *Excavations at Garforth: A High-Status Roman burial and The Kingdom of Elmet*. CBA: Yorkshire Fireside Chats. 'Season 4'.

129. Bromwich, R. ed. (2014). *The Triads of the Island of Britain*. University of Wales Press.

130. Breeze, A. (2002). The kingdom and name of Elmet. *Northern History*, 39(2), pp.157-71.

131. Williams, R. and Lewis, G. trans. (2019). *The Book of Taliesin: Poems of Warfare and Praise in an Enchanted Britain*. Penguin UK.

132. Gruffydd, R.G. (1994). 'In search of Elmet'. *Studia Celtica*, 28, pp.63-79.

133. James, A.G. (2009). *Egles/Ecles and the formation of Northumbria. *The Church in English Place Names*. ed. Quinton E.

134. Henson, D. (n.d.). *Place-names & the Anglian takeover of Elmet*. Unpublished.

135. Jenkins, D. (1986). *The Laws of Hywel Dda*. Gomer Press.

136. Sims-Williams, P. (2019). *The Book of Llandaff as a historical source*. Boydell & Brewer.

137. Lambert, L. (2022). *Ergyng to Archenfield: National Identity in an Early Medieval Borderland*. Leeds International Medieval Congress.

138. Molyneaux, G. (2011). 'The Ordinance concerning the Dunsæte and the Anglo-Welsh frontier in the late tenth and eleventh centuries.' *Anglo-Saxon England*, 40, pp.249-72.

139. Lambert, T. (2018). Frontier Law in Anglo-Saxon England. *Crossing Borders: Boundaries and Margins in Medieval and Early Modern Britain* (pp. 19-42). Brill. eds. Butler, S. and Kesselring, K.J.

140. Hunt, J. (2009). 'A figure sculpture at Upton Bishop, Herefordshire: continuity and revival in early medieval sculpture'. *The Antiquaries Journal*, 89, pp.179-214.

141. Bassett, S. (1997). Continuity and fission in the Anglo-Saxon landscape: the origins of the Rodings (Essex). *Landscape History*, 19(1), pp.25-42.

142. Rippon, S. (2022). *Territoriality and the early medieval landscape: The countryside of the east Saxon kingdom*. Boydell & Brewer.

143. Mirrington, A.D. (2019). *Transformations of Identity and Society in Anglo-Saxon Essex: A Case Study of an Early Medieval North Atlantic Community.* Amsterdam University Press.

144. Hamerow, H. (1993). *Excavations at Mucking. Vol 2. The Anglo-Saxon Settlement.* English Heritage.

145. Hirst, S. and Clark, D. (2009). *Excavations at Mucking. Vol 3. Anglo-Saxon Cemeteries.* MOLA.

146. Crabtree, P.J. (1996). Production and consumption in an early complex society: animal use in Middle Saxon East Anglia. *World Archaeology*, 28(1), pp.58-75.

147. Leroy, I. (2024). *Quentovic and after: Early Medieval occupation on the Canche.* Fourth Dorestad Congress. 'The Year 1000'.

148. Clarkson, T. (2023). *'A mighty fleet and the king's power': the Isle of Man AD 400-1265.* Birlinn.

149. Symonds, L. *et al.* (2014). Medieval migrations: isotope analysis of early Medieval Skeletons on the Isle of Man. *Medieval Archaeology*, 58(1), pp.1-20.

150. Davey, P.J. (1999). *Rushen Abbey, Ballasalla, Isle of Man: first archaeological report.* University of Liverpool.

151. Freke, D. (2002). *Excavations on St Patrick's Isle, Peel, Isle of Man, 1992-98.* Liverpool University Press.

152. Carpenter, H. ed. (2006). *The Letters of J.R.R. Tolkien.* HarperCollins.

153. Rollason, D.W. (1978). Lists of saints' resting-places in Anglo-Saxon England. *Anglo-Saxon England*, 7, pp.61-93.

154. Morris, R. ed. (1880). *The Blickling Homilies of the Tenth Century. Early English Text Society.* Oxford University Press.

155. Leeds, E.T. (1940). 'Two Saxon cemeteries in north Oxfordshire'. *Oxoniensia*, 5, pp.21-30.

156. Hughes, S.S. *et al.* (2014). 'Anglo-Saxon origins investigated by isotopic analysis of burials from Berinsfield, Oxfordshire, UK.' *Journal of Archaeological Science*, 42, pp.81-92.

157. Leslie, R.F. ed. (1966). *The Wanderer.* Manchester.

158. Brunner, B. (2022). *Extreme North.* WW Norton & Co.

159. Carver, M. (2008). *Portmahomack: Monastery of the Picts: Monastery of the Picts.* Edinburgh University Press.

160. Bower, W. (1510). *Scotichronicon.* MS 186. f. 12v: Book I – f.305v: Book XVI

161. Hull, V. (1941). 'The Exile of Conall Corc'. *PMLA*, 56(4), pp.937-50.

162. Evans, N. (2013). 'Circin and Mag Gerginn: Pictish Territories in Irish and Scottish Sources'. *Cambrian Medieval Studies*. 66. pp.1-36.

163. Barney, S.A. trans. (2006). *The Etymologies of Isidore of Seville.* California State University.

164. Gilbert, M. trans. (1998). The Miracles of St Nynia the Bishop (c. 780?). *The Triumph Tree: Scotland's Earliest Poetry, 550–1350.* Clancy, T.O. ed. Edinburgh: Canongate. pp.126–39.

165. Offer, C.J. (2002). *In Search of Clofesho: The Case for Hitchin*. Tessa Books.

166. Fitzpatrick-Matthews, K.J. and Haarer, F.K. (2014). The experience of "small towns". Utter devastation, slow fading or business as usual. *AD 410. The history and archaeology of late and post-Roman Britain*. eds. Haarer, F.K. and Collins, R. pp.43-60.

167. Kennett, D. H. (1970). 'Pottery and other finds from the Anglo-Saxon cemetery at Sandy, Bedfordshire'. *Medieval Archaeology*. 14. pp.17-33.

168. Mills, D. (2010). *A Dictionary of London Place-Names*. Oxford University Press.

169. Peresztegi, J. and Featherby, R. (2019). The Green, Southall, London UB2. Archaeological Desk Based Assessment. *Archaeology*, 1.

170. Switsur, R. (1989). 'Early English boats'. *Radiocarbon*, 31(3), pp.1010-18.

171. Savage, H.L. ed. (1974). *St Erkenwald*. Hamden: Archon Books.

172. Falileyev, A. (2020). 'Three notes on the Gododdin'. *Studia Celtica*, 54(1), pp.81-98.

173. Aitchison, N. (2023). 'Urbs Giudi: text, translation and topography'. *Anglo-Saxon England*, 50. pp.1-41.

174. Driscoll, S.T. *et al.* (1997). *Excavations within Edinburgh Castle in 1988-91*. Society Antiquaries Scotland.

175. Hunter, F. (2013). *Hillfort and hacksilver: Traprain Law in the late Roman Iron Age and early prehistoric period*. Society of Antiquaries of Scotland.

176. Coe, J.B. and Young, S. (1995). *The Celtic Sources for the Arthurian Legend*. Llanerch Publishers.

177. Woolf, A. (2007). *From Pictland to Alba, 789-1070*. Edinburgh University Press.

178. Alcock, L. *et al.* (1990). 'Reconnaissance excavations on Early Historic fortifications and other royal sites in Scotland, 1974-84: 3, Excavations at Dundurn, Strathearn, Perthshire, 1976-77'. *Proceedings of the Society of Antiquaries of Scotland*. 119, pp.189-226.

179. Best, R.I. and Bergin, Osborn, eds. (1929), *Book of the dun cow*.

180. Schlesinger, A. and Walls, C. (1997). 'An Early church and Medieval farmstead site: excavations at Llanelen, Gower'. *Archaeological Journal*. 153 (1). pp.104-47.

181. Fisher, C. (1926). 'The Welsh Celtic Bells'. *Archaeologia Cambrensis*. 81 (2).

182. Petts, D. (2009). *The early medieval Church in Wales*. Stroud: The History Press.

183. Seaman, A. (2013). Dinas Powys in context: settlement and society in post-Roman Wales. *Studia Celtica*, 47(1), pp.1-23.

184. Campbell, E. *et al.* (2023). A new chronology for the Welsh hillfort of Dinas Powys. *Antiquity*, 97(396), pp.1548-63.

185. Evans, E. *et al.* (1985). A third-century maritime establishment at Cold Knap, Barry, South Glamorgan. *Britannia*, 16, pp.57-125.

186. Leardini, M. (2022). *The Roman expansion into Wales and the legionary base of Caerleon*. Undergraduate Dissertation. Ca' Foscari University of Venice.

187. Youngs, S. (1989). *Work of the Angels*. London.

188. --- (10th c.). Bamberg, Staatsbibliothek, MS H. J. IV 11

189. Charles-Edwards, T.M. (2014). *Wales and the Britons, 350-1064*. Oxford University Press.

190. Denison, S. (1997). 'Welsh fort identified as citadel of Dark Age king'. *British Archaeology*. 29.

191. Murad, K. (2024). *A Crisis of Opportunity: Ireland and the Mediterranean.* Borderland Communities. International Medieval Congress, 'Crisis'.

192. Richards, M. (1965). 'Early Welsh territorial suffixes'. *The Journal of the Royal Society of Antiquaries of Ireland*. 95 (2).

193. Davies, D. (2016). *Welsh place names and their meanings.* Ceredigion: Y Lolfa.

194. Guy, B. (2019) 'Rheinwg: The Lost Kingdom of South Wales'. *Peritia*. 30. pp.97-121.

195. Ellerd-Cheers, H. (2024). *Listing Identity: How Early Medieval texts influence national imaginations.* Listing the World. International Medieval Congress, 'Crisis'.

196. Mullen, A. and Woudhuysen, G. eds. (2023). *Languages and Communities in the Late-Roman and Post-Imperial Western Provinces*. Oxford University Press.

197. Bourne, C. (2023). *A Network of Cattle Ranches: The Vaccary Enclosure System in Early Medieval Wales*. Leeds International Medieval Congress, 'Networks and Entanglements'.

198. Davies, W. (1990). *Patterns of power in early Wales*. Oxford University Press.

199. Bourne, C. (2024). 'Chapter 3: The Early Medieval Kingdom of Gower'. Personal Communications (24/7/24).

200. Halsall, G. (2008). *Warfare and society in the Barbarian West 450-900*. Routledge.

201. Mellows, W.T. trans. (1941). *The Peterborough Chronicle of Hugh Candidus*.

202. Healey, H. (1999). 'An Iron Age salt-making site at Helpringham Fen, Lincolnshire: excavations by the Car Dyke Research Group 1972-7'. Lincolnshire Salterns: Excavations at Helpringham, Holbeach St Johns, and Bicker Haven. Report No. 89.

203. Upex, S.G. *et al.* (2011). The Praetorium of Edmund Artis: A Summary of Excavations and Surveys of the Palatial Roman Structure at Castor, Cambridgeshire 1828–2010. *Britannia*, 42, pp.23-112.

204. Golding, B. (2017). Remembering the Battle of Hastings: Memorialization, Le Souvenir Normand, and the Entente Cordiale. *Anglo-Norman Studies XXXIX.* ed. van Houts, E.M.C.

205. Hudson, M. (2014). 'Conquerors and Conquered: Early Perspectives of the Battle of Hastings'. *The Saber and Scroll Journal*, 3(2).

206. Tyson, K. trans. (2018). *Carmen Widonis-The First History of the Norman Conquest*. Granularity Limited.

207. Liddy, C.D. (2008). *The bishopric of Durham in the late Middle Ages: lordship, community and the cult of St Cuthbert*. Boydell & Brewer Ltd.

208. Breeze, A. (1999). 'Was Durham the broninis of eddiu's life of St Wilfrid?'. *Durham archaeological journal*, (14), pp.91-2.

209. O'Brien, C. (2002). 'The early medieval shires of Yeavering, Breamish and Bamburgh'. *Archaeologia Aeliana*, 30, pp.53-74.

210. James, A.G. (2007). 'The Brittonic Language in the Old North'. *Scottish Place-Name Society*. 2.

211. Woodman, D.A. (2015). Charters, Northumbria and the Unification of England in the Tenth and Eleventh Centuries. *Northern History*, 52(1), pp.35-51.

212. Rozier, C.C. (2020). *Writing History in the Community of St Cuthbert, C. 700-1130: From Bede to Symeon of Durham*. Boydell & Brewer.

213. Lacey, B. (2014). *Constructing Communities: Identification and Self-Understanding in the Twelfth-Century North of England*. PhD Thesis. University of Sheffield.

214. Offler, H.S. ed. (1968). 'Durham Episcopal Charters, 1071-1152'. *Publication of the Surtees Society, Vol 179*. Gateshead.

215. Dobbie, E.K. (1942). 'Anglo-Saxon Minor Poems'. *Anglo-Saxon Poetic Records*. 6. New York.

216. Higham, N. (2006). Northumbria's southern frontier: a review. *Early Medieval Europe*, 14(4), pp.391-418.

217. Bullen, K.F. (2024). A Survey of the place-names of the Isle of Axholme, Lincolnshire. PhD Thesis. University of Nottingham.

218. Blair, Peter Hunter, ed. (1959). *The Moore Bede: Cambridge University Library Kk. 5. 16. Volume 9 of Early English manuscripts in facsimile*. Rosenkilde and Bagger.

219. Loveluck, C. (2007). *Rural Settlement, Lifestyles and Social Change in the Later First Millennium AD at Flixborough, Lincolnshire: Anglo-Saxon Flixborough in its Wider Context*. Historic England.

220. Atkinson, D. (2007). *The early medieval settlement remains from Flixborough, Lincolnshire: the occupation sequence, c. AD 600-1000*. Historic England.

221. Johnstone, C. *et al.* (2007). *Farmers, monks and aristocrats: the environmental archaeology of Anglo-Saxon Flixborough*. Historic England.

222. Loveluck, C. (2001). Wealth, waste and conspicuous consumption. Flixborough and its importance for Middle and Late Saxon rural settlement studies. *Image and Power in the Archaeology of Early Medieval Britain*, Oxford: Oxbow, pp.79-130. H. Hamerow and A. MacGregor. eds.

223. Neville, J. (1999). *Representations of the Natural World in Old English Poetry*.

224. Turner, R.C. and Rhodes, M. (1992). A bog body and its shoes from Amcotts, Lincolnshire. *The Antiquaries Journal*. 72. pp.232-40.

225. Buckland, P. (1979). Thorne Moors: a palaeoecological study of a bronze age site: a contribution to the history of the British insect fauna. Working paper. University of Birmingham.

226. Colgrave, B. trans. (1968). *The earliest life of Gregory the Great*. Cambridge University Press.

227. Coates, R. (2013). 'The name of the Hwicce: a discussion'. *Anglo-Saxon England*, 42, pp.51-61.

228. Bassett, S. (2023). 'The hidation of the Hwicce: investigating its halving between the eighth century and 1086'. *Anglo-Saxon England*, 50. pp.1-33.

229. Carver, M. *et al.* (2009). *Wasperton: A Roman, British and Anglo-Saxon Community in Central England.* Boydell Press.

230. Hooke, D. (2009). *The Anglo-Saxon Landscape: the Kingdom of the Hwicce.* Manchester University Press.

231. Meaney, A. (1964). *A Gazetteer of Early Anglo-Saxon Burials.*

232. Hanlon, B. (2024). *Diffusing the Alfredian Woodland Crisis.* Leeds International Medieval Congress, 'Crisis'.

233. Hawkes, S.C. and Pollard, M. (1981). The gold bracteates from sixth-century Anglo-Saxon graves in Kent, in the light of a new find from Finglesham. *Frühmittelalterliche Studien*, 15(1), pp.316-370.

234. Gelling, M. *et al.* (1982). *The place-name volumes for Worcestershire and Warwickshire: a new look. Field and Forest.*

235. Halsall, G. (2013). *Worlds of Arthur: facts and fictions of the Dark Ages.* OUP Oxford.

236. Hawkes, S.C. *et al.* (1961). 'Soldiers and settlers in Britain, fourth to fifth century: with a catalogue of animal-ornamented buckles and related belt-fittings'. *Medieval Archaeology*, 5(1), pp.1-70.

237. Witney, K.P. (1982). *The Kingdom of Kent.* Phillimore & Co. Ltd.

238. Brookes, S. and Harrington, S. (2010). *The Kingdom and People of Kent, AD 400-1066: Their History and Archaeology.* The History Press.

239. Harrington, S. and Welch, M. (2014). *The Early Anglo-Saxon Kingdoms of Southern Britain AD 450-650: Beneath the Tribal Hidage.* Oxbow Books.

240. Tschan, F. ed. (2002). *History of the Archbishops of Hamburg-Bremen.* Columbia University Press.

241. Fleming, R. (2020). The movement of people and things between Britain and France. *The Oxford Handbook of the Merovingian World*, pp.370-88. eds. Effros, B. and Moreira, I.

242. Parfitt, K and Brugmann, B. (1997). *The Anglo-Saxon Cemetery on Mill Hill, Deal, Kent.* Society for Medieval Archaeology.

243. Vince, A.G. ed. (1993). *Pre-Viking Lindsey.* Council for British Archaeology.

244. Leahy, K. (2008). *The Anglo-Saxon Kingdom of Lindsey.* The History Press.

245. Green, C. (2008). 'The British Kingdom of Lindsey'. *Cambrian Medieval Celtic Studies*, 56.

246. Green, C. (2020). *Britons & Anglo-Saxons. Lincolnshire 400-650.* Lincoln: History of Lincolnshire Committee.

247. Leahy, K. (2007). *Interrupting the Pots: The Excavation of Cleatham Anglo-Saxon Cemetery, North Lincolnshire.* Council for British Archaeology.

248. Halkon, P. (2024). *Pocela's farm?.* Pocklington District Heritage Trust, 'Seeking the Anglo-Saxons and Vikings'.

249. English, R. (2024). 'Elephant ivory rings in early medieval graves reconsidered'. *Early Medieval Europe.* 32 (3). pp.306-36.

250. Cooper, N. (2000). *The Archaeology of Rutland Water: Excavations at Empingham in Gwash Valley, Rutlan, 1963-73 and 1990.* Leicester Archaeology Monographs. University of Leicester.

251. Wright, D.W. *et al.* (2022). 'Laughton-en-le-Morthen, South Yorkshire: Evolution of a Medieval Magnate core.' *Landscapes*. 23 (2).

252. Windell, D. J. (2018). Ethnonyms as Toponyms. The case of Vandals in Late Antique Britain.

253. Green, C. (2011). 'Tealby, the Taifali, and the end of Roman Lincolnshire', *Lincolnshire History and Archaeology*, 46. pp.5–10.

254. Jarvis, E. (1850). 'Account of the discovery of ornaments and remains, supposed to be of Danish origin, in the parish of Caenby, Lincolnshire'. *Archaeological Journal*, 7(1), pp.36-44.

255. Sherlock, S. (2024). *Recent Saxon Discoveries*. Pocklington District Heritage Trust, 'Seeking the Anglo-Saxons and Vikings'.

256. Rickman, A. (2024). *Illuminating the Material: An Enlightened Re-examination of 'Apotropaic' Bird-of-Prey Ornamentation on Anglo-Saxon Weaponry and Armour*. MA Thesis, University of Montana. Unpublished.

257. Clarke, D. (2021). 'Loidam Civitatem: Leeds From Tribal Capital To Viking Backwater'. *Northern History*, 58(2), pp.169-96.

258. Watt, S. ed. (2011). *The Archaeology of the West Midlands*. Oxford: Oxbow Books.

259. Hookway, E.N. (2015). *An archaeological analysis of Anglo-Saxon Shropshire AD 600–1066: with a catalogue of artefacts*. PhD Thesis. University of Birmingham.

260. Stanford, S.C. *et al.* (1982). 'Bromfield, Shropshire—Neolithic, Beaker and Bronze Age sites, 1966–79.' *Proceedings of the Prehistoric Society.* 48. (1). pp.279-320.

261. Lane, A. (2014). 'Wroxeter and the end of Roman Britain'. *Antiquity*, 88(340), pp.501-15.

262. White, R.H. (2022). Wroxeter: Ashes Under Uricon: a Cultural and Social History of the Roman City. Archaeopress Publishing Ltd.

263. Bassett, S. (2000). 'How the west was won: The Anglo-Saxon takeover of the west midlands'. *Anglo-Saxon Studies in Archaeology and History*. 11. pp.107-18.

264. Baker, J. (2015). 'The *Meresæte of northwest Shropshire.' *Notes and Queries*. 260. pp.207–11.

265. Friedrich, M. and Harland, J.M. eds. (2020). *Interrogating the 'Germanic': A Category and its Use in Late Antiquity and the Early Middle Ages*. Walter de Gruyter GmbH & Co KG.

266. Aldsworth, F. G. and Welch, M. G. (1978). 'Droxford Anglo-Saxon cemetery, Soberton, Hampshire'. *Proc Hampshire Fld Club Archaeol Soc.* 35, pp.93-182.

267. Mainman, A. (2024). *Anglian York*. Pocklington District Heritage Trust, 'Seeking the Anglo-Saxons and Vikings'.

268. Addyman, P. (1968). *Saxon Southampton: a review of the Evidence. Part 1, History, Location, Date and Character of the Town*. Hampshire Field Club & Archaeological Soc.

269. Machling, T. *et al.* (2024) Nicked and 'nicked': The Knaresborough gold ring and a possible Viking-redeposited Iron Age hoard from eastern England. Zenodo.

270. Smyth, A. trans. (2001). *The Medieval Life of King Alfred the Great: A Translation and Commentary on the Text Attributed to Asser*. Springer.

271. Kennedy, M. (2022). 'Tossing Waves and Earthen Caves: Loss, Nature, and Identity in The Wife's Lament'. *The English Languages: History, Diaspora, Culture*, 8, pp.1-7.

272. Johnson, D. (2024). Personal Communications (8/8/24).

273. McDonell, G. (n.d.) *Slag recovered from excavations near Kettlewell*. Unpublished. Bradford University, Department of Archaeology.

274. Barnatt, J. and Smith, K. (2004). *The Peak District: Landscapes Through Time*. Windgather Press.

275. Higham, N.J. (1993) *The origins of Cheshire*. Manchester: Manchester University Press

276. Hodges, R. (1991). Notes on the Medieval Archaeology of the White Peak. *Recent Developments in the Archaeology of the Peak District*. pp.111-22. R. Hodges and K. Smith. eds.

277. Hooke, D. (1990). *Worcestershire Anglo-Saxon Charter-Bounds*. Boydell Press.

278. Ekwall, E. (1985). *The Concise Oxford Dictionary of English Place-names*. University Press Oxford.

279. Rowland, J. (1990). *Early Welsh Saga Poetry: A Study and Edition of the 'Englynion'*. Cambridge: Brewer.

280. Poweli, D. ed. (1806). *Itinerarium Cambriae*. Gulielmi Bulmer.

281. Matthews, J. (2020). *The Book of Merlin: Magic, Legend, & History*. Amberley Publishing.

282. Alcock, L. (1971). *Arthur's Britain*. Penguin Classics.

283. Halsall, G. (2007). *Barbarian migrations and the Roman West, 376–568*. Cambridge University Press.

284. Jones, O. (2009). 'Hereditas Pouoisi: the Pillar of Eliseg and the history of early Powys', *Welsh History Review*. 24(4). pp.41-80.

285. Edwards, N. (2009). 'Rethinking the pillar of Eliseg'. *The Antiquaries Journal*, 89, pp.143-77.

286. Kirby, D.P. (1976). 'British dynastic history in the pre-Viking period'. *Bulletin of the Board of Celtic Studies*, 27, pp.81-114.

287. Stephenson, D. (2015). 'Re-thinking thirteenth-century Powys'. *Transactions of the Honourable Society of Cymmrodorion*. 21, pp.9-26.

288. Stanford, S.C. (1991). *The Archaeology of the Welsh Marches*. William Collins Sons & Co.

289. Williams, I. trans. (1999). *Armes Prydein o Lyfr Taliesin*. University of Wales Press.

290. Breeze, A. (2012). 'The Name and Battle of Arfderydd, near Carlisle'. *Journal of Literary Onomastics*, 2(1), pp.1-9.

291. McCarthy, M. (2011). 'The Kingdom of Rheged: a landscape perspective'. *Northern History*, 48(1), pp.9-22.

292. Wilmott, T. ed. (2013). *Hadrian's Wall: archaeological research by English Heritage 1976-2000*. English Heritage.

293. Toolis, R. and Bowles, C. (2017). *The lost Dark Age kingdom of Rheged: the discovery of a royal stronghold at Trusty's Hill, Galloway.*

294. Breeze, A. (2020). *British Battles 493-937.* Anthem Press.

295. Moore, E. (2024). *Early Medieval Stone Sculptures as Markers of Stability.* Borderland Communities. International Medieval Congress, 'Crisis'.

296. Moore, E. (2025). *The Influence of the Physical and Historical Landscape on the placement of Early Medieval Stone Sculpture in the Kingdom of Northumbria.* PhD Thesis. University of Lancaster.

297. Pythian-Adams, C. (1986). *Norman Conquest of Leicestershire and Rutland.* Leicestershire Museums Art Galleries and Records Service.

298. Bourne, Jill. (2003). *Understanding Leicestershire and Rutland. Place-names.* Heart of Albion.

299. Trubshaw, B. (2015). *Minsters and Valleys. A topographical comparison of seventh and eighth century land use in Leicestershire and Wiltshire.* Heart of Albion.

300. Leeds, E.T. and J.L. Barber. (1950). 'An Anglican Cemetery at Glaston, Rutland'. *The Antiquaries Journal.*

301. Rahtz, P. (1970). 'Excavations on Glastonbury Tor, Somerset, 1964–6'. *Archaeological Journal*, 127(1), pp.1-81.

302. Austin, M. (2014). 'Rethinking Hardown Hill: Our westernmost early anglo-saxon cemetery?'. *The Antiquaries Journal*, 94, pp.49-69.

303. Bassett, S. (2009). Prestetone: land of the clerics of Wooton Wawen. *The Church in English Place Names.* ed. Quinton E.

304. Clark, A. (2024). *The journey as the destination.* Story Worlds. International Medieval Congress, 'Crisis'.

305. Tickle, J. (2024). *Mobilising subregnum in 9th-to 10th-Century Wessex.* (Sub) rulerships in crisis. International Medieval Congress, 'Crisis'.

306. Bailey, H. (2024). *Botolph & Beyond.* Story Worlds. International Medieval Congress, 'Crisis'.

307. Curran, C. (2024). *What is an Early Medieval Breton manuscript?* Early Medieval Brittany. International Medieval Congress, 'Crisis'.

308. Chatwin, D. and Gardiner, M. (2005). 'Rethinking the early medieval settlement of woodlands: evidence from the western Sussex Weald'. *Landscape History*, 27(1), pp.31-49.

309. Semple, S. (2008). 'Polities and princes AD 400–800: New perspectives on the funerary landscape of the South Saxon kingdom'. *Oxford Journal of Archaeology*, 27(4), pp.407-29.

310. Stevens, S. (2006). 'Excavations at the former site of Tribes Yard, Bersted Street, Bognor Regis, West Sussex'. *Sussex Arch Coll*, 144.

311. Shapland, M. (2023). 'Selsey Cathedral and the Early Medieval Kingdoms of Sussex'. Society for Church Archaeology Lectures.

312. Hines, J. (2004). The foundations of Surrey. *Aspects of Archaeology and History in Surrey: Towards a Research Framework for the County.* Surrey Archaeological Society. pp.91-102. eds. Cotton, A. *et al.*

313. Graham, T. (2002). 'A Rho-cross Engraved on a Jet Finger-ring from Bagshot, Surrey'. *Oxford journal of archaeology*, 21(2).

314. Cash, C.G. (1913). 'Notes on some Yarrow Antiquities'. *Proceedings of the Society of Antiquaries of Scotland.* 47, pp.360-84.

315. Clarkson, T. (1995). 'Local folklore and the Battle of Arthuret'. *Transactions of the Cumberland and Westmorland Antiquarian and Archaeological Society.* 95. pp.282-4.

316. Campbell-Howes, F. (2024). *Reconstructing Ros, Materialising Moreb: The case for two lost early medieval kingdoms in the Moray Firthlands, north-east Scotland, 700–1000 AD.* MA Thesis. University of Birmingham. Personal Communications (31/10/24).

317. Rennie, E. (1998). *Cowal: a historical guide.* Birlinn.

318. Clarkson, T. (2014). *Strathclyde and the Anglo-Saxons in the Viking Age.* Birlinn.

319. Morris, C. ed. (1949). *The Journeys of Celia Fiennes.* Cresset.

320. Blair, J. and Hamerow, H. eds. (2007). *Waterways and canal-building in Medieval England.* Oxford University Press.

321. Kenyon, D. (1991). *The origins of Lancashire.* Manchester: Manchester University Press.

322. Cook, O.E. (2020). Archaeological excavation report: 2-4 Chester Road, Castlefield, Manchester.

323. Smith, I.G. (1997). 'Some Roman place-names in Lancashire and Cumbria'. *Britannia*, 28, pp.372-83.

324. Davies, S. (2010). 'The Battle of Chester and Warfare in Post-Roman Britain'. *History*, 95(318), pp.143-58.

325. Coase, K. (2019). *2,000 Years of Manchester.* Pen and Sword.

326. Edwards, B.J.N. (1973). 'A canoe burial near Lancaster'. *Antiquity*, 47(188), p.298.

327. Coates, R. (2014). 'Oundle, Northamptonshire'. *Journal of the English Place-Name Society*, 46, pp.40-4.

328. Mahoney, M.C. (2016). *Animals at Ashton: diet and human-animal dynamics in a Romano-British small town.* PhD Thesis. University of Leicester.

329. Russell, J.C. (1947). 'The Tribal Hidage'. *Traditio*, 5, pp.193-209.

330. Millett, M. and James, S. (1983). 'Excavations at Cowdery's Down Basingstoke, Hampshire, 1978–81'. *Archaeological Journal*, 140(1), pp.151-279.

331. Cole, G. *et al.* (2020). 'Summary justice or the King's will? The first case of formal facial mutilation'. *Proceedings of the American Philosophical Society*, 42(174), pp.378-96.

332. B. Cox (1994). *The Place-Names of Rutland.*

333. Grimmer, M. (2005). 'British Christian continuity in Anglo-Saxon England: the case of Sherborne/Lanprobi'. *Journal of the Australian early medieval Association*, 1, pp.51-64.

334. Davies, G. *et al.* (2020). 'From 'House of Caves' to nexus of central England: future research directions for Nottingham, c. AD 650-1250.' *Transactions of the Thoroton Society of Nottinghamshire*, 123, pp.55-75.

335. Baker, C. (2020). 'More on the Tribal Hidage'. https://profchrisbaker. com/2020/06/30/more-on-the-tribal-hidage/

336. Oosthuizen, S. (2016). *The Anglo-Saxon Fenland*. Windgather Press.

337. --- (1609). Survey of the lordship of Halcetor, co. Montgomery. *Powys-Land Clb Collec Hist Archaeol* 37.

338. Coates, R. (2008). Invisible Britons: the view from linguistics. *Britons in Anglo-Saxon England*, pp.172-91. ed. Higham, N.J.

339. Guest, P. (2019). Hoarding in Later Roman Britain and beyond. *The Staffordshire Hoard*, pp.325-34. eds. Dickinson, T. *et al.*

340. Booth, P. *et al.* (2010). *The late Roman cemetery at Lankhills, Winchester.*

341. Andrews, P. *et al.* (2019). *A Prehistoric Burial Mound and Anglo-Saxon Cemetery at Barrow Clump, Salisbury Plain, Wiltshire*. English Heritage.

342. Ulmschneider, K. and Youngs, S. (1999). 'Archaeology, history, and the Isle of Wight in the Middle Saxon period'. *Medieval Archaeology*, 43(1), pp.19-44.

343. Harrington, S. (2020). A Well-Married Landscape: Networks of Association and 6th-Century Communities on the Isle of Wight. *The Land of the English Kin*. Brill. pp. 95-111. eds. Langlands, A.J. and Lavelle, R.

344. McGurk, P. and Woodman, D.A. eds. (2024). *The Chronicle of John of Worcester*. Oxford University Press.

345. Shelley, P.B. (repr. 2022). *Selected Poetry*. Alma Classics.

Dear Reader,

We hope you have enjoyed this book, but why not share your views on social media? You can also follow our pages to see more about our other products: facebook.com/penandswordbooks or follow us on X @penswordbooks

You can also view our products at www.pen-and-sword.co.uk (UK and ROW) or www.penandswordbooks.com (North America).

To keep up to date with our latest releases and online catalogues, please sign up to our newsletter at: www.pen-and-sword.co.uk/newsletter

If you would like a printed catalogue with our latest books, then please email: enquiries@pen-and-sword.co.uk or telephone: 01226 734555 (UK and ROW) or email: uspen-and-sword@casematepublishers.com or telephone: (610) 853-9131 (North America).

We respect your privacy and we will only use personal information to send you information about our products.

Thank you!